The Terministic Screen

The Terministic Screen

Rhetorical Perspectives on Film

Edited by David Blakesley

Southern Illinois University Press
Carbondale and Edwardsville

Copyright © 2003 by the Board of Trustees,
Southern Illinois University
All rights reserved
Printed in the United States of America
06 05 04 03 4 3 2 1

Library of Congress Cataloging-in-Publication Data

The terministic screen : rhetorical perspectives on film /edited by David Blakesley.
        p. cm.
Includes bibliographical references and index.
    1. Motion pictures. 2. Rhetoric. 3. Film criticism. 4. Motion pictures—Philosophy.
I. Blakesley, David.
PN1994 .T47 2003
791.43—dc21
ISBN 0-8093-2488-1 (cloth : alk. paper)   2002009397

Printed on recycled paper. ♻

The paper used in this publication meets the minimum requirements of American National
Standard for Information Sciences--Permanence of Paper for Printed Library Materials,
ANSI Z39.48-1992. ∞

To Julie,
for the eyes, the ayes, and the I's

Contents

Acknowledgments

WITH TIME I HAVE COME TO VIEW EDITING not only as an exercise appended to the act of writing but as a critically important aspect of the professionalization and collaboration that helps give shape to a discipline. So much of the process occurs offstage, where the performance is planned and rehearsed, where people grapple with the finer points of interpretation and persuasion, where we collaborate at the moments of creation. It has been my great pleasure to work with the authors whose work appears in this book, all of whom have been patient coconspirators in our attempts to identify the value of taking rhetorical perspectives on film. I want to thank in particular Alan Nadel, whose advice during the early stages of this project was offered enthusiastically and always with the grace of a seasoned scholar.

My teacher at San Diego State University, Thomas Nelson, helped me appreciate the finer points of film interpretation long before I'd even heard of rhetoric. I recall his enthusiasm fondly and hope that he sees some merit in his former student's effort. At Southern Illinois University Carbondale, Richard Peterson gave me the opportunity to teach film even though (or in spite of the fact that) I was primarily a rhetorician by training. Tony Williams offered good advice about this project in its early stages. My students there taught me as much as I taught them; they have included Phil Simpson (who has an essay in this volume), Scott Furtwengler, Chris Costello, David Tietge, Jeff Townsend, Roger Pugh, Kathy Kageff, Jackie Pieterick, Tim Donovan, and Robert York, as well as many others whose enthusiasm was contagious. Karl Kageff, now my editor at Southern Illinois University Press, was also among them and has now become a rhetorician in his own right, not to mention a supportive and perceptive editor. Carol Burns and Kristine Priddy have been excellent editors as well. My many fine colleagues at Purdue have supported my work in film and rhetoric, providing me with the opportunity to study and teach visual rhetoric. Students in my visual rhetoric course in spring 2002 helped me formalize some of the key distinctions I make in the introduction to this work.

Throughout it all, my wife, Julie, has shared her love and her love of film with me, even though (it seems) I spend much more time writing about films than I do watching them. My brother, Roger, took me to my first film, either *Grand Prix* or *The Gypsy Moths,* and my parents, Pearl and Merrill, shared their enthusiasm for Hitchcock films when I was much too young to understand their brilliance.

My father-in-law, Charles Reiske, helps me appreciate how profoundly central identification is to film spectatorship, while my mother-in-law, Martha, manages to maintain the all-important critical distance. My daughter, Meagan, and son, Matthew, remind me every day that we enjoy films in no small way because they teach, delight, and persuade. Meagan and Matt not only want to be in movies, they want to be *inside* them, in the worlds they create. Lately, they want to make them as well, and with the help of digital imaging technologies, they're well on their way.

The Terministic Screen

Introduction: The Rhetoric of Film and Film Studies

David Blakesley

Even as they offer interpretations of particular films, cultural periods, cinematic technique, or the nature of rhetoric itself, the essays collected in *The Terministic Screen: Rhetorical Perspectives on Film* also address implicitly (and often explicitly) what have become common refrains in film studies: What constitutes film theory? What does film theory make possible? Is film theory even possible or useful in the wake of the rhetorical (or linguistic) turn? What is the social value of film theory and interpretation? In the last decade or so, film theorists have asked these questions frequently, with their answers ranging from pronouncements about the desperate need for the unification and synthesis of theoretical approaches under the guise of new, albeit somewhat loose, theoretical formulations (such as cultural studies) to suggestions that film theory has run its course—that it has already suffered from too much rehearsal of the trendy—and that we are effectively in a period of "Post-Theory."[1] In this introduction, I hope to contextualize this debate with reference to the emergence of rhetorical theory as a terministic screen for the analysis and interpretation of film, as well as to provide a framework for understanding the rhetorical emphases in recent film criticism and in the essays presented here. Introductions to each of the three parts of the book—"Perspectives on Film and Film Theory as Rhetoric," "Rhetorical Perspectives on Film and Culture," and "Perspectives on Films about Rhetoric"—provide the rationale for the division of the book into three sections and more detailed previews of each essay.

Collectively, our answers to these questions about film theory and criticism in this volume suggest that the need for unifying film theory in the interest of film studies (as a discipline) is a valiant effort, but it is at best unnecessary to do so, and perhaps even misguided. Alternatively, *The Terministic Screen* suggests that the power and value of film theory as a generative set of principles for the analysis and interpretation of film is borne from a dialectic of competing perspectives, from the very richness and diversity of approaches to film that have been made possible by the very theory that has been castigated so frequently, and often justly, by critics, such as David Bordwell and Noël Carroll. The essays in this volume are not shy about articulating theoretical approaches to film—psychoanalytic, semiotic, hermeneutic, phenomenological, cultural, or otherwise. They do so, however, without making totalizing claims on behalf of theory itself or without claiming some disciplinary motive. Instead, we see in taking rhetorical perspectives on film the opportunity—even the necessity—of using all that is there to use as we grapple with complex and important questions about the nature and function of film and other visual media in our society. The argument, then, is not about which theory ought to be elevated to disciplinary reverence, but about how best to use the terministic resources theory makes available.

Many of the contributors find in the suppleness and eclecticism of rhetorical theory the chance to articulate an approach to film study that is both theoretically sound and hyperconscious of its own strategies of containment. Each perspective on film and film theory typically draws from the rich traditions of film, literary, and rhetorical theory, enacting its own synthesis of approaches in the interest of adapting analysis and interpretation to the situation a film, series of films, or type of film presents to its viewers. A rhetorical perspective on film usually focuses on problems of appeal in the broadest sense, as symbolic gestures involving the familiar components of any communicative act: an address with a variety of means for a purpose in a context and situation that ranges from the internal world of the film to the external world of the viewer and critic. A rhetorical perspective—however broad the field of thought from which it derives its terminology—is still just one perspective among many, and while some would argue that it is perhaps the perspective on perspectives that philosophers like Richard Rorty so desperately seek, the contributors to this volume are aware of rhetoric's function as a filter or screen, enabling some things to pass through clearly, obscuring or repressing others. As we seek to articulate the range of rhetoric in film studies, we have all been hyperconscious of the human predisposition to see the self in the other, or to see in a film, for example, an acting out of some theoretical formulation that we already hold dear, some bizarre reenactment of our own theoretical sensibility. The authors in *The Terministic Screen* have been too well trained as rhetoricians not to recognize the pitfalls of that sort of ritualized incantation of subjectivity and the accompanying dangers of rationalizing all experience as self-fulfilling prophecy.

We have exercised such restraint by bearing in mind the concept that is named in the main title of the book, *The Terministic Screen*. The phrase "terministic screen" comes from Kenneth Burke's well-known essay, "Terministic Screens," in *Language as Symbolic Action*. In that essay, Burke's central contention is this: "Not only does the nature of our terms affect the nature of our observations, in the sense that the terms direct the *at*tention to one field rather than to another. Also, *many of the 'observations' are but implications of the particular terminology in terms of which the observations are made*" (46). In alluding to Burke, *The Terministic Screen* would thus elaborate these two premises about symbolic action: our terms direct the attention and jump to particular conclusions. Film rhetoric—the visual and verbal signs and strategies that shape film experience—directs our attention in countless ways, but always with the aim of fostering identification and all that that complex phenomenon implies. Film theory—the interpretive lens through which and with which we generate perspectives on film as both art and rhetoric—likewise functions as a terministic screen, filtering what does and does not constitute and legitimize interpretation and, thus, meaning.

Rhetorical Perspectives on Film

To this point, there has been a substantial body of work devoted to the rhetorical analysis of film and to the rhetoric of film interpretation. That work is scattered across a wide range of disciplinary thought, so as a field of study, it has remained on the periphery of interest, especially in film studies proper, which as some have noted is itself an amalgam of interdisciplinary perspectives.[2] Some works with a strong rhetorical emphasis do sneak through to the limelight, however. Bill Nichols has been at the center of that attention with books on the documentary film and popular culture, such as *Ideology and the Image: Social Representation in the Cinema and Other Media* (1981), *Representing Reality: Issues and Concepts in Documentary* (1992), and *Blurred Boundaries: Questions of Meaning in Contemporary Culture* (1994). What I find most "rhetorical" about his work is its attention to the presence or absence of reflexivity in both film and film theory, the idea that when you look carefully, you discover that films and our interpretation of them say as much about the attitude of the director and viewer as they say about their referential subject, with that attitude implicit in the pseudo-realist documentary and explicitly problematized in the reflexive film (and in reflexive theory, I would add). Barry Brummett's *Rhetorical Dimensions of Popular Culture* (1991) is only partly about film, but it is also wholly rhetorical in approach and thus an excellent model for what constitutes a rhetorical perspective on film. Likewise, work by Thomas Benson and Carolyn Anderson (*Reality Fictions: The Films of Frederick Wiseman,* 1989, 2002), Martin J. Medhurst ("Image and Ambiguity: A Rhetorical Approach to *The Exorcist,*" 1973; "*Hiroshima Mon Amour:* From Iconography to Rhetoric," 1982; and "The Rhetorical Structure of Oliver Stone's *JFK,*" 1993), and Thomas Rosteck (See It Now *Confronts McCarthyism: Television Documentary and the Politics of Representation,* 1994) demonstrate the usefulness of rhetorical criticism as social and cultural criticism in film studies. By nature interdisciplinary (rhetoric, suggested Aristotle, has no subject matter of its own), rhetorical perspectives are implicitly woven throughout works like Kaja Silverman's *The Subject of Semiotics* (1983), Tania Modleski's *The Women Who Knew Too Much: Hitchcock and Feminist Theory* (1988), Vivian Sobchack's *The Address of the Eye: A Phenomenology of Film Experience* (1992), and Jo Keroes's *Tales Out of School: Gender, Longing, and the Teacher in Fiction and Film* (1999). David Bordwell's *Making Meaning: Inference and Rhetoric in the Interpretation of Cinema* (1989) uses *rhetoric* in the dismissive and popular sense (as biased, motivated, disingenuous, or empty phraseology), so his work is useful as one approach to the study of the ways that the production of theory functions rhetorically, even though we may contest the idea that there is some way to avoid that rhetoricity in any theoretical or interpretive discourse. In the emergent field of visual rhetoric, W. J. T. Mitchell's *Picture Theory: Essays on Verbal and Visual Representation* (1994) and Ann Marie Seward Barry's *Visual Intelligence: Perception, Image, and Manipulation in Visual Communication* (1997) both examine the function of the perception and the moving image from a rhetorical-cognitivist perspective. Both suggest new directions for rhetoric and film theory in the age of the pictorial turn and the digitized image.

Across such a broad range of work, and in light of the diverse approaches represented in *The Terministic Screen*, it would seem no small task to extract and synthesize common theoretical principles sufficiently precise to mark a perspective on film as "rhetorical." Like so many other titular terms (psychoanalysis, semiotics, phenomenology, cultural studies, and so on), the meaning of the term *rhetoric* is itself hotly contested, and so what constitutes "rhetorical analysis" will also be in dispute.[3] Nevertheless, it may be useful to suggest an outline or range of rhetorical perspectives on film in the interest of distinguishing them from, for example, semiotic or phenomenological perspectives. Each of the works in *The Terministic Screen* share some emphases with other approaches described under each of the following four categories, which I offer here with some brief explanation and references to work in film studies that might be considered in allegiance with, if not models, of the approach. I also point to essays in this volume that share, extend, or reconstruct key theoretical insights with regard to, for example, the ways that efforts to construct film language should account for language's social function (as rhetorical, in other words). Each of these categories—film as language, film as ideology, film interpretation, and film identification—should probably be thought of as leanings or orientations (in the sense Burke discusses orientations in *Permanence and Change* [part one]), rather than as precisely defined and practiced philosophical foundations.

Film as Language

Advanced by the work of Christian Metz (*Film Language,* 1971, 1974; *The Imaginary Signifier: Psychoanalysis and the Cinema,* 1977, 1982), Stephen Heath and Patricia Mellencamp (*Cinema and Language,* 1983), Vivian Sobchack (*The Address of the Eye: A Phenomenology of Film Experience,* 1992), Stephen Prince ("The Discourse of Pictures: Iconicity and Film Studies," 1993; *Movies and Meaning: An Introduction to Film,* 2000), and others, this approach treats film both semiotically and phenomenologically as a grammatical system of signs, with attention to spectatorship and perceptual processes. Metz's work in particular has been enormously influential, mostly for his attempts to develop a sign system for film spectatorship, drawing heavily from Lacanian psychoanalysis (concepts such as the mirror stage and the insistence of the letter in the unconscious). In tying this semiotic system to the imaginary (the realm of secondary identification), Metz shifts our focus to the construction and reception of film and, thus, the ways that film functions not only as a language (in its sign system, with cinematic technique the analogical equivalent of a grammar) but also as a rhetorical appeal to or an assertion of identity in the audience. In *The Terministic Screen,* Ann Chisholm's "Rhetoric and the Early Work of Christian Metz: Augmenting Ideological Inquiry in Rhetorical Film Theory and Criticism" shows how Metz's insufficient treatment of the rhetorical/ideological component of perception in his semiotic system might be rescued for future scholarship. Byron Hawk's "Hyperrhetoric and the Inventive Spectator: Remotivating *The Fifth Element*" moves a step beyond Metz as well, arguing for the plasticity of the imaginary signifier in the spectator's invention of the filmic text. Davis W. Houck and Caroline J. S. Picart's "Opening the Text: Reading Gender, Christianity, and American Intervention in *Deliverance*" draws from the semiotic/hermeneutic perspective proffered by Umberto Eco to examine *Deliverance* as embedded text in a broader cultural critique, which also aligns their essay with others that would see film ideology as usefully examined from a rhetorical perspective.

Film as Ideology

This approach views film as serving ideological functions in both its content and technical apparatus. The task of film criticism is to expose film's complicity with or deconstruction of dominant ideology. Rhetorical analyses (of film, texts, speeches, or any other symbolic activity) are typically concerned with both how works achieve their effects and how works make their appeals to shared interests (the margin of overlap) among people. This attention to agency in concert with ideological analysis and critique make this perhaps the most common way to approach a film rhetorically. In film studies, its practitioners include Brummett, Nichols, and Robert Stam (*Reflexivity in Film and Literature: From Don Quixote to Jean-Luc Godard,* 1985; *Subversive Pleasures: Bakhtin, Cultural Criticism, and Film,* 1989). As cultural expression, films reveal not only the predispositions of filmmakers but they also serve ideological functions in the broader culture (as critique, as hegemonic force, as symptomatic) that can be analyzed as having a rhetorical function, especially to the extent that rhetoric serves as the means of initiating cultural critique and stabilizing cultural pieties. In *The Terministic Screen,* essays by Ekaterina V. Haskins ("Time, Space, and Political Identity: Envisioning Community in *Triumph of the Will*"), Thomas Benson ("Looking for the Public in the Popular: The Hollywood Blacklist and the Rhetoric of Collective Memory"), Philip L. Simpson ("*Copycat,* Serial Murder, and the (De)Terministic Screen Narrative"), Friedemann Weidauer ("From 'World Conspiracy' to 'Cultural Imperialism': The History of Anti-Plutocratic Rhetoric in German Film"), Harriet Malinowitz ("Textual Trouble in River City: Literacy, Rhetoric, and Consumerism in *The Music Man*"), and Granetta L. Richardson ("Screen Play: *Ethos* and Dialectics in *A Time to Kill*") most succinctly represent the approach to film as ideology, although nearly all of the essays in the collection broach the subject of film ideology as rhetorical critique. For example, my essay, "Sophistry, Magic and the Vilifying Rhetoric of *The Usual Suspects,*" deconstructs that film's condemnation of rhetoric as a symptomatic form of ideological maintenance in its own right, complicitly with the sophistry the film seeks to expose. Likewise, Benson and Weidauer track cultural attitudes through a series of films, showing how widespread cultural anxiety translates into cinematic technique and narrative style. In a similar vein, Simpson builds upon his work in *Psycho Paths: Tracking the Serial Killer through American Film and Fiction* (2000) to show how the serial killer narrative in *Copycat* "falters when it eschews complex sociopolitical criticism and instead blames one, perhaps two 'viral' agents for the perpetuation of violence."

Film Interpretation

This approach treats film as a rhetorical situation involving the director, the film, and the viewer in the total act of making meaning. Its subject is often the reflexivity of interpretation, both as it is manifest on screen and in the reception by the audience/critic. In addition to Nichols's treatment of documentary film rhetoric, J. Hendrix and J. A. Wood's "The Rhetoric of Film: Toward a Critical Methodology" (1973), Bordwell's *Making Meaning* (1989), Seymour Chatman's *Coming to Terms: The Rhetoric of Narrative in Fiction and Film* (1990), and Bordwell and Carroll's *Post-Theory* (1996) each examine the film experience as a rhetorical situation. As I have already mentioned, Bordwell is perhaps most concerned with the role of the critic in that situation. Chatman attempts to show that film interpretation should account for audience reactions, the formal elaboration and function of genre, and the symbolic representation of meaning on screen. Chatman, however, shies away from rhetoric's role in articulating the situational nature of film (or any text), preferring instead to imagine rhetoric as useful for translating linguistic tropes and forms into their visual equivalents. In *The Terministic Screen,* Alan Nadel's "Mapping the Other: *The English Patient,* Colonial Rhetoric, and Cinematic Representation" and Bruce Krajewski's "Rhetorical Conditioning: *The Manchurian Candidate*" explore the ways that rhetorical perspectives provide more than merely another terminology for guiding the critic's analytical moves. Krajewski, for instance, criticizes the lack of attention to the critic's implication in elaborating filmic meaning:

> Practicing visual theory or rhetorical analysis of films becomes an ideological substitute for a lack, that lack being specific considerations of what the results of such practicing are, or ought to be. Change the world to what? What effects different forms of thinking take, even rhetorical ones, on the whole— call this whole global living conditions—*those* remain grossly underdetermined, untheorized, and ungrounded philosophically or politically, in the practical sense of *any* party politics.

Nadel argues that mainstream cinematic narrative "evokes the same ethos as mapping, in that both forms of representation create symbolic spaces that mask the arbitrary authority ceded, *a priori,* to the place whence the (geographic, historiographic, or cinematographic) discourse emanates." The colonizing rhetoric of mapping in *The English Patient* is emblematic of mainstream narrative's desperate attempt to wrest control from the spectator by asserting power over interpretation in a film's diegetic narrative. Both Nadel and Krajewski see rhetoric not merely as a system of analytical tools, but as a metasystem that helps us interpret our interpretations, as viewers and as theorists.

Film Identification

This approach considers film rhetoric as involving identification and division. Film style directs the attention—or not—for ideological, psychological, or social purposes. Identification has been paired with discourses on the postmodern subject in work by critics such as Kaja Silverman (again, *The Subject of Semiotics*), Laura Mulvey ("Visual Pleasure and Narrative Cinema," 1975), Tania Modleski (again, *The Women Who Knew Too Much,* 1988), and many other works influenced by Metz and found often in feminist and psychoanalytic studies. While the notion of the subject in film studies has received its due share of attention, the meaning of identification, particularly as it functions rhetorically, has yet to be closely scrutinized. For Metz, identification occurs in the imaginary realm of the signifier, where film narratives create the conditions for identification to occur in a secondary order of reality. It would be useful, I think, to compare identification in the imaginary with the function of identification rhetorically. Kenneth Burke saw identification as both the condition and aim of rhetoric, and with it, the corresponding division. The desire for identification, which Burke calls consubstantiality, is premised on its absence, on the condition of our division from one another (there would be no need for the rhetorician to proclaim our unity, Burke says, if we were already identical) (*A Rhetoric of Motives* 18–29). Consubstantiality, with its root in the ambiguous *substance* (sub-stance), may be purely an expression of desire, an identity of attitude and act in a symbolic realm, much like Metz's secondary order. In *The Terministic Screen,* various essays examine identification as the key term (and desire) in the total film narrative, which includes the spectator's subject position, as well as the film's attempt to articulate it. Byron Hawk's "Hyperrhetoric and the Inventive Spectator: Remotivating *The Fifth Element,*" in addition to describing an alternative grammar of reception (see "Film as Language"), draws from Gregory Ulmer's *Heuretics* to argue for remaking the process of identification as, or in spite of, film's assertion of normative responses to division. James Roberts ("On Rhetorical Bodies: *Hoop Dreams* and Constitutional Discourse") shows how the filmic gaze fosters identification of/with bodies, so that, for example, the spectator's identification with the protagonists of *Hoop Dreams* is more than merely imaginary, but has a physical, bodily basis as well. In my own essay ("Sophistry, Magic, and the Vilifying Rhetoric of *The Usual Suspects*"), I explore the conflicting attitudes toward identification represented in Bryan Singer's 1995 film, which associates the manipulation of identification with evil even as it uses that rhetoric to make its appeal to the unsuspecting audience. Kelly Ritter ("Postmodern Dialogics in *Pulp Fiction:* Jules, Ezekiel, and Double-Voiced Discourse") continues this examination of identification in her exploration of the self-representational, dialogic discourses on identity offered by Jules (Samuel Jackson).

These four categories—film as language, film as ideology, film interpretation, and film identification—represent broad categories of interest among those who proclaim to be practicing rhetorical analysis on film and film theory. Interesting exchanges across essays in this book should stimulate further discussion (for example, the critique of ideological inquiry in film theory offered by Ann Chisholm touches on prior work by Benson and Medhurst on film and cultural criticism). In the end, the point here is not to define what a rhetorical perspective on film should or must be, but to offer the reader the opportunity to judge whether rhetoric might offer an alternative and supple terminology for discussing film in an age when many proclaim (i.e., desire) the death of theory. I also see no reason to attempt to mark the territory of the possible or worthy in rhetorical studies of film, which comes across as far too dismissive and paternalistic. Arguments like Bordwell and Carroll's in *Post-Theory* suggesting that theory (by which they mean psychoanalytic, cultural studies, and semiotic approaches to film) is dead (or certainly ought to be) is a disingenuous act of appropriation, an attempt to restructure film studies in their own image (as we're perhaps all vain enough to attempt at some point, I admit) and to introduce theory by a kind of counter-espionage. In the next section, I will explain more precisely why I see arguments about the direction of disciplinary interest as more about the writers' attitudes toward the discipline than about the scholarship itself. I also discuss why I see in rhetoric opportunities for responding in interesting and provocative ways to the problems of interpretation posed by postmodernism.

The Rhetorical Turn

The Terministic Screen is very much about seeing and interpreting, about visual rhetoric and making meaning. It is about "ways of seeing," to borrow a phrase from Burke (later popularized by John Berger et al.), and how these ways of seeing may be determined locally by a film as an isolated, substantive, and symbolic form of expression, but also by more general cultural, psychological, and rhetorical frames, ones that guide interpretation and that shape our understanding of what meanings film makes possible. The essays in this book consider films rhetorically, as acts that dramatize and interrogate the ways people use language and images to tell stories and foster identification. They also examine how, as Burke put it, "[a] way of seeing is also a way of not seeing—a focus on object A involves a neglect of object B" (*Permanence and Change* 49).

As I mentioned at the outset, *The Terministic Screen* responds to the frequently expressed feeling among film theorists that many of the theoretical approaches to film so popular during the 1970s and 1980s have run their course, or at least are in need of some refreshing synthesis. In the early 1990s, Stephen Prince, for instance, sensed that "the paradigms that have been central until now—structural linguistics, Althusserian Marxism, Lacanian psychoanalysis—have taken the field about as far as they can and that some major realignments of approach are slowly forming" ("Contemporary Directions in Film Theory" 3). More recently, Richard Allen and Murray Smith note the wide recognition that "the field of film studies is in a state of flux, or even crisis or impasse" (1). It is impossible to pinpoint precisely why film studies has reached this state of dispersion. Paradigm shifts do not take place as neatly or as resolutely as they might in more scientific disciplines, which themselves are subject to the inexplicable forces of anomaly, personality, and persuasion. The emergence of a new generation of film scholars will naturally bring new allegiances and anxieties to the fore. Films themselves will precipitate re-alignments in approaches to the extent that they problematize our conventional ways of interpreting them. And yet in spite of these disparate forces of change, it is clear that there have been currents and eddies to follow, perhaps most noticeable among them, the burgeoning interest in cultural and media studies, an interest motivated at least in part by the desire to examine the social nature of spectatorship, which transcends the immediacy of the film spectator as the (psychological) subject of semiotics. Even so, as Thomas Rosteck argues, cultural studies itself remains "a murky set of practices, alternately vague and unsettling, even threatening" (386).

Across the broader field of the humanities, there has also been a shift of sorts that would explain the blurring of perspectives within film studies and at the same time suggest an emergent movement more particular than cultural studies but motivated by some of the same concerns. This movement is sometimes identified as a *turn* of "linguistic," "rhetorical," "critical," or even "pictorial" proportions (e.g., by Rorty in *Philosophy and the Mirror of Nature;* Eagleton in *Literary Theory;* Angus and Langsdorf in *The Critical Turn: Rhetoric and Philosophy in Postmodern Discourse;* Simons in *The Rhetorical Turn: Invention and Persuasion in the Conduct of Inquiry;* and W. J. T. Mitchell in *Picture Theory: Essays on Verbal and Visual Representation*). This turn—which I think of as primarily rhetorical—is marked by heightened consciousness of the ways in which all symbolic acts (including film) are functions of rhetorical power (i.e., best understood as situated, partisan acts by virtue of their expression in comprehensible and social symbol systems). In contradistinction to the linguistic turn in film studies, which drew from structuralist and post-Saussurean linguistics in the 1970s, the rhetorical turn signifies a revised relationship between the interpretive method and the products of critical inquiry. What theory "produces," in other words, is very much a consequence of its terministic screen. Likewise, for example, the effect a particular film might have on viewers depends upon an aesthetic that itself is a product of social forces, an amalgam of (rhetorical) appeals whose subject matter is residually ideological and whose maintenance and power are hegemonically scripted. Our ways of seeing—

and of knowing and interpreting—are ultimately acts of identification, which Burke names as the central aim in a rhetoric of motives (*Rhetoric* 20–29).

The self-reflexivity of rhetorical theory, something which Burke often noted was its chief analytical strength and social value, makes it especially appealing now, as across the humanities and sciences we come to terms with the implications of postmodernism and deconstruction for epistemology, perception, and visual rhetoric. These two related but interanimating attitudes—postmodernism and deconstruction—have forced traditional methods of analytical and humanistic study to run the gauntlet of skepticism. It simply is no longer possible to ignore the (socalled) problem posed by our symbol systems, which represent and deflect meaning always and inescapably. Now, it is as if every assertion we make must unwrite itself if it is to have any integrity. Or rather, it must acknowledge its unwritability, that the presence (meaning) it would invoke must recede the moment it is asserted. It is certainly possible to wish things otherwise and to claim objectivity—for certain perceptual processes, for example—but as a friend of mine (Bruce Appleby) always put it, macho subjectivity masquerades as objectivity. What responses to this rhetorical turn can we imagine? Other than browbeating one another about the deficiencies of the latest fad, what might we do?

In *Post-Theory: Reconstructing Film Theory* (1996), David Bordwell and Noël Carroll assemble an eclectic and provocative set of essays that contest the preeminence of psychoanalytic and cultural studies approaches to film in the late twentieth century. Bordwell and Carroll aim to rearticulate what can best be called a neoformalist and cognitivist approach to film, though the charge of being *neoformalist* is one both have strenuously tried unsuccessfully to deflect.[4] In the grander scheme of things, it probably matters very little (to anyone else) whether Bordwell or Carroll are genuinely neoformalists. What does matter, I believe, is that they have managed in some degree to dictate the terms in which film theorists account for their own activity as film critics, in much the same way that Allan Bloom, with his fabulously popular *The Closing of the American Mind* in the late 1980s, set the terms for the tired rehashing of why higher education was failing society (and especially its "impoverished" youth). It is a tried-and-true tactic of debunkers to exploit the naturally ambiguous concept of a movement or trend by casting it in a dramatic narrative, the intention of which is to clear the stage for their next act. Such narratives gloss over and reduce uncertainty by wrenching terms from their contexts to weave them in a contrastive terminology that jumps to conclusions of its own in the enlightened interest of "restructuring" (or of recovering, as from an addiction or an illness). The problem that remains repressed in *Post-Theory* is that such a rearticulation of the past is itself unreflexively situated and partisan. While that may be an unavoidable consequence of theoretical (or any) discourse, it is not one that should be so easily dismissed as "grand theory" in a work that smuggles in theory of its own. I want to spend a moment on Bordwell's and Carroll's arguments in *Post-Theory* (in each author's introductory essay) to suggest that their antitheory movement (rehearsed as it is by almost every generation) fails or refuses to acknowledge the consequences of the rhetorical turn, which in a fundamental way has altered our sense of coherence and means of judging the merits of theoretical discourse.

It is somewhat surprising to hear from someone like Bordwell this apocalyptic tale of endings and new beginnings because his book *Making Meaning: Inference and Rhetoric in the Interpretation of Cinema* (1989) effectively elaborates the situatedness (i.e., rhetorical nature) of film interpretation, even if it does attempt to wriggle free by asserting an alternative rhetoric that is arhetorical (the problem with interpretation is that it is *too* rhetorical). Still, in *Making Meaning,* there is a measure of resistance to totalizing claims about the activity of film theory that unfortunately surfaces boldly in *Post-Theory* and makes the book—especially Bordwell's own "Contemporary Film Studies and the Vicissitudes of Grand Theory" and Carroll's "Prospects for Film Theory: A Personal Assessment"—read like fire-and-brimstone laments from scowling critics who can't understand why someone might find something useful for film study in the theoretical and terminological currency of our times.

In "Contemporary Film Studies and the Vicissitudes of Grand Theory," Bordwell argues persuasively against paying undue allegiance to theoretical terminology that makes unmodulated claims for what Carroll will call in his personal assessment "monolithic conceptions of film theory" (38). Such conceptions argue, for example, that any theory of film interpretation (what we bring to bear on the act) must be intrinsically a theory of film, not a theory of language or psychology transported from contexts they were not meant to explain (38). Bordwell prefers instead what he calls "middle-level research," work that draws on smaller scale theories (of metaphor, narrative, ideology, style, for example) to explain the nature or function of cinema:

> The middle-level research programs have shown that *you do not need a Big Theory of Everything to do enlightening work in a field of study.* Contrary to what many believe, a study of United Artists' business practices or the standardization of continuity editing or the activities of women in early film audiences need carry *no* determining philosophical assumptions about subjectivity or culture, *no* univocal metaphysical or epistemological or political assumptions—in short, no commitment to a Grand Theory. (29)

I would qualify such a pronouncement and suggest that such programs needn't articulate such assumptions in order to produce useful insights, but those assumptions have to be there playing some determinative role because anyone who writes selects terminology that seeks to represent reality (or subjectivity), and as a selection from among alternatives, such representations express choice (conscious or not), and thus deflect the attention from one thing to another. It is the nature of definition that we must explain one thing in *terms* of something else. Our choice of terms is a rhetorical one, operating by exclusion and as an expression of desire. So producing a study of United Artists' business practices need not invoke grand theory, but it will be the end result of choices from among alternative explanations, and there will be philosophical assumptions shaping them. If it were possible to reproduce such business practices in the fullness of their unfolding in time, mapped across all of the personalities, documents, social practices, and historical situations that contained that business practice, then one might be able to argue for such a study's being uncontaminated by theory. But such a study would be indistinguishable from the event/practice it sought to describe (recall Pierre Menard's efforts to produce the perfect interpretation of *Don Quixote* in Jorge Luis Borges's short story, "Pierre Menard, Author of the *Quixote*," by reliving every aspect of Cervantes's life). It may be possible to produce a good study of United Artists' business practices without explicitly mentioning grand theory (e.g., capitalism), but that is not the same as producing a good study without the shaping influence of some philosophical assumptions (about, for instance, what we mean by *business* and *practice,* who and what we invoke when we make reference to United Artists, and so on). The rhetorical turn teaches us that ignoring this shaping influence of terminology at the point of utterance is to ignore the determinative power of ideology on the production of knowledge. One important function of criticism is to be self-critical, so Bordwell's insistence that middle-level research can be theory-free is tantamount to saying that it should be uncritical (and that it is uncritical). At the end of the essay, he notes that "literary studies, art history, musicology and many other disciplines within the humanities developed rich research traditions before Grand Theory intervened" (38). To suggest that the research traditions in literary study, for instance, were theory-free is to ignore completely not only the shaping influence of rhetoric, philosophy, psychology, and aesthetics on the production of literary appreciation but also the work of the many scholars who have written and rewritten the history of the discipline of literary study to show the consequences of such theories on our understanding and use of literature.

I would like to mention one more case in point, this time with reference to Noël Carroll's introductory essay in the same volume, "Prospects for Film Theory: A Personal Assessment." In this essay, Carroll argues for film criticism that would draw conceptual strategies from a variety of fields of knowledge. He argues as well that there needn't be some totalizing filmic theory in order for film interpretation to deliver useful insights. His case for approaches to film that use what is there to use is convincing. Yet one senses a profound distrust of any intervening terministic screen because, Carroll claims, there are aspects of film experience that can be untainted by ideology. To refute the charge that he is a "rank formalist," Carroll argues that the claims of the "proponents of the Theory" (that every aspect of cinema is implicated in ideology) are empirically insupportable. In mounting his defense of cognitivism's assertion that some aspects of cinema are in fact detachable from ideology, he writes:

> Surely, the perception of cinematic movement, the recognition of the cinematic image, and the comprehension of narrative will have the same bio-

logical, psychological, and cognitive foundations in any humanly imaginable, nonrepressive, classless, egalitarian utopia that those perceptual and cognitive processes have in present-day Los Angeles. (51)

For quite some time, perceptual theorists, art historians, and critical theorists have recognized that even perceptual processes, such as the observation of movement or depth, are not simply automatic, biological processes, but they also function as assertive acts, guided by belief, experience, and desire. Richard L. Gregory's work in perceptual psychology (e.g., *The Intelligent Eye*, 1970) and, more recently, Mitchell's *Picture Theory* (1994) and James Elkins's *The Object Stares Back: On the Nature of Seeing* (1997) provide empirical evidence as well as sound arguments for the conclusion that "simple" perception is hardly innocent or disinterested. If we do have anything in common with each other with regard to the perception of movement, the recognition of the image, or the comprehension of narrative, it is that our perception is thoroughly imbued with ideological (and other forms of) purpose. What Carroll's complaint reveals, ultimately, is that for him ideology is merely the explicit expression of a political viewpoint (i.e., propaganda), and not— as Kenneth Burke, Raymond Williams, Louis Althusser, Fredric Jameson, and others have argued—a shaping force at the point of conception or consciousness. For Carroll, it seems that any light that enters the eye does so unimpeded by a belief system because beliefs don't reside outside of the body (after all). It is not necessary to read Stephen Hawking to know, however, that light is reflected off of objects from a source. Where you choose to shine the light determines what you will ultimately see.

As the essays in *The Terministic Screen* demonstrate, the consequences of the rhetorical turn for film studies are significant and provocative. While they represent a range of approaches within rhetorical studies itself, these essays share a common recognition that a rhetorical approach to film can help us draw together some of the theoretical perspectives on film that have previously been isolated to particular approaches within film studies or dispersed throughout academic areas, such as communication, literary studies, rhetoric, art history, linguistics, and composition. None of the essays simply reduces film to a language, or to a system of signs, and yet some of them draw on that perspective to articulate what might be called a "film rhetoric," a perspective that would account for the function of the sign psychologically (as in cognitive studies) and socially (as in cultural studies). For others, the film spectator is not merely the subject of the semiotic or the unwitting participant in the reification of the film director's gaze, glance, or hail. Nevertheless, such a perspective might inform a revision of spectatorship to include the ways that film language works rhetorically to reconstitute the subject, which itself might either be the secondary reality of the film world or the primary reality that molds the film-viewing experience of the spectator. The essays in *The Terministic Screen* also share a central concern for the processes of rhetoric itself, rhetoric here conceived as either the exploitation or elaboration of ambiguity to foster identification. It is our hope that readers will find herein an emergent field within film studies that cuts across traditional disciplinary bound-aries to provide unity and direction without sacrificing the complexity or preci-sion that theory demands.

In one sense, the range and scope of the essays presented in *The Terministic Screen* will work against any neat conception of what it means to study film rhe-torically. Sometimes rhetoric aims for closure and to produce conviction and cer-tainty, outcomes that clearly are important for any theoretical perspective that would lay claim to status as theory. At the same time, however, it is important to remember that rhetorical inquiry has, in the philosophical sense, always been concerned with multiplying perspectives, for elaborating and exploiting ambigu-ity. Assembled in *The Terministic Screen* are rhetoricians whose overall aim is per-haps best described by Burke, who sees the rhetorician as but one voice in a dia-logue: "Put several such voices together, with each voicing its own special assertion, let them act upon one another in co-operative competition, and you get a dialec-tic that, properly developed, can lead to views transcending the limitations of each" ("Rhetoric—Old and New" 63). In the end, we share the belief that taking rhe-torical perspectives on film creates alchemic possibilities, new ways of understand-ing film as a visual and verbal medium that can impact our lives profoundly.

Notes

1. In *Post-Theory: Reconstructing Film Studies,* David Bordwell and Noël Carroll argue, for example, that the question before film studies now is not the end of film theory (with a small *t*), but "the end of Theory, and what can and should come after" (xiii).

2. Bordwell suggests this interdisciplinarity in his introduction to *Post-Theory* (3–4).

3. See, for instance, Edward Schiappa's discussion of these contests in "Second Thoughts on the Critiques of Big Rhetoric."

4. Noel King makes the case for Bordwell's and Carroll's neoformalism in "Hermeneutics, Reception Aesthetics, and Film Interpretation."

Works Cited

Allen, Richard, and Murray Smith. "Introduction: Film Theory and Philosophy." *Film Theory and Philosophy.* Ed. Richard Allen and Murray Smith. Oxford and New York: Clarendon P, 1997.

Angus, Ian, and Lenore Langsdorf, eds. *The Critical Turn: Rhetoric and Philoso-phy in Postmodern Discourse.* Carbondale: Southern Illinois UP, 1993.

Aristotle. *The "Art" of Rhetoric.* Trans. John Henry Freese. Loeb Classical Library. New York: G. P. Putnam, 1926.

Benson, Thomas, and Carolyn Anderson. *Reality Fictions: The Films of Frederick Wiseman.* 2d ed. Carbondale: Southern Illinois UP, 2002.

Berger, John. *Ways of Seeing.* 1972. New York: Penguin, 1995.

Bordwell, David. *Making Meaning: Inference and Rhetoric in the Interpretation of Cinema*. Cambridge: Harvard UP, 1989.

Bordwell, David, and Noël Carroll. *Post-Theory: Reconstructing Film Studies*. Wisconsin Studies in Film. Madison: U of Wisconsin P, 1996.

Borges, Jorge Luis. "Pierre Menard, Author of the *Quixote*." *Collected Fictions*. Trans. Andrew Hurley. New York: Penguin, 1999. 88–95.

Brummett, Barry. *Rhetorical Dimensions of Popular Culture*. Tuscaloosa: U of Alabama P, 1991.

Burke, Kenneth. *Language as Symbolic Action: Essays on Life, Literature, and Method*. Berkeley: U of California P, 1966.

————. *Permanence and Change: An Anatomy of Purpose*. 1935. 3d ed. Berkeley: U of California P, 1984.

————. *A Rhetoric of Motives*. 1950. Berkeley: U of California P, 1969.

————. "Rhetoric—Old and New." 1950. *New Rhetorics*. Ed. Martin Steinmann, Jr. New York: Scribners, 1967. 59–76.

Chatman, Seymour. *Coming to Terms: The Rhetoric of Narrative in Fiction and Film*. Ithaca: Cornell UP, 1990.

Eagleton, Terry. *Literary Theory: An Introduction*. 1983. 2d ed. Minneapolis: U of Minnesota P, 1996.

Gregory, Richard. L. *The Intelligent Eye*. New York: McGraw-Hill, 1970.

Heath, Stephen, and Patricia Mellencamp, eds. *Cinema and Language*. Frederick, MD: University Publications of America, 1983.

Hendrix, J., and Wood J. A. "The Rhetoric of Film: Toward a Critical Methodology." *Southern Speech Communication Journal* 39 (1973): 105–22.

King, Noel. "Hermeneutics, Reception Aesthetics, and Film Interpretation." *Film Studies: Critical Approaches*. Ed. John Hill and Pamela Church Gibson. Oxford: Oxford UP, 2000.

Medhurst, Martin J. "*Hiroshima, Mon Amour:* From Iconography to Rhetoric." *Quarterly Journal of Speech* 68 (1982): 345–70.

————. "Image and Ambiguity: A Rhetorical Approach to *The Exorcist*." 1937. *Rhetorical Dimensions in Media*. Ed. Martin J. Medhurst and Thomas W. Benson. 2d ed. Dubuque, IA: Kendall/Hunt, 1991. 495–507.

————. "The Rhetorical Structure of Oliver Stone's *JFK*." *Critical Studies in Mass Communication* 10 (1993): 128–43.

Metz, Christian. *Film Language*. 1971. Trans. M. Taylor. New York: Oxford UP, 1974.

————. *The Imaginary Signifier Psychoanalysis and the Cinema*. 1977. Trans. Celia Britton, et al. Bloomington: Indiana UP, 1982.

Mitchell, W. J. T. *Picture Theory: Essays on Verbal and Visual Representation*. Chicago: U of Chicago P, 1994.

Modleski, Tania. *The Women Who Knew Too Much: Hitchcock and Feminist Theory*. New York: Methuen, 1988.

Mulvey, Laura. "Visual Pleasure and Narrative Cinema." *Screen* 16.3 (1975): 618.

Nichols, Bill. *Blurred Boundaries: Questions of Meaning in Contemporary Culture.* Bloomington: Indiana UP, 1994.

———. *Ideology and the Image: Social Representation in the Cinema and Other Media.* Bloomington: Indiana UP, 1981.

———. *Representing Reality: Issues and Concepts in Documentary.* Bloomington: Indiana UP, 1992.

Prince, Stephen. "Contemporary Directions in Film Theory: An Introduction." *Post Script* 13.1 (Fall 1993): 3–9.

———. "The Discourse of Pictures: Iconicity and Film Studies." *Film Quarterly* 47.1 (Fall 1993): 16–28.

———. *Movies and Meaning: An Introduction to Film.* Boston: Allyn and Bacon, 2000.

Rorty, Richard. *Philosophy and the Mirror of Nature.* Princeton, NJ: Princeton UP, 1979.

Rosteck, Thomas, ed. *At the Intersection: Cultural Studies and Rhetorical Studies.* New York: Guilford, 1999.

———. "Cultural Studies and Rhetorical Studies." Review-Essay. *Quarterly Journal of Speech* 81 (1995): 386–403.

———. *See It Now Confronts McCarthyism: Television Documentary and the Politics of Representation.* Tuscaloosa: U of Alabama P, 1994.

Schiappa, Edward. "Second Thoughts on the Critiques of Big Rhetoric." *Philosophy and Rhetoric* 34.3 (2001): 260–74.

Silverman, Kaja. *The Subject of Semiotics.* New York: Oxford UP, 1983.

Simons, Herbert W., ed. *The Rhetorical Turn: Invention and Persuasion in the Conduct of Inquiry.* Chicago: U of Chicago P, 1990.

Simpson, Philip L. *Psycho Paths: Tracking the Serial Killer Through Contemporary American Film and Fiction.* Carbondale: Southern Illinois UP, 2000.

Sobchack, Vivian. *The Address of the Eye: A Phenomenology of Film Experience.* Princeton: Princeton UP, 1992.

Stam, Robert. *Reflexivity in Film and Literature: From Don Quixote To Jean-Luc Godard.* Ann Arbor: UMI Research P, 1985.

———. *Subversive Pleasures: Bakhtin, Cultural Criticism, and Film.* Baltimore: Johns Hopkins UP, 1989.

Ulmer, Gregory. *Heuretics: The Logic of Invention.* Baltimore: Johns Hopkins UP, 1994.

Part One

Perspectives on Film and Film Theory as Rhetoric

THIS BOOK BEGINS WITH ESSAYS THAT READ FILMS RHETORICALLY, drawing terminology from rhetoric proper and from its elaborations in film theory itself. Taken together, they act as initial gestures, exemplifying the range and scope of the rhetorical approach to film. Since a particular concern of this book is to map the emergent field of rhetorical studies of film, each essay is careful to articulate its terministic screen, with an eye for encouraging readers to see the rhetorical principles at work in other films, ones that may not be obviously propagandistic or didactic. Each of the essays in part one also views film and filmic technique as implicitly rhetorical: acts of representation and communication to audiences (spectators) in scenes and contexts using techniques that direct attention, shape interpretation, and foster identification or division. None of the essays reduces the scope of rhetoric such that only films that make explicit arguments (e.g., propaganda films) count as "rhetorical." This first set of six essays typify approaches Thomas Benson likely has in mind when he suggests that rhetorical criticism entails more than attention to the explicitly persuasive dimensions of film:

> A much broader approach encompasses rhetoric as the study of symbolic inducement, reaching beyond films that are didactic or propagandistic, and employing the whole range of tools common to humanistic inquiry into cultural forms and investigating issues of text, genre, myth, gender, ideology, production, authorship, the human subject, meaning, the construction of cinematic ways of knowing, response, and reception. (620)

The essays comprising part one do share a common interest in these last few subjects: ways of knowing, response, and reception. As such, they have much in common with rhetorical criticism and theory whose focus is purely textual, yet they must contend as well with the temporal and visual dimensions of filmic meaning. While it would not be accurate to say that the essays in part one treat film "like a text" (reducing them to rhetorical figures, for example), it would be fair to say that each views film as necessarily invoking a rhetorical situation in which form, content, and technique function as symbolic action or inducement.

I have divided the book into its three sections—"Perspectives on Film and Film Theory as Rhetoric," "Rhetorical Perspectives on Film and Culture," and "Perspectives on Films about Rhetoric"—to distinguish between those approaches that study film through the terministic screen of rhetoric (part one) from those that view film as a form of cultural production that expresses cultural perspectives with designs also on shaping public attitudes (part two) and those that focus on films whose content is rhetoric itself (part three). Essays in part two practice the rhetorical criticism of culture, and thus, they share with cultural studies interests in film as the product of ideological lines of force. The essays in part three of the book share common interests in films that self-reflexively direct our attention to processes of interpretation, identification, and literacy. Their approach is more clearly distinguishable because the films discussed share that common content.

While they certainly share sentiments and terminology, there is an important difference between the essays that comprise parts one and two. For the sake of illustration, consider that both Haskins and Weidauer write about German film from rhetorical perspectives. Haskins's focus is on the ways that Riefenstahl's *Triumph of the Will* constructs community with the strategic use of rhetorical and aesthetic appeals, showing the film to be a carefully and complexly constructed rhetorical act sometimes at odds with the explicitly propagandistic uses for which it was intended and challenging the presumption that the film's audience was easily swayed. Weidauer's focus, however, is on films of the Weimar era as themselves symptomatic of widespread cultural anxiety about the nature and social function of film generally. On the one hand, then, we have film viewed as the embodiment of symbolic action, as a rhetorical act in its own right; on the other, we have films viewed as the artistic expression of cultural attitudes, with the focus on what these films reveal about their cultural circumstances rather than their means of representation or ways of knowing.

Part one opens with Alan Nadel's "Mapping the Other: *The English Patient*, Colonial Rhetoric, and Cinematic Representation." Nadel articulates colonization as symbolic action, showing the strategies of containment implicit in mapping and cinematic representation:

> The narrative of colonization thus consists of innumerable acts, for example, of definition, redefinition, assimilation, appropriation, and exclusion, that facilitate the creation and definition of mapped space, so that to map is to participate in the rhetoric of colonialism, in that mapping extends and represents the gaze of the colonizer in the name of objectivity, neutrality, science.

Ann Chisholm's "Rhetoric and the Early Work of Christian Metz: Augmenting Ideological Inquiry in Rhetorical Film Theory and Criticism" closely examines Metz's efforts to articulate a film language. Her essay shows that within his initial semiotic theory, rhetoric assumes multiple roles:

> It is at once synonymous with a 'strict' or normative grammar, with disposition, and with connotative operations. [. . .] Although he appears to actualize several dimensions of this overdetermined concept, Metz tacitly reifies rhetoric both insofar as its second definition adjoins its first and insofar as its third definition is effaced, in the last analysis, by other aspects of his theory.

Building on this analysis, Chisholm surveys work that draws from Metz and/or rhetorical theory to suggest ways we might better define the range and scope of rhetoric as ideological inquiry. In "Temptation as Taboo: A Psychorhetorical Reading of *The Last Temptation of Christ*," Martin J. Medhurst taps the resources of psychoanalytic terminology to show how that film is "structured by a complex calculus of myth, metaphor, and sign, the structural relationships of which must be understood if one is to evaluate this work of cinematic art on its own terms." Medhurst, whose previous work is discussed by Chisholm in her chapter, also models ways that insights from psychoanalysis may be conjoined with rhetorical analysis to deepen our understanding of identification as both a rhetorical and psychological principle. Drawing from the work of Gregory Ulmer in *Heuretics: The Logic of Invention*, Byron Hawk ("Hyperrhetoric and the Inventive Spectator: Remotivating *The Fifth Element*") shows how the notion of the spectator can be expanded to include the possibilities for radical reconstruction of the film as object and the spectator as subject. "The filmic narrative," writes Hawk, "is constructed in order to allow viewers to suture themselves onto a character and identify with that subject position. [But] once identification is made with the character, the spectator has the potential to remotivate that subject position into a context distant from the initial filmic context."

Part one continues with essays that examine films as what Burke would call representative anecdotes—narratives that stand by themselves but that also contain insights into wider cultural forces. Ekaterina V. Haskins draws from Burke's conceptualization of "scene" in a symbolic of motives and Mikhail Bakhtin's notion of the "chronotope" to examine the rhetoric of identification in "Time, Space, and Political Identity: Envisioning Community in *Triumph of the Will*." Haskins analyzes Leni Riefenstahl's film to demonstrate that "the presumption of 'irrationality' with regard to fascist discourse relies on a shaky warrant—the belief in an autonomous rational individual whose identity is given prior to any participation in the political" (2). As aesthetic propaganda, the film manufactures collective consciousness by inscribing individuality always and already in a political process of identification more complex than normally assumed by those who would attribute its "success" to individual weakness. In the concluding essay of part one, James Roberts explores the ways in which bodies, both on-screen and in the audience, are rhetorically constituted by virtue of their explicit visual and proxemic representation. His essay, "On Rhetorical Bodies: *Hoop Dreams* and Constitutional Discourse," associates the idea that cinematic narratives materially construct bodies with the hegemonic practices of culture at large to position people like William Gates and Arthur Agee (the subjects of *Hoop Dreams*) as stereotypical (and thus containable) "inner-city youth."

Each of the essays in part one illustrates the variety of ways that rhetoric may usefully generate provocative viewings of the film object. Along the way, they also teach us that rhetoric is a rich terministic screen for both the analysis of film and the film theory that directs our attention.

Work Cited

Benson, Thomas W. "Rhetoric of Film." *Encyclopedia of Rhetoric and Composition: Communication from Ancient Times to the Information Age.* Ed. Theresa Enos. New York: Garland Publishing, 1996. 620–21.

1

Mapping the Other: *The English Patient,* Colonial Rhetoric, and Cinematic Representation

Alan Nadel

O<small>NE CANNOT COLONIZE WITHOUT A MAP, A GAZE, AND A NARRATIVE.</small>
Since colonization is a symbolic action—albeit with innumerable material consequences—it requires a symbology. To say that Columbus discovered America, for example, is to say that he participated in a symbolic relationship in which his European sponsor was, *a priori,* superior and his "America" was, *a posteriori,* subordinate. According to the understanding of space encoded by European maps, in other words, if Columbus landed on an "unmapped" place, whatever he discovered there, by definition, would be subordinate, for maps make initial distinctions, distinctions that organize a gaze. And these distinctions, Michel de Certeau makes clear, are of a historiographic nature. They divide the nations with written "history" from those nations with unwritten history, so that the mapping of the new space is the writing of the colonizer's history. Because the discovery of "America" extends the map of Spain, it becomes part of the history of Spanish—or more generically European—exploration and conquest. The mapping of the New World—and by extension the bodies of those others who inhabit it—organizes the historiographic gaze just as the nominal rubric, "The Age of Exploration," thematizes it.

The narrative of colonization thus consists of innumerable acts, for example, of definition, redefinition, assimilation, appropriation, and exclusion, that facilitate the creation and definition of mapped space, so that to map is to participate in the rhetoric of colonialism, in that mapping extends and represents the gaze of the colonizer in the name of objectivity, neutrality, science.[1] Maps project a representation as though the referents existed in nature, as though the matrix of measurement and gridwork simply reflected what was there—what was discovered to be there—rather than that they create the space on which the narrative of discovery can unfold by virtue of representing the other.

Just as the codes of mapping are thus rhetorical devices providing colonial narratives with a scientific ethos, so the codes of cinematic representation, especially in mainstream Hollywood-style cinema, are rhetorical devices providing the illusion of omniscience or, to state it differently, the ethos of objectivity to narratives that subordinate the deigesis to the desires of the spectator. Mainstream cinematic narrative, in other words, evokes the same ethos as mapping, in that both forms of representation create symbolic spaces that mask the arbitrary authority ceded, *a priori,* to the place whence the (geographic, historiographic, or cinematographic) discourse emanates. The spectator, as visitor to the symbolic space, is invited to share the privileged gaze of the colonizer.

In this light, *The English Patient* presents an extended rhetorical argument about the dimensions of colonial discourse in such a way as to connect that discourse to the codes of cinematic representation, thus revealing the seductive quality of colonial discourse as a form of cinematic romance from which the rhetorical tenets of mainstream cinema allow no escape. Since mapping is the literal act of turning the other into a representation, it is a rhetorical process, one that is requisite to traditional narrative cinema. That cinema constructs its narrative by means of plotting coordinates between a vast and unviewable world and a manageable, contained temporal and physical space. This coordination only becomes legible by virtue of its compliance with elaborate semantic and syntactic conventions. Since filmmaking, in this regard, is identical to mapmaking, the fact that the central characters in *The English Patient* are engaged as mapmakers thus underscores the ways that filmmaking and mapmaking participate in colonial rhetorical practices.

If mapmaking is the quintessential colonialist activity—the construction of a gridwork and taxonomy aimed at naming the other, at turning the other into the same—then the International Sand Club, as Almasy's pre–World War II, North African exploration group euphemistically names itself, is, despite its claims of apolitical internationalism, devoted in the most abstract and concrete ways to colonialism. This devotion is so transparent as to render itself invisible in the same way that cinematic rhetoric (at least in mainstream cinema) renders its privileged gaze invisible in order to make it one with the diegesis it presumes to render. That presumption, of course, is merely rhetorical; mainstream narrative cinema constructs a world through a series of rhetorical conventions so that that world may appear to be "captured." The same is true of the cartographer whose symbolic representations name and delimit a site that then may be claimed, transgressed, acquired, owned, exchanged, exploited, or renounced; cartography creates the external perspective from which the indigenous people can be distinguished and in whose name the concept of the primitive and/or role of the subaltern can be created.

The film interweaves two stories, one of Almasy, a Hungarian who in the 1930s worked as part of an international team exploring and mapping North Africa, and the other of Hana, a Canadian nurse who served in an Allied medical corps in Europe during World War II. In the final weeks of the war in Europe, distraught by the fact that, as the English patient states, "anybody she ever loves tends to die on her," Hana opts out of the war, taking refuge in an abandoned Italian monastery. There she plans to tend, in his final days, to the nameless "English patient," suffering from profound and extensive burns incurred in a plane crash in North Africa six years earlier. That English patient is Almasy, who had had an affair, just prior to the outbreak of the war, with a married British woman, Katherine Clifton. Through a complex interplay first of crosscutting and then of flashbacks, the film interweaves the events in North Africa in the late 1930s and in the Italian monastery at the end of World War II.

The North African events start with Almasy's plane crash in the desert (he's shot down by German troops), which causes his burns. Next he is rescued by ostensibly nomadic people who treat the burns with nonwestern ointments and transport him out of the desert via camel. These segments are crosscut with segments of Hana's treating wounded soldiers in Europe. The use of crosscutting, according to standard cinematic rhetoric, would suggest that the two events are simultaneous, separated by space but not by time. Only when Hana and the English patient occupy the same place—"Italy 1944," a title tells us—can we discern that their events took place in different times, simultaneous only from the privileged perspective of the cinematic spectator.

As a rhetorical device, in other words, the initial crosscutting simultaneously establishes and diminishes difference. The contrasts between Almasy's adventures and Hana's are underscored by their apparent simultaneity, so that we are encouraged to construct an allegorical equation: her suffering equals his. This allegorical move—the act of making the other the same—of course, is requisite to colonizing. In revealing the rhetorical convention as misleading, the "1944" subtitle does not remove the illusory construction of similarity/difference; instead it reorients its axis, such that the two sequences, in sharing the same cinematic space, are united in their separation from the spectator. The spectator's position thus becomes historical, since the writing of history necessarily creates temporal distinctions within the unity of the historical text that allows history to exist *qua* history.[2]

The viewer thus replicates, in relation to Almasy's story (and to Hana's), Almasy's own relationship to his book of Herodotus, who, he tells Hana, is "the father of history." This is especially so because Herodotus provides the allegorical scaffold for Almasy's romance with Katharine. When, around the campfire in the desert, the members of the International Sand Club entertain each other, Katharine does so by telling a story of adultery and death recorded by Herodotus: In order to demonstrate the beauty of his wife to Gyges, Candeles, the king of Lydia, arranges to hide Gyges in his wife's bedroom while she is undressing. When the queen beholds Gyges observing her naked body, she tells him, in Katharine's words: "either you must submit to death for gazing on what you should not or else kill my husband, who has shamed me, and become king in his place. So Gyges kills the king, marries the queen, and becomes ruler of Lydia for twenty-eight years. End of the story." Through crosscutting and sound bridges, the film links Hana's reading the story from Herodotus in the monastery and Katharine's telling it in the desert, thus creating an ostensive parallel between Hana's love for the English patient and Katharine's love for Almasy. This odd triangulation of Herodotus, Hana, and Katharine, moreover, situates the English patient/Almasy in the peculiar position of being both the auditor and the projector of the scene of the storytelling, in other words, as both the site of the cinematic apparatus and the site of the cinematic spectator. Because, moreover, the matrix that unifies the sites of the two narratives is his identity—in other words, the connection between "Almasy" and "the English patient"—the cinematic devices foreground how as spectator Almasy occupies the role of the Lacanian split subject, which, many argue, is endemic to the experience of the cinematic spectatorship.[3] The story that Almasy *heard* becomes the memory the English patient *projects,* into which he inserts Almasy—himself and not himself, as he claims no memory of his name—as the spectator. That story is about the relationship of death and power to the act of "gazing upon what you should not." It is thus a template for the circulation of lack that, in the Lacanian model, binds death and pleasure through the mechanism of desire, and it is also a metonymic moment in the film's rhetoric for the specific circulation of desire that will consume Katharine and Almasy.

This metonymic moment, contextualized by the symbolic order under the name of "the father of history," Herodotus, situates Almasy not only as the psychological subject of the events to which he was spectator but also as the historical subject of them, in that he has interleaved his life into Herodotus's text. Between the pages of his edition of Herodotus, Almasy has put letters, notes, and pictures that comprise his personal history prior to becoming the English patient. Just as the book of Herodotus becomes the text that integrates truth, fable, allegory, personal history, and public history for the English patient, the film becomes the same synchronic text for the viewer. Like the characters, we are put in the position of ceding authority to a text, so that it may allow us to construct from it a fictive history. Constructing the history of the English patient, furthermore, becomes a theme in the film, such that most of the significant characters are engaged in the same enterprise, from the English officer who is interviewing the English patient in Italy, to Hana, Caravaggio, and Kip. One could even argue that the English patient himself is reconstructing his history through years of scorched denial; that he too is filling in the blank spaces and giving a name and a meaning to the events. Since Almasy is not English, to discover how he came to be called the English patient is to understand the rhetoric of colonialism—the process of discovering, of claiming, and of naming that authorized his activity in North Africa and organizes colonialism in general. That is the same activity, rhetorically, that the viewer must go through to understand why the film is named *The English Patient*. The film guides its viewers, in other words, to an understanding of the same arbitrary acts of nominalism that the plot guides its characters toward. Those acts involve the rhetorical power to name and to claim, and the rhetorical implications of being named and being claimed.

Since the film is so extensively engaged in the rhetoric of naming and claiming, the opening credits become very significant. While the credits appear, we see a close-up of a brush drawing with black (India?) ink on a rough tan parchment. The sequence is compelling because of the vividly contrasting textures, so that as the wet ink touches the parched, tan surface, we watch not just an inscription but a conversion; the ink makes the light, dry, rough, heterogeneous surface dark, smooth, wet, and homogeneous. It performs this act of conversion, moreover, through an unseen agency, as only the tip of the brush is visible and we do not know who marks the surface or when or why. The marks themselves are also cryptic. We cannot tell at first if they resemble figures, designs, or letters in some alphabetic or pictographic language. Only as the drawing is completed is it possible to discern—although one certainly might have guessed—that the black inscription resembles a human figure lying horizontally, arms extended above his/her head. Although later in the film, similar figures will be found decorating the walls of a cave, named by the European explorers "The Cave of Swimmers," we have no way of knowing what the figure represents. It could be a human swimming or screaming or dead. It might not represent a human at all but rather some anthropomorphic god or demon in the history or religion of the people who drew the figures in the cave. At the outset, however, even this questionable naming and claiming is withheld. We simply have a black figure superimposed on a light surface, a foreign substance with an unseen and unnamed agent occupying and symbolically reorganizing an alien space.

This act of inscription, furthermore, stands in sharp contrast to a simultaneous but very different act of naming and claiming: the presentation of the film's credits. This takes place within a recognizable symbology—standard letters of an English alphabet, arranged to present comprehensible messages in a recognizable order: stars, film title, featured players, chief production personnel in ascending order of importance, culminating with the name of the director. The letters, unlike the ink figure, moreover, seem detached from the surface on which they appear and absent of the sign of the agent that produced them. In the symbology of film rhetoric they are the *a priori* owners of the space that is being claimed, *a posteriori*, by the brush and black ink. In these opening credits, therefore, the nondeigetic world is artificially made simultaneous with the deigetic in the same way that the crosscutting that follows will artificially make the 1930s Africa and the 1940s Europe simultaneous. The opening credits thus demonstrate the authority of cinematic rhetoric to subordinate time and space to the ends of its symbolic representation, in other words, to demonstrate the way in which mainstream cinema replicates the act of mapping endemic to the rhetoric of colonialism.

When the credits are finished, the parchment with the black image dissolves into another space, similar in hue but different in texture, smooth but full of curves, highlighted by dark shadows. The scene at first seems to be the close-up of a naked and hairless (hence, probably female) body. In a gesture of visual chiasmus, in other words, the imagery of the black body on the tan parchment seems inverted, such that the tan surface now represents the body while the black highlighting indicates its parameters. The shadow of the drawn body lingers, moreover, after the parchment has dissolved, such that it becomes a large shadow floating across the new surface. While the camera pans back, it becomes clear that the surface is not the body of a woman but of a continent, the rippled sands of the Sahara, which appear smooth when viewed from adequate distance, in this case the height of an airplane. Rhetorically, this inversion turns the making of the black inscription into an act of mapping, in other words, a symbolic representation of a place. It suggests, in addition, that in both the version and the inversion, the informing metaphor for the mapped site is the female (or at least feminized) body.[4] In presenting the drawn (i.e., symbolic) version of the body as black and the land itself as light, the film also puns visually on the nominal representation of Africa, in colonial discourse, as "the dark continent." Finally, the visual chiasmus suggests the gesture of the entire film, to create an alternative imagery that inverts traditional colonialist rhetorical assumptions and, through them, inverts colonialism's seductive hegemonic argument.

In so doing, however, it also relies on the power of the camera to create analogies, to invert images, to distance, and to abstract. Only through the standard codes of cinematic rhetoric can we establish the sites in North Africa and Italy, for the purpose of comparison and scrutiny, and, even more so, only by reliance on those codes can we place those sites in time. In other words, the geography acquires its historicity not by virtue of the events that occurred on/to it but by virtue of its appropriation into a symbolic system, one that aims at passing for transparent reality, in the same way that mapping and colonizing do. The opening sequence thus suggests that even inversion and critique depend on discursive practices that replicate the activity being critiqued. In the same way, the alternative (or anti-) colony set up in Italy by Hana to escape the "world war" of colonial empires simultaneously inverts and replicates the colonialist rhetoric that underpins the war. In the end, that common rhetoric emerges as the only constant amid the political and economic vicissitudes of the warring nations.

This motif is made explicit late in the film, during a flashback in which Almasy remembers the farewell dinner of the International Sand Club. Arriving late and drunk at this black-tie dinner in Cairo, Almasy vents his anger at Katharine for having ended their affair through a general denunciation of the whole group. When Almasy's best friend, Madox, proposes a toast, "To the International Sand Club: May it soon resurface!" Almasy responds: "Misfits, buggers, fascists, and fools—God bless us everyone." As part of his diatribe, he further states, "The people here don't want us. You must be joking. The Egyptians are desperate to get rid of the colonials." Madox's toast parallels an earlier set of toasts in which the members of the club celebrated the funding of a new expedition. First they drank "to mapmaking" and then to their having acquired the funds to support the project: "To arm-twisting!" Just as Almasy's toast glossed Madox's toast, "arm-twisting" all-too-precisely connects the colonial investment in mapping Africa with acts of coercion.

Madox represents the international interest in Africa in a more positive way when he breaks camp for the final time, in order to return to England: "We didn't care about countries, did we? Brits, Arabs, Hungarians, Germans—none of that mattered, did it? It was something finer than that." Their international club was indeed devoted to something finer than nations; it was devoted to sand, the fine sand of North Africa, those nearly microscopic grains that slip as easily through a hand as through an hourglass, those grains that could make the wind visible or hide an entire expedition, that equally could be vast or suffocating. Brit, Arab, Hungarian, and German were united in their dedication to the white amorphous matter that covered the top third of the dark continent. As Madox had pointed out earlier to Almasy in regard to the value of their maps, "In war if you own the desert, you own North Africa."

This remark not only underscores the connection between mapping and colonizing but also indicates Madox's tacit assumption that the ownership of North Africa is limited to those who produce the map, who participate in its codes and are authorized to do so by its set of coordinates and its process of representation. In World War II, the warring parties are the mapmakers, not the mapped. Represented as other by the process of mapping, subordinated, *a priori*, the indigenous Africans can neither own the maps nor the sites that the maps represent. Since "ownership" is a form of acquisition, those who are part of the dark continent, who comprise its dark population, cannot own it. And although Madox did not live to appreciate the prophetic nature of his words, the postwar period of the late-1940s and of the 1950s proved him correct. As he wished in his final toast, the club does resurface, for whatever their differences, between 1939 and 1945, the warring Caucasians quickly forget them after the war as they return to their common interests. If from the perspective of the International Sand Club the war destroyed the spirit of internationalism that allowed collaborative mapping of Africa, the war was only a brief hiatus in practices spanning centuries— in some ways dating back to Herodotus—that unified the Western powers in their shared interest in controlling and using, in dividing up and owning, the dark continent according to the boundaries that they had mapped.

In contrast to Madox's affection for the internationalism of the Sand Club, then, Almasy's caustic rebuke could be read as a renunciation of colonialism, but I think it is more apt to regard it as a form of ire about the fact that the club's principles were not sufficiently universal. Unlike North Africa, Katharine could not be owned by virtue of having been mapped. Although Almasy claimed that he hated ownership, he could not resist the desire to trace, name, and claim parts of Katharine. "I claim this shoulder blade," he said to her when they were in bed, "No wait—turn over. I want *this*—this place—what's it called? This is mine. I'm going to ask the king permission to call it Almasy Bosphorous." At the same dinner party in which he drunkenly abused the Sand Club, Almasy later cornered Katharine to tell her, "I want to touch you. I want the things which are mine, which belong to me." He could not have what he called "mine," of course, because his claim was rhetorical, emanating from conventions and assumptions that relate acts to claims. The colonizer climbs the mountain or plants his foot on the "foreign" shore and stakes his claim. Having planted the flag, having penetrated the unmapped region, having named what he has mounted and penetrated, the unmapped site becomes his. It becomes his, moreover, only because his actions are authorized by the name of a nation or monarch, in other words, by a historiography that seals and gives sovereignty to the borders of the colonizer's origin so that that historiography may open the borders of the unmapped space to the narrative of the colonizer's destiny. This narrative, known generically as the quest, has longstanding status in Western discourse and is requisite to our understanding of romance, as Wlad Godzich succinctly explains:

> Western thought has always thematized the other as a threat to be reduced, as a potential same-to-be, a yet-not-same. The paradigmatic conception here is that of the quest in romances of chivalry in which the adventurous knight leaves Arthur's court—the realm of the known—to encounter some form of otherness, a domain in which the courtly values of the Arthurian world do not prevail. The quest is brought to an end when this alien domain is brought within the hegemonic sways of the Arthurian world: the other has been reduced to (more of) the same. (qtd. in de Certeau, *Heterologies* xiii)

The quest is also endemic to mainstream cinema in that the mainstream cinema posits a unity wherein the goals and adventures of the principals are connected to the totalizing of their triumph: to win the day is to couple happily, whether that coupling is the goal of the initial quest or simply its ancillary reward.[5]

In this sense, for Almasy to succeed, he needed to triumph over all obstacles to attain what he called "mine," the Katharine attached to the body on which he has already staked his claim. That claim was staked, of course, with indifference to or in defiance of prior claims. Katharine was married, bore the name of her husband, and her marriage carried the legal sanctions of the state, sanctions that, like the International Sand Club, were supposed to transcend national borders. In staking his claim, Almasy was thus throwing into conflict two historical narratives, one grounded in legal precedent and the other in romantic precedent. Nor was this conflict lost on Katharine, who tried to negotiate it by disengaging the worlds that authorized each claim: "This is a different world is what I tell myself," she told Almasy, "a different life, and here I am a different wife." For Katharine, in other words, the map provided a provisional solution.

The Anglo-European world represented the place where warrants emanated from legal contracts, whereas the exotic elsewhere of the dark continent warranted its sanctions, in her mind, with the transcendent laws of romance.

In this way, the world of cinema itself is aligned rhetorically with the dark continent, the place where a romantic narrative may be projected onto the un-mapped space of the other with the confidence that such appropriative behavior is consistent with the apparatus of the filmmaker or cartographer and with the romantic narrative that circumscribes the spectator in classical cinema.[6] For this reason, it is easy to identify with Almasy's position as romantic quester/hero, even when Katharine eliminates the warrant for that position, first by breaking off the affair and subsequently by writing, as she lay dying in the Cave of Swimmers, that "We are the real countries, not the boundaries drawn on maps, the names of powerful men." The connection between maps and bodies reiterates the visual equation made at the outset, when the drawing of the black body is marked on, and then translated into the feminized body of North Africa. Although the low-flying biplane that replaces the shadow carries Katharine in the front seat, we do not learn until late in the film that she is already dead, so that her final message renouncing mapping (and also asking to be buried in England) turns the opening scene retrospectively into a tribute to failure. Having placed what turns out to be both an unshakable and a fatal claim on Katharine, Almasy was incapable of supporting the narrative upon which that claim was based. In returning to the repressed memories of his last days in Africa, the English patient in the Italian monastery confronts the way in which his claim on Katharine led to the death of her and her husband, Geoffrey. In a suicide attack, Geoffrey killed himself and seriously injured Katharine by trying to crash their plane into Almasy. Almasy, who escaped the crash, had to leave Katharine in the Cave of Swimmers and cross the desert by foot in order to get help.

He could not secure that help, however, because he was completely embedded in the romantic narrative that had motivated his actions as a member of the International Sand Club and, as well, as Katharine's lover. He believed, in other words, in the transcendent role of his work and values, constructing a rhetorical position in regard to the object of his scrutiny that exempted him and his work from national interests or political implications. He treated his roles as explorer, cartographer, and lover cinematically, in other words, only in terms of his personal quest. Thus, when British soldiers refused to give him a car to return to Katharine, when they regarded his lack of papers and his foreign (to them) name with suspicion, he could respond only with violence that subordinated their concerns to his values.

One could argue in fact that his experiences as a colonizer had prepared him for no other kind of response. But the occupying troops had indeed turned his position from that of colonizer into that of subaltern. The British were, at that moment, the colonial powers, and he was the other whose authority and credibility, whose very identity, was contingent on his ability to participate in, rather than transcend, their rules and discursive practices. Nor did his beating and arrest by the British in any way disabuse him of this informing narrative. His commitment to return to Katharine, even after there was no chance that she was still alive, dominated his sense of purpose and, as is customary in mainstream cinema, the film's, such that his murdering of a British soldier so that he could escape and return to Katharine, or his trading maps of North Africa to the Germans in exchange for help, are valorized under his commitment to his dead lover.

Almasy thus continued to act as though he occupied the rhetorical position of the colonizer rather than that of the colonial subject. He continued to treat the fulfillment of his romantic destiny as a right rather than as the aborted narrative of a claimed place and people. This sense of transcendent authority, the sense that he could place himself above the material events of the space he had mapped, led to catastrophe: "There was a trade. I had our expedition's maps. After the British made me their enemy, I gave their enemy the maps. [. . .] so I got back to the desert and to Katharine in Madox's English plane with German gasoline."

Shot down by the Germans, because of his plane's British insignia, he was a victim of the rhetoric of mapping, that is, the ascribing of nominal identity to an other in order to align it with the assumptions of a national narrative. Once he took to the air in a British plane, even though the British had marked him as a German spy, even though the Germans had provided his gasoline, even though his citizenship was neither English nor German, he was by definition the product of his markings. The fact that his personal history might run counter to the assumptions of those who shot him down was irrelevant because, by virtue of his subordinate position, his story had no place in their discourse; he existed only as a part of their unfolding history and, even then, only nominally so.

The film's rhetoric anticipates this conversion from Almasy to the English patient, from colonizer to subaltern, not only through the chiasmus of the opening sequence but also through the repeated framing of Almasy by visual crossgrids that imply that he, and thus everyone who maps, is potentially subject to being mapped. Repeatedly we see him shot through openings crosshatched with iron, framed by windows' checkered bars, or viewed through the cross beams exposed by the bombed out parts of the Italian monastery. We are made to see him, in other words, arranged along a set of arbitrary, perpendicular coordinates, the longitude and latitude of his identity.

Almasy's nominal identification with England thus renders him its colonial subject, completely dependent on the English for care and for identity. He thereby manifests the hybridity that for Homi Bhabha defines the colonial subject's position. To be the English patient means to be in the care of the English and/or to be of their identity. The severity of his burns makes Almasy permanently the former and the political confusion of his identity makes him passively and conveniently the latter. He has by the war's end been mapped and cross-referenced by their gridwork of priorities, by their laws and assumptions, ultimately by their national interests. He has become what he always already was: the subject of colonial rhetoric.

For the final weeks of his life, however, Almasy becomes a member of an alternative colony, an oxymoronically anticolonial colony, one that creates a site from which he can reassemble his past and the film can interrogate colonialism's rhetorical assumptions. This colony initially has two members, Hana, the Canadian nurse, and her English patient. Rather than cart the suffering patient from hospital to hospital, as the Allies advance through Italy in the final weeks of the war, Hana decides to stay with the English patient in an abandoned, partially bombed-out monastery. Although she never fully articulates her complex motives, she acts as if, by caring for the scorched English patient and thus easing the pain of *his* purgatory, she can suffer through her own. In part, she seems to be escaping not so much death as its uncertainty; she knows the English patient will die (as he later says to Caravaggio, "You can't kill me. I died years ago"), and hence she can care for him without hope or expectation. More generally, the bombed-out monastery seems to be her place of sanctuary from the brutal defeat of hope and expectation that characterizes war in general.

In constructing this unofficial sanctuary, therefore, she attempts to take herself (and the English patient) off the contested map of Europe and thereby exempt herself from the rhetoric of war, aggression, and subordination endemic to making empires. Ironically, Hana has chosen for the site of this anticolony the historical home of the Roman Empire and the Holy Roman Empire. She is embedded, moreover, in colonial assumptions from which, unlike the war, per se, she cannot find escape. In making the monastery habitable, for example, she repairs the staircase by stacking it with books from its library. In other words, she appropriates for her own pragmatic ends the cultural artifacts that she cannot understand, thus replicating a fundamental act of colonization. When the English patient suggests that she might think of reading the books to him, she indicates that there may not be any in English, that is, any culturally suitable for their community.

Like colonies everywhere, the anticolony cannot maintain its social configuration any more than could the desert colony of the International Sand Club. Shortly after Hana sets up the household, David Caravaggio arrives. Like Hana, he is Canadian; like Almasy, he worked in North Africa before the war; like the monastery, he is nominally linked to the Italian Renaissance. He has also been a spy, a thief, and an assassin. He lived in the same neighborhood as Hana in Montreal and he worked in the same office as Clifton, during the time Almasy was having an affair with Clifton's wife. Like the English patient, Caravaggio has also been deformed because of his experiences—he lost his thumbs as the result of Nazi torture in North Africa—and like the English patient, Caravaggio depends on morphine. In many ways, Caravaggio is the mark of all the history that Hana and her English patient are trying to escape and, like the English patient, his body bears the scars and track marks of that history.

Caravaggio functions, in other words, as the inescapable mark of colonialism's historicity. On a map, a colony may be clearly delimited and nominally attached to the colonial power, but its representation is far from complete, and the attachment it represents is far from stable. To inscribe on a map the colonial site as bordered and connected is to obliterate the bodies on whom the marks of the colonizer have inscribed the colonizer's history as the ostensive substitute for that of the indigene's. Although there is no escape from this mark of the colonizer, no way of returning to the site of an unspoiled origin, Caravaggio is particularly interesting because he brings with him the hybridity of the colonial powers rather than that of the colonial subjects.

This is one more moment of chiasmus, in which the film, having first inverted the relationship of the monastery to the war in Italy further inverts the nature of its sanctuary when the monastery incorporates the same forces that it is trying to exclude. Because these are exactly the forces that have turned Almasy into the English patient, they are, of course, impossible to exclude; Caravaggio merely makes visible through his scars the identity that the scars on the English patient obscure. Even the arbitrary excuse that the Nazi officer uses to remove Caravaggio's thumbs—(that it is the Muslim punishment for adultery or, he ponders, "Is it for theft?")—evoke Almasy's crimes: Almasy has committed adultery and stolen the maps for the Germans.

The flashback, as a device of cinematic rhetoric, thus inserts Almasy into the monastery colony, itself situated within the context of World War II, which finally the film contextualizes within the cognitive map of twentieth-century Western imperialism. The construction of the film thus echoes in the symbolic register what the interleaving of Almasy's life between the pages of his volume of Herodotus does in the metonymic register: it implicates inextricably the historical subject in the colonizing enterprise of history.

The parallels between the Italian and African colonies further underscore that relationship by problematically foregrounding the hybridity of any rhetorical position relating colonizer to colonized. The flashlight examination of the drawing of the Cave of Swimmers, for example, parallels Hana's torchlight examination of the Renaissance painting on the walls and ceiling of an Italian church. She is hoisted up to that ceiling by Kip, the Indian lieutenant in the British Army, who has camped on the monastery grounds while he dismantles bombs and mines left in the region by the Germans.

In 1945, of course, India is still part of the British Empire and Kip is thus a British subject, risking his life to make Italy safe for Allied occupation. As a representative of the culture outside of the Western Renaissance, his act of exploration and discovery reveals the implicit assumptions that informed the International Sand Club's "discoveries." But the critical position established by Kip cannot be maintained any more successfully than can the anticolonial configuration of Hana's monastery colony, for Kip is always artificially the British subject in the same way that Almasy is artificially the English patient. Like Almasy he shares a nominal and legal identity with exactly those people who had made him their enemy. If the author who represents Almasy's life as the colonial subject is Herodotus, then the author who represents Kip's is Kipling. For that reason, Kip tries to explain to the English patient that he finds Kipling impossible to read. The English patient, however, mistakenly believes that the problem arises from Kipling's prose style. "You have to read Kipling slowly," he explains, repeating the sentence with the punctuation: "'the wonder house, comma, as the natives called the Lahor Museum.'" But the problem, Kip makes clear, lies not in recognizing the proper punctuation but in realizing the historically specific conditions that the punctuation effaces: "It's still there, the cannon outside the museum; it was made of metal cups and bowls taken from every household in the city of Staks and melted down, and later they fired the cannon at my people, comma, the natives, full stop."

Whereas Kipling's sentence attributes to the Indians an act of inappropriate naming (they call the museum a "wonder house"), Kip's sentence reveals the inappropriateness of Kipling's naming the Indians "natives." In addition to making visible Kipling's misnaming, Kip indicates its material consequences. The property of the Indians was confiscated in the interest of subjugating and killing its original owners. Under the appropriative conditions of colonialism, the Indians thus provided the means for their own subjugation. Kip reveals the arbitrary nature of this subjugation by demonstrating that the same punctuation applies to both forms of appropriation or misappropriation, but that the cannon—like the canon, however it is punctuated—exists in a unidirectional relationship to the colonized; it is not a function of logical punctuation but of power. Thus Hana, regardless of her personal beliefs, as part of the occupying forces in Italy is empowered to turn the canonical works of Italian literature into her private staircase.

But if Kip's objection to Kipling is that "the message of your book, however slowly I read it, is that the best thing for India is to be ruled by the English," he also cannot avoid recognizing the ways in which his history is interleaved with that of Great Britain, something that becomes apparent when Kip's assistant, Hardy, was killed in the square of the nearby Italian village, as part of the celebration over the German surrender, when Hardy attempted to plant an English flag on what turned out to be a booby-trapped statute. If Hardy was killed by one of the bombs Kip had failed to find and dismantle, that bomb also suggests the tenuous relationship between Kip and the empire in which he is a citizen.

Earlier, Kip was nearly killed when he had to dismantle a bomb stuck under a bridge. The German surrender had just been announced and an American tank, with celebrating soldiers piled on it, was rumbling toward the bridge, its vibrations sure to set the bomb off. The tank refused to be stopped and Kip had dropped his wire cutters in the pool of water surrounding the bomb. When he found the cutters, he only had time to cut one wire, not knowing if it would incapacitate the bomb or explode it. Hana had not wanted him to go that morning, but Kip replied, "It is what I do. I do this every day." Kip does, in other words, the same thing the cups and bowls in the city of Staks or the staircase of books in the monastery do: make the environs suitable for colonial occupation. Appropriately, therefore, the bomb Kip is defusing bears his own name (serial number "KKIP 2600"); and the explosion he forestalls, as much through arbitrary luck as skill and guile, is the immanent blowup of the colonial world.

For the time being, however, it is Hardy, not Kip, who is blown up in an act of nationalism coming on the heels of the moment when Kip dismantled the bomb named KKIP. The juxtaposition of these events, coupled perhaps with Kip's relationship to Hana and to the English patient, forces Kip to realize not only how nominal was his relationship to Hardy but also how endemic that nominalism is to Kip's role as nominal British subject:

> I was thinking yesterday—yesterday—the patient and Hardy—everything that was good about England. I couldn't even say what that was—we didn't even exchange two personal words and we'd been through some terrible things together, some terrible things. He was engaged to a girl in the village. I mean—and us—he never once asked me if I could spin the ball at cricket or Karma Sutra—or—I don't even know what I'm talking about.

To this Hana responds, simply, "You loved him."

The film doesn't question the accuracy of Hana's pronouncement so much as problematize its meaning by making it roughly analogous to Almasy's love for Katharine, that is, a love not only for a dead person but for the impossible ideal that Katharine dies imagining, the world without maps. Only in such a world could Hardy and Kip find common ground, but Hardy dies imagining exactly the opposite, the world in which the British flag flies in the Italian village square. Hardy's death at the end of the war and Katharine's at the beginning—both the result of imposing British rule on foreign terrain—are thus counterbalancing ideals, the war's bookends, between which we find Herodotus and Kipling, Almasy and the English patient.

The film translates those historical fictions and fictional histories into the text of the postcolonial world, located in the subject position not of the explorers but of the lost historical subjects, Hana and Kip. Their dilemma is captured in two segments. The first is an interchange that takes place when Hana asks Kip what he would do if one night she didn't come to him.

> *Kip:* I'd try not to expect you.
> *Hana:* Yes, but what if it got late and I hadn't shown up?
> *Kip:* Then I'd think there must be a reason.
> *Hana:* You wouldn't come to find me? Hmm. That makes me never want to come here. Then I tell myself: he spends all day searching and at night he wants to be found.
> *Kip:* I do want you to find me. I do want to be found.

Being found, of course, means being subject to the laws of discovery, claiming, owning. Almasy finds Katharine, and follows her to the marketplace, and goes back to find her again and again, even after she is dead. And the English patient finds her once more in his memory in the events that comprise the film's cinematic narrative. What has been lost materially has been recovered rhetorically through the conventions of cinematic representation. So Kip's desire to be found can be seen as his desire to be the subject of cinematic narrative, the agent in the colonial romance; equally, however, it can be seen as his desire to be discovered independent of the colonial narrative that appropriates him, like the metal cups and bowls in the city of Staks, in the interest of making the landscape safe for the British. Kip is in the untenable position of being the colonial subject defusing the explosive legacy of World War II, at the very moment when colonialism, itself, is about to explode. The post–war era will mark the collapse of the British Empire, to be replaced by the hegemony of American cold war imperialism. The world of the English patient will die, to be replaced by a world in which American tanks barrel obtusely in every direction over fragile bridges under which lie thousands of KIPPS ready to be triggered.

But we live in an age when nations are mapped cinematically (or televisually) more than geographically. Bosnia and Serbia, or Kuwait and Iraq, for example, claim their national identity not by virtue of scientifically assayed and contractually demarcated borders (any more than by the virtue of historical or topographical ones) but by appeal to the warrant of a composite narrative image best understood cinematically. Today, national identity, it could be argued, can be seen as a cinematic metonym, wherein the foregrounding of the romantic subject makes transcendent and ubiquitous the idea of a common yet specific identity.

The process of cinematic identification thus functions in the same way as the rhetorical question can; the process of acquiring the image on the screen is the process of being owned by it, named by it, mapped by it. The moviegoer is thus always already the colonial subject assuming the imaginary position of the colonialist with the invisible ease upon which hegemony depends. This phenomenon by definition distinguishes the film *The English Patient* from the Ondaatje novel, in that the film necessarily participates in the colonialist qualities of film rhetoric, a rhetoric that more and more pervasively extends beyond the limits of the cinematic experience itself.

Notes

1. See de Certeau, "Introduction," *The Writing of History.*
2. "Modern Western history essentially begins with differentiation between the *present* and the past [. . .] This rupture also organizes the content of history within the relations between labor and *nature*" (de Certeau, *Writing* 2).
3. See, for example, Metz and Žižek.
4. In *Containment Culture,* I discuss at great length, in terms of American post–World War II foreign policy, the connection between colonialism (in the form

of cold war "containment") and gendered narratives. Annette Kolodny makes similar points about America's westward expansion in earlier centuries.

5. Bordwell et al. show that this structure is a fundamental aspect of the narrative in films produced in what they call the "classical style" of Hollywood cinema.

6. Hence, Mulvey's (widely echoed) claim that in mainstream cinema the cinematic object is feminized and subject to a masculine scopheliac gaze.

Works Cited

Bhabha, Homi. *The Location of Culture.* London: Routledge, 1994.

Bordwell, David, Janet Staiger, and Kristin Thompson. *The Classical Hollywood Cinema: Films Style and Mode of Production to 1960.* New York: Columbia UP, 1985.

de Certeau, Michel. *Heterologies: Discourse on the Other.* Trans. Brian Massumi. Minneapolis: U Minnesota P, 1986.

———. *The Writing of History.* Trans. Tom Conley. New York: Columbia UP, 1988.

Kolodny, Annette. *The Lay of the Land: Metaphor as Experience and History in American Life and Letters.* Chapel Hill: U of North Carolina P, 1975.

Metz, Christian. *The Imaginary Signifier: Psychoanalysis and the Cinema.* Trans. Celia Britton, et al. Bloomington: Indiana UP, 1982.

Mulvey, Laura. "Visual Pleasure and Narrative Cinema." *Screen* 16.3 (1975): 6–18.

Nadel, Alan. *Containment Culture: American Narratives, Postmodernism, and the Atomic Age.* Durham: Duke UP, 1995.

Žižek, Slavoj. *Enjoy Your Symptom! Jacques Lacan in Hollywood and Out.* 2d ed. New York: Routledge, 2001.

———, ed. *Everything You Always Wanted to Know about Lacan (But Were Afraid To Ask Hitchcock).* London: Verso, 1992.

———. *Looking Awry: An Introduction to Jacques Lacan Through Popular Culture.* Cambridge: MIT Press, 1991.

2

Rhetoric and the Early Work of Christian Metz: Augmenting Ideological Inquiry in Rhetorical Film Theory and Criticism

Ann Chisholm

COINCIDENT WITH RHETORICAL THEORISTS' RENEWED INTEREST IN IDEOLOGY, the question of ideology and its relation to filmic texts has gained prominence among rhetorical film theorists and critics (e.g., Charland, Crowley, Hariman, McKerrow, Ono and Sloop, Strine). Janice Hocker Rushing and Thomas Frentz, for example, have explored this problem in their efforts to integrate ideology and archetype. Likewise, while identifying means to investigate the rhetorical dimensions of popular culture, Barry Brummett also has advocated ideological analyses of filmic texts.[1]

Although there is much to admire in the recent achievements of rhetorical film theorists and critics, this fact does not militate against the need for further inquiry regarding the relations between rhetoric, cinema, and ideology. Accordingly, my concern here is to establish sites of substantial convergence between rhetorical film theory and a body of film theory expressly committed to ideological exegeses of cinema-contemporary film theory.[2] Because such an endeavor must be grounded in the early discourses fundamental to contemporary film theory, I begin with the germinal and exceedingly influential treatises of Christian Metz.[3]

In this essay, I examine Metz's early work and his conceptualization of rhetoric. After providing a brief overview of Metz's project, I find that within his initial semiotic theory, rhetoric assumes multiple roles: It is at once synonymous with a "strict" or normative grammar, with disposition, and with connotative operations. I then determine that, although he appears to actualize several dimensions of this overdetermined concept, Metz tacitly reifies rhetoric both insofar as its second definition adjoins its first and insofar as its third definition is effaced, in the last analysis, by other aspects of his theory.

This exegesis of Metz's work, then, detects the often implicit, contradictory, and problematic means through which he delimits his early description of rhetoric. In the same moment, I ascertain that two bases for supplementing Metz's limited view of rhetoric can be found, ironically, in the very definitions of rhetoric that Metz invokes and yet substantially enervates—flexibility and connotation. I do not deny, however, that Metz's inventory of cinematic structures (the "Grande Syntagmatique") and the narrow definition of rhetoric it comprises are useful to rhetorical film theorists. Rather, by recuperating and rethinking the concepts of flexibility and connotation in relation to rhetoric and by attending to contemporary film theorists' critiques of Metz's work, I not only develop additional means to enrich rhetorical film theorists' and critics' ideological inquiries but also situate the subject of rhetoric squarely within the early debates concerning cinematic representation and realism.

Specifically, while reconsidering and invigorating Metz's early views pertaining to rhetoric in these ways, I reveal that they furnish rhetorical film theorists and critics with the means to apprehend and discuss the representational import of cinematic structures that underwrite the spatial and temporal organization of filmic narratives, with the means to consider the ideological ramifications of those structures in realist, fiction films, and with the means to conceptualize rhetorical resistance through his notion of flexibility. More importantly, by reanimating the links that Metz has forged between rhetoric and connotation, I ascertain that he also offers rhetorical film critics the means to investigate the ways that filmic writing re-articulates filmic images, while reinforcing, extending, or revising prevailing cultural codes and ideologies.

Metz's Early Cine-Semiotics

Central to the theses of his book *Film Language*[4] is Metz's characterization of cinema as a language without a langue (65). As opposed to a language system comprising "*signs* used for *intercommunication*," cinema, according to Metz, is one-way communication comprising a partial system that incorporates "very few true signs" (75). Explaining this claim, Metz asserts that, due to its iconic nature, the cinematic image does not manifest the double articulation necessary to a full-fledged language system or langue (61–65, 88). Filmic images are likened instead to sentences or events and, in turn, are understood to be the minimal units of cinematic narrative (24, 61–67, 81).[5] This description of the cinematic image, intensified by the conviction that cinematic movement and temporality subordinate individual images to narrative, prompts Metz to emphasize and to investigate the various mechanisms of spatial and temporal organization that typify realist, fiction films (45, 89).

Specifically, Metz advances the Grande Syntagmatique,[6] an inventory of relations between shots. The Grande Syntagmatique designates eight varieties of autonomous segments: the autonomous shot, the parallel syntagma, the bracket syntagma, the descriptive syntagma, the alternate syntagma, the scene, the episodic sequence, and the ordinary sequence (*Film* 119–33, 145–46). Each constituent of the Grande Syntagmatique provides a partial answer to the principal question that guides Metz's semiotic inquiry: "How does the cinema indicate successivity, precession, temporal breaks, causality, adversative relationships, consequence, spatial proximity, or distance, etc.?" (98). In other words, the Grande Syntagmatique identifies the ways that realist, fiction films function as narrative.

Metz's statement that cinematic language differs from languages encompassing langues introduces several additional claims, many of which are tied conceptually to his concern with narrative. Referring to the aforementioned discrepancy, he both contrasts cinema with ordinary, daily communication (such as that used in conversation) and associates cinema with literature (83–84, 213). These comparisons then lead him to underscore cinema's rhetorical and poetic qualities (65, 75–84).

Concurrently, Metz posits that the cinema is an "art that tends toward a language" and that the language of cinema is "a language of art" (*Film* 59, 64, 135). Art, for Metz, is linked with composition and connotation. When he equates cinema ("the art of images") with literature ("the art of words"), therefore, he does so not only by remarking that both are "driven upward" via connotation but also by subtly associating both with "arrangement" or "ordering" (*Film* 58, 76–77, 81). Concomitantly, because he considers art, connotation, and ordering to be crucial features of cinema, his cine-semiotics stresses filmic *discourse*, which he deems a "rich message with a poor code"—speech rather than langue (*Film* 65, 84–90).[7]

In spite of Metz's assertions to the contrary, the opposition he poses between langue and discourse is not unequivocal. Given his overall purposes, Metz cannot help but to ascribe grammatical qualities to cinematic language. Accordingly, Metz eventually discounts many of his claims pertaining to cinema's artistic and connotative attributes. Both of these tendencies impinge upon his thoughts about rhetoric.

Syntax, Grammar, *Dispositio*, and Rhetoric

Metz asserts that, as they established and standardized the narrative functions of various cinematic figures, the earliest filmmakers introduced and conventionalized a cinematic syntax (*Film* 40, 95). He consequently maintains that cine-semiotics should be rooted in the study of syntactics (*Film* 70). Because he both emphasizes cinematic narrative and insists that cinema does not comprise a langue, however, he must modulate the meaning of the term syntax. Nevertheless, as he does so, he minimizes and restricts the effects of his revised interpretation.

In much the same way, and by means of a series of moves that are not unrelated to his treatment of syntax, Metz similarly tempers the definition of grammar as it pertains to the Grande Syntagmatique. Through correspondences with two ostensibly different conceptions of rhetoric, Metz introduces a subtle distinction between the idea of a normative grammar and the character of the Grande Syntagmatique—a distinction that, on the whole, he does not uphold in any substantial way.

Metz subsumes cinematic syntax, described as "a certain number of *filmic constructions,*" under the broader category of syntagmatics, which he regards as the guarantor of discursive intelligibility (*Film* 67, 209, 222). Syntagmatic arrangements of images and visual elements are important to Metz because, as signifiers of narrative and filmic denotation, they furnish the infrastructure for cine-semiology (*Film* 111, 222–23).

The overall movement from syntax to syntagmatics not only incorporates denotations that constitute the temporal and spatial aspects of narrative plots but also introduces a pivotal tension between semantics and syntactics. Even though the semantic pole is crucial to his project, Metz ultimately resolves this theoretical tension in favor of syntax (and, eventually, grammar). He does so by radically restricting the semantic impulses of his theory in two ways: first, by reasserting the primacy of *cinematic* signifiers (constituents of the Grande Syntagmatique), and second, by emphasizing the "literalness" of plot over and above the "artistic effects" that also contribute to filmic narratives (*Film* 99, 143–44). Syntagmatics, therefore, do not supplement or transform traditional definitions of syntax as much as become substantially equivalent to them.

Just as Metz endeavors to alter and yet to retain cinematic syntax, he aims to modify and also to sustain cinematic grammar. Moreover, I propose that the tension between syntax and semantics, which mirrors the precarious balance between langue and language in Metz's work, fuels the complex relationship that emerges between grammar and rhetoric (*Film* 208). The terms of this relationship can be discerned in the following:

> Cinema has never had either a grammar or syntax in the precise linguistic sense of these terms [. . .] rather it has always obeyed, and today still obeys, a certain number of fundamental semiological laws [. . .] that are extremely difficult to isolate, but whose models are to be sought in general linguistics, or general semiotics, and not in the grammar or normative rhetorics of specific languages. (*Film* 208–9)

Here, he draws a distinction between the general cinematic laws of ordering or composition, which exist on a level prior to the differentiation of verbal languages from other semiotic systems, and the normative rules of rhetorics that are presumably analogous with idiomatic grammar (*Film* 209).

Elsewhere, a second view of rhetoric, one aligned with Metz's own formations rather than opposed to them, appears as he explains cinematic grammar. "The grammar of cinema," he resolves, "is a rhetoric rather than a true grammar" (*Film* 117). In this context, he proposes that his second definition of rhetoric allows for both an almost unlimited freedom regarding the internal composition of minimal cinematic units and a relative degree of freedom concerning the ordering of those units (*Film* 81, 117).

Metz's corresponding interest in syntagmatic arrangements causes him to address rhetoric exclusively in terms of the classical concept *dispositio.* Discussing *dispositio,* he circumvents the fact that it is conceived fundamentally with respect to a speaker's needs in relation both to the particular subject matter and to the specific audience at hand. As a result, Metz not only restricts rhetoric by conflating it with a narrow definition of *dispositio* but also expedites the transformation of rhetoric into a sort of semiotic code.

Using "judiciary discourse" as an example, Metz both defines rhetoric as the "determined ordering of undetermined elements" (images) and facilitates links between rhetoric and narration (*Film* 97–98, 117–18).[8] In conjunction with the initial transformation from rhetoric to syntagmatics, this second metamorphosis from rhetoric to narration equates rhetoric with the semiosis of cinematic narrative proposed by Metz's Grande Syntagmatique, neglects processes of persuasion or influence, and returns rhetoric to the realm of grammatical precepts and structures. Thus, Metz concludes that "*this rhetoric I have just mentioned is also, in other aspects, a grammar*" (*Film* 117).

In sum, Metz writes that, although it is not a "pure grammar," cinematic language is an "indiscernible mixture between grammar and rhetoric" (*Film* 224). Within cinematic language, therefore, rhetoric ostensibly offsets normative definitions of grammar and admits cinematic freedoms, "flexible" syntagmatic rules that permit innovation.

Nevertheless, Metz fails to describe this proposed relationship between rhetoric and cinematic freedom, delimits the scope of rhetorical flexibility substantially, and reverts to the idea of a predetermined, regulative grammar. Accordingly, while Metz contends that "cinematic grammar is not a real grammar [. . .] but simply a body of partially codified semantic implications," he refers to the latter as "*fine grammatical rules*" (*Film* 225; italics added). In the same vein, he states that "*various degrees of agrammaticism*" occur when these rules are transgressed (*Film* 225). To put it differently, cinematic freedom (syntagmatic evolution) must be governed by grammar because, like its subspecies syntax, grammar is necessary for intelligibility (*Film* 135, 217, 223).

Metz's objection to traditional understandings of grammar and syntax, therefore, belies his ultimate commitment to the underlying thrust of those concepts.[9] Concomitantly, Metz's first and second definitions of rhetoric are not unrelated: His supposed aversion to both a normative rhetoric and a normative grammar heralds the identity he asserts between rhetoric and *dispositio,* an identity that subsequently approximates the regulative conception of grammar and the corresponding definition of rhetoric that he allegedly rejects.

Filmic Images, Denotation, Connotation, and Rhetoric

Combining rhetoric and grammar, Metz grants a greater degree of freedom to the internal composition of filmic images than to the ordering of those minimal units. Unlike phonemes and monemes, he argues, filmic images are neither finite in number nor likely to impart a determinable amount of information (*Film* 26, 88, 101, 115–16). Furthermore, because they cannot be reduced to anything less than assertive, actualized statements or sentences, even the constituent parts of filmic images are not analogous to phonemes or monemes (*Film* 26, 66–67, 88, 101, 115–16). For these reasons, he considers the internal configurations of filmic images to be products of invention impervious to cine-specific precepts (*Film* 26, 69, 115).

Even so, the cinematic image is significant to Metz's theories.[10] Although it is not cine-specific, the image is linked to two pivotal concepts that form the nucleus of his claim that cinema is an art that tends toward a language—connotation and denotation.

Metz vacillates between integrating and differentiating connotation and denotation. On the one hand, he explains the necessary relationship between these two signifying operations; on the other hand, he emphasizes denotation in lieu of connotation. In fact, the more closely connotation and denotation are allied in Metz's work, the more dispensable *connotation* becomes. This circumstance has important implications for rhetoric.

Metz initially proposes that filmic connotations, like literary connotations, are superimposed over denotations (*Film* 79–81, 96). Cinema is unique for Metz, however, in that its connotations and its denotations are homogeneous: Both, he maintains, are expressive (*Film* 79). Developing this point, he argues that the natural expressiveness of the filmed object, iconic denotation via analogy, precedes connotation, which stylistically expresses the filmmaker's intended message (*Film* 76, 79–80).

Metz extends these assertions while discussing a shot from Eisenstein's *Que Viva Mexico*. He describes that image as "a famous shot of the tortured, yet peaceful faces of three peasants buried to their shoulders being trampled by the horses of their oppressors [. . .] a beautiful triangular composition, a well-known trademark of the great director" (*Film* 79). In this case, the denotative plane comprises the relationship between the expressions on the motionless faces (the denotative signifiers) and the suffering and death they naturally convey (the denotative signifieds). The connotative plane, in turn, signifies the nobility of the landscape, the greatness of the Mexican people, and the promise of an eventual Mexican triumph (the connotative signifieds). These layers of meaning issue both from the triangle of faces (the connotative signifier) and from the martyrdom (signified of denotation) those faces exhibit (signifiers of denotation).

Referring to this example, Metz asserts that, because each retains its own signifier and signified, connotation and denotation are distinct operations (*Film* 80). At the same time, he also concludes that, even though it is "vaster" than denotation, connotation is tied to denotation because it relies on the denotative signifier and signified (*Film* 80, 96–97). Along these lines, Metz contends that the cinema is neither exclusively connotative nor exclusively denotative. He writes that "one is forever shifting from art to non-art, and vice versa": Utilitarian, denotative images are organized, framed, and lit through techniques that afford some measure of connotative or artistic effect; aesthetic, connotative images serve as denotative representations (*Film* 82, 97). The last assertion and the correlative argument that connotation is reliant upon denotation function is not to establish that those signifying operations are equally valuable but to justify Metz's effort to ground his cine-semiotics in denotation (97).

Considering cultural codes after he abandons his initial belief in the natural expressiveness of profilmic objects, Metz revises his conception of denotation and connotation. He then introduces a third definition of rhetoric, one synonymous with connotation.

Insofar as it assumes that iconic analogy motivates the denotations indicated by the image track, Metz's second explanation of denotation resembles the first. However, he amends his view of analogy in other ways. In particular, he argues that analogy smuggles iconological[11] and perceptual[12] codes into films (*Film* 111–12). These extra-cinematic codes of representation, recognition, and identification create the seemingly "natural" appearance of filmic images (*Film* 78, 111). Therefore, although it is now coded, analogy continues to function as analogic denotation "in relation to the codes of the superior level"—in other words, in relation to *cinematic* codes (*Film* 111–12).

Metz not only recasts his theory of denotation but also revises his account of connotation. He begins by defining connotation as "motivated overtaking" or symbolism (109–10). Metz's second explanation of connotation, "the signified motivates the signifier but goes beyond it," now refers not to the presence of additional connotative signifiers such as compositional schemes, but to the evocation of an already established relationship between a prior (denotative) signifier and significate (109–10). That prior relationship motivates connotative significations generated either throughout the course of a film or within the cultural contexts imported and invoked by the film.

An example from the film *Sex, Lies, and Videotape* illustrates Metz's description of connotative operations engendered within films. In that film, Ann Meleney's husband, John, conducts a secret affair with her sister, Cynthia. Each time they meet illicitly, John gives Cynthia a lush, exotic plant. Eventually, these plants,[13] strewn around Cynthia's apartment throughout the film, signify more than John's overtures to intimacy (the motivation). They also indicate, with resonant connotations, the overall character of the affair itself (the overtaking). This instance of "overtaking" is depicted most clearly during a scene in which the unknowing Ann visits Cynthia's apartment and becomes anxious and irritated, for no apparent reason, while looking at the plants.[14]

According to Metz, then, the connotative or symbolic meaning (the character of the affair) neither counters nor disregards the prior denotative meaning established within the film (John's prelude to illicit intimacy).[15] Rather, the connotative meaning overtakes and supplements the initial denotation.

Similarly, Metz submits that visual images also import extra-filmic connotations, explained once again through references to the process of motivated overtaking (*Film* 109, 113).[16] Metz asserts that before cinematic language orders the denotations of shots and images, before symbolic signification is fostered (as in the previous example) within the film itself, various connotations or symbolisms also exist as elements of cultural codes (113, 142, 213–15). Filmed objects, characters, patterns of light, clothing, et cetera, their extra-cinematic denotations discerned through perception, retain these connotations, which contribute to "the total understanding" of any particular film (*Film* 111–13, 212–13).[17]

Thus, Metz resolves that connotations and denotations are comprehended simultaneously, that connotations are situated at the core of iconic analogy, and that connotations play a major role in the understanding of filmic images (113–14, 213). Furthermore, he states that "the semiotics of cinema can be "conceived of either as a semiotics of connotation or as a semiotics of denotation" (*Film* 96, 111).

Metz nevertheless strays from his own proposition that viewers perceive connotations and denotations simultaneously. As is more clear in his illustration of filmic connotation and somewhat less explicit in his description of extra-filmic connotation, he in fact supposes that the discernment of denotation precedes the discernment of connotation.

Once more, in tandem with positing the interdependence between connotation and denotation, Metz offers grounds for both prioritizing denotation and marginalizing connotation. Revitalizing his earlier claim that filmic images are both denotative and connotative, he contends that even lackluster and minimally connotated images engender denotations (*Film* 213). Connotations, he therefore maintains, neither function at the "deepest mechanism of filmic intellection" nor serve as necessary counterparts to the Grande Syntagmatique (*Film* 213). Instead, connotations are "pure rhetoric," cultural stereotypes that are reproducible in a variety of media (*Film* 141, 142–43, 213). In this respect, we must ask the following question: Why is such a rhetoric deemed "pure"? Certainly, this rhetoric can be no purer than the rhetoric Metz links with both the grammar of cinema and the Grande Syntagmatique.[18]

For the second time, Metz reinstates the model of cine-semiotics he actually pursues and develops—a semiotics of denotation (*Film* 96, 109, 213–14). Here, he does not postulate that the denotations of filmic images furnish an infrastructure for cinematic language. Studies of filmic images per se, Metz insists, invariably bypass cine-specificity because "general" cultural codes constitute those images, their denotations, and their connotations, whereas "specialized codes" of cinematic language function "beyond" images (*Film* 111–13, 226–27). Concomitantly, the denotations of filmic images are understood to oscillate with the denotations of cine-specific codes and, in the process, to participate in the construction of filmic plots (*Film* 97–99, 143–44, 226–27). The connotative significations of filmic images, in turn, are then superfluous, essentially ornamental, third-order operations.[19]

The circumstances of connotation determine the fate and the scope of rhetoric in Metz's early semiotics. Recall that, in lieu of characterizing cinema as a language containing a langue, he aligns cinema with connotation and art. Also remember that he is somewhat ambivalent about eliminating completely all vestiges of langue. Thus, his principal concerns are not various forms of connotation, as one might surmise from many of his own statements, but extra-cinematic denotation and, still more important to his aims, cinema-specific denotation. Concurrently, he suppresses the third definition of rhetoric in favor of the second, which I have argued is merely a subtle variant of the first.

Metz, Rhetorical Film Theory, and Ideological Criticism

Overall, Metz advocates a rhetoric of grammatical organization. He therefore subsumes rhetoric under the Grande Syntagmatique and binds it securely to the denotative significations that engender filmic narratives.[20] I do not mean to imply here that grammar, disposition, and narrative are devoid of rhetorical force. Indeed, I assert that if *supplemented,* the Grande Syntagmatique (and attendant cinematic figures of punctuation) may enhance the three methodologies that seem to dominate rhetorical film theory.

Hendrix and Wood's neo-Aristotelian methodology, for instance, features arrangement and narration, yet the authors' call for "terms appropriate to the vocabulary and syntax of the filmic medium" remains unanswered (110–11). In this regard, the Grande Syntagmatique (and cinematic punctuation) may provide a necessary rejoinder to Hendrix and Wood's petition. Like the neo-Aristotelian perspective, the participatory stance,[21] delineated most fully in Brummett's *Rhetorical Dimensions of Popular Culture,* does not advance cine-specific versions of either disposition or grammar. Nonetheless, because it is rooted in narrative and "social logics," the participatory stance may integrate the cine-specific codes identified by Metz (28, 30–33, 71–75).[22] The mythic perspective, best exemplified in the works of Rushing and Frentz, promotes the most comprehensive structural theory of narrative used by rhetorical film theorists to date. Metz's project may be of interest in this case because, although it highlights *mythic* structures quite well, Rushing and Frentz's methodology slights *cinematic* structures.

Metz's early theories eventuate in a cautionary note that pertains not only to his early works but also to rhetorical film theorists' and critics' recent ideological investigations. As other contemporary film theorists remark in their responses to Metz's early work and as he consequently realizes, filmic narratives constituted by components of the Grande Syntagmatique are ideologically suspect (e.g., Cegarra 129–87; Heath, "Film" 116 and "Work" 22–23). Of particular note in this respect is Stephen Heath's view that cinematic narratives both depict "reality" through ideological representational systems and, simultaneously, conceal those ideological operations ("Film" 117–21; "Work" 26–27).

Rhetorical film theorists and critics also assume that narratives naturalize ideologies and ideological contradictions (e.g., Brummett, *Rhetorical* 13–14, 59–62; Frentz and Rushing, "Part II" 77; Rushing and Frentz, "Integrating" 394–97). These scholars typically seek to unmask and to diagnose those concealed ideologies and contradictions. Many times, these same scholars also contend that particular types of narrative closure illustrate, to greater or lesser degrees, potential solutions to ideological crises and inconsistencies. Their critical agendas notwithstanding, these theorists and critics often do not consider that specific *cinematic* processes are complicit in the naturalization of ideologies (e.g., Cegarra 150–53; Heath "Film" 101; Heath "Work" 9–10).

If incorporated into rhetorical film theory, Metz's thoughts about the "avoidance" or the "relaxation" of the Plausible, about those moments of invention or radical quotation that evade cinematic conventions authorizing naturalization, may be quite useful (*Film* 238–52). From this vantage point, the Grande Syntagmatique (and attendant codes of punctuation) may be a valuable guide for ideological criticism. Syntagmatic chains and figures comprised by the Grande Syntagmatique may be seen to function rhetorically in filmic texts that naturalize ideology. Conversely, filmic texts may be understood to engage the Grande Syntagmatique rhetorically for oppositional, counterideological ends. In other words, the potential "flexibility" of cinematic conventions permits rhetorical film theorists and critics both to address the ideological import of those conventions and to locate potent sites of resistance in cinematic practice.

Metz's initial concern with cine-specificity caused him to disregard not only filmic images but also connotation and his third definition of rhetoric. Just as many contemporary film theorists urged him both to reexamine this theoretical surplus and to enable his methodological project to absorb it, I ask rhetorical film theorists to pursue similar objectives.

Initially, scholars might reconsider the status of the cinematic image in rhetorical film theory. The earliest rhetorical film critics, particularly those relying on neo-Aristotelian precepts, seldom mention filmic images (e.g., Carpenter and Stalzner; Hendrix and Wood; Free). Proponents of later methodologies recognize the importance of the image. The participatory perspective, for example, explicitly encourages analyses of visual representational codes (Brummett, *Rhetorical* 12, 28). Likewise, the mythic perspective furthers analyses of filmic images through archetypes (Rushing and Frentz 406). In actual critical practice, however, both perspectives favor exegeses of plot, character, and dialogue. As a result, there are few references to filmic images in those studies applying either mythic or participatory methodologies.[23]

In light of these circumstances, and particularly in light of the fact that Metz characterizes filmic images as assertions or "arguments," I submit that rhetorical film theorists and critics might enrich their analyses by emphasizing filmic images to a greater extent (*Film* 4–6, 14).[24] Furthermore, I maintain that rhetorical film theorists and critics may extend their ideological analyses by recuperating and rethinking Metz's description of the various cultural codes that constitute filmic images.

In short, like many contemporary film theorists responding to Metz's early work, I argue that filmic images and cultural codes are crucial to ideological considerations of film texts (e.g., Cegarra, Eco, Heath, Wollen). In this view, filmic texts must be regarded as sites of intersection between heterogeneous codes. Accordingly, as they investigate this conception of the filmic text, rhetorical film theorists and critics cannot avoid the vital issue impinging upon rhetoric and ideology—connotation.

Metz's first explanation of connotative operations discounts connotative signifiers and stresses denotative signifiers and signifieds, which are central to his project, instead. Similarly, as they posit an identity between the connotative signifier and the denotative signifier and signified, Metz's subsequent accounts of connotation facilitate reductions from connotation to denotation. In the first instance, the signifier of connotation is overlooked; in the second, it is absent.

Accepting Barthes's edict that connotative signifiers are the "signifiers of ideology," many contemporary film theorists not only charged that Metz's early work rendered ideological processes insignificant but also endorsed sustained investigations of connotation (e.g., Barthes 49; Cegarra 170–75; Heath, "Film" 115–17). Such investigations are also essential to rhetorical film theory because rhetoric is linked with connotation both in Metz's work and in the treatises of other contemporary film theorists (Barthes 49–50; Cegarra 160–61; Heath, "Film" 116; Wollen 146–47). Unquestionably, for many contemporary film theorists, rhetoric is rendered suspect because of the following equation: rhetoric = connotation = ideology. Ironically, these very circumstances suggest that rhetoric may be used as a template to trace those filmic and social symbols that impel classical filmic texts while reinforcing, extending, and revising prevailing ideologies.

Additionally, rhetoric and connotation might be considered in the context of filmic writing, a concept briefly mentioned in the footnotes of *Film Language* (81, 224) and discussed at length in Metz's later work *Language and Cinema*. Borrowing liberally from Barthes and Kristeva, Metz describes filmic writing in the following manner:

> The process [. . .] *displaces* codes, deforming each of them by the presence of the others, contaminating some by means of others, meanwhile replacing one by another, and finally—as a temporarily "arrested" result of this general displacement—*placing* each code in a particular position in regard to the overall structure, a displacement which thus finishes by a positioning which is itself destined to be displaced by another text. (103)

In short, filmic writing is the process of codical integration, displacement, and alteration unique to each filmic text. Thus, the idea of filmic texts working with and against established conventions, the notion of flexibility, reappears. In this case, however, Metz does not insist that cine-specific codes take precedence over cultural codes (*Film* 105–11). Therefore, the denotations and connotations of extra-cinematic codes participate in and, more important, may be altered by the process of filmic writing.[25] To put it differently, through filmic writing, textual systems transform codes contributing to filmic naturalization, including cultural codes that confer both literal (denotative) and symbolic (connotative = ideological) values to filmic compositions and images.[26] By examining filmic writing, then, rhetorical critics may identify filmic sites of ideological modification and change.

Conclusion

Overall, in Metz's early work, rhetoric serves three purposes: it epitomizes the outlook of the earliest film theorists, whom Metz describes as proposing a cinematic langue or grammar; it establishes the differences between those scholars' theories and Metz's perspective by embodying the "flexible" character of his cinesemiotics; and it assumes synonymy with extra-cinematic connotation. Although he introduces a second definition of rhetoric to underscore differences between languages comprising a langue and cinematic language, Metz substantially mitigates those discrepancies. Then, as he siphons off an abundance of semantic and artistic significations by marginalizing connotation, he enervates the third conception of rhetoric.

While maintaining that Metz's Grande Syntagmatique and the narrow definition of rhetoric it comprises are useful to rhetorical film theorists, I recover two ideas essential to the rhetorics that his theory relinquishes—flexibility and connotation. In other words, I identify the means through which Metz's three definitions of rhetoric may enrich rhetorical film theory by explaining the rhetorical significance of Grande Syntagmatique in relation to the following: the Plausible, the filmic image, the connotative stratum of cultural signification, and the process of filmic writing. In doing so, I not only augment conceptions of filmic rhetoric but also underscore the crucial ideological problem of cinematic realism, heretofore neglected by rhetorical film theorists and critics. Moreover, I demonstrate that rhetorical film theorists and critics may benefit from sustained, direct examinations of germinal works in contemporary film theory.

Scholarship of this kind would do well to engage Metz's later theoretical studies, which augmented his concern with the formal characteristics of cinematic discourse emphasized in this study.[27] In the end, as Sandy Flitterman-Lewis reminds us, Metz ultimately viewed the cinematic apparatus as a social institution, one best understood through "a notion of cultural communication [that] emphasizes the interdependence between . . . economic relations of production, ideological institutions and expectations, and the productions of symbolic forms" ("Tribute" 4). Here, we are reminded of Stuart Hall's "Encoding/Decoding," which stresses textual conditions of production, textual structures (discussed at length in terms of connotation, rhetoric, and ideology), and conditions of reception (Hall 90–103). Here, too, objections to Hall's essay notwithstanding, we encounter the necessity of adopting an interdisciplinary approach to the rhetoric film: one that recognizes the import of cinematic structures, while also acknowledging the filmic text's status as a cultural phenomenon; one that potentially identifies and establishes intersections between rhetorical (film) theory and criticism, film theory and criticism, and cultural studies. Therefore, just as Metz's earliest works inspired the wide range scholarship that is constitutive of film studies today, so also his earliest conceptions of rhetoric in relation to filmic texts can serve as resources for animating and for broadening the scope of rhetorical film theory and criticism committed to ideological inquiry.

Notes

1. Here, I am arguing not that earlier works in rhetorical film theory and criticism do not have ideological implications but that the essays I mention explicitly advance methodologies that theorize the critique of ideology.

2. This field of investigation comprises those works generated since the mid-1960s that have legitimized film studies as a discipline, that have dislodged the romantic assumptions that dominated film theories up to that point, and that have inherited the ideological legacy fostered in France during the political upheavals of May 1968.

3. Metz's influence can be discerned from Stephen Heath's declaration that "a consideration of semiology in relation to the particular signifying practice of cinema passes inevitably through reference to the work of Christian Metz" ("Introduction" 9–10). "To say this," Heath maintains, "is to acknowledge at once the pioneering nature of that work and its importance" (9–10). Andrew corroborates and extends Heath's assertion by referring to Metz as "the center of an organized, international, quasiscientific approach to film theory" (180–81). "It would be impossible to try to summarize the directions, both scholarly and political, into which semiotics has branched," Andrew contends, "but all these directions owe much of their original impetus to Metz" (180–81). Similarly, Lisa Block De Behar writes of a "fervent admiration for the soundness of the epistemological bases on which Metz laid a discipline which has extended and solidified after his formulations, thus endorsing the universality of Metz's *recherche* [. . . and] the subsequent cleavage of numerous investigations, different from each other, which does not conceal their common origin" (3).

4. Because it is constituted by a number of individual essays, *Film Language* embodies the initial progression of Metz's thoughts concerning cinema. Footnotes subsequently added by Metz, some reflecting modifications made in light of his later work *Language and Cinema,* also attest to these developments. These refinements are discussed throughout this essay.

5. Instead of manifesting equivalences to either phonemes or monemes in verbal language, Metz argues, the cinematic shot is equivalent to an (assertive) statement or an utterance. Therefore, a close-up of a revolver does not mean "revolver," but "here is a revolver!" (*Film Language* 26, 66–67). In this vein, Metz writes that "cinema begins where ordinary language ends: at the level of the 'sentence,' the filmmaker's minimum unit" (81).

6. Metz has developed several versions of the Grande Syntagmatique. Although he does mention the first, Metz delineates the second in *Film Language.* Metz's analysis of Jacques Rozier's *Adieu Philippine* illustrates his description of the improved Grande Syntagmatique (*Film* 149–82).

7. At times, Metz fails to distinguish between the terms *langue* and *code*. This flaw in his work has no bearing on my arguments, however.

8. There are strong links between judiciary discourse and narration in classical rhetoric. For example, judiciary discourse is the single rhetorical genre from which Aristotle does not exclude narration. "Narration," Aristotle writes, "is surely part of a forensic speech only: how in a political speech or a speech of display can there be narration in the technical sense?" (199). Although Aristotle does address the possibility of including narration within the other two genres, he emphasizes the resulting difficulties to a greater degree. Therefore, deliberative oratory and narration are discussed as follows:

> In political oratory there is very little opening for narration; nobody can "narrate" what has not yet happened. If there is narration at all, it will be of past events, the recollection of which is to help the hearers to make better plans for the future. Or it will be employed to attack someone's character, or to eulogize him—only then you will not be doing what the political speaker has to do. (210)

9. This assertion is important because the presence of grammar, particularly in conjunction with the existence of a paradigmatic dimension, may indicate the presence of a langue. The resulting deterioration of Metz's supposed antagonism toward langue is reinforced by the fact that he retracts his initial skepticism concerning the viability of paradigmatic relations in cinema (*Film* 68, 71, 99, 102). Only his view of the cinematic image fully corresponds with his proposed rejection of langue with respect to de Saussure's conception of that term. In many studies of narrative and myth, however, the notion of langue, or of comparable deep structures, and the possibility of equivalency between minimum units and sentences are not mutually exclusive.

10. Metz maintains that individual images provide a base over which cinematic language is superimposed (*Film* 101, 213).

11. Metz defines these codes as "the more or less institutionalized modalities of object representation, the processes of recognition and identification of objects in their visual or auditive 'reproduction,' and, more generally, the collective notions of what an image is" (*Film* 111).

12. Metz identifies perceptual codes as "visual habits of identification and construction of forms and figures, the spatial representations peculiar to each culture, various auditory structures, and so on" (*Film* 111).

13. The images of the plants denote through analogy the idea "plant." Therefore, although Metz does not discuss this possibility, the denotation discussed in this example may also be considered connotation.

14. In this example, the affair is symbolized by the plants. Because the plant plays a role in the affair, the symbol is not totally arbitrary. Conversely, because other visual or auditory elements depicted during John and Cynthia's encounters might also serve to symbolize their affair, the relationship between the con-

notative signifier and the connotative signified, between the plant and the affair, is partially arbitrary (Metz *Film* 109–10).

15. Likewise, the symbolic meaning neither counters nor disregards the signified of the analogic denotation—"plant."

16. Metz provides the following example: "One says that the cross is the symbol of Christianity because, although Christ died on a cross (the motivation), there are many more things in Christianity than there are in a cross (the overtaking)" (*Film* 109). Here, again, Metz does not say that the motivation may also be connotative.

17. Inversely, Metz argues, the overall character of a particular filmic text determines which cultural connotations assume symbolic status (*Film* 104).

18. The latter, according to Metz, is influenced by cultural codifications as well (*Film* 71–72, 215).

19. This is not to say that connotation is entirely inconsequential to Metz's theory. He posits the importance of this signifying operation in his discussions of the parallel syntagma, the bracket syntagma, the episodic sequence, and the ordinary sequence (*Film* 124–33).

20. Metz describes the connotative and denotative significations of specialized, cinematic codes in much the same way. In this context, he considers connotation "a form of denotation" (*Film* 118). The various means available for structuring the same cine-specific denotation, according to Metz, engender different connotative effects (118–19). Therefore, Metz once again stresses denotation rather than connotation.

21. The participatory perspective is a consolidation of epistemic views of rhetoric (Scott "On Viewing Rhetoric as Epistemic" and "On Viewing Rhetoric as Epistemic: Ten Years Later"), Becker's textual mosaic, and early postmodern rhetorical theory (Brummett "Electric"). Although concerned with a variety of media, Brummett's recent work also features extended discussions regarding the rhetoric of film (*Rhetorical* 109–71).

22. This consolidation is necessary because Brummett's participatory stance ultimately promotes thematic exegesis (*Rhetorical* 76, 112). Brummett's analyses of filmic texts illustrate this fact.

23. The works of Benson and Medhurst provide thorough analyses of cinematic images. Additionally, several of these analyses are relevant to the discussion of connotation that follows. Nevertheless, a single, comprehensive methodology advocating both cine-specific analysis and ideological critique has not emerged in these works.

24. This is not to say that rhetorical film theorists should acknowledge the image as a potential basis for cinematic grammar. Metz's arguments against such a move are quite compelling and have been upheld, for the most part, by contemporary film theorists.

25. In *Film Language,* Metz admits only once the possibility that connotative variance may be conferred by films (222).

26. I do not maintain, however, that denotation can be excluded from ideological considerations.

27. One might, for example, map potential relations between Metz's later work concerning filmic enunciation, rhetorical film theory, and rhetorical film criticism (Metz "Impersonal" 747–72). I in no way wish to imply, however, that Metz's work is the only scholarship in film studies that might be useful to rhetorical film theorists.

Works Cited

Andrew, J. Dudley. *The Major Film Theories: An Introduction.* London: Oxford UP, 1976.

Aristotle. *Rhetoric.* Trans. W. Rhys Roberts. New York: Modern Library, 1954.

Barthes, Roland. *Image, Music, Text.* Trans. Stephen Heath. New York: Hill, 1977.

Becker, S. L. "Rhetorical Studies for the Contemporary World." *The Prospect of Rhetoric: Report of the National Developmental Project.* Ed. Lloyd. F. Bitzer and Edwin Black. Englewood Cliffs, NJ: Prentice-Hall, 1971. 21–43.

Benson, Thomas W. "The Rhetorical Structure of Frederick Wiseman's *High School.*" *Communication Monographs* 47 (1980): 233–61.

———. "The Rhetorical Structure of Frederick Wiseman's *Primate.*" *Quarterly Journal of Speech* 71 (1985): 204–17.

Block De Behar, Lisa. "Introduction." *Semiotica* 112 (1996): 3–7.

Brummett, Barry. "Burke's Representative Anecdote as a Method in Media Criticism." *Critical Studies in Mass Communication* 1 (1984): 161–76.

———. "Electric Literature as Equipment for Living: Haunted House Films." *Critical Studies in Mass Communication* 2 (1985): 247–61.

———. *Rhetorical Dimensions of Popular Culture.* Tuscaloosa: U of Alabama P, 1991.

———. "Some Implications of 'Process' or 'Intersubjectivity': Postmodern Rhetoric." *Philosophy and Rhetoric* 9 (1976): 21–51.

Carpenter, Ronald H., and Robert V. Stalzner. "Nixon, Patton, and a Silent Majority, Sentiment about the Vietnam War: The Cinematographic Basis of a Rhetorical Stance." *Central States Speech Journal* 25 (1974): 105–10.

Cegarra, M. "Cinema and Semiology." *Screen* 14 (1973): 129–87.

Charland, Maurice. "Finding a Horizon and Telos: The Challenge to Critical Rhetoric. *Quarterly Journal of Speech* 77 (1991): 71–74.

Crowley, Sharon. "Reflections on the Argument That Won't Go Away: Or, a Turn of the Ideological Screw." *Quarterly Journal of Speech* 78 (1992): 450–65.

Eco, Umberto. "Articulations of the Cinematic Code." 1970. Rpt. *Movies and Methods.* Ed. Bill Nichols. Los Angeles: U of California P, 1976.

Flitterman-Lewis, Sandy. "Tribute to Christian Metz." *Discourse* 16.3 (1994): 1–8.

Free, W. "Aesthetic and Moral Value in *Bonnie and Clyde.*" *Quarterly Journal of Speech* 56 (1968): 220–25.

Frentz, Thomas S. and Janice Hocker Rushing. "Integrating Ideology and Archetype in Rhetorical Criticism, Part II: A Case Study of *Jaws*." *Quarterly Journal of Speech* 79 (1993): 61–81.

Hall, Stuart. "Encoding/Decoding." 1990. Rpt. *The Cultural Studies Reader.* Ed. S. During. New York: Routledge, 1993.

Hariman, Robert. "Critical Rhetoric and Postmodern Theory." *Quarterly Journal of Speech* 77 (1991): 67–78.

Heath, Stephen. "Film/Cine/Text." *Screen* 14 (1973): 99–123.

———. "Introduction: Questions of Emphasis." *Screen* 14 (1973): 9–13.

———. "The Work of Christian Metz." *Screen* 14 (1973): 5–29.

Hendrix, Jerry, and James A. Wood. "The Rhetoric of Film: Toward a Critical Methodology." *Southern Speech Communication Journal,* 39 (1973): 105–22.

McKerrow, Raymie E. "Critical Rhetoric: Theory and Praxis." *Communication Monographs* 56 (1989): 91–111.

Medhurst, Martin. J. "*Hiroshima, Mon Amour:* From Iconography to Rhetoric." *Quarterly Journal of Speech* 68 (1982): 345–70.

———. "Image and Ambiguity: A Rhetorical Approach to *The Exorcist.*" *Southern Speech Communication Journal* 44 (1973): 73–92.

———. "The Rhetorical Structure of Oliver Stone's *JFK.*" *Critical Studies in Mass Communication* 10 (1993): 128–43.

Medhurst, Martin J., and Thomas W. Benson. "*The City:* The Rhetoric of Rhythm." *Communication Monographs* 48 (1981): 54–72.

Metz, Christian. *Film Language.* 1971. Trans. M. Taylor. New York: Oxford UP, 1974.

———. "Impersonal Enunciation, or the Site of Film." *New Literary History* 22 (1991): 747–72.

———. *Language and Cinema.* Trans. D. J. Umiker-Sebeok. Paris: Mouton, 1974.

Ono, Kent. A., and John M. Sloop. "Commitment to *Telos*—A Sustained Critical Rhetoric." *Communication Monographs* 59 (1992): 48–60.

Rushing, Janice Hocker. "*E. T.* as Rhetorical Transcendence." *Quarterly Journal of Speech* 71 (1985): 188–203.

———. "Evolution of the "New Frontier" in *Alien* and *Aliens:* Patriarchal Co-optation of the Feminine Archetype." *Quarterly Journal of Speech* 75 (1989): 1–24.

Rushing, Janice Hocker, and Thomas S. Frentz. "The Frankenstein Myth in Contemporary Cinema." *Critical Studies in Mass Communication* 6 (1989): 61–80.

———. "Integrating Ideology and Archetype in Rhetorical Criticism." *Quarterly Journal of Speech* 77 (1991): 385–406.

Scott, Robert. L. "On Viewing Rhetoric as Epistemic." *Central States Speech Journal* 18 (1967): 9–16.

———. "On Viewing Rhetoric as Epistemic: Ten Years Later." *Central States Speech Journal* 27 (1976): 258–66.

————. "The Tacit Dimension and Rhetoric: What It Means to be Persuading and Persuaded." *Pre/Text* 2 (1981): 115–23.

Strine, Mary. "Critical Theory and 'Organic' Intellectuals: Reframing the Work of Cultural Critique. *Communication Monographs* 58 (1991): 195–201.

Wollen, Peter. *Signs and Meaning in the Cinema*. 3d ed. Bloomington: Indiana UP, 1972.

3

Temptation as Taboo: A Psychorhetorical Reading of *The Last Temptation of Christ*

Martin J. Medhurst

ON AUGUST II, 1988, 25,000 PROTESTERS MARCHED ON UNIVERSAL STUDIOS in Hollywood, California. The object of their ire was the latest in a long line of provocative films by director Martin Scorsese, *The Last Temptation of Christ*.[1] Replicated on a smaller scale at theaters throughout the country, the protests—staged mostly by theologically orthodox Christians—drew national media attention, rekindled freedom-of-expression issues, and highlighted just how far Hollywood had retreated from its previous Production Code standards.[2] While each of these issues is an important subject in itself, none can be understood completely apart from the object that reanimated them: the film.

Trying to understand Scorsese's *Last Temptation* is no easy matter, for the cinematic text has been overshadowed by the production company's none-too-subtle publicity campaign, the protesters' charges of blasphemy and historical inaccuracy, and the media's seeming preoccupation with its First Amendment rights.[3] Nevertheless, *The Last Temptation* is a film worthy of serious analysis. The central interpretive problem, it seems to me, is that of finding an appropriate point of comparison against which to judge the film in the midst of PR slogans, protests, and countercharges.

Several legitimate modes of reading the film are suggestive. Is the film to be judged with respect to its fidelity to the original novel by Nikos Kazantzakis? Is it to be evaluated according to the parameters of a particular cinematic genre such as the biblical epic, looking back to DeMille, Stevens, and Zeffirelli for generic touchstones? Should we compare *The Last Temptation* to other Scorsese films, searching for the motifs and cinematic vision that mark the true auteur? Or, is the proper point of comparison the picture of Jesus' life and ministry as found in the Bible—a sort of literary or historical realist standard?

Reviewers and critics have adopted each of these perspectives in attempting to come to grips with the most controversial film of the 1980s. Each perspective reveals something of import about the film, but each also reduces a complex work of art to a set of standards that if not totally inappropriate is at least incomplete for purposes of evaluation.

Those who compare the film to the novel often note, for example, the high fidelity that exists between Kazantzakis's 1955 novel (translated into English in 1960) and Scorsese's 1988 film version. Each reflects Kazantzakis's view of life as "the unyielding, inextinguishable struggle of the naked worm called 'man' against the terrifying power and darkness of the forces within him and around him" (Helen Kazantzakis 507).[4] As Lawrence Meredith, writing in *The Christian Century,* notes: "In the gospel according to Kazantzakis, sin is the inability *to choose* the very freedom which is the Christ event" (800). Under this view, "it is not God who will save us—it is we who will save God, by battling, by creating, and by transmitting matter into spirit" (Kazantzakis, *Saviors* 106). This perspective is enlightening as far as it goes, but if pushed too hard, it leads to the conclusion that the novel and the film convey basically the same message, a conclusion that is, at best, questionable.

Likewise, those who attempt to locate the film either with respect to its genre—the biblical epic—or with respect to the totality of Scorsese films—his vision as an auteur—reveal individual points of interest and enlightenment but fail to account for either the overall structure or the cinematic details of the film. Several reviews have noted how much *The Last Temptation* departs from the expectations generated by earlier biblical epics, how it strips "the biblical epic of its encrusted sanctimony and show biz" by restoring "the immediacy of that time, the stern wonder of that land, the thrilling threat of meeting the Messiah on the mean streets of Jerusalem" (Corliss 36). For others, *The Last Temptation* is, in essence, a remake of *Mean Streets,* or *Raging Bull,* or *The Color of Money* in a different guise. Under this view, Scorsese's films are "thematically, the same film." According to Richard Corliss, they are a "kind of buddy movie" where "two men are bound by love or hate" and "one must betray the other and thereby help certify his mission" (Corliss 36).

Finally, there are the numerous critics, primarily fundamentalist or evangelical Christians and conservative newspaper columnists, who fault the film for its departure from the Christ story as found in the Bible. Jerry Falwell, for example, has labeled the film "utter blasphemy of the worst degree" (qtd. in Ansen 56), while radio personality Dr. James Dobson finds the film to be "the most blasphemous, evil attack on the church and the cause of Christ in the history of entertainment" (qtd. in Ankerberg and Weldon 2). Conservative columnist and commentator Patrick Buchanan agrees, arguing that "the movie represents an act of cinematic vandalism against the beliefs that Christians hold sacred; it is a deliberate profanation of the faith" (qtd. in Ankerberg and Weldon 2).

The outrage expressed in such statements found its praxis in the boycott effort organized by Reverend Donald Wildmon of the American Family Association. Wildmon, by his own accounting, "distributed 4,000,000 petitions to local theatres, distributed spots to approximately 900 Christian radio stations, and provided a 30-minute special which aired on approximately 50 Christian television stations" ("Focus") in an effort to compel withdrawal of what he and others considered an intentionally blasphemous film. This perspective, too, despite the histrionics of some of its advocates, teaches us important lessons, most centrally that the Christ of *The Last Temptation* is not the Christ of the Bible.

Of course, the film, itself, announces that fact at the outset when an introductory credit states that the film is "not based upon the Gospels" but is a "fictional exploration of the eternal spiritual conflict."[5] The credit tells us what the film is not, but that is far from explaining what it is—or what it might mean. For while this film is indeed based upon a story—what Aristotle called a mythos—it is not the Kazantzakis story of "a laborious, sacred, creative endeavor to reincarnate the essence of Christ" (Helen Kazantzakis 505). Nor is it the story of the biblical Christ as seen through the lens of Hollywood glitz. Nor is it even the story of the radical teacher of God's kingdom found in the biblical narratives of Matthew, Mark, and Luke. No, Scorsese's story of *The Last Temptation of Christ* is an allegory, an allegory that requires close attention to details to understand fully. As with all good allegories, *The Last Temptation* is structured by a complex calculus of myth, metaphor, and sign, the structural relationships of which must be understood if one is to evaluate this work of cinematic art on its own terms. For as Harry Cheney has noted, "The Jesus of the movie is a metaphor entirely separate from the historical Savior." "What we are dealing with here," says Cheney, "is allegory, not biography" (56).

Jesus as Everyman

If we are, in fact, in the presence of allegory rather than biography, what are we to make of this man, Jesus? If he is not the Christ of the Bible, then who is he? I shall argue that Scorsese's Christ is Everyman, a metaphor for universal humanity in both its ontological and psychological dimensions. At the level of myth, two paradigmatic narratives structure the film: the Edenic myth of Adam and Eve in the Garden and the central myth of Freudian psychoanalysis, the Oedipus complex. Each myth informs and transforms the other and each is necessary for a full understanding of the film.

Specifically, I shall argue that the Christ of the film is suffering from a crisis of identity brought on by an unconscious desire for his mother, Mary, and resulting in an estrangement from his father, God. The loss of identity is representative of the universal state of humankind: drawn to the immanent things of this earth (represented by the mother, Mary), but conscious of a higher, transcendent spiritual calling, a calling that can never be fully realized (represented by the heavenly Father). At the level of metaphor, four specific typologies inform the text: Christ as the Second Adam; Mary as the innocent but beguiling Eve; the Cross as a type of Man's burden as well as the way to transcend that burden; and the serpent or Devil as the advocate of the uninhibited, pleasure-seeking desires of the Id—that which seeks to unleash the restraints imposed by the Super-Ego (i.e., God consciousness) and to form the Ego or self after its own image.

This is the story of Everyman in that all humans ask three questions: 1) Who am I?, 2) Why am I here?, and 3) How do I fulfill my mission in this life? In *The Last Temptation,* Jesus struggles to answer these questions, but he is only a man, a man suffering from the same repressed desires and fears as suffered by all men. The film is a story of how this one man confronts his desires and fears and in so doing comes to understand who he is, what his purpose is, and how he must fulfill that purpose.

That the Jesus of the film has serious identity problems has been clear to nearly every reviewer, even if they do not recognize—which most do not—the psycho-analytic implications of the symptoms.[6] The film opens with Jesus lying on the ground, curled up, thinking about the pain in his head, the claws that seem to dig in and tear. After a cut, the voice-over says: "First I fasted for three months. I even whipped myself before I went to sleep. At first it worked. Then the pain came back and the voices. They call me by name, Jesus. Who is it? Who are you? Why are you following me?" From the outset, the viewer is confronted with a man who hears voices, voices that speak of a calling, a destiny. A little further into the film, Jesus says, "I'm a liar, a hypocrite; I'm afraid of everything. I don't ever tell the truth, I don't have the courage. When I see a woman, I blush and look away. I want to, but I don't take her—for God. . . ." This is the Jesus of the film; a man with severe identity problems who has repressed the natural desire for women in an effort to find peace with God, his heavenly father.

Film critics clearly recognize that something is wrong with this Jesus, but they cannot quite put their collective finger on what it is. References abound in the reviews to Jesus as a "tortured soul" (Neff 13) who is "racked by doubts" (Ansen 57), "apprehensive and fundamentally confused about his message and his mission" (Leo 35) and a "tormented, neurotic blunderer" (Blake 100) who is presented as an "existential searcher after self knowledge" (O'Brien 470). As Michael Morris puts it: "The film's Jesus questions himself so much that it's sort of like watching *The Three Faces of Eve*" (qtd. in Leo 36). That this Jesus does have identity problems is clear. The question then becomes why? Why is this man the way he is, and by implication, why are all people the way they are? The answer is provided in a close reading of the filmic text itself.

The Oedipal Situation

A careful reading of the visual, auditory, thematic, and metaphorical elements reveals that this Jesus is struggling to form a whole, integrated self. This struggle pits the pleasure-seeking instincts of the Id against the admonishing and rule-governed strictures of the Super-Ego. In the film, Mary the mother is the repressed object of desire. As the film opens, we find that Jesus lives with his mother, apparently alone, in a village where he supports both of them by making crosses for the Romans. Although Joseph does not appear in the film (a rhetorical choice that also functions as a sign of the filmmaker's intentions), Kazantzakis tells us in the novel that Joseph was paralyzed by a lightning bolt on his wedding day, thereafter to sit motionless in the house striving to utter the only word ever again to pass from his lips: "Adonai"—God. So Joseph is out of the picture and it is just Jesus and Mary living alone in the house. When Jesus' head pains start again, Mary cradles him in her arms and gently strokes his head.[7] As Jesus helps the Romans carry a cross to Golgotha to crucify another would-be messiah, Mary tries to protect him from the angry crowd. "Don't touch him—get away from him," she warns. Hence, at the very outset of the film, there is a close bond between mother and son, a bond that the rest of the film will demonstrate to have been unconsciously sexual in nature and one that will systematically decrease as Jesus symbolically transfers his love for his mother to a mother substitute, Mary Magdalene.

Now, before we go further into the film, it is important to be clear about the precise dimensions of the Oedipus complex. Victoria Hamilton provides a succinct summary:

> The Oedipus complex maps out the vicissitudes of triangular relationships which have their origins in the relationship between the child and his two parents. The child of three to five years of age is engaged in a three-person relationship in which the father plays an increasingly focal role. The child wants to get in between his parents. This wish entails the idea that he gets rid of one parent so as to enjoy an exclusive love relationship with the other. The resolution of this dilemma has far-reaching implications for the child's view of reality. In order to come to terms with the "reality principle," he must abandon his early attempts to organize the world about him in accordance with the "pleasure principle" (Freud 1911), through which his selfish or "narcissistic" wishes and needs are fulfilled. The Oedipus complex is resolved or "dissolved" by a renunciation of childish, sexual wishes, which are inherently anti-social, and by an "identification" with the parent of the same sex. The little boy no longer wishes to eliminate his father but to be just like him. (16)

Ilham Dilman further points out that "the conflict that a person still feels with regard to his parents lies at the basis of his later emotional and sexual difficulties in life. Those difficulties represent an enactment of this conflict in his current life, the repercussions of his doing so, and his reactions to them" (Dilman 43).

In the film, Jesus, now a grown man, clearly has both emotional and sexual difficulties. His emotional difficulties center around his relationship with his father (God). His sexual difficulties center around three symbolic representations of the mother: Mary Magdalene, Mary the sister of Lazarus, and Martha her sister. The film itself announces this symbolic equivalence when it twice proclaims: "There's only one woman in the world—one woman with many faces." The one woman is, of course, the mother. The other three women are symbolic equivalents not only because they have the same or a similar name but because they are all the objects of sexual desire; repressed in the case of mother Mary, but manifest in Jesus' dream life in the cases of Magdalene and the sisters, Mary and Martha.

That Jesus' sexual encounters with the two Marys and Martha happen during a dream merely reinforces the symbolic nature of the liaison. By marrying first Magdalene, then Mary, and then taking Martha as a sex partner, Jesus is symbolically acting out his repressed desires for his mother. These repressed desires are pictured in the film as being checked by fear of the father. As Jesus says, "I want to rebel against you, against everything, against God, but I'm afraid. You want to know who my mother and father are? You want to know who my God is? Fear! You look inside me and that's all you'll find." Magdalene recognizes this relationship between the repressed sexual desires and the emotional fear of the father when she tells Jesus: "If you weren't hanging onto your mother, you were hanging on to me, now you're hanging onto God."

The fear of the father, representative of the claims of the Super-Ego, prevents Jesus from engaging in the desires of the flesh and results in an identity crisis wherein the Ego is so underdeveloped that it experiences great anxiety. And the "two main sources of anxiety," as Dempsey notes, are "the erotic or aggressive instinctual impulses of the 'id,' and the menace of the superego parental, collective or individual, directed against the impulses or instincts" (167). The anxiety, apprehensiveness, and neurotic behavior noted by many of the film reviewers is a direct result of the Oedipal situation within which Jesus finds himself. The recognition that such neurosis is "the 'psychoanalytic analogue' of the theological doctrine of original sin" (Homans 128) allows the critic to discover the link between the use of the Oedipus myth and its Edenic counterpart, the story of Adam and Eve in the Garden.

Biblical Typology

The very title of Scorsese's film, *The Last Temptation of Christ,* announces the presence of a typology.[8] For as Christ, the biblical Second Adam, is tempted while on the cross, so the first Adam was tempted in the Garden. Whereas the tempter in the biblical garden was Satan in the form of a serpent, on Scorsese's cross Christ is tempted by Satan in the form of an angel. Whereas the first Adam disobeyed his father, God, and gave in to the temptation, partaking of the fruit of the tree of the knowledge of good and evil, the Second Adam, Christ, was obedient to the father, even unto his death on a cross. But the analogy does not stop there.

The story of the Garden is the story of humankind's creation, of harmony between humans and God, humans and the environment, humans and themselves. It is the story of the rupturing of that harmony by an act of will: an act of deliberate and willful disobedience of the children of God for which they suffer estrangement from God, estrangement from the Garden, and, eventually, estrangement from one another.

In the Garden story, God is the father. The mother, however, is the earth, for Genesis 2:7 declares that "then the Lord God formed man of dust from the ground." The association between the earth and motherhood is made explicitly in the novel, where Kazantzakis writes: "Leaning over, he kissed the earth. 'Mother,' he said softly, 'hold me close, and I shall hold you close. Mother, why can't you be my God?'" (455). It was from mother earth that the first man was made and it would be to mother earth that the Second Adam would return in death. The earth/mother image thus represents both life and death simultaneously. It is from her that life is drawn, but it is also by her that temptation, sin, and death are made manifest. Hence, in the Scorsese film, a serpent and garden tree appear to Jesus during his sojourn in the desert. The serpent speaks with the voice of Mary Magdalene. The original temptation in the Garden is thus replicated in the life of Jesus. The temptation, in both cases, is forbidden knowledge: knowledge of the tree of good and evil in the one case and incestuous knowledge of the mother in the other. In both cases it is the command of the father that stands between the desire and its fulfillment. In both cases it is the woman— Eve in the Garden and the symbolic substitute for the mother, Mary Magdalene, in the film—that is the vehicle for the temptation. Eve entices Adam to disobey, while the dream of being married to Magdalene and raising a family of his own is dangled before the crucified Christ in a final attempt to derail him from what he now understands to be his mission. The difference, of course, is that the first Adam succumbs to the temptation; the Second Adam does not.

That we are to understand Christ's last temptation as parallel to humankind's first is clear in the visual narrative of the film and the written narrative of the novel. As Christ comes down from the cross in the film, he is led by the angel (Satan) into a clearing in the wilderness. Mist rises from the ground, just as it does in the Garden (Genesis 2:6), and a sparkling newness gives the impression of a world freshly created. As Jesus enters the clearing, he sees that a wedding is going on and asks, "Who's getting married?" "You are," replies his angelic guide. Kazantzakis's novel gives an even more sharply drawn portrait of the parallel with Eden: "'Let us go,' said the angel, and he began to stride nimbly over the blossoming meadow. 'Great joys await you, Jesus of Nazareth. God left me free to allow you to taste all the pleasures you ever secretly longed for. Beloved, the earth is good—you'll see. Wine, laughter, the lips of a woman, the gambols of your first son on your knees—all are good'" (*Last* 446). In this passage Kazantzakis captures the refrain of God's pronouncement upon his creation as recorded in Genesis, where the writer uses the rhetorical device of epistrophe as he repeatedly emphasizes "And God saw that it was good" (Genesis 1:12, 18, 21, 25, 31).

Kazantzakis also links the ceremony in the meadow and the consummation of the marriage that immediately follows with "the pleasures you ever secretly longed for." Those pleasures are to have intercourse with the mother, which, by transference, Jesus does after he weds Magdalene. But this secret longing is the greatest of taboos. Just as Adam's disobedience brought with it an intimate knowledge of the earth mother, so Jesus in his dream on the cross acquires intimate knowledge that will cause him to be forever estranged from his true father, God Almighty. It thus becomes clear that the filmmaker employs two great myths— the Garden of Eden and the Oedipus complex—which are, in essence, the same myth. Thomas J. J. Altizer states the case most succinctly when he observes that "the Oedipus complex is at bottom a desire for the primal paradise, and the sexual desire for the mother is fundamentally a desire for union with unfallen being" (qtd. in Homans 181–82). Scorsese is not, therefore, telling two stories, but rather a single story in two distinct (but closely related) mythic forms, one ancient and one modern; one theologically based, the other psychologically based. Both involve fundamental questions of identity, of who I am in relationship to those who created me—my parents. As Homans puts it: "The Oedipus myth articulates for all men the innermost problematic depths of selfhood and, as such, is the psychoanalytic counterpart of Biblical myth" (27).

That this film really is about identity and its formation is clear from the opening segment. Jesus is a cross maker. Within the first few minutes of the film, we observe Jesus not only making a cross but actually measuring himself on a *cross of his own making*. Scorsese is engaging in a visual pun of sorts, but it is anything but funny. Jesus, as representative of all humanity, is announcing that humankind's burdens—its crosses—are ones that all of us make for ourselves. Our crosses are those things we most fear. Christ makes crosses because he fears and hates his father and the ever-present voice within that tells him, "You're not a man, you're the son of man. And more, the Son of God. And more than that, God!" Christ makes crosses because it is his form of rebellion against the father. The father bids him to grow up into manhood, to be what he was created to be— the Messiah. But Jesus seeks to keep the commands of the father at bay by assisting in the crucifixion of all would-be messiahs. "I want him to hate me," Jesus says. "I fight him. I make crosses so he'll hate me. I want him to find somebody else, I want to crucify every one of his messiahs." The cross thus represents rebellion against the father and his wishes. Eventually, of course, the very vehicle of rebellion will become the vehicle of identification with and obedience to the father.

The centrality of the cross as the testimony to the son's identification with and obedience to the father is affirmed when Satan uses the crucifixion as the opportunity for temptation. In symbolic terms, the cross of Jesus is equivalent to the tree in the Garden of Eden. Just as the cross is the mark of obedience, so was the tree the test of Adam's willingness to obey. As humans became separated from God through the first tree, so by being lifted up on this new tree, the cross, Christ reestablishes that broken relationship. The Devil, not wanting the rupture to be healed, naturally selects the cross as the site of his last temptation. It is his last chance to keep father and son apart and, by extension, to keep God separated from all of his children, the universal humanity embodied in Jesus Christ.

To accomplish his ends, Satan takes on a disguise as "an angel of Light" (2

Cor. 11:14). That the angel in the film (unlike the one in the novel) is feminine may also be significant, for it is the pleasures of the earth (mother) and flesh (Magdalene/mother) that Satan chooses to use as enticement. Just as the serpent was said to be "more subtle" than any other creature, so this angel (Satan) seems to be the most innocent, harmless creature of God. She is, however, the reverse image of the serpent in the Garden where, as the advocate of unrestrained pleasure, Satan showed Eve fruit that was a delight to the eyes (Genesis 3:6). This same serpent, now in angelic form, shows Jesus the pleasures of the earth and says to him: "Your Father is the God of mercy, not punishment," a phrase that echoes Genesis 3:4: "But the serpent said to the woman, 'You will not die.'" The angel's response to Jesus' first question as he enters into the meadow is significant, for it is both a lie (identifying the angel with Satan, the "Father of Lies") and it focuses on a question of identity. "I'm not the Messiah?" Jesus queries. "No, no you're not," says the angel. Since Messiahship is equivalent to identification with the father and thus the sign of having successfully passed through the Oedipal period, it is not surprising that Satan immediately invites a regression by overseeing the wedding of Jesus and Mary Magdalene. It is an attempt to keep Jesus from developing into a whole self, a self not bound by repressed desire for the mother or hatred for the father. For what the Oedipus complex really amounts to is "one of the crises in an individual's life in his development towards independence and autonomy" (Dilman 45). By the time Jesus reaches the cross he has acquired such autonomy. He has rejected the self-defining enticements of the Zealots, who bid one to come and lose his life in the revolution ("Remember, you once told me that if I moved one step from revolution, you'd kill me. . . . Remember? . . . I've strayed, haven't I?"). He has rejected the self-defining character of the Jewish Law ("Then the Law is against my heart"). And he has rejected the self-defining limitations of family ("I don't have a mother. I don't have any family"). He has chosen the cross freely, on his own. He has come to a consciousness of who he is, why he was born, and what he must do ("I have to die on the cross. . . . Remember, we're bringing God and Man together. They'll never be together unless I die. I'm the sacrifice."). But the possibility of regression to a former state always exists, and it is this fact upon which the Devil seems to be counting. The satanic angel is fully aware of the instinctual draw toward the mother, earth, and procreation, an instinct that has exerted a profound influence on Jesus' life. The last temptation is merely an amplified version of all the temptations with which Jesus has struggled his entire life. The dream sequence on the cross is a compression of all Jesus' desires, fears, anxieties, and pleasures into a split second. But to understand the full significance of the last temptation one must return to the text of the film itself.

Rhyme Patterns and Visual Correlates

Throughout the film, various signs are provided that indicate Jesus' strong attraction to things of the earth, especially those centered in sexuality. Two pair of rhyme patterns are instructive in this regard: semen/demon and womb/tomb.[9] Both have significance for the final dream sequence.

The semen/demon pair occurs by implication throughout the film. It is Jesus' desire for his mother, symbolically transformed into his desire for Martha and the other Marys, that forms the core of his identity problems. This repressed desire is his demon—that which must be exorcised if he is to come into full adulthood, to be a wholly integrated and independent self. The scenes of prostitution in Mary Magdalene's house and Jesus' temptation in the desert both point to the connection between semen and demon. In the house of prostitution, for example, Jesus literally closes his eyes to what is going on roundabout him. But the demon is *inside* his head, not in the external actions. To exorcise the demon, Jesus asks for Magdalene's forgiveness, forgiveness for not being able to perform sexually as an adult man. "I want you to forgive me," says Jesus. To which Magdalene replies: "He [God] already broke my heart. He took you away from me, and I hate both of you [Jesus and God]. . . . You're the same as all the others, only you can't admit it. You're pitiful."

Jesus cannot take Magdalene as his sexual partner precisely because the Father, God, forbids him from doing so. The Father stands between the son and the symbolic representation of the mother. It is because of this set of relationships that semen, a sign of physical, earthly sexual desire becomes Jesus' demon—that which must be exorcised or overcome before he can be a fully functioning autonomous self. The rule of the semen/demon is the sign of his continuing attraction to the mother and the things of this earth, as well as a sign of his continuing estrangement from his father in heaven. This is made explicit during the scene at Nazareth when, after listening to Jesus preach, a man in the crowd says: "Go get somebody from his family to take him away. . . . See, this is what happens when a man doesn't get married, the semen backs up into his brain." A few lines later, another man charges Jesus with having a demon. And so he does, but the film has already shown us what that demon is: the desire for his mother transferred to the other women in his life and the reproach of the father that stands between Jesus' developing Ego and the satisfaction of the instincts of the Id. If he were married and had a family, the dialogue suggests, he would not have this problem, no demon would exist. This semen/demon pair is also linked to the womb/tomb imagery.

The womb is that part of the mother from which life comes forth. Adam was drawn from the womb of mother earth; the Second Adam from the womb of Mary. But the fate of all such earthly men is the tomb. To come from the womb is to end in the tomb. The two are symbolically equivalent. In the Kazantzakis novel, the womb is viewed as a place of imprisonment that only a man can unlock. What is the key? Semen. Here is what the serpent says to Jesus: "God created man and woman to match, like the key and the lock. Open her. Your children sit huddled together and numb inside her, waiting for you to blow away their numbness so that they may rise and come out to walk in the sun" (257).

The imagery here is precisely parallel to the Lazarus scene in the film. Lazarus lies dead in a tomb, dead in the womb of the earth. Even the visual framing of the tomb's opening is in the shape of a woman's womb. As Jesus reaches out for Lazarus's hand, he is almost pulled into the womb/tomb. The womb, the earth, the feminine is reaching out, beckoning Jesus. And he almost succumbs. But to be lured into the womb is also to be propelled into a tomb. To remain forever caught up in an identity crisis, to be forever desirous of the womb of the mother is to invite the death and entombment of the Ego, the self. Hence, like the se-men/demon pair, the womb/tomb coupling is also a symbolic equivalent, though one is linked with life and the other with death. Lazarus, therefore, when asked whether he prefers life or death, is made to say that there is not much difference between the two. Total identification with either the womb or the tomb is to be other than a whole self, for the self is formed by the day-to-day struggles of that which occurs between womb and tomb. Kazantzakis clearly means these to be symbolic equivalents, for he writes in his book *The Saviors of God:* "I once set out from a dark point, the Womb, and now I proceed to another dark point, the Tomb. A power hurls me out of the dark pit and another power drags me irre-vocably toward the dark pit" (54). Whether womb or tomb, both are dark pits requiring release. The human seed, semen, releases the self from the womb. The heavenly seed, love, frees the self from the tomb.

Becoming an Integrated Self

As the final dream sequence nears completion, Jesus looks at his second wife, Mary, and says: "Don't ever leave me." As the camera focuses on his wife it is apparent that Mary the sister of Lazarus now appears exactly as Mary the mother of Jesus did in the beginning of the film. They are the same person, both visually and sym-bolically. The final temptation is to be forever caught up in the Oedipal love and desire for the mother, to never gain true selfhood, to be forever unsure, anxious, and dependent on the mother's love and protection, never to identify with the father and take on his identity. This is the temptation that Jesus rejects.

As one who has already passed through the Oedipal period during the course of the film, Jesus is no longer attracted to the mother, no longer hates the father, and no longer fearful of the future. He has struggled to become who he was in-tended to be: the Messiah, the Son of God. As he crawls from his bed, pulling himself back up Golgotha's hill, Jesus calls out to the father: "I fought you when you called. I resisted. I thought I knew more. I didn't want to be your son. Can you forgive me? I didn't fight hard enough. Father, give me your hand. I want to bring salvation. Father, take me back. Make a feast. Welcome me home. I want to be your son." And, indeed, with his reappearance on the cross, Jesus is shown to be God's son, to have chosen to obey the voice of the Father rather than suc-cumb to the enticements of the earth and the desires of the flesh.

But this Jesus is not divine, but fully human. He is not the Christ of the Bible who was both fully God and fully Man, but, rather, the symbolic representation of Everyman, of universal humanity. He is the metaphorical representative of all who seek for their true selves, who question their purpose for living, who strive to discover why they are on this earth and what their mission, their goal in life, is to be. Although cloaked in a complex work of visual artistry, Scorsese's basic point is straightforward: We are all in the process of searching for who we are, of developing a whole, integrated self, a self that can function apart from the dictates of family but that always, in a very profound way, is an outcome of having been part of a family and of having gone through the Oedipal period. As members of the human family, we must decide who we are and what our purpose in this life is. It will not be easy, says Scorsese, but we must struggle, fight, ascend, always remembering that, in the words of Kazantzakis: "The doors of heaven and hell are adjacent, and identical: both green, both beautiful. Take care, Adam! Take care! Take care!" (*Last* 280).

Conclusion

Humanity must both will and choose the good. Merely discovering the truth about oneself is not enough. One must act on that discovery in order to be a fully integrated self. Scorsese has given the cinematic audience a profound statement of the problem of achieving human selfhood. If this statement has disturbed large numbers of people, it may be that unconsciously they recognize the Oedipal impulses that lay at the heart of the film and wish to further repress those impulses by striking out at the artist—the father, so to speak—and his creation. Or, perhaps some audience members have taken what Scorsese clearly intends as a statement of the problem to be, instead, a statement about the solution.

If this were primarily a film about the Christ of the Bible, it would be easy to see why so many Christians object and to understand why a professional critic like Kenneth Chanko could conclude that "if the film were viewed in a vacuum, it would be difficult to come away from this version of the Jesus story with the certainty that this prophet was the Son of God. Indeed, given the film's portrayal, it is difficult to believe that Jesus exerted the kind of spiritual power necessary to attract millions to his cause" (551). But this is not primarily a film about the Jesus of the Bible. It is a film about a universal dimension of humanity that the filmmaker, for whatever reasons, has chosen to communicate through the symbolic, metaphorical, and typological aspects of the Christ story. By weaving an intricate allegory that operates on two separate levels, Scorsese has demonstrated a basic cinematic truth: seeing and understanding are not the same thing. What some see as pure blasphemy against God the Son can, instead, be understood as a powerful statement about the problems of human identity formation, of coming to know who we are in a mean and dirty world filled with internal urges, social expectations, and spiritual aspirations.

Clearly not everyone "reads" *The Last Temptation of Christ* in the same way. And perhaps that should not be surprising, for as Kazantzakis wrote in the novel:

Everything is of God, he reflected; everything has two meanings, one manifest, one hidden. The common people comprehend only what is manifest. They say, 'This is a snake,' and their minds go no further; but the mind which dwells in God sees what lies behind the visible, sees the hidden meaning. (150)

Scorsese invites us to go beyond the manifest, beyond what can be seen with our eyes, and to understand through an act of mind the deeper significance of the struggle for human selfhood.

Notes

The author wishes to thank Amy Melissa Tilton for her assistance in preparing the final version of this chapter.

1. *The Last Temptation of Christ* was directed by Martin Scorsese, director of such films as *Mean Streets, Taxi Driver, Raging Bull,* and *The Color of Money,* among others. The screenplay was written by Paul Schrader from the novel by Nikos Kazantzakis. For details on the film's opening and the protests and counter-protests that accompanied it, see Chandler and Easton; Dart and Chandler.

2. From 1930 until 1968, the Motion Picture Association of America (MPAA) subscribed to a Production Code that set guidelines and limitations on what film-makers could portray on the screen and how such portrayals could be presented. The portion of the Production Code dealing with religion stated, in part, that "No film or episode shall throw ridicule on any religious faith." For a reproduction of the complete code, see Schumach.

3. If one were to rely strictly on the publicity releases from MCA-Universal, one would encounter the repetition of three themes: sincerity, seriousness, and power. The studio's PR message was clear: Scorsese is a man who is sincere about his faith in Christ and who has made a serious film that relates his personal vision in a most striking and powerful way. To the audience member who, amidst the voices raised in protest, was unsure about the propriety of seeing the film, Universal advised: "Now, See For Yourself."

Over against this PR image were the equally vociferous protests of a large segment of the Christian community that found the film "offensive," "blasphemous," "outrageous," "evil," "dangerous," "unfair," and "inaccurate." Virtually all of the protest leaders urged their followers to stay away from the film, while some, such as the Rev. Donald Wildmon of the American Family Association and Dr. James Dobson of Focus on the Family, urged a general boycott of all MCA-Universal products.

The response to such calls for action from MCA-Universal, as well as other media representatives, was to charge the protesters with trying to subvert First Amendment guarantees of freedom of expression and with practicing censorship. As film director Sydney Pollack said: "What's at stake is the very essence of what we mean when we talk about a free society"(qtd. in Chandler and Easton 1).

Producer Michael Mann was even more vociferous when he charged: "For some of these groups to foist themselves upon us as some kind of thought police is reprehensible" (qtd. in Chandler and Easton 1). For these and other views, see Chandler and Easton.

4. This description is found in a letter from Kazantzakis to his friend Borje Knos dated 4 January 1952.

5. All quotations from the film are based on a transcription of the videotape release of *The Last Temptation of Christ* distributed by MCA Home Video, Inc. 1989.

6. One exception to this generalization is Ilene Serlin. I want to thank Professor Thomas S. Frentz for drawing my attention to her fine Jungian critique of *The Last Temptation of Christ*.

7. Later in the film, Jesus is held in much the same manner by Mary Magdalene. The visual correlate of the film is also present in written form in the novel, as the following two examples show: "'Help me light the fire and we'll cook.' Her [Magdalene's] voice was tender and attentive, *like a mother's*" (Kazantzakis, *The Last Temptation of Christ* 93; emphasis added). And again: "All night long she [Magdalene] listened to him breathe tranquilly, restfully, like an infant nursing at the breast; and she, lamenting softly within herself with tender, protracted sighs, lay awake and lulled him to sleep *like a mother*" (Kazantzakis, *The Last Temptation of Christ* 93; emphasis added).

8. For an excellent introduction to typological criticism see Frye. For an application of typological analysis in rhetorical criticism, see Reid.

9. Kazantzakis's novel, *The Last Temptation of Christ*, was originally written in Greek. The Greek text makes heavy use of rhythm and rhyme schemes that can only be dimly approximated in an English translation. For an explanation of Kazantzakis's method, see Bien. Nevertheless, some rhyme schemes are retained in the English translation and are adapted to the film version. Womb/tomb and semen/demon are only two of the more prominent examples. That Kazantzakis himself was aware of what he was doing with language seems clear from his various writings.

Works Cited

Ansen, David, et al. "Wrestling with 'Temptation.'" *Newsweek* 15 Aug. 1988: 56.

Bien, Peter. *Kazantzakis and the Linguistic Revolution in Greek Literature.* Princeton: Princeton UP, 1972.

Blake, Richard A. "The Universal Christ." *America* 27 Aug. 1988: 100.

Buchanan, Patrick. "Hollywood Levels Sleazy Assault at Christian Community." *The Facts on "The Last Temptation of Christ."* Ed. John Ankerberg and John Weldon. Eugene, OR: Harvest House, 1988. 2.

Chandler, Russell. "25,000 Gather at Universal to Protest Film." *Los Angeles Times* 12 Aug. 1988: 4 + 26.

Chandler, Russell, and Nina J. Easton. "Protest, Debate Greet Premiere of 'Temptation.'" *Los Angeles Times* 12 Aug. 1988: 1.

Chanko, Kenneth M. "The Last Temptation of Christ." *Films in Review* Nov. 1988: 551.

Cheney, Harry M. "Scorsese's Scorcher: *The Last Temptation of Christ.*" *Eternity* Oct. 1988: 56.

Corliss, Richard. "A Critic's Contrarian View." *Time* 15 Aug. 1988: 36.

Dart, John, and Russell Chandler. "Full Theatres, Protests Greet 'Temptation.'" *Los Angeles Times* 13 Aug. 1988: 1 + 29.

Dempsey, Peter J. R. *Freud, Psychoanalysis, Catholicism.* Chicago: Henry Regnery, 1956.

Dilman, Ilham. *Freud and Human Nature.* Oxford: Basil Blackwell, 1983.

Dobson, James. "Focus on the Family Radio Broadcast, 11 July 1988." *The Facts on "The Last Temptation of Christ."* Ed. John Ankerberg and John Weldon. Eugene, OR: Harvest House, 1988.

Frye, Northrop. *The Great Code: The Bible and Literature.* New York: Harcourt, 1982.

Hamilton, Victoria. *Narcissus and Oedipus: The Children of Psychoanalysis.* London: Routledge and Kegan Paul, 1982.

Homans, Peter. *Theology after Freud: An Interpretive Inquiry.* Indianapolis: Bobbs-Merrill, 1970.

Kazantzakis, Helen. *Nikos Kazantzakis: A Biography Based on His Letters.* Trans. Amy Mims. New York: Simon, 1968.

Kazantzakis, Nikos. *The Last Temptation of Christ.* Trans. P. A. Bien. New York: Simon, 1960.

———. *The Saviors of God: Spiritual Exercises.* Trans. Kimon Friar. New York: Simon, 1960.

Leo, John. "A Holy Furor." *Time* 15 Aug. 1988: 35.

Meredith, Lawrence. "The Gospel According to Kazantzakis: How Close Did Scorsese Come?" *The Christian Century* 14–21 Sept. 1988: 800.

Neff, David. "Scorsese's Christ." Editorial. *Christianity Today* 7 Oct. 1988: 13.

O'Brien, Tom. "Jesus as Hamlet: *The Last Temptation.*" *Commonweal* 9 Sept. 1988: 470.

Reid, Ronald F. "Apocalypticism and Typology: Rhetorical Dimensions of a Symbolic Reality." *Quarterly Journal of Speech* 69 (1983): 229–48.

Schumach, Murray. *The Face on the Cutting Room Floor: The Story of Movie and Television Censorship.* New York: De Capo, 1974.

Scorsese, Martin, dir. *The Last Temptation of Christ.* Universal Pictures, 1988.

Serlin, Ilene. "At the Movies." *The San Francisco Jung Institute Library Journal* 8.3 (1989): 67–75.

Wildmon, Donald. "1988 Accomplishments of the American Family Association." Printed material distributed by mail and in author's possession, 1988.

4

Hyperrhetoric and the Inventive Spectator: Remotivating *The Fifth Element*

Byron Hawk

Domination and Paradox

MANY THEORISTS IN THE SPACE OF CULTURAL STUDIES NOW ACCEPT the active role spectators can play in their interaction with dominant cultural forms. As Linda Williams notes in *Viewing Positions* (1995), "The issue that now faces the once influential subfield of spectatorship within cinema studies is whether it is still possible to maintain a theoretical grasp of the relations between moving images and viewers without succumbing to an anything goes relativism" (4). This is the same question that confronts Kenneth Burke in "Terministic Screens." He recognizes such potential relativism, but nevertheless attempts to theorize it. He concedes that "no one's 'personal equations' are quite identical with anyone else's"; but then in order to sidestep this relativity, he goes on to argue that "all members of our species conceive of reality somewhat roundabout, through various *media* of symbolism" (55). Language is posited as a given and particular differences derive from it. Starting from this assumption, Burke makes the distinction between persons/action and things/motion and gives it quasi-universal status in human culture—a distinction that enables him to propose his dramatistic theory as a means to encompass all readings of symbolic action. Even though the dramatistic approach allows Burke a retrospective theoretical grasp on "personal equations," it is still caught in the paradox that troubles Williams: we are at once divided by our bodies and our specificity and yet united under the omnipresent symbolic.

As Mark Poster points out in *The Mode of Information,* this is the paradox of poststructuralism: "It promises a new level of self-constitution, one beyond the rigidities and restraints of fixed identities, but also makes possible the subordination of the individual to manipulative communications practices" (65). On the one hand, media discourse is ubiquitous in our current culture, and hence prefigures potential subject positions. The filmic narrative, for example, is constructed in order to allow viewers to suture themselves onto a character and identify with that subject position. On the other hand, once identification is made with the character, the spectator has the potential to remotivate[1] that subject position into a context distant from the initial filmic context. The spectator can re-suture the filmic images onto hir[2] prior knowledge and experience—memory. The problem, as Williams notes, becomes how to theorize this inventive potential in the viewer as a process, not just in retrospect.

Headway can be made in this area by linking Gregory Ulmer's methods to the subfield of spectatorship within film studies. Ulmer says that the key to "working heuretically is to use the method that [one is] inventing while [one is] inventing it, hence to practice hyperrhetoric" (*Heuretics* 17). Thinking through this *hyper-active* position, he devises an inventional tactic for writing. I argue that his method can provide an attractive perspective on film spectatorship as an inventive process. It can give academics "theoretical grasp" on (active) spectatorship, as well as give spectators an initial method for taking images out of their ideological or filmic context and remotivating (or re-suturing) them within the context of the spectators' own "personal equations" or mythologies. And, if this active spectatorship is pushed to its limit to become hyperrhetoric, spectators can transform Ulmer's method into new methods. Hyperrhetoric, then, proposes a way out of reductive either/or perspectives on film theory. Theory neither constitutes the viewer and viewing process nor provides a transparent window on them. Film is neither just a forum for dominant ideology nor a site open to any interpretation. Spectatorship is neither a site for passivity nor a space for resistance. Reader response theory is too relative, resistance to hegemony too oppositional. As a mode of both invention and criticism, hyperrhetoric approaches the complex situation of spectatorship as a moment of emergence. All of the above elements are at play in the inventive act of active spectatorship.

But not everyone will read so actively. Consequently, I take from Henri Bergson and Gilles Deleuze a distinction between automatic recognition and attentive recognition and argue for a third possible mode, hyper-attentive recognition. This third mode of spectatorship begins to blur the boundaries between ideology/spectator, theory/application, objective/subjective, motion/action and even male/female. Utilizing Roland Barthes's notion of the punctum, and Ulmer's reinscription, the puncept, this third mode allows the spectator to practice a "writerly" model of invention.[3] If we take Ulmer's notion of hyperrhetoric seriously, there is no way to completely theorize a method that is being invented while it is being deployed. But by accepting this paradox of hyperrhetoric, academics (and spectators) can begin to think methodically about the blurring of these boundaries, especially between applying a prescribed theory and using a method for inventing a method. As an example of this process, I use Ulmer's heuretic CATTt (Contrast, Analogy, Theory, Target, tale) to read *The Fifth Element* in a way that remotivates the five elements of classical rhetoric (invention, arrangement, style, memory, delivery) and produces a theory of attentiveness.

The Inventive Spectator

In cultural studies, much work has been done on the inventive potential of the consumer of culture and its images. Michel de Certeau, for example, is generally given credit for inspiring much of the work that emphasizes fan remotivation of corporate mass culture. In *The Practice of Everyday Life*, he sees the individual as "subjected" by institutional "strategies" molded to the current political and economic tendencies. Rather than assuming a passive role for the subject, however, he focuses on the "tactics" employed by consumers to reappropriate mass culture artifacts. De Certeau follows Michel Foucault's dual notion of the subject. Foucault writes, "There are two meanings of the word *subject:* subject to someone else by control and dependence, and tied to his own identity by a conscience or self-knowledge. Both meanings suggest a form of power which subjugates and makes subject to" (212). But even though the subject is constructed through strategies, its knowledge of itself makes it more than a site of passive acceptance. Subjectivity is an active site that participates in the reproduction of discourses and practices. De Certeau's now well-known notion of this contemporary subject hints at Deleuze's work: "readers are travelers; they move across lands belonging to someone else, like *nomads* poaching their way across fields they did not write" (*Practice* 174; my emphasis).

De Certeau's focus on the active consumer has spawned many followers. Thomas McLaughlin, for example, focuses on what he terms "vernacular theory" in *Street Smarts and Critical Theory.* One of his examples is the fan as critic. Most fanzines—self-produced magazines focused on particular styles, bands, or actors–"are obsessed with the *business,* in spite of the fact that 'fans' are supposed to be obsessed with the product" (58). Punk fans know that their music gets co-opted, and this becomes a big focus of much of the music, subculture, and fan criticism. McLaughlin also cites an example that shows fan/writer Mark Mahaffey making a "flash of theoretical insight" writing about G. G. Allin.[4] According to McLaughlin, Mahaffey rejects "the consensus interpretation (violence is bad, art is uplifting) [. . .] in favor of an oppositional reading (violence is fun, art can be psychotic)" (60). In both cases, fan subjectivity is revealed as an active site for the practice of discourse and knowledge production. Henry Jenkins, in *Textual Poachers,* also addresses the ways in which "fans raid mass culture, claiming its materials for their own use, reworking them as a basis for their own cultural creations and social interactions" (18). He discusses an active fan culture around remotivated *Star Trek* characters. Some fans write new narratives that create a sexual relationship between Spock and Captain Kirk and support this remotivated identification by purchasing fanzines and gathering at *Star Trek* conventions.

Remotivation is not restricted to fan culture and written discourse, however. In "TV's Anti-Families," Josh Ozersky provides a good example while discussing *The Simpsons:*

A black Bart soon began to turn up in unlicensed street paraphernalia. In the first of the unauthorized shirts, Bart was himself, only darkened. The novelty soon wore off, however, and in successive generations Bart found himself ethnicized further: "Air Bart" had him flying toward a basketball hoop exclaiming, "In your face, home boy." Another shirt had Bart leering at zaftig black women, loutishly yelling "Big Ole Butt!" at their retreating figures. And in later versions, Bart has a gold tooth, a razor cut, and an angry snarl—the slogan "I got the power!" juts overhead in an oversized balloon. (205–6)

This shows that cultural representations are not static or purely deductive. Media images evolve as they come into contact with people and social situations. Public texts intersect private bodies for the purpose of identity construction, and private bodies intersect social groups via the reconfiguration of public texts, blurring the lines between those (public) discourses and those (private) spaces. These remotivated texts can provide the very basis of social interaction from conversations with friends to huge fan conventions.

This type of social phenomenon applies to the solitary viewer sitting in a theater in two predominant and somewhat obvious ways. A spectator does not go into a theater as a blank slate. S/he has a backlog of prior knowledge (a mythology or image repertoire specific to hir) that is constructed through a combination of dominant culture, social interaction, and life experience. The spectator brings this mythology to the film, and the filmic images are connected to it. Then, once out of the theater, the spectator discusses hir reading of the film with other friends who have seen it, and they often try to make sense of the film/reading.

I am thinking of an example from my own experience. In the summer of 1997, I saw *The Fifth Element*. The movie essentially parodies sci-fi films by making many references to other films like *Stargate, Star Wars,* and *Blade Runner*. As I was watching the film, I was puzzled by the opening references to *Stargate;* then when references to *Star Wars* and *Blade Runner* appeared, I recognized the necessity for an ironic reading. After seeing the film, I discussed my reading with various friends who had seen the movie. They were disturbed by the derogatory nature of the love relationship: the girl needed Bruce Willis to not only be the savior/hero but also her savior/hero. It was not just that she need help being the hero; the representations of her lack were completely over the top (for my tastes as well as my friends'). They attributed this representation to bad Hollywood filmmaking, which is believable enough. But I, on the other hand, read it as a parody of such representations of women given that the entire film seemed to rest on such punning and cheap gags. This correlates to my two points above: 1) There was a certain amount of cultural information necessary for me to read the film, (familiarity with the other referenced movies, an understanding of parody/irony, and a familiarity with stereotypical filmmaking), which allowed me to read the romantic representations in the film in a specific way; and 2) The film provided a source of material for social interaction. People do not merely walk away from a film. They think about it, discuss it, and derive different conclusions from it. Moviegoers practice "vernacular theory."

(hyper)Rhetoric and Heuristics

I would like to propose Ulmer's work as one stepping-off point for theorizing such active spectatorship, which is at root an inventional process. In *Teletheory,* he proposes "mystory"—a text that integrates public discourse (films, myths, events, etc.), private biographies (memory—real or fantasy), and disciplinary discourse (the discipline does not matter, it simply provides another terministic screen or two to the matrix)—as an inventional method that helps students to combine and recombine the ready-made images of electronic culture and link them to the academic discourses under consideration, while incorporating them into their own image-repertoires. Following Derrida, Ulmer proposes "the proper name as the *inventio* [. . .] most basic [to the] strategy of teletheory" (166; my emphasis). A person's name can be used as a conceptual starting place (a topos) to begin to link these discourses because it contains double meanings and decomposes into other words. For example, "Hawk" can be linked to the eagle as the symbolic bird of prey in our public discourse, or it can also mean to pawn something, or it can decompose into "ha"—laughter. From here, I can link to the space shuttle Challenger as a technological eagle functioning within our cultural mythology, to the fact that I used to buy all of my musical equipment at a pawn shop in Dallas where my friend worked because I was a broke student, and to Ulmer's use of the pun and laughter as critical tools. The name provides a set of conceptual starting places that can link various public, private, and disciplinary narratives and discourses.

In Ulmer's practice, "Once the inventory is brought together, the *arrangement* follows [. . .] as selection and combination, including images as well as words" (211; my emphasis). This montage technique of selection and combination follows the model of decomposition–"deconstruction extended from a mode of criticism to a mode of composition" (Ulmer, *Applied Grammatology* 59).[5] Like the name, images, common words, and narratives carry excess meanings, which the arrangement process of selecting something from one context and combining it with other elements and contexts reveals. Through this process, these once disparate discourses begin to make sense together, and the fact that these other discourses appear to be connected to you creates pleasure—a bliss-sense (jouissance): "Bliss-sense, as distinct from sense or common sense, concerns the pleasure of the text, the love of learning, the subject's desire for knowledge, which is grounded not in a specialized discipline but in the family story and everyday life" (*Teletheory* 96). It should be no surprise that this everyday form of invention through arrangement is pleasurable: it is the identification of identity through the process of inventing identity.[6] For Ulmer, "human identity is a function of a life story that people believe in and tell about and to themselves. The story operates less by referentiality than by coherence, has more in common with myth than with history [. . .] consisting not of one fixed account but of the relationship among the various stories we tell in an ongoing practice" (34). Ulmer's approach to mystory in *Teletheory* is one way of actively engaging in the practice of mythos, or identity construction, as a "mode of composition"—the ongoing practice of "coherent" arrangements.

An important part of inventing and composing identity is the role of *memory*. In Ulmer's example of the mystory genre, "Derrida at Little Bighorn," he draws on the three "storehouses" of memory: mental (personal), oral (cultural), and textual (disciplinary). For a private biography, he relies on his personal memories of being a truck driver for his father's company in Miles City, Custer County, Montana. Though his public story, Custer's Last Stand, has been spread via texts, its primary location is in our oral, cultural mythology. And I see his disciplinary story, Derrida's grammatology and its dissemination through American academia, as primarily a textual dispersal, even though it too has its element of orality within the discipline. Without these storehouses for memory, identity formation would be impossible. Without experiences and memories of the concert, there would be nothing to report in a fanzine. Without TV as a storehouse and oral dispenser of cultural memory, there would be no Bart Simpson to remotivate into a T-shirt display of identity or no Kirk/Spock to spin into a narrative. And likewise without academia and its privileging of texts, there would be no Derrida for Ulmer to remotivate through his mystory, or no Ulmer for me to write with in this essay.

This vital role of memory is remotivated in Ulmer's follow-up to *Teletheory*, *Heuretics*. Generated out of the term *chora*, which Derrida gets from Plato's *Timaeus*, "chorography" becomes Ulmer's new characterization of the practice of memory. As a "term," chorography is "a rhetoric of invention concerned with the history of 'place' in relation to memory" (*Heuretics* 39). As a "strategy," it "consider[s] the 'place' and its 'genre' in rhetorical terms—as a topos" (33). From a Platonic viewpoint, the chora is the space where the philosopher's eternal truths are stored, a metaphysical memory bank, and the topos is the situated, literal place the sophists use as memory aids. In *Teletheory*, memory as topos is already in use: Miles City, Little Bighorn. A personal place that resides physically on the earth and in the person's memory is used as the scene for invention. What makes chorography distinct in the context of *Heuretics* is how the concept of place is theorized and put into practice.

Ulmer retheorizes place via the relationship between chora and topos. Following Derrida's characterization of chora as "the spacing which is the condition for everything to take place" (qtd. in *Heuretics* 71), Ulmer conflates the binary of chora as space and topos as place. Rather than chora as metaphysical space and topos as literal place, Ulmer sees the chora as the cultural space that emerges between metaphysical and physical space. For him, "In order to foreground the foundational function of location in thought, choral writing organizes any manner of information by means of the writer's specific position in the time and space of a culture" (33). In practice, this space creates a different rhetorical approach than Plato's recollection through metaphysical memory or the sophists' use of topoi, which are metaphorical mental places where formulaic arguments are stored and retrieved. Rather than use abstract models of species/genus analytics or stock positions for arguments (opposition, definition, cause/effect), Ulmer creates a heuristic—a set of topoi—that specifically situates invention within a cultural time and place. Rather than use the proper name and its decomposition as the single topos as in *Applied Grammatology*, or the mystory as in *Teletheory*, Ulmer's *heuretic*—or heretical heuristic—combines both of these approaches in a way that further aids the organization of invention.

The CATTt—Contrast (opposition, inversion, differentiation), Analogy (figuration, displacement), Theory (repetition, literalization), Target (application, purpose), and tale (secondary elaboration, representability)—is proposed as a pedagogical aid for the practice of invention in general and the practice of mystory in particular. To provide an example of this approach to writing a mystory, Ulmer fills in the categories (C = argumentative writing; A = Method acting; T = Derrida; T = hypermedia; t = cinema remake). As he proceeds through the book, he fills in these general topics with specifics and links them together in ways similar to his work in *Teletheory*. A student can use this same set and select different particulars, "a different popular work for the remake, different emotional memories for the rehearsal, a different aspect of Derrida's writings, and so on" (*Heuretics* 39). Or, the student can fill in the categories differently, pick and choose which categories to use, or possibly even devise a whole new set of topoi out of the process of implementing the initial heuretic. In each case, the CATTt, more explicitly than the mystory, encourages the reader/writer to break down and identify discourses, to place them in one's own space, and to think about their relationships. The CATTt, then, is a more explicit aid to invention via the arrangement of memory.

Theorizing the Untheorizable

I am interested in Ulmer's methods because they enable an interesting perspective on theorizing film spectatorship. Initially, they can provide a model for the process of remotivation as it functions both at unconscious and conscious levels. Through living in the conflated space of chora/topos that encompasses the three storehouses of memory, a spectator habitually remotivates images or characters by placing them in hir own image-repertoire. The images of Kirk and Spock, for example, are placed within a cultural space specific to each fan or group of fans. In the case of the fanzine writers who are predominantly heterosexual women, their experience cannot be separated from a cultural mythos that inscribes homosexuality as a possible identity. Constance Penley attributes the fact that most of the writers who imagine a Kirk/Spock relationship are heterosexual women to a fantasy/desire for equality in their own sexual relationships.[7] They are unconsciously writing their wish-fulfillment identities into a "mystory" via the popular characters. Their cultural space/place provides the conditions of possibility for those narratives to emerge.

Though these mystories are not necessarily conscious moves, the CATTt can function as a conscious way to retrospectively read such remotivations. For example, I can break my reading of *The Fifth Element* down into the five topoi of the CATTt: (C = literal or straight reading; A = pun/gag; T = Ulmer; T = a theory of attention structures; t = sci-fi movies). I was not explicitly thinking of the CATTt as I was watching the movie or discussing it with my friends or even when I was writing this essay. But, in retrospect, I can see that I broke the movie down by contrasting my reading with a straight reading, made an analogy to punning and cheap gags, implemented Ulmer's theoretical model for the purpose of my own theory of spectatorship, and placed it all in the context of sci-fi movies (and the history of rhetoric). Someone else reading the film is going to fill in these topoi differently, use other topoi, or link them in different ways based on hir own places. But theorists can use the CATTt to analyze the connections and arrangements a spectator makes among various discourses as a part of the viewing process.

It would also be possible to use Ulmer's methods as explicit inventional devices. A spectator could go into the theatre with the mystory and CATTt in mind and engage in a conscious, ongoing reading process that turns the rhetoric of the film back onto the film. This hyperrhetorical move is what spectators do when they watch a film and ask themselves, what is going on? They formulate a possible answer to that question based on their prior knowledge and then turn that possibility back on to the screen to see how it holds up. Spectators do this unconsciously; it is a way of reading. The CATTt can, however, be useful as a reading strategy throughout the film to allow for a more active (conscious) utilization of the linking process. It could even be used as a pre-reading strategy prior to watching the film, or as a post-reading strategy to rethink the film across memory.

Interestingly enough, these possibilities disclose the problem of theorizing the untheorizable. None of these possibilities are ostensibly applying a theory. The first is working unconsciously off of instinct—no theory is "applied." The second is the application of a theory, in a certain sense, but by someone who is not the spectator, not unlike Burke's use of dramatism.[8] The third places the spectator in the active role of spectatorship but still does not participate in the particular application of a pre-scribed theory—no predetermined outcome or generalization is assumed, produced, or desired. The method of controlling something in advance (or producing a generalization that can then control something in advance) is part of the ideology of science (induction and deduction), which runs antithetical to the processes of hyperrhetoric. Initially, mystory might be characterized as working from specific to general: lay out various discourses, look for connections and combinations based on the happenstance of a pun or a supplemental link, select/collect certain details into a set or narrative. A spectator can then generalize a method from that process, as Ulmer does in *Heuretics,* but the generalization does not pre-figure future inventions. It is a function of hyperrhetoric—of creating a method as it is being invented, a during-thought that can only be proposed as a pedagogical tool as an afterthought.

Rather than deductively guide the invention, rather than simply produce a narrative (or mystory), the method should produce another method. As Ulmer notes, the difference between "Derrida at Little Bighorn" and his mystory in *Heuretics* is that chorography shows how to use the mystory to produce a method:

> The chorographer uses the mystory to guide the exercises of the Method (actively searches for or creates repetitions among discourses of society). And these repetitions do not produce 'grand designs' but 'miniaturizations' bringing the heterogeneous items of information into order around a detail or a prop (a strange actor) in the setting. (*Heuretics* 139–40)

A grand design (theory) would function deductively and produce a predicted outcome or narrative. A miniaturization (method) would produce another miniaturization because it would be based on a different, nomadic "strange actor" from a different space/place. Theory is only one element of the CATTt—one cannot predict how it will combine with other elements.

The fact that chorography is at once an applicable and ungeneralizable method points to the paradox of hyperrhetoric. Even Ulmer says, "Chorography is an impossible possibility" (26). But its inventive possibility lies in the very fact that choral writing "must be in order neither of the sensible nor the intelligible but in the order of *making,* of *generating.* And it must be transferable, exchangeable, without generalization, *conducted* from one particular to another" (67; my emphasis). In order to illustrate this concept, Ulmer formulates a word to replace the binary of induction/deduction—conduction: "Conduction [. . .] carries the form of the pun into a learned extrapolation in theory" (*Teletheory* 63). To explain this notion, Ulmer puns on the term: conduction as an electrical term is the ground, the circuitry, for connecting "disparate fields of information; it is also implicated in conduct, behavior, how one follows one's desire"; and the term also brings to mind the conductor, leader of the group, someone who "guides the flow of significance from one semantic field to another" (65). The paradox of the conductor, the strange actor, is that s/he is both topos—the founding place of action/invention—and the empty space of the chora that allows discourses to pass through and reconnect to other circuits based on the supplemental meanings within language and the aleatory (accidental) connections within life. Conduction (which is the conductor) emerges between chora and topos, unconscious and conscious, induction and deduction.

Three Modes of Spectatorship

This paradox of the spectator, at once conduit and conductor, requires some further attention. Rather than function through an unconscious or conscious subject, the three possible uses of the CATTt noted above co-exist along a continuum of modes of action: automatic, attentive, and hyper-attentive modes of spectatorship (or conduction). One argument against my use of the CATTt could be that my friends and I are academics and trained to do a variety of "attentive" readings. But it does not take an understanding of Ulmer or Derrida to "automatically" appropriate the image of Bart Simpson, Kirk, or Spock. In either case, images are integrated into a person's own image-repertoire. This process is going on all the time. Even at the level of Burke's motion, there is an automatic recognition of the links between the world and our bodies. But there are times when the spectator, of a film or life, is snapped out of this automatic mode. Something triggers a more attentive process. The important detail is to determine what triggers this wake-up call, this move from automatic to attentive recognition, in the viewer. What is it that becomes a conductor or conduit?

Craig Saper, in *Artificial Mythologies,* discloses the necessary link. He builds his theory of cultural invention out of a mixture of early and late Roland Barthes by asking the question, what if Barthes lived and went back to his early work in the light of his later work? This perspective allows Saper to recognize that Barthes's work is not the inventional process of a psychological individual, but a de-individualized notion of the self—what Saper calls the trickster, an "artificial mythologist." For Saper, "Instead of simply debunking a myth about love, [the artificial mythologist] poses as a lover waiting in vain for the beloved to return" (9). The trickster mocks the myth. The subject becomes conductor—the conduit for the myth who endlessly redirects it. But the important piece of the puzzle is what functions as the conduit between myth and conductor—Barthes's notion of the punctum in *Camera Lucida.* Saper spots a crucial detail here. Typically the punctum is seen as the detail in a photograph that opposes the studium, the aesthetic or social meaning of the overall image. But this is a false opposition. It is precisely because of the studium that the punctum shows up. How else would Barthes recognize the oddity of a shirt collar or "the hand at the right degree of openness" (*Camera* 58) without a cultural mythology that situates the out-of-*place*ness of the punctum? The intersection between all the particular images in a photo and all the cultural connotations creates the punctum as "something not quite in harmony, a problem or an impasse, always pointing to other routes and destinations [. . . that] provoke[s] something like, but not identical to, involuntary memories" (Saper 16).

The typical relation assumed between an actual image and a recollection image is one of analogy—the standard Freudian approach. But the punctum does not necessarily work off of this model. The punctum plugs into a circuit of other images and brings these linkages to the attention of the spectator. It links the conductor and the myth but may not trigger what is analogous. A shirt collar might prick Barthes, stir a feeling, a memory, that has no associational link to a shirt or a collar. Rather than follow the logic of the master tropes, the punctum plugs into a circuit based on an aleatory logic, and it is the oddity of the accidental link that captures the conductor's attention. Precisely because the detail is set against a studium like the master tropes, the conductor is at attention—

recognizes the link the punctum creates—but does not necessarily have control over it. Saper claims that what Barthes is interested in is not the detail, but "where the detail promises to take him. [. . .] [T]his place of other places functions as a relay of desire: always pointing to something outside itself" (17). As Saper notes, "Barthes does not merely record his ego's subjective wanderings; instead, he gets the last *laugh* on those critics [. . .] by demonstrating with careful precision how to write about cultural invention without a psychological subjectivity centering creativity" (19; my emphasis). This de-individualized, a-psychological space is neither subjective nor objective: it is Ulmer's chora/conductor—the space that is erased yet allows lines to be crossed. The detail is the primary agent and its random pattern cannot point to something inside the subject because the chora is empty. The chora exists only as traces of the crossings that pass through it. Consequently, there is no individualized un/conscious that functions across the master tropes, only a continuum of levels of attentiveness to the process of the punctum.[9]

What I have tried to propose is a way to think through the process of invention that accounts for these three modes of spectatorship. In automatic recognition, a movement-image (an object/image in the world) is appropriated as a time-image (a movement-image stored in memory) and then linked via a random connection to other movement-images and recollection-images (recalled time-images).[10] This process is largely habitual (low on the attentiveness continuum) and can accidentally be associational but is not always or necessarily so. Analogy is only one element of the CATTt—the outcome of its combination with other elements may not necessarily be analogous. Attentive recognition moves away from these automatic connections via the punctum. Something about the random connection startles us, affects us, brings us to attention. In our heightened awareness, descriptions no longer simply refer to the object-world but to time-images that do not reside in our minds but in time (duration) as the conflation of topos and chora, personal and cultural memory.[11] For me, what Ulmer brings to the table is the possibility for hyper-attentive recognition. Once we have become aware of the punctum, the next step is to begin to actively arrange and reconnect the images and discourses. The CATTt can be used as a more attentive heuristic—a *heuretic*—to filter, organize, and redirect a punctum across a field of discourses and images. A more aware, active approach will trigger different time-images and make different (and more) connections than an automatic or attentive mode of spectatorship—to become hyper-attentive the conductor must remain open to all the possible links that a detail enacts.

From Punctum to Puncept

In all three modes of spectatorship—automatic, attentive, and hyper-attentive—the agency is in the conduction among discourses, image-repertoires, and bodies, but at varying degrees of attentiveness. The conductor is neither subject to someone else's control nor tied to a conscious identity. Spectators can never be the fully conscious, autonomous, rational individuals of scientific discourse; can never know or predict what the punctum will prick; cannot theorize it. A spectator can only hope to aid the process, to try and arrange discourses, image-repertoires, and bodies for faster processing in a world of hypermedia, and something like the CATTt can fill the space of the chora and help conduct the barrage of incoming images by grouping them together in randomly related sets. What Ulmer is doing/describing in both *Teletheory* and *Heuretics* functions in all three modes of attentiveness. But in order for attentiveness to be hyper-attentive, a spectator must practice hyperrhetoric, which carries with it an implied reflexiveness, a playful inventiveness that works with Ulmer's remotivation of the punctum, the puncept—a set of fragments collected from the sting of memory.

Barthes recognizes the possibility for a hyper-attentive mode of spectatorship but does not make the move from punctum to puncept. Instead, he claims that his method does not work with film (or movement-images), only with photography. The punctum requires that a spectator sit and meditate and be able to return to the image again for further contemplation. Barthes asks,

> Do I add to the images in movies? I don't think so; I don't have *time:* in front of the screen, I am not free to shut my eyes; otherwise, opening them again, I would not discover the same image; I am constrained to a continuous voracity; a host of other qualities, but not pensiveness; whence the interest, for me, of the photogram. (*Camera* 55; my emphasis)

In hyperrhetoric, there is no time in the sense Barthes is using it here. In a media culture, there is no time for melancholy. Spectators have to be hyper-attentive, fast on their feet, practitioners of *kairos*.[12] Kairotic elements always carry the potential for recognition, linkage, or flight, and hyper-attentive spectators have to be open and aware of the punctum that flows through them.

Hence, Ulmer's important shift away from Barthes. The punctum is no longer associated with melancholia: "laughter replaces melancholy as the mark of the sting of the punctum (the sign of memory in cognition)" (*Teletheory* 73). Barthes acknowledges the possibility that "the logical future of the metaphor would [. . .] be the gag" (qtd. in *Teletheory* 73). He recognizes this need for open-ended play, especially in language:

> Each time [we] encounter one of these double words, [we should keep] both meanings, as if one were winking at the other and as if the word's meaning were in that wink, so that one and the same word, in one and the same sentence, means at one and the same time two different things, and so one delights, semantically, in the one by the other. (qtd. in *Teletheory* 75)

But he ultimately prefers to stay on the side of seriousness and mourning as exhibited in *Camera Lucida.* The fact that Barthes sets aside the possibility that the punctum also produces laughter positions him to play the straight man for Ulmer's comedic *delivery.* Because "the cognitive style of teletheory—conduction—involves a reordering of emotional experience of the entry into the Symbolic away from mourning and melancholia toward wit and humor," *style* becomes a mode of conduct toward desire, images, and discourses that privileges laughter as bliss-sense (74). Style and delivery, as modes of conduct, become the endless play of name, place, and memory gathered together in the puncept.

Barthes, then, leaves Ulmer to develop the puncept as a way to deal with the comical speed of media culture. The pun is open-ended,[13] but the puncept is not limited to puns; it is a set of links collected around a motif—some details follow the logic of the pun, some the logic of the master tropes, some no logic at all. The puncept, then, is a set of puns, jokes, gags, images, and memories that offset the melancholy practice of both induction and deduction. In such a (hyper)-rhetorical enterprise, logic is displaced by style and delivery. Style becomes the central rhetorical principle because its process of selection and deployment of words and images grounds the utilization of invention, arrangement, and memory through the act of delivery—the aural and visual use of voice and gesture. Hence, the centrality of laughter—delivering one-liners and cheap gags: the style of comedic delivery grounds the selection and deployment of puncepts. And the centrality of speed: the puncept is hyperrhetorical—gathered while it is being deployed. Style must have quick wit, and puncepts allow conduction to be more attentive. In a hyper-attentive mode of spectatorship, the conductor selects memories induced through the process of the punctum and arranges them into a puncept that is used for invention through the continuous generation, the total flow, of style through delivery.

The Puncept in Practice

A key element in hyperrhetoric is to provide an example, produce a "miniaturization." Simply using a theory to read an object, discussing theory as if it were separate from practice, runs antithetical to theorizing the untheorizable. But an artificial myth operates "in the order of making, or generating" (Ulmer, *Heuretics* 67). Consider Ulmer's and Barthes's productions. As one goes on to read the rest of *Heuretics,* there is no clear, step-by-step explanation as to how the CATTt provides a theory that is applied to Ulmer's mystory. It seems as though he could have written the mystory without it, as he did in *Teletheory.* This methodology is consistent with hyperrhetoric—the CATTt is a method he invented through the process of writing his mystory in *Heuretics* that was then placed at the beginning of the process/book). Barthes provides a clearer picture of how the punctum might work, but critics characterize his example as a re-turn-ing back to modernism and subjectivism, rather than a method in the a-subjective process of becoming, one that is particular to the production of Barthes's book. Following their lead, I would like to work through a particular methodical reading of *The Fifth Element* as an example of using a method for reading a film that goes beyond applying a theory to creating new concepts.

In film, the punctum becomes the puncept—without time to reflect, the spectator has to gather striking images as they come at hir. An entire scene can even become a punctum. Barthes is right that in film a small detail is not likely to initiate a prick, but he does not seem to consider the fact that size is relative. The speed of film still provides an impression of a scene: as an image flashes, it pricks the viewer and then moves on—like the first scene in *The Fifth Element*. The contrast of space and desert punctured through to a recollection image. But I did not quite have time to recall it. On to the next scene/image: inside the temple; the row of columns; the boy hiding. Is this *Stargate*? What are they doing ripping off *Stargate*? I asked myself. The scene flashes: the Black Hole that Evil passes through; the desert people. Or wait. Is this supposed to be Indiana Jones? And who is this Obi-Wan Kenobi character? The movie is setting a precedent for itself. It comes out of the gate punning self-referentially on other sci-fi movies. But the clincher for me was the cheesy aliens. Now I know they cannot be serious. How can they with these waddling duck-billed aliens that look so goofy they entirely negate the serious and ominous music in the background? All these are questions that I delivered to the screen. My attention was now raised. There had to be an element of play in the film.[14]

For those who have not seen the movie, the plot line is fairly straightforward. Pure Evil is descending on the earth to wipe out all life. The duck-billed aliens are the caretakers of the five elements necessary to defeat evil. Four of the elements are triangular stone statues that represent earth, air, fire, and water. The fifth element, however, takes human form in the guise of the perfect woman. But of course, this perfection is still lacking. Bruce Willis has to provide the all too human hero to help the perfect heroine save the world. In the early scenes I described above, before the viewer learns that Dallas's help is needed, the archaeologist initially reads a glyph that points to a central fifth element that connects all four other elements/cardinal points. But before he can figure out that the four elements are in the temple, the duck-billed aliens descend on the temple and take them for safe keeping until Evil returns three hundred years later.

As the aliens take off, their ship hangs in the sky, and for a split second, it looks just like the Challenger, slowly ascending through the clear sky, waiting for disaster. I remember the day still. I had just come home from school (I was an undergraduate at the time) and turned on the TV while I grabbed some lunch. I had forgotten the launch was that day, so I was glad I caught it just in time to see it take off. Then the scene in *The Fifth Element* jumps to three hundred years in the future showing a ship in space—an analogous scene to the Challenger image and now also a pun on *Star Wars*. The ships in each movie are identical. The film is both serious and playful at the same time. The captain on the deck of the ship, surely a reference to *Star Trek,* looks out through the video monitor/windshield to witness an explosion. A sphere in space disintegrates before their eyes as the Challenger did before mine on the video storehouse of cultural vision and memory. I still remember how I felt. Strange. How could I be sad? It was a blip on the TV screen, a puff of smoke, then nothing. But there was a cultural melancholy. Technology may not save us after all. In the movie, however, the image of the Challenger is displaced onto the sphere/planet that is Evil itself. Another play on *Star Wars*. The Death Star equated evil, technology, and death, all of which are conflated in images portrayed in this scene. The success of the scene rests on triggering the cultural references in our memory.

After this scene, the spectator finally gets introduced to Bruce Willis's character—the poor bum, cab driver, ex-military man living in a small efficiency, Corbin Dallas. Dallas is the place I was born, the place where I grew up. Dallas is my place, my site for invention. I used to always go to a pawnshop in Dallas to buy my musical equipment because I was a broke student. No matter how broke I was, I always needed my tools for invention (and arrangement). Music was my creative and inventive outlet. I will always remember the music scene in Dallas as my place for invention. Could Corbin Dallas also be this space? this conduit? As Evil now approaches, the duck-billed aliens are returning, presumably with the five elements to save the world. But just as the perfect, alien heroine, Lelu, needs a human cohort, so does Evil. A scene blips on the screen. Zorg, the owner of a multinational corporation who looks like a cyberpunk Hitler with a hick southern accent, stands in front of a circular window that looks out onto a cityscape. Given the southern accent, I imagine that it is *Dallas*—surely the movie is punning on that iconic series and the ruthless character J. R. Ewing. But what could be the connection between the apparently opposing characters of Corbin Dallas and Zorg as conductors of invention?[15]

Zorg's hired henchmen shoot down the ship returning with the five elements. The only thing that remains from the crash site is a hand, closed around a handle. From the DNA, the government recreates the Supreme Being, the fifth element. But the government, of course, makes the mistake of trying to contain her, to keep her closed, to FIX her. She escapes, falls in Corbin Dallas's cab—which floats along the sky in a Blade Runneresque cityscape—and they are chased by the police. Corbin's first chance to save the Supreme Being results in his cab resting upright on its trunk. He looks back for the girl but the moviegoer sees a shot of her right hand, now open, blurred in the foreground. Another piece of the puzzle—the open hand of rhetoric. Could Lelu represent the coming together of the five elements of rhetoric under one primary element? For Ulmer, this fifth, central element is style. But not the style of Ramus. Ulmer writes:

> In an electronic apparatus, the fact that rhetoric has been reduced to style is not the weakness it was in literacy. When rhetoric served face-to-face oratory, speakers studied with actors to learn *pronunciatio* (delivery), whereas in the representational conditions of the electronic, acting serves *elocutio* (style); this is indicative of the specific way that rhetoric is replacing logic in the postmodern trivium. (*Heuretics* 211)

Ulmer even equates style with argumentation. An actor or performer gains celebrity status because of a certain style. (I am of course thinking of music. All of the harmonies and rhythms have been played out. The only thing left to do is repackage them through style). Support or proof in entertainment discourse is essentially an effect of ethos derived from fashion. All the other rhetorical elements are subsumed under style. It seems ironic for me to equate style with Lelu. Her character is culturally clumsy. But "in chorography, the actor's style [. . .] becomes a map to insight and invention" (212). In chorography, even the style of no style opens the way to the elevation and invention of style: "If rhetoric was reduced to style in the print era, then it is the actor's style in particular that rhetoric's recovery of the powers it lost to logic will begin (the means of the recovery must be invented)" (212). The open space left by the devaluation of style is the condition of possibility for its return.

It is this invention that I call for in my reading of *The Fifth Element*. But to pull it together I still need to introduce two more characters. In the opening scene(s), the "Obi-Wan Kenobi" character is the temple priest and the main contact for the duck-billed aliens. When they left with the four elements (there are four stone elements representing earth, air, fire, and water—the fifth element is the girl representing life), they instructed him to pass down the knowledge of their existence and future return through a succession of priests. So as expected, Corbin and Lelu stumble across a priest who becomes their sidekick—somewhat bungling and aged, but an important element. Zorg calls the priest into his office. Earlier he had contacted the priest about the four elements he was trying to steal for Evil. When called into his office, the priest does not remember Zorg. But when he does recall him, Zorg replies, "Glad you got your memory back." Though on the one hand an inconsequential remark for the plot of the film, it signifies the priest's role as the storehouse of cultural memory—his duty is to collect and pass on ancient knowledge. The priest confronts Zorg about his evil plan, garnering a response from him. His rationale for destruction is that it is necessary for creation. He knocks an empty glass onto the floor. It shatters and a pack of robots scurry out to clean it up. Zorg represents decomposition. The necessary element of destruction in invention—that chance we all must take, just as the passengers on the Challenger did.

The final character I need to introduce is the ever so elated Ru B. Rod. As the plot moves on, we find out that the other four elements are in the possession of a diva who is giving a concert on the luxury space liner Fhloston Paradise. Corbin is pulled into the mission by the government, who reinstates his military duty and sets him up to win a trip to the vessel. Ru B. Rod is the flamboyant radio announcer/personality who follows Corbin around to broadcast the spectacle. It does not take much to see the puns in Ru B. Rod. The combination of a rubbed red phallus and the obvious pun on the transgendered RuPaul make Rod the personification of the pun and the gag. As the hyperbolic talk-show host, he is the king/queen of delivering the cheap gag. This is an important element for my reading in two primary ways. The entire movie articulates itself around one cheap gag after another. There are simply too many to recount. But, for example, earlier in the film Lelu is changing clothes and the priest and Dallas quickly turn their heads in embarrassment, as Dallas delivers the line "So, you want a cup of coffee?" as they both display quirky facial expressions with raised eyebrows. It's a cheap gag, but one that raises one of the main problematic situations of the film—the awkwardness and oddity of the female hero. She always seems out of place within our patriarchal cultural mythology. In a similar scene, the priest is sitting at a bar after Corbin and Lelu take off for Fhloston Paradise. The priest throws back a drink and says to the robot bartender, "I know she's made to be strong but she's also so fragile, so human. Know what I mean?" The camera pans up to the bartender's TV-screen face as he shakes his head. It's another cheap gag, but one that exemplifies this same problematic.

The fact that the movie articulates itself across such jokes and gags is precisely the thing that got my attention. Just as Ulmer indicates, the punctum is no longer the detail but the gag, the puncept—a collection, or set, of such puns that trigger memory, thought, and invention. But the second important thing is the blurring of gender roles. The cheap gags try to call attention to it try to call us to *attention.* Many of the characters are emblematic of the blurring. Diva is depicted as a tall blue alien with multiple phallic tubes off of her body, who before her death metaphorically gives birth to the four elements/stones from her body. Ru B. Rod is characterized as a flighty gay male, yet his hyper-sexual escapades are with women. Lelu is strong when fighting Zorg's henchmen and the government's men but is fragile and needs Corbin's love. Corbin, the hardened, individual hero we have come to know through popular representations, is actually a hopeless romantic and has a hard time reconciling his need for Lelu as a mate and his need for her as a fellow hero. His gender ambiguity rests in his name: Dal-las, a girl, Dal/gal, las/girl. This collection of characters provides one puncept arranged around the blurred lines of gender.

In addition to the puncept gathered around my name, the one around the movie's puns and cheap gags, and the one that gathers the gender problematic is the puncept that revolves around the primary characters' relationship to hyperrhetoric. Corbin as the conductor, the arranger: he connects the "disparate fields of information"; he worries about his conduct toward Lelu repeatedly throughout the movie; and he functions as the leader of the group. He embodies the arranger of elements in the culturally acceptable image of the hyperbolic action hero. Lelu as not only the embodiment of style but the embodiment of hyperattentiveness: in two scenes, Lelu is parked in front of a TV monitor, the storehouse of cultural/world memory; the images fly by her à la MTV as she absorbs our language and history. The priest as the embodiment of memory: metaphorically he is the harbinger of the ancient cult and literally he provides a safe haven that allows Lelu to consume our culture through media events. Zorg as the evil, chaotic representation of invention: he is the destructor of old, traditional values always in search of the new at all costs. Ru B. Rod as the deliverer of one-liners, cheap gags, and gender spoofs. All of them are necessary for the movement of the film toward conduction.

But Zorg is the only element that does not make it to the final scene. Besides the above noted puncepts, another key puncept is the juxtaposition of de struction/creation. When the ship takes off for Fhloston Paradise, the spectator is presented with another Challenger image. As they arrive at the spaceship/ cruise ship, the film displays a conflated image of the Challenger and the Titanic. In an attempt to blow up the ship and rid himself of style and arrangement (Lelu and Corbin), Zorg inadvertently, and perhaps necessarily, destroys himself along with the ship. On the way back from escaping the destruction, Lelu again reverts back to a hyper-attentive mode and receives images of war and devastation from the screen and comments, "Humans are so strange. Everything you create you destroy." Ignoring the cheesy moral to this typical scenario, the film embodies the role of decomposition as the outcome of rhetoric. In a media age, an age where rhetoric becomes hyperrhetoric, invention stems from de composition.

In the denouement scene, Corbin fulfills his role as arranger. He figures out how to arrange the symbols and match the four elements to actions. In order to start the machine, engage the five elements as the conduit of invention, and destroy the abstract notion of evil, each character has to create a simulation of earth, air, fire, and water. The priest's understudy comes in to fill the void left by Zorg (memory as the basis for invention), as Corbin, the priest, and Ru B. Rod assume an elementary position. But Lelu, the fifth element, cannot fulfill her central role alone. Corbin runs in to hold her up so that she can become the conductor, the conduit for the inventive energy of the combined elements of rhetoric through the central element of style, providing again another image that blurs male and female. Zorg—invention, creation from decomposition— then symbolically returns as the force that results from conduction and de stroys Evil.

From every destruction comes a third, post-meaning. For me, this means that invention does not come from an isolated mind/memory. It has to come from multiple sources, Corbin, Lelu, Zorg (via the understudy), Ru B. Rod, the priest. The opposites of male/female and good/evil are represented and at the same time run after each other, need each other for definition, description, and invention. The fifth element—style, the feminine hero—defeats Evil, the closed logic of a rhetoric shut off from all its elements, and gives life, invention, creation. All the countless cheesy love scenes just do not add up to a negative stereotype of women. They are so hyperbolically serious that I can only read them across the key puncept of the movie, the cheap gag. The final scene where Corbin and Lelu are back in the cylinder recovering from their ordeal and making love as the presi dent waits to go live on TV is so hyperbolic that it becomes hyperrhetorical—it laughs at itself. The ending of *The Fifth Element* did not disgust me because the woman needed the man; it made me laugh! Its ridiculousness, its out-of-*place*ness, was the punctum, the gag, that destroyed the stereotype and sparked my read ing, my invention.

Conclusion: Hyperrhetorics

Invention, arrangement, style, memory, and delivery—the five elements of classical rhetoric. How could Bruce Willis have known that throughout rhetoric's history, these elements have been modified to fit various rhetorical situations? How could he have known that rhetoric outlived its original context that spawned Aristotle's definition of rhetoric as "the art of discovering all the available means of persuasion in any given case," that the ascendance of writing slowly relegated memory and delivery to the side of the stage, and that Peter Ramus negated invention in the sixteenth century, leaving rhetoric with arrangement and style? This form of literacy virtually ignored images as means to rhetorical ends. But, and luckily for Bruce, in our current media culture, images have come to play a prominent role in the revitalization of rhetoric. Richard Lanham perhaps says it best:

> Indeed, if we were to define rhetoric using a strictly contemporary terminology, we might call it the "science of human *attention*-structures." Such a definition [restores] to rhetoric's domain in full force the last two of the traditional five parts, delivery and memory. [. . .] Memory, we are coming to see, is an active agency of creation not a passive curator of the past. Delivery, in its turn, would now include all that we think of as "non-verbal communication." (134; my emphasis)

By now it should be fairly clear how important these elements are to rhetoric, the current situation, and the arguments (connections, compositions) I have been making in this essay. The present historical phase of hyper-attentive recognition requires the reintegration of memory, delivery, and above all invention back into the elements of rhetoric. Hyperrhetoric remotivates the five elements of classical rhetoric into the new context of media culture.

Memory is the site, the place of invention. Memory is a place: the place I was born, the university I attended, the house I lived in as a child. In classical rhetoric, such physical places served as mnemonic devices—literally sites of memory. The move from orality to literacy led to a shift in place. The site of memory became the written text and Peter Ramus's tree diagrams. But in videocy—Ulmer's word for the world of hyperrhetoric—film and TV (and of course the Internet/computers) have become the primary sites, the main storehouses of world memory. The place of the chorographer arranges these memories that float between the cultural and the personal. As active participants in this reintegration, spectators are no longer shackled to the seriousness of the literate text. A conductor is free to roam nomadically through the world of words and images and let style be the engine of hir delivery, a delivery predicated on the pun, the joke, the gag, and remotivation as a form of bliss-sense.

Most importantly, invention becomes something neither unconscious nor conscious. It becomes attentive—a way of being-in-the-world, a way of becoming—and in a world of hypermedia, it becomes hyper-attentive. In such a context, invention has to be more than a set of prescribed schemata for reading and writing, more than a rigid formula for thinking. One could make the argument that Ulmer's CATTt, as the new five elements, functions as a remotivated rhetorical canon for the new media culture. This is so only in the sense that using "the method that [one is] inventing while [one is] inventing it" is about becoming, thinking, reading, living. It does not matter whether invention emerges automatically as when people remotivate Bart and Kirk/Spock, or whether invention is conducted attentively to read readings, or whether invention springs from hyper-attentiveness before, during, or after the experience of a film. All of them are becoming-inventive. The key for hyperrhetoric, however, is that it uses a theory to generate a remotivated theory via practice—a method. Ulmer's method is sly; it is not simply a theory to be applied. By making the theory only one of the discourses being utilized, the method becomes inherently inventive and kairotic. The spectator selects the other discourses, and inevitably combines, links, conducts them in various ways through the articulation inherent in practice. In this essay, for example, I used Ulmer's methods but linked them to my past experience and the cultural myth of the individual un/conscious and read them in the context of *The Fifth Element* to invent a notion of hyper-attentiveness—one possible hyperrhetoric among many possible hyperrhetorics. Bruce, the man who made *Hudson HAWK,* should be proud.

Notes

1. See Saussure's *Course in General Linguistics* (67–68) for definitions of the terms *motivated* and *unmotivated.*

2. Throughout the essay, I use "hir" to denote a conflation between her and his. Aside from the practical reasons, it is also emblematic of the gender problematic I see in *The Fifth Element.*

3. See Barthes's *S/Z* for the notion of writerly texts. See Silverman's *The Subject of Semiotics* (248–49) for a link between writerly texts and the filmic notion of suturing.

4. G. G. Allin was a punk rock performance artist known for extremist, anarchic behavior.

5. See Ulmer's *Applied Grammatology* (63–64) for more on decomposition.

6. See Burke's *Rhetoric of Motives* for a discussion of identification as a key rhetorical term.

7. See Penley's "Feminism, Psychoanalysis, and the Study of Popular Culture" (488) in which she argues that women can suture themselves into a variety of subject positions.

8. In *A Grammar of Motives,* Burke uses the pentad ratios to situate (arrange) the history of philosophy. In a similar way, I am using the CATTt to read my reading of the film.

9. Rather than theorizing the unconscious as a host of individual libidinal drives or wish-fulfillments, I am opening the concept to include all possible recollection-images.

10. See Gilles Deleuze's *Cinema 2* (44–46) for Bergson's distinction between automatic/habitual and attentive recognition. For an excellent discussion of Deleuze's books on cinema, see D. N. Rodonowick's *Gilles Deleuze's Time Machine.*

11. For Deleuze and Bergson, "Memory is not in us; it is we who move in a Being-memory, a world-memory" (*Cinema 2* 98). See also Bergson's *Matter and Memory.*

12. *Kairos* is Greek for "timing"—the right or opportune time to speak or write. It implies chance—being at the right place at the right time—but also the ability to recognize it.

13. See Lanham (127–28) for the pun as a key rhetorical concept.

14. The term play not only refers to joking, laughter, and frivolity but also to textuality. Play is the pliability of terms—the room to stretch terms that leaves them open to decomposition.

15. All of my questions are meant to simulate my interaction with the filmic images—which, of course, does not precisely follow any of my actual readings/watchings of the film.

Works Cited

Barthes, Roland. *Camera Lucida: Reflections on Photography.* New York: Hill and Wang, 1995.

———. *S/Z.* New York: Hill and Wang, 1974.

Bergson, Henri. *Matter and Memory.* New York: Zone, 1994.

Burke, Kenneth. *A Grammar of Motives.* 1945. Berkeley: U California P, 1969.

———. *A Rhetoric of Motives.* 1950. Berkeley: U California P, 1969.

———. "Terministic Screens." *Language as Symbolic Action.* Berkeley: U of California P, 1966. 44–62.

Certeau, Michel de. *The Practice of Everyday Life.* Trans. Steven F. Rendell. Berkeley: U of California P, 1984.

Deleuze, Gilles. *Cinema 2: The Time-Image.* Minneapolis: U of Minnesota P, 1995.

The Fifth Element. Dir. Luc Besson. Columbia, 1997.

Foucault, Michel. Afterword. "The Subject and Power." *Michel Foucault: Beyond Structuralism and Hermeneutics.* Ed. Hubert Dreyfus and Paul Rabinow. 2d ed. Chicago: U of Chicago P, 1983. 208–26.

Jenkins, Henry. *Textual Poachers: Television Fans and Participatory Culture.* New York: Routledge, 1992.

Lanham, Richard. *A Handlist of Rhetorical Terms.* Berkeley: U of California P, 1991.

McLaughlin, Thomas. *Street Smarts and Critical Theory: Listening to the Vernacular.* Madison: U of Wisconsin P, 1996.

Ozersky, Josh. "TV's Anti-Families: Married with Malaise." *Signs of Life.* 2d ed. Boston: Bedford Books, 1997. 205–13.

Penley, Constance. "Feminism, Psychoanalysis, and the Study of Popular Culture." *Cultural Studies.* Ed. L. Grossberg, et al. New York: Routledge, 1992. 479–500.

Poster, Mark. *The Mode of Information: Poststructuralism and Social Context.* Cambridge, MA: Polity, 1990.

Rodonowick, D. N. *Gilles Deleuze's Time Machine.* Durham: Duke UP, 1997.

Saper, Craig. *Artificial Mythologies: A Guide to Cultural Invention.* Minneapolis: U of Minnesota P, 1997.

Saussure, Ferdinand de. *Course in General Linguistics.* La Salle, IL: Open Court, 1972.

Silverman, Kaja. *The Subject of Semiotics.* New York: Oxford UP, 1983.

Ulmer, Gregory. *Applied Grammatology: Post(e)-Pedagogy from Jacques Derrida to Joseph Beuys.* Baltimore: Johns Hopkins UP, 1985.

———. *Heuretics: The Logic of Invention.* Baltimore: Johns Hopkins UP, 1994.

———. *Teletheory: Grammatology in the Age of Video.* New York: Routledge, 1989.

Williams, Linda. *Viewing Positions: Ways of Seeing Film.* New Brunswick: Rutgers UP, 1995.

5

Time, Space, and Political Identity: Envisioning Community in *Triumph of the Will*

Ekaterina V. Haskins

IT IS IMPOSSIBLE TO DENY THAT IN THE ERA OF TELEVISION, most of what we come to know and feel about the political and our own place within it is tied to visual and aural images. If one surveys the political landscape of the pretelevision period, film "propaganda" in Nazi Germany remains one of the most notorious examples of the political spectacle in the twentieth century. For most contemporary viewers, celluloid images of parades and rallies of the Third Reich are inevitably linked to ghastly pictures of Auschwitz; hence, critical scholarship tackling Nazi rhetoric encounters the risk of a schizophrenic split between the demands of moral judgment and the demands of theory. As one critic has remarked, "It is as if one is left tainted and guilty by association" (Lorentzen 162). Indeed, many rhetorical theorists in the past—with the exception of Kenneth Burke ("The Rhetoric of Hitler's 'Battle'")—were puzzled and outraged by the "irrational" persuasive powers of Nazi visual pageantry, contrasting it with the putatively rational process of deliberation and free political discussion in western democracies.

Yet there is more than irrational seduction to what Walter Benjamin termed the "aestheticization of politics" represented by Nazi films, where the masses are brought "face-to-face with themselves" (Benjamin 251). In order to challenge the irrationality presumption, as well as to offer a more critically useful way of reading visual propaganda, I will inquire into the rhetoric of identification deployed in the well-known Nazi "documentary" *Triumph of the Will*. Building upon the Burkean understanding of rhetoric as "identification," I will explore how political identity is dramatized and shaped through the manipulation of time and space in cinema. As distinct from other readings of this disquieting classic, my interpretation centers not on the relationship between the masses and the "Führer" but on the ways viewers are invited to identify with *their* cinematic representation as the folkish community, the collective body of "das Volk." The essay's critical approach combines Burke's insight into the constitutive properties of the "scene," developed in *A Grammar of Motives,* and Bakhtin's concept of "chronotope" (literally, "time-space"), developed in the essay "Forms of Time and Chronotope in the Novel" *(The Dialogic Imagination).* By focusing on how the spectator's experience is framed and guided by the medium of film, my argument also contributes to the rhetorical theorizing of political identity construction as "subject positioning." Before I turn to the rhetoric of identification in *Triumph of the Will,* however, I must explain my opposition to what I referred to above as the irrationality presumption as well as justify my choice of the "chronotopic" lens for interpreting the film.

From Irrationality to Identification: A Turn to Visual Rhetoric

The majority of rhetorical analyses of fascist rhetoric registered bafflement and moral disdain at the Nazis's capacity to turn the presumably rational German people into rabid supporters of the "Führer." Consistently, Nazi rhetoric has been described as a propagandistic perversion of humanistic creativity or as an irrational albeit effective tool of ideological enslavement of the German masses.[1] To an extent, such reaction is understandable: Nazi rhetoric appears overtly "irrational" in comparison with traditional forms of political address in western liberal-democratic nations. Even more disconcerting is the thought that success of such rhetoric defies any guarantee of a rhetorically sustained democracy. Yet, I suggest that the presumption of "irrationality" with regard to fascist discourse relies on a shaky warrant—the belief in an autonomous rational individual whose identity is given prior to any participation in the political.

Let me illustrate this point with two examples: Bosmajian's study of Nazi marching as a form of rhetoric and Mayo's dramaturgical analysis of the physical setting of the Nazi political rally. Bosmajian correctly insists on the need to critique the visual symbolism deployed by the Nazis, not only their speechmaking. However, his argument about the force of visual symbolism remains circular. He seems to suggest that Nazi rhetoric was persuasive because it was . . . persuasive. In the end, Bosmajian's analysis amounts to pointing out the absence of an expected pattern of political decision-making involving rational citizenry and sober analysis of issues. He thus concludes that the persuasion of Nazi marching

> took those millions of Germans *who succumbed to this persuasion* into a phantasmagoria where *there simply was no place for discussion or debate regarding the social and political issues confronting the German people.* [. . .] In this phantasmagoria created by the Nazis where force and sentimentality, fire and blood, sword and flag prevailed, *there simply was no place for the meaningful use of language or rational decision-making by the populace.* (17; my emphasis)

The terms aligned with the "rational"—"meaningful use of language," "discussion," "debate"—are contrasted with the words connoting irrationality: "succumbed," "phantasmagoria." In this way, the critic seals off Nazi rhetoric from any claims to political meaning by implying its utter otherness and irrationality.

While Bosmajian constructs a rational-irrational binary, Mayo proceeds by distinguishing between authentic and inauthentic identity. The surrounding "stage," constructed for the participants of the Nazi rally through monumental set design and the use of various insignia of the Third Reich, argues Mayo, is a false one: the reality created in the process of this gigantic performance is "temporary and lacks substantive normative content" (357). Inherent here is a charge of inauthenticity of the collective identity as well as its intrinsic inferiority to private, supposedly authentic identity, of which participants are "robbed" as they enter the spectacular "pseudo-event" (357). While using the Burkean notion of the scene to highlight the relationship between the setting and the action (a concern to which I will return later), Mayo nevertheless does not follow Burke's insight into the rhetorically constitutive quality of the scene, but falls into the trap of the irrationality presumption. His conclusion is not very different from Bosmajian's: "With appropriate stimulation from selected charismatic actors, the crowd becomes an *action-oriented mass* rather than a listening body comprised of *autonomous individuals*. Coordinated stage design can become *spellbinding* under the supervision of charismatic actors who respond to the scene and know how to guide the rally play" (357). As this passage demonstrates, individual rational consciousness is assumed as an a priori condition of participants in a spectacle *before* they are seduced into relinquishing their individuality.

By opposing this rational-irrational binary, I by no means wish to exonerate Nazi rhetoric. I insist, on the contrary, that such a view ignores the dialectical nature of individuality and sociality and, by so doing, dismisses Nazi visual rhetoric by explaining it away. By the same token, it would be just as mistaken to assume that millions of Germans were inherently irrational, and thus easily convinced by the mythology of the mass spectacle unleashed by the Nazi propaganda machine.[2] The following discussion, then, offers a different critical matrix for reading visual propaganda, based on Burke's notion of identification and its postmodern corollary, the "subject position."

For Burke, identification conjured by "propaganda" is not an invasive force to which one surrenders authentic individual identity. Rather, it is a necessary, even constitutive, process that compensates for the original difference. Indeed, Burke's indictment of the premise of an a priori rationality, unspoiled by any unwholesome impulse or motive, is very clear: "If men were not apart from one another, there would be no need for the rhetorician to proclaim their unity. If men were wholly and truly of one substance, absolute communication would be of man's very essence" (*Rhetoric* 22). More than a decade before he wrote this statement, before World War II and Auschwitz, Burke published a critical piece entitled "The Rhetoric of Hitler's 'Battle.'" In the introduction, Burke admonished his compatriots against simplistic assumptions about democratic processes:

> We are "beyond" the stage where we are being saved from Nazism by our *virtues*. And fascist integration is being staved off, rather, by the *conflicts among our vices*. Our vices cannot get together in a grand united front of prejudices; and the result of this frustration, if or until they succeed in surmounting it, speaks, as the Bible might say, "in the name of" democracy. (211)

The study of the rhetoric of identification, therefore, should address not the loss of an already given extra-rhetorical identity but the constitution of a collectivity through assimilating differences.

This orientation is certainly not new; much theoretical and critical work has been done in this vein. McGee's essays "In Search of the 'People'" and "The 'Ideograph,'" as well as Charland's study of constitutive rhetoric of the *Peuple Québécois,* set the tone by seizing upon *identification* as Burke's key term for rhetoric. Their material, however, is confined to ideographs and textual narratives; such a focus pushes the visual dimension of identification to the margins of critical studies.[3]

Osborn's "Rhetorical Depiction," especially the section that addresses depiction as identification, is perhaps the most notable exception to the rule. Importantly, Osborn turns to *Triumph of the Will* to illustrate the "depiction-as-identification" exhibited by "culturetypes" such as "Führer," "youth," "obedience," "future," and "racial purity" (90). Osborn's analysis, though it contains useful insights into pictorial culturetypes and archetypes, nevertheless does not delve into the ways in which the film shapes the experience of seeing these images to promote identification. Osborn simply asserts that the "sharing of symbols must be a profoundly satisfying experience" and that "just to merge in the use of certain symbols is deeply reassuring" (89). If, indeed, the innate desire to "merge in the use of certain symbols" accounted for the identificatory process, there would be no need for a rhetorically crafted unity. In other words, one must look at the dialectic of identification and division to elucidate the identification function of visual rhetoric.

To account for complexities of identification, some rhetorical critics have turned to the notion of "subject position" to explain how viewers or readers are enabled by texts to take on discursively constructed social and political roles. As Brummett and Bowers point out, texts offer a spectrum of subject positions to their readers, ranging from "an identified subject position" of a desirable character or role model to a subversive subject position "in which a subjectivity is assumed that is at odds with, and often directly opposed to, the call of the text" (118–19). If the viewer assumes the identified subject position, she will, temporarily, gain a sense of authority, motivation, and voice offered by the narrative.[4] Thus, an unemployed worker or an office clerk in Germany of 1935 may be empowered by a vision of joyous men, women, and children filling the festive streets of the Nuremberg of *Triumph of the Will.* By contrast, an exiled Marxist intellectual in Paris or a Jewish shopkeeper in Berlin may resent or fear the spectacle of Germany's unification under the aegis of the Nazi party.

One film, to be sure, is not sufficient to render millions of spectators into Nazi subjects, since the acquiring of identity is not a simple unidirectional process.[5] However, *Triumph of the Will* no doubt assisted in the transformation of the fragmented identity of the Weimar Republic into the unified identity of "das Volk." In keeping with the theory of identification and subject position outlined above, we will further examine how visual narrative may construct "identified subject positions." Burke's discussion of the "scene" and Bakhtin's notion of "chronotope" will be of particular relevance to our argument about *Triumph of the Will* as a calling forth of a new German identity.

Unlike traditional dramaturgical conceptions of "stage," Burke's "scene" does not involve concealment of "real" identity in the service of a public image. Instead, Burke views the scene as an environment that both implicitly contains the quality of the action (direction of the narrative) and synecdochically determines the identity of the agent-actor (*Grammar* 7). Furthermore, the scene is not confined to a stage-set, but can also be understood "in the sense of the relationships prevailing among the various *dramatis personae.* For the characters, by being in interaction, could be treated as scenic conditions or 'environment,' of one another" (*Grammar* 7). Significantly, Burke urges the critic to conceive of the "container and thing contained" as a tension, so as not to collapse one into the other: "Our terms lending themselves to both merger and division, we are here trying to divide two of them while recognizing their possibilities of merger" (*Grammar* 7). Burke's *Grammar* thus promotes our appreciation of the formal, aesthetic appeal of the scene. On the formal level, the scene arouses the viewer's expectations by suggesting a certain logic to the development of the plot and the actor's role, thereby influencing the viewer's identification with the actor.

While the Burkean "scenic" perspective allows us to examine the rhetoric of identification dialectically by recognizing the tension between the scene and the collective identity that the scene forshadows or contains, Bakhtin's chronotope probes the spatiotemporal dynamic of the visual narrative in both the aesthetic and historical sense. Because of his attention to aesthetic as well as sociohistorical aspects of symbolism, Bakhtin's approach supplements particularly well the Burkean insight into the rhetorical properties of the scene. Bakhtin describes chronotope as "the intrinsic interconnectedness of temporal and spatial relationships": "spatial and temporal indicators are fused into one carefully thought-out, concrete whole. Time, as it were, thickens, takes on flesh, becomes artistically visible; likewise, space becomes charged and responsive to the movements of time, plot, and history" (85). The use of the term *history* is very significant here, for Bakhtin presents chronotope not as a purely aesthetic category, but as an artistic distillation and assimilation of social time and space. The scene, once it acquires temporal dimension, lends itself to both artistic and sociopolitical meanings. By the same token, we can speak of formal-aesthetic as well as political identification. Indeed, Bakhtin presents the ancient city—the polis—as such a real-life chronotope, in which "all the most elevated categories, from that of the state to that of revealed truth, were realized concretely and fully incarnated, made visible and given a face" (132). In classical times, as Bakhtin points out, there was no split between the individual and the collective: within this all-encompassing chronotope, the individual was "utterly exteriorized, but within a human element, in the human medium of his own people" (135).

Disturbingly, it is precisely the archaic model of the polis as the real-life, all-encompassing chronotope that is invoked in Nazi political rallies and, especially, the "documentary" *Triumph of the Will.* With the advent of "mechanical reproduction," especially film, complexities of modern society, it was hoped, would find their visual representation in the moving image.[6] Leni Riefenstahl's classic, on the contrary, aims at simplification. As if the concrete sociohistorical context—the larger scene—had suddenly fallen out of sight, the viewer is presented with an aesthetic distillation of history-in-the-making, the model for which is the aestheticized German and classical past. Yet, as I have insisted earlier, distinctions between rational-irrational or authentic-inauthentic do a disservice when it comes to Nazi political spectacle. What matters is how political and social differences become obliterated or flattened out visually through the manipulation of the scenic environment and how this environment, in turn, invites viewers to occupy identified subject positions. Accordingly, I will now focus on the ways in which *Triumph of the Will* collapses historical and mythical senses of time by recontextualizing the events at Nuremberg as the beginning of "Germany's rebirth" and reinforcing the mythical logic through the depiction of the city and the people.

Envisioning "das Volk"

Triumph of the Will to this day remains the most memorable cinematic rendering of Nazi political spectacle. Commissioned by Hitler himself, the film claims to recreate the events of the 1934 National Socialist Party Congress in Nuremberg. Thirty years after the making of *Triumph,* Riefenstahl stressed that she had merely tried to capture a historical event: "Everything is real. And there is no tendentious commentary for the simple reason that the film has no commentary at all. It is history. A purely historical film" (qtd. in Taylor 189). In a recent documentary about her life and work, Riefenstahl added that once given this task, she only wanted to fashion the material into something "better than the newsreel," which meant making it "mobile and thus more interesting."[7] We should be less concerned, however, with revealing how Riefenstahl's editing creates a virtually seamless narrative out of the footage shot by her crew over the period of seven days, nor should we ask whether such a rendition constitutes a political fiction or a cinema verité. The former question makes us blind to the ideological implications of Riefenstahl's aesthetics, the latter poses a dead-end binary of fiction versus realism. Instead we must examine how the "staging" of the events at Nuremberg and Riefenstahl's "fashioning" of the images recorded on celluloid converge in their aesthetic and political effect of conjuring the "folkish" identity.

Let us begin with the spatiotemporal logic of Nuremberg as the constitutive site of the "das Volk." Hitler's selection of Nuremberg as the site for the mass display of national unity under the leadership of the Nazi party is significant in its own right.[8] As the imperial seat of German Kaisers, this medieval city lends Hitler the identity of Germany's long-awaited "Führer" and serves as a stage for unifying various identities of the Germans into "ein Volk." Nuremberg functions as a symbolic container whose own historical magnitude, and its difference from modern Berlin with its bourgeois-democratic flare, suggests an orientation toward the past. By virtue of association with the scene, Hitler and the people assembled to greet him take on a premodern identity, despite the ubiquity of modern technological symbols such as the airplane and the automobile. Terry Eagleton explains this incongruity, "It is precisely such correspondences between the archaic and the avant garde which characterize Nazi ideology, as the sensuous specificity of blood and soil is coupled to technological fetishism" (333). In Riefenstahl's rendering, however, Nuremberg is not a static background for display of national unity by the "faithful"—it is a centripetal force controlling the viewer's experience of and participation in the political spectacle of "Germany's rebirth."

The centripetal pull is created from the very outset in the film. After the musical overture, the eagle and the swastika appear on the screen, followed by the titles: "On the 5th September 1934, 20 years after the outbreak of the War, 16 years after the beginning of German suffering, 19 months after the beginning of Germany's rebirth."[9] The titles orient the viewer not only toward the momentousness of the Congress but in effect suggest the historical logic of National Socialism—the return to the ideal of the mythical past. Accompanied by the "Horst Wessel Song," Hitler's airplane descends literally and visually from the clouds onto the medieval city, whose cathedral spears rise as if to greet the viewer. Though the titles before the opening of the scene inform us that it is Hitler who "flew to Nuremberg to survey the columns of his faithful followers," for a brief moment the *viewer* is the one flying over Nuremberg. Hence it would be limiting to say that this scene depicts Hitler's arrival as the return of a messiah; religious overtones notwithstanding, the imagery here has more than one level of meaning due to the positioning of the viewer. In a way, it is the spectator who is "returning" to Nuremberg, and the vertical trajectory of this return—as if out of nowhere one is dropped into the scene of vibrant and festive gathering—adds a dreamlike quality to this experience. Classical commentaries on the opening scene highlight Riefenstahl's depiction of Hitler as a "man above men, as well as a man among men" (Barsam 33). From a chronotopic perspective, however, the scene contains the elements that visually *constitute* Hitler's "Führer" identity: the mythical aura of the city coupled with the seemingly endless stream of people flooding Nuremberg.

Medieval Nuremberg is an ideal place, one is invited to believe; it is a magnet drawing to itself thousands of people. Indeed, as the airplane is flying over the city, the viewer sees the columns marching through the streets in a continuous current. The shot suggests that streets are the city's arteries and the faithful flowing through them are its blood, which is plausible given the recurrent symbolism of "blood" and "soil" in Nazi aesthetics. On the other hand, panoramic shots of the city's magnificent cathedrals, monuments, and bridges, intercut with the shots of Hitler's cortege riding through the streets, point toward the artistic genius of the people who created these monuments.

These scenic elements justify the temporal trajectory of the "return" to the once lost greatness. Spatial symbolism fleshes out abstract ideals of the past as guiding principles for the future. Bakhtin described this type of spatiotemporal organization as a "historical inversion":

> The essence of this inversion is found in the fact that mythological and artistic thinking locates such categories as purpose, ideal, justice, perfection, the harmonious condition of man and society and the like in the *past.* [. . .] [W]e might say that a thing that could and in fact must be realized exclusively in the *future* is here portrayed as something out of the *past,* a thing that is in essence a purpose, an obligation. (147)

In the film, the vertical, "otherworldly" spatial arrangement conveys a desirable vision of history: one must go back to the past to construct the future. Indeed, in the beginning of the *Triumph,* the viewer follows the airplane descending from the skies, whereas the ending depicts the marching S. A. troops as if they were ascending to the clouds, thereby asserting the immortality of the "Thousand-Year Reich." Germany's history becomes mythologized, while the myth of the noble past, visualized through vertical spatial structures, is presented as history.

A discussion of spatiotemporal peculiarity, however, does not exhaust the identificatory appeal of the film. To fully address identification as a counterpart of division, we must now turn to the depiction of the mass "actor," the German people. It is the third scene of *Triumph of the Will* that most fully develops the ideal of the city as the center of German identity. From a strictly sequential point of view, the function of the scene is to build up the anticipation of the Congress. Interestingly, the "Führer" does not make his appearance until the very end of the scene; for the period of almost three sequences, the viewer becomes a witness to the lives of those who either live in Nuremberg or who have arrived there to participate in the festivities. More than any other part of Riefenstahl's film, these three sequences—the city of Nuremberg awakening, the morning in the tent city of the troops and workers, and the arrival of peasants from various regions—reinforce "folkish" identity. This collective identity, as I suggested above, should be viewed not as an irrational subjugation of individuality, but as an effect of visual leveling of contemporary social and cultural differences. In fact, one of the fundamental modern distinctions—that between the private and the public—is symbolically obliterated early on in the film.

The externalization of the private life is a key principle of the premodern real-life chronotope, as Bakhtin describes it in relation to the Greek polis. Here it is fleshed out most vividly in a shot of a window opened to a flutter of swastika-adorned banners and a panorama of smoking chimneys and cathedral towers. Perhaps in a different setting, a shot of a hand opening a window would be a matter of simple visual metonymy, since this is a normal morning ritual—morning has arrived. But, accompanied by a hymn from Wagner's *Die Meistersinger von Nürnberg* and followed by a display of Nazi flags, the image cannot be regarded as a politically neutral interlude. On the contrary, it conveys a message of the "opening up" of the private world to the community and of an "awakening" to a new German era. Again, as in the beginning of the film, the viewer is invited to identify with the invisible "actor's" position.

In the next sequence, which continues the evocative theme of the morning, the viewer's attention is turned to the city of tents housing the "faithful"—the troops and workers of the German Labor Front. These young men, too, are waking up and getting ready for a new day, both literally and symbolically. The viewer gets to see them washing, shaving, combing each other's hair, eating a hearty German breakfast—all to the accompaniment of energetic military songs and marches. In addition to affirming the principle of openness and exteriority introduced by the previous sequence, the scene repeatedly stresses the men's playfulness. All mundane activities are carried out with enjoyment and overt satisfaction. The grim years of "German suffering" are over, as the prologue declared, but how does "Germany's rebirth" translate into such unbridled joy? The simple answer would be that the job-creation scheme helped to reduce unemployment. However, on the symbolic level, this sequence is proclaiming that a new generation, Germany's future, draws no separation between work and play, between the productive and the expressive.

Commenting on the fascist tendency to introduce aesthetics into political life, Walter Benjamin wrote: "Fascism attempts to organize the newly created proletarian masses without affecting the property structure which the masses strive to eliminate. Fascism sees its salvation in giving these masses not their right, but instead a chance to express themselves" (241). However, in *Triumph of the Will*, the "masses" are given "a chance to express themselves" only in a particular manner—a manner that suggests and inspires unification rather than division. Expression is portrayed as natural and universal, as an essential need of a healthy human body. Consider, for instance, how Riefenstahl aestheticizes the workers' muscular torsos, so that they appear less as laborers and more as athletes. Whether the sequence was staged for the camera or not, one sees Hitler's followers as actors in both aesthetic and political senses. Thanks to visual conflation of the roles of the worker and the actor, one receives an impression of the virtual absence of class differences among the "faithful." This impression is confirmed in a later, more formal scene when Hitler responds to the address of the members of the Labor Front with a declaration that "labor is no longer a divisive concept, but a unifying one."

The manner of cheerful display is sustained in the next sequence, as peasants from different districts, dressed in their region's traditional costumes, are entering Nuremberg. The transition from the virile beauty of the young men in the camp to the picturesque garments of German peasants bolsters the ideal of a united people, undivided by differences of class or territory. Just as the troops marching through the streets, seen in the aerial shots, or the workers in the camp outside Nuremberg, these country people are coming to the city to perform their share of political duty. Flowers and fruit—the bountiful products of German soil—are offered to the city and to the "Führer." Furthermore, although their costumes and music mark them as representatives of Germany's rural and politically divided past, the peasants by their performance of unity with the rest of the people are in effect denying that any divisiveness ever existed in the first place. Their *implicit* testimony to the absence of regional differences is amplified visually and verbally in the fifth scene, as panoramic shots alternate with close-ups of the Labor Service troops.

The display of loyalty to "ein Volk, ein Führer, ein Reich" brings together young men from all over Germany. As individual representatives announce their home region ("Friesland," "Bavaria," "Kaiserstuhl," and so on), the camera brings into focus their chiseled Aryan features. The underlying leitmotif of the close-ups here as well as in other scenes—the crowds cheering Hitler in the streets, the peasants in their folk dress, the workers, the soldiers, and the boys of the youth forces—is the supposedly natural homogeneity of the Germans, of their "blood." Indeed, racial purity of the Germans becomes a scenic element in itself, providing the most common of grounds for collective identity. Non-Aryan faces are conspicuously absent, which, by the logic of visual representation, connotes their political nonexistence. As Lacoue-Labarthe points out, National Socialism takes the organic interpretation of the political to an extreme, by equating *physis* [nature] with race, and thus makes racism a counterpart of "a massive unleashing" of collective expression (69). Accordingly, annihilation of the Jews is a counterpart of the Nazi aesthetic of the communal space: the Jews are constituted as a "topological monstrosity," they are "literally unlocatable or—and this comes down to the same thing—forbidden to exist from the outset" (75).[10] In sum, the collective image of "das Volk" ambiguously contains identification and division, invocation of a community and an expulsion of difference.

The camera's eye sees a joyous and proud people gathered in a beautiful medieval city. Yet the place is not a mere backdrop. Nuremberg is presented as a quasi-mythical center that beckons the German people and their "Führer" back. Furthermore, panoramic shots and close-ups erase distinctions between the individuals and the collective body of "das Volk." As a result of the mythologization of the events at Nuremberg, concrete sociohistorical differences are suspended in favor of a people's community *(Volksgemeinschaft)*. Nuremberg becomes a Rome to which all roads lead, toward which all Germans direct their gaze. As such, the city invokes the supposedly idyllic German past, presenting this past as a noble imperative for the future. Cinematic spectator positioning in *Triumph of the Will* thus yields "access to a world where disenfranchised modernites can fancy themselves going primitive again. As a result, modern apparatuses help align the viewers' discontent with modern civilization with contemporary constructions of a homogeneous and ornamental body politic, the *Volksgemeinschaft*" (Koepnick 437). The spectacle communicates to the Germans what they should be by showing them what they can be. The film's rendering of the Nuremberg Congress thus fosters nonrational (as opposed to "irrational") identification by offering the viewers an aestheticized vision of themselves as political performers.

Conclusion: The Interpretive Stakes

I have addressed a forbidding and fascinating topic of fascist spectacle in order to open up an alternative way of discussing—and critiquing—the visual rhetoric of identification. To view Nazi visual symbolism in terms of identification means going beyond the unproductive, often self-congratulatory, binary of the rational-irrational. Identifying political discourse in western democracies as a rational standard against which the irrational excesses of dictatorships are to be judged, the critic risks discounting the resources of mass appeal that may some day be turned against democracy.[11]

Many intellectuals, who witnessed Hitler's ascension to power—among them Walter Benjamin and Kenneth Burke—saw in Nazi rhetoric more than the ravings of a fanatic masquerading as a messiah. What they saw was more enlightening than debilitating: the capacity of rhetoric in the "age of mechanical reproduction" to offer to the masses, for the first time, an *image* of themselves as political performers. Burke's conception of identification, I believe, stems from an appreciation of the image's power to constitute political reality. The rhetoric of identification, as a counterpart of social division, is a continuous battle over the images of our reality, where the stakes are not only the policies and their outcomes but the polity itself. To understand the polity, then, one must attend to the images that strive to define it.

The adoption of the chronotopic interpretive lens has allowed me to delve into the spatiotemporal dynamics characteristic of a moving image. As distinct from the ideographic perspective, which typically limits interpretation to the ideologically constitutive effects of verbal rhetoric, I sought to elucidate both aesthetic and political aspects of identification. However, the analysis of the cinematic narrative in *Triumph of the Will* further supports the conclusions drawn by scholars using ideographs to explain collective identity: the "people" is a rhetorical effect rather than an extrarhetorical entity composed of autonomous individuals. Hence, my reading addressed the visual properties of the scene, which constitute "das Volk" and project its historical mission, as well as the positioning of the viewer vis-á-vis the scene.

The impact of the film on the viewer is by no means purely formal. In *Triumph of the Will*, as I have shown, we find a paradoxical yet particularly powerful deployment of space and time, whereby the folkish community is called into being. The disturbing peculiarity of the symbolic "container" for the new German identity is that its aesthetic ideal, the Aryan body, and its historical trajectory, the unattainable mythical past demand exclusion of any excess or difference to sustain their purity. And it is risky to bracket such implications, for as Susan Sontag deftly put it,

> [I]t is dishonest and tautological to say that one is affected by *Triumph of the Will* [. . .] only because [it was] made by a filmmaker of genius. Riefenstahl's films are still effective because their longings are still felt, because their content is a romantic ideal to which many continue to be attached. [. . .] The exaltation of community does not preclude the search of absolute leadership; on the contrary, it may inevitably lead to it. (320)

Notes

1. Analyses of Nazi speechmaking abound, but few studies focus on the visual rhetoric of the Nazi movement and Nazi political spectacle after 1933. See Bosmajian on the persuasiveness of Nazi marching, Bytwerk on rhetorical aspects of Nazi meetings, Mayo on Nazi rallies, Stuart on rhetorical aspects of Nazi architecture, and Zortman on theater in Nazi Germany.

2. See, for example, Ernest A. Menze's *The Cultural Roots of National Socialism*. In a chapter entitled *"Mythos* against *Logos"* Menze gives the following synopsis of the slippery slope towards Nazism:

> The demands of reason deprive the petit bourgeois of his philistine contentedness; escaping from enlightenment he seeks his support in *Mythos;* but the *Mythos* to which he clings is false: confused rambling takes the place of religion. Trusting in the sublime, he descends to the vulgar; from nationalism the path leads to bestiality; brutality, initially a rhetorical gesture, becomes reality in the end. (97)

Criticizing such pronouncements as "based on a tabloid-type national psychology," Wilfred van der Will proposes to "bear with the complexities of German social, political, and cultural history" (103). He points out that art, architecture, literature, music, broadcasting, the press, and film were brought into line with the Nazi organization of society through the strategy of *Gleichschaltung* (ideological incorporation) (111).

3. On the limitations of the ideograph, with regard to the visual, nondiscursive forms of rhetoric, see Edwards and Winkler.

4. Brummett and Bowers note that subject positions they outline are distinct from "decoding positions" presented by Stuart Hall and those who build on his work: "Hall's scheme is keyed to the reader's relationship to power structures as mediated through a text. Our scheme is keyed to the reader's relationship to a text that has an effect on power structure" (119).

5. Murray proposes to view the process of Nazi subject position formation dialectically, as a process in which rhetorical texts and performed actions are intertwined the same way utterances in a dialogue prompt and answer each other. Murray's focus is on the anti-Semitism aspect of Nazi ideology formation (i.e., on the construction of the "ordinary German" by way of a construction of "the other"). It is equally important, however, to attend to the "positive" construction of the subject position of the "ordinary German." Indeed, since the ideology of the Third Reich and its implication in the Final Solution "are mutually interdependent and inextricably bound together *in history,* it is important to understand how and why they have been played off and against each other" (Elsaesser 156).

6. Benjamin describes the emancipatory potential of cinema thus: "By close-ups of the things around us, by focusing on hidden details of familiar objects, by exploring commonplace milieus under the ingenious guidance of the camera, the film, on the one hand, extends our comprehension of the necessities that rule our lives; on the other hand, it manages to assure us of an immense and unexpected field of action" (236).

7. *The Wonderful, Horrible Life of Leni Riefenstahl* was directed by Ray Muller.

8. Kenneth Burke, in his "Rhetoric of Hitler's 'Battle,'" points out the rhetorical significance of Munich for the National Socialist movement:

> Every movement that would recruit its followers from among many discordant and divergent bands must have some spot toward which all roads lead. Each man may get there in his own way, but it must be the one unifying center of reference for all. Hitler considered this matter carefully, and decided that this center must be not merely a centralizing hub of ideas, but a mecca geographically located. (212)

9. These titles are from *Triumph of the Will,* directed by Leni Riefenstahl, 1935.

10. In his provocative film entitled *Architektur des Untergans* (The Architecture of Doom), director Peter Cohen, in a way similar to Lacoue-Labarthe, explains the gas chambers of Auschwitz as a culmination, indeed a rational conclusion, of the Nazi aesthetic program.

11. Postmodern representations of the Third Reich often point out parallels between mass spectacles of the Nazi era and contemporary media events in western democracies. As Thomas Elsaesser describes it, Hans Jurgen Suberberg's film *Our Hitler* (1977) implicitly suggests

> [t]hat Hollywood cinema and more recently television, in the name of democracy and the right to consume, have made the Riefenstahl aesthetic of *Triumph of the Will* (1935) the international television norm: politics has become a series of photo opportunities, public life a perpetual festival of presence, action, live-ness, where spectacle of destruction, or feats of prowess and the body beautiful are feeding national and individual fantasies of omnipotence. (161)

Works Cited

Architektur des Untergans [The Architecture of Doom]. Dir. Peter Cohen. First Run/Icarus Films, 1991.

Bakhtin, Mikhail. "Forms of Time and of the Chronotope in the Novel." *The Dialogic Imagination*. Ed. Michael Holquist. Trans. Caryl Emerson and Michael Holquist. Austin: U of Texas P, 1981. 84–258.

Barsam, Richard Meran. *Filmguide to Triumph of the Will*. Bloomington: Indiana UP, 1975.

Benjamin, Walter. "The Work of Art in the Age of Mechanical Reproduction." *Illuminations*. Ed. Hannah Arendt. Trans. Harry Zohn. New York: Schocken, 1969. 217–51.

Bosmajian, Haig A. "The Persuasiveness of Nazi Marching and Der Kampf Um Die Strasse." *Communication Quarterly* 16 (1968): 17–22.

Brummett, Barry, and Detiene L. Bowers. "Subject Positions as a Site of Rhetorical Struggle: Representing African Americans." *At the Intersection: Cultural Studies and Rhetorical Studies*. Ed. Thomas Rosteck. New York: Guilford, 1999. 117–36.

Burke, Kenneth. *A Grammar of Motives*. New York: Prentice-Hall, 1952.

———. "The Rhetoric of Hitler's 'Battle.'" *On Symbols and Society*. Ed. Joseph R. Gusfield. Chicago: U of Chicago P, 1989. 211–31.

———. *A Rhetoric of Motives*. 1950. Berkeley: U of California P, 1969.

Bytwerk, Randall L. "Rhetorical Aspects of the Nazi Meeting: 1926–1933." *Quarterly Journal of Speech* 61 (1975): 307–18.

Charland, Maurice. "Constitutive Rhetoric: The Case of the *Peuple Québécois*." *Quarterly Journal of Speech* 73 (1987): 133–50.

Eagleton, Terry. *The Ideology of the Aesthetic*. Oxford: Blackwell, 1990.

Edwards, Janis L., and Carol K. Winkler. "Representative Form and the Visual Ideograph: The Iwo Jima Image in Editorial Cartoons." *Quarterly Journal of Speech* 83 (1997): 298–310.

Elsaesser, Thomas. "Subject Positions, Speaking Positions: From *Holocaust, Our Hitler*, and *Heimat* to *Shoah* and *Schindler's List*." *The Persistence of History: Cinema, Television, and the Modern Event*. Ed. Vivian Sobchack. London: Routledge, 1996. 145–83.

Glazer, Hermann. *The Cultural Roots of National Socialism*. Trans. Ernest A. Menze. Austin: U of Texas P, 1978.

Koepnick, Lutz P. "Siegfried Rides Again: Westerns, Technology, and the Third Reich." *Cultural Studies* 11 (1997): 418–42.

Lacoue-Labarthe, Philippe. *Heidegger, Art, and Politics: The Fiction of the Political*. Trans. Chris Turner. Oxford: Basil Blackwell, 1990.

Lorentzen, Justin J. "Reich Dreams: Ritual Horror and Armoured Bodies." *Visual Culture*. Ed. Chris Jenks. London: Routledge, 1995. 161–69.

Mayo, James M. "Propaganda With Design: Environmental Dramaturgy in the Political Rally." *Life as Theater*. Ed. Dennis Brisset and Charles Edgley. 2d ed. New York: Aldine de Gruyter, 1990. 353–63.

McGee, Michael C. "The 'Ideograph': A Link between Rhetoric and Ideology." *Quarterly Journal of Speech* 66 (1980): 1–17.

———. "In Search of the 'People': A Rhetorical Alternative." *Quarterly Journal of Speech* 61 (1975): 235–49.

Murray, Jeffrey W. "Constructing the Ordinary: the Dialectical Development of Nazi Ideology." *Communication Quarterly* 46 (1998): 41–59.

Osborn, Michael. "Rhetorical Depiction." *Form, Genre, and the Study of Political Discourse*. Ed. Herbert W. Simons and Aram Aghazarian. Columbia: U of South Carolina P, 1986. 79–107.

Sontag, Susan. *A Susan Sontag Reader*. New York: Vintage, 1983.

Stuart, Charlotte L. "Architecture in Nazi Germany: A Rhetorical Perspective." *Western Journal of Speech Communication* 37 (1973): 253–63.

Taylor, Richard. *Film Propaganda: Soviet Russia and Nazi Germany*. London: Croom Helm, 1979.

Triumph des Willens [Triumph of the Will]. Dir. Leni Riefenstahl. 1935.

van der Will, Wilfried. "Culture and the Organization of National Socialist Ideology 1933 to 1945." *German Cultural Studies*. Ed. Rob Burns. Oxford: Oxford UP, 1995.

The Wonderful, Horrible Life of Leni Riefenstahl. Dir. Ray Muller. Kino on Video, 1995.

Zortman, Bruce H. "The Theater of Ideology in Nazi Germany." *Quarterly Journal of Speech* 57 (1971): 153–62.

6

On Rhetorical Bodies: *Hoop Dreams* and Constitutional Discourse

James Roberts

Slow motion shots of William Gates and Arthur Agee slam-dunking the basketball intercut with scenes from the 1989 NBA All-Star Game attune viewers early on of *Hoop Dreams*'s focus on the body and its movements. The way in which this documentary is filmed, moreover, allows the room necessary to engage critically the manner in which the filmic body gets rhetorically constituted. *Hoop Dreams*'s rhetoric, that is, does not focus critical acumen onto a dissection of the social body in a direct way, but through critical address, we can examine the evolution of this body as it develops during the film. This essay seeks to examine several bodies in this film in order to reveal how rhetorical discourse contributes to their interior and exterior augmentation. The essay considers the topological construction of cinematic subjects and bodies through rhetorically motivated and driven productive discourse. By better understanding the constitution of these entities in general, we might better unsettle our contemporary understanding of them and, then, initiate new possibilities of film-thought that can lead to new ways for bodies and subjects to make a difference and to gain valid recognition. Discussing bodies as rhetorically constituted, values as social, general language as formative, it does not necessarily call attention, in this elementary instance, to rational, ethical, or particular languages. I will lay out first an ecumenical elaboration of discursive body formations before proceeding to a specific, textual discussion. Thus, we will move from a discussion of general rhetorical bodily configuration toward a specific discussion of the cinematic constitution of bodily configuration. Before proceeding on this line, though, it is necessary to work through some of the often tricky and confusing terms employed in this essay and in other rhetorical criticism.

For the purposes of this essay, I use the term rhetorical to reference the wide array of forces that constitute, outline, and give substance to filmic bodies. That is, the camera, dialogue, editing, body postures, voice-over commentary—all of these contribute rhetorically in some way to the formation, guidance, and understanding of Arthur and William as both cultural and cinematic subjects. With such an outline, however, I do not spend much space discussing the crucial constructions of Arthur and William as racial bodies. Certainly, events, comments, and other constructions create these boys as particular types of racially coded bodies; this is the topic of many well-argued essays (in particular, see bell hooks's "Dreams of Conquest"), but it is not the focus here.

In the first claim of this essay—that film rhetoricians are concerned with the formulation and characterization of cinematic subjects through rhetorical discourse—I use several terms that can be vague and confusing. For instance, what does it mean to consider the "topological construction" of a thing, a being? What is topological about a body? If we are to discuss the body or the subject as a construction of discourse and rhetoric, we must first think about how bodies come to know and be known.

Rhetoric and Discourse

The materiality of bodies as subjects is not simply linguistic. Discourse can be seen in its materiality and includes within itself the linguistic and the nonlinguistic. As we work our way through a consideration of *Hoop Dreams,* it should become evident that the cinematic apparatus itself contributes to the constitution of bodies as subject in extra- or nonlinguistic terms. However, even outside of films, nondiscursive practices play important roles in constructing social bodies. Desire, if viewed as a prior-to-discourse practice, for example, provides extant bodies with articulation previous to constitution through language. In a cinematic realm, camera angles or positionings that present matter in a particular mode are doing so in nondiscursive fashions. So, discourse is used to refer not solely to special or particular vocabularies but also to the way in which the use of language in a particular domain helps to constitute the subjects or objects to which it refers. There are a number of films that employ an essentialist notion of a discourse of the inner-city neighborhood in order to effect a type of response. In films such as *Juice, Kids,* and *Colors,* specific modes of a discourse of inner-city youth are employed in an effort to elicit generalized portraits of the subjects presented Ironically, though, within this very presentation there is also a creation that often remains unexamined. Seen in this sense, discourse is used by its speakers (whether they are community leaders, film directors, or individual film characters) as "an attempt to dominate the field of discursivity, to arrest the flow of differences, to construct a centre" (Laclau and Mouffe 112).

This essay is not an attempt to fix the obviously recognizable proliferation of differences within cinematic bodies; rather, it is a sort of thinking-through of how discourse attempts to locate and situate differences contained within subjects as moments of stable articulatory structure. Rhetorical ploys contained within discourses also figure in the formation of bodies. However, rhetorical employment is never merely a contemplative entity in discursive practices; it is an articulatory practice[1] that constitutes and organizes bodies as well as social and familial relations. Thus, we can view rhetoric as a constitutional aspect of larger arenas of discourse. Moreover, through the temporality of rhetorical bodily formations, there are real, consequential social legitimacy issues at stake;[2] we will be able to recognize these concerns in specificity when we turn our attention to *Hoop Dreams.* Additionally, I will map out some of the terrain in which rhetoric as articulation gets employed in social relations. This notion of temporality as a factor in producing bodies is important to keep in mind, as it is *in* time that subjects become constituted. If the constitution of bodies were simply a succession of rhetorical experiences occurring *through* time (instead of *in* time), exploring the constitution of social bodies would not present much of a challenge. If this linearity were indeed so, we could predict or trace a projection of these bodies without needing to consider their inclusive differences. However, as constructed in multiple, simultaneous discourses—some of which verify existing realities, some of which erase previous positions—bodies are always shifting in their movement. By exploring the ways in which rhetoric has recourse to bodies, we are not working to reveal a determined subject located in time; we are, though, revealing its constitution, simultaneously making visible the subject's (the body's) contingent and alterable character.

The issues raised by questions of bodily formations are not explicitly questions concerning rhetorical constructionism or essentialism; rather, we will do better to investigate more complex questions with regard to the rhetoric that constitutes bodies through a specifically filmic discourse. Arthur and William, the two primary characters of *Hoop Dreams,* are sites of contestation: as bodies in the social field, they are the matrices of a variety of forces impinging upon them as they interact, exist, and attempt to move within and outside of their social domain.

Initial Sightings

As the opening credits roll, Arthur is playing basketball with several other youths obviously older than he. Several onlookers stand in amazement as they watch Arthur move effortlessly around the court with the ball, dribbling, shooting, and dunking with the grace of a much older body. One of the people watching Arthur is Earl Smith, who says that part of his job is to "help young people on the road to success." Smith is so impressed with Arthur's basketball abilities that he will "bet you a steak dinner you'll be hearing from [Arthur] in four to five years, and I don't know anything about him." There are several important moves made in these statements, claims that provide viewers with the initial groundwork on which Arthur will be rhetorically constructed throughout the rest of the film.

All Smith knows about Arthur is what he sees: an athletic body seemingly mature beyond its years. On court, Arthur glides smoothly with the ball around the other players. As a group, the players, of which Arthur is the camera's main focus and, seemingly, the rest of the gallery's as well, are on display. As such, Arthur's body, both in its physicality and as a subject (of the camera), is the body that becomes the rhetorical focus for the others involved in his future. In this inner-city arena, replete with asphalt court and a netless rim, Arthur moves comfortably. The other players are sportingly respectful of his abilities as they watch him perform dunks and slashing moves that seem styled for the audience their game has attracted. Intermittently shot through a fence that surrounds the court, this scene begins to frame the cityscape that will be referenced throughout the film. In this manner, the camera has already contributed to Arthur's cinematic formation.

As we speak of bodies emerging from specific and general modes of rhetorical discourse, we too in a sense are bound to talk of subjects. Much of our writing concerning bodies and subjects overlaps in film criticism. When examining bodies as constituted by and through rhetoric, we are also, almost ipso facto, talking about subjects that we create as we encounter them. Bodies and subjects, that is, are not merely constituted by and through those in direct contact with them: we as audiences or viewers also participate in (re)constituting that which we encounter. Particularly in referencing the peculiar interactions of rhetoric and film, we are obligated to talk about the subjects of film. The very "representationality" of the cinema from its beginnings has been conceived as (re)presenting subjects. Variously, these subjects (as matter, that matter) in film have been shown in their interaction with the world, other subjects, or objects at hand. It would be an easy trap to fall into: bodies as subjects are interpellated by discourse and, as such, by default become discernible and articulated as singularities within that discourse. Thus, we need to examine the polyvalence of subjects.

For the purposes of this essay, we will use the term subject to refer not to one simply interpellated by discourse (as sort of homogeneously encoded with a specific ledger) but rather as one constituted as the transcendent point of a mélange of often contradictory discourses, hence the term's polyvalence. Thus, to use Deleuze and Guattari's term, a subject is "nomadic": it has no home, no reference point, no destination.[3] As a social body accepts, rejects, ignores, incorporates, and idealizes particular discourses, it vacillates between not two but many positions as possibilities of its own being. Again, Deleuze: a subject or "a body penetrates another and coexists with it in all of its parts" (5–6). That is, subjects are not chronologically or sequentially born of rhetorical discourses that they are introduced to through social interaction; but subjects are, instead, always involved in creating their own oscillating locations as subjects. This is not to suggest that subjects as such can self-constitute outside discursive conditions. But the subject does maintain a temporal character of agency in its constitution. All subject identity is relational. This theoretical position should allow us the room needed to talk about agency (as opposed to the free will of a preconstituted subject) in these beings. In scientific terms, a subject is a victim of Heisenberg's uncertainty principle: we cannot know its position and speed (or directional movement) simultaneously. By the time we have figured a position for a subject, that subject has slipped into a new, changed position. Whenever I refer to subjects, therefore, I am referring to multiple subject(ive) positions within rhetorically formulated structures.[4] Thinking of subjects in this manner permits us to discuss particular reflections of the subjects of our investigations; and, simultaneously, thinking of fluctuating positionality encourages us to recognize the shifting, foundering nature of the very subjects we create. Generally, this theoretical move authorizes us to talk of specific modes of the construction of subjects without impugning them with forced stasis or location as some forms of essentialism might proffer. To talk of subjects as constituted, as emergent from discourse, is not to believe that they are fixed; rather, a subject's construction is the very production of its abilities. Each of these protean subject positions is a rhetorically constituted position, as this essay will demonstrate through its analysis of *Hoop Dreams*. As we move into this analysis, we will discover the ways in which cinema produces subjects and bodies as particular modes of discourse peculiar to filmic rhetoric. We will come to see how it is that bodies are made both through presentation in film and as consequences of, as materializing from, the cinematic apparatus itself.

Three days after he meets Arthur for the first time, Earl Smith, an "independent talent scout," takes the thirteen-year-old boy and his family on a recruiting visit to St. Joseph's School, a prestigious preparatory school in suburban Chicago. It was from this school that Isiah Thomas would later go on to fame at Indiana University, where he won a national championship in basketball, and with the Detroit Pistons, where he won several world championships. The visit to St. Joe's is an important step for Arthur to show others how he can, as the recruiter puts it, "perform."[5] As we ride with Earl Smith and Arthur, we watch the passing scenery as we move from confined inner-city Chicago to plush, open suburbia. These shots provide us with a visual presentation of the physical and subjective move Arthur makes from the inner-city court on which Smith "discovers" him.

During the recruiting visit to St. Joe's, Arthur's body again is the focus of a rhetorical construction that begins to constitute him as subject, for both the audience of the game and us as the film's audience. Initially, Arthur plays another game of basketball with a group of teens. This game, however, takes place inside a gymnasium designed specifically for basketball: glass backboards and new nets on the rims. We once again watch Arthur as a body on display, as a show of abilities. The coach of St. Joe's basketball team is Gene Pingatore, the same who coached Isiah Thomas many years before. As Arthur plays, we listen to Ping, as he is called throughout the film, talk about the young player: "I can see the playground in him. I see the talent but not the confidence. With Isiah, I just knew he'd be great." Here, we get a similar comment to that made by Earl Smith about Arthur's play. Ping, though, makes a rather remarkable claim that he can "see" a part of Arthur in the way that he plays. Could we disagree? Ping's comment is at once remarkable in its claim and yet its rhetoric isn't remarkable at all. We accept the idea that he can, as a trained and successful coach, see certain things we as untrained novices might not recognize. His comment, made during a casual interview while viewing a game, contains within it elementary (at least) theoretical assumptions about the body as temporally and discursively constituted. Like Coach Pingatore, we have casual theories about the body as social agent, but we need to understand better how these theories can be put to productive (read: beneficial) use rather than as (prede)termination and (de)limitation.

Rhetorical criticism should be concerned with being able to recognize subjective positions that emanate from bodies. Ping's comment, it seems, is not made as a recognition of Arthur's constitution but rather ends up partially constituting the very subject that it seeks to label. That is, as he traces a past Arthur—the one of the playground—to the current Arthur—the one playing here, now—Ping situates Arthur for us as viewers by showing a historical, temporal, and rhetorical body. The playground is not merely a place but a discursive, affective entity that moves with and within the bodies it contacts. Ping's comment also comes as a rhetoric of foundationalism that locates a pregiven, interrogating construction of Arthur as subject. In order to understand what I am seeing, Ping seems to be saying, you must be able to see Arthur's past.

This past that Ping references is not static, though. Inherent in the claim is the idea that the subject shifts: "I can see the playground in him" allows other things to be seen as well. The playground, or neighborhood in which we watched Arthur play earlier, is a discursive rather than rhetorical production. This returns us to our conceptions of the subtle differences between subjects and bodies. Why these terms are not necessarily synonymous lies in the fact that a subject does not necessarily need a body; in certain forms, bodies are the enemies of subjects. The subject is often leftover, moreover, when we remove the body. Thus, the leftover cultural playground that Ping recognizes in Arthur is a subject defined within a discursive proposition. Here we get some initial notions of the differences between rhetoric and discourse. The playground is referred to as a discourse that produces bodies. As Ping claims to "see the playground," he then makes it a rhetorical effect. Discursive production, which also can be thought of as a type of subject thematization, does not aim at freeing bodies from constraints; rather, it designs to *subject* bodies in such a way that they can become objects. Discursive thematization objectifies. It does not first consider social bodies but attempts to locate them in such as way as they become objectively or ontologically subject to questioning and definition. Ping's "physical" statement about Arthur constitutes a center of him as subject that is central to its very definition: the playground is "in" Arthur.

Physical Rhetoric

My analysis of *Hoop Dreams* began with a description and explication of Coach Pingatore's comment about Arthur and the playground because it is a particularly strong example of how rhetoric and discourse constitute bodies and subjects. Ping's own personalized rhetoric will continue to imbue both Arthur and William as the film progresses. However, when we are first introduced to William, he is instantly being constructed by his mother and brother, and throughout the film, William will continue to emerge from this familial (and expectorant) rhetoric.

Fourteen-year-old William Gates, like Arthur Agee, wants to play in the NBA. His family is in full support of his dream, as his mother, Emma, declares, "He's just doing something he loves, and I'm happy for him." This statement comes across as typical support from a mother devoted to supporting her child's dreams and goals. Then, we meet William's brother, Curtis: "If someone can understand the way William plays, then that'd make me feel a lot better. I'd say, 'They should've understood the way I play.'" Emma and Curtis are the two most prevalent familial voices we listen to as we follow William's story. These two introductory comments parallel statements they will make throughout the film concerning William's basketball abilities. Curtis's understanding of William's abilities are filtered through his own abilities and, as we will come to discover, his own failures. The next time that we see Curtis, in fact, he admits that "all my basketball dreams are gone. All my dreams are in [William]." So, as we are being introduced to the other character, William, who will lead us through this film, we come to understand him as a subject already being put into play by external rhetorical forces. Curtis's desire to live his dreams through his younger brother will partially encourage William through the remainder of the film.

Curtis is a good means to examine how William, as a subject and a body, gets rhetorically constituted. In an interview during his sophomore year at St. Joe's, William tells the viewers that "it seems like everybody's my coach." Cut as it is between Emma Gates's comment that Curtis is "all the time telling [William] what to do" and Curtis's claim that "I guess I'm a pro in my mind, I've thought about it so many times," William's comment has particular poignancy. Visually, William falls in the middle of his mother and brother: rhetorically, as well, William seems caught in a struggle within the two familial rhetorics that impinge on him. One the one hand, Emma's dreams are constructed *for* the support of her son; on the other, Curtis's dreams, if they come to fruition, will have been *for* himself. As a body that gets made continually throughout the film, William is quite right that "everybody's my coach." In this comment, William provides us with evidence that he and we, as community members, have (at least vague) conceptions and theories of the body. Earlier we discovered how remarkable and simultaneously pedestrian Ping's comment about "seeing" the playground in Arthur is. Here, in William's comment that "everybody's my coach," we get another glimpse of how it is that bodies are thought, that is, how we conceive—outside of initially theoretical or critical languages—of body production. On the one hand, this comment can be taken at face value: all people act as if they are my coach; they offer much advice, many rules, and a great deal of influence. This is innocent thinking about the body as a protean entity. On the other hand (and in more theoretical terms), we can view it as critical awareness of how we think of bodies: as beings rhetorically constructed in time. Bodies are trained, taught, and tested over and over. Sometimes this pressure comes in the form of verbal

tirades from athletic coaches, as Ping frequently berates William for not practicing well; but, more regularly, this rhetorical training comes from other bodies
that we come in contact with in daily interaction.

Important questions arise when attempting to document, in some way, how
bodies become rhetorically constituted. For example, do we watch Arthur's and
William's bodies, initially at least, being read by the camera and by viewers as
basketball bodies rather than as other types of bodies? To answer this question
we must understand that we use and employ our "bodies for the assignment of
all sorts of roles, tasks, duties, and strategies" (Harre 257). William and Arthur
use their bodies for themselves—they are not mere pawns of rhetorical inscription placed on them from the outside. But, it is important and profitable work
to investigate how these bodies get (re)constituted though particular cinematic
rhetoric as well.

Subjective Objects

Arthur and William both begin attending St. Joe's the same academic year; they
are freshman in this predominantly white, middle- to upper-class Catholic school.
They are required to take a full load of courses, practice team basketball every
day, and commute daily the three-hour round-trip from their homes in Chicago.
The two must also make a myriad of other social "commutes" as they attempt
to make the transition from their neighborhoods to the lifestyle offered at St. Joe's.
One particular transition that they must make in order to succeed (i.e., play
basketball for the school's team) is to place importance on their education. We
find out that both William and Arthur have educational deficiencies that start
them out well behind other students at school. During his freshman year, William claims that "when I first got here, I said 'I want to go home.'" This comment is placed over a shot of William in a New Testament class in which the
teacher is asking questions about the Bible. In this shot, William is the only black
student and one of the few not to raise his hand in response to the teacher's
queries. An African-American nun offers further perspective on William's academics: she tells him that he "must be one great basketball player to get into this
school with these grades." This type of verbal narration situates William academi-
cally in relation to those students around him in the camera's frame. Cinematically, both visually and verbally, William, as a filmic subject, is being constructed
by the camera as a position on the outside. He looks disinterested in this shot,
and his voice-over certainly adds to the construction of William as a particular
type of body: a basketball body rather than an academic body. Here, the term
body is used because it allows the movement between two or more positions that
something like "basketball player rather than student" does not. That is, student/
athlete sets up a binary that limits the possibilities of each, as separate/separable
individuations of the same being. Employing the term "body" here and elsewhere
permits fluctuating and simultaneous manifestations of movement and possibility.

Emerging from rhetorical discourse, bodies gain (or learn) their abilities, limits, and positions with reference to other bodies and the rhetoric presented by these others. Working from within this perspective is not as much as an advocation of a philosophy that finds the subject in the I-Thou Project[6] as it is an understanding that bodies are always already found (that is, constituted and mappable) in reference to other bodies. As it learns the morays and means of those around it, a body takes on characteristics that it then shows to the world as its own. This body learns how to act, respond, and create from within itself and onto those bodies around it. There is an infinite matrix of forces impugning this body with various discursive and nondiscursive formations. In this general discussion, we can think of the topography of bodies as the ontologically revealed and epistemically created layer of the social body.

But this body is more like an onion than an apple. As a layer, the topology under investigation does not give way to other layers that eventually disclose a center or core of the body as some sort of fundamentally attributive source or locus. Rather, bodies thought of in this manner are social constructs through and through. This is not to deny bodies their corporeality at all: it is to recognize that a corporeal, bodily structure is a material surface that is terrain for molding and formation. Obviously, physical bodies are comprised of blood, organs, and skin. Additionally, society, through rhetoric and discourse, vies for influence, constitution and construction, on bodies. The questions that accompany these bodies concern the mapping of material transformations that constitute lived experience. We can think of this materiality, this corporeality (this meat, as it is coming to be known in an increasingly cyber-oriented culture), as a site or surface through which and on which construction works. Feminist scholar Elizabeth Grosz writes quite thoughtfully about the body as a site of cultural inscription, as "an externality that presents itself to others and to culture as a writing or inscriptive surface" (10).[7] Specific rhetorical structures, as will be developed in a discussion of cinema later in this essay, constitute and organize social bodies as the result of particular articulatory practices.

The often confusing multiplicity of bodies designated by the terms of constitution, presentation, and (re)presentation (especially in a focus on cinematic bodies[8]) can be unraveled only if our conception of bodies is understood from the very beginning as the constitution of effects on bodies or, more precisely, as bodies that emerge from site-specific discursivity. By understanding bodies in this manner—as constituted phenomena of language and other (sign) systems—we might then be able to access more thoroughly the ways in which cinema itself creates and presents these bodies. Psychology, anthropology, philosophy, and poetry have all attempted to pursue in different ways and to varying degrees of success the behavior, faculties, powers, possibilities, and densities of bodies. Two questions remain for this essay to investigate within this formulation of bodies: have these interpretations been explored in the ontological manner from which they set out; and, what of rhetoric's involvement in the building of bodies?

The series of shots of William in his high school classroom highlights the racial disparity at St. Joe's, a school that is able to, by William's second year, provide the star basketball player with a support network so that his family can defer the entire cost of his education. The more time we spend at St. Joe's, the more we come to recognize that the black students who are shown on camera are predominately associated with the various sports teams at the school. Thus, the school itself is constructed as a cinematic subject just as the playground was constructed by Coach Pingatore earlier in the film: as an objective "place," the school is transformed into a cinematic subject by putting into play various rhetorical devices that create and constitute the bodies that inhabit it.

It is important to keep in mind that I am not seeking to establish an overarching rhetorical reading of *Hoop Dreams*. Rather, I am concerned with the rhetorical production of the film and its contained subjects and bodies. Thus, we look for the ways in which things such as the playground and school (in addition to William and Arthur) gain their discursive and rhetorical constitution throughout the film. One question that arises from this point is this: Do the school and playground, once thought of as objects that exist ontologically outside of sign systems, get made into subjects by the filmic representations of their own transcendence? This question takes us back to our earlier claim that subject identity is relational. The playground is talked about by Pingatore as viewers watch play in an updated, indoor, and institutionalized gymnasium. The "subject" playground is both literally and figuratively "viewed" in contrast to other subjective relations. Hence, we find that subjects are produced from rhetoric about objects. The playground's transcendent subjectivity, as referenced in Ping's comment about Arthur, reveals its rhetorical constitution as that which produces bodies such as Arthur.

Apparatus Rhetoric

Near the beginning of his sophomore year at St. Joe's, Arthur is forced to leave the school because his father has been laid off from work several times in recent months: the family can no longer afford to send their son to the expensive private school. Arthur, additionally, owes the school part of his tuition payments from his freshman year. In debt and out of St. Joe's, Arthur is required to attend his neighborhood high school. When we first visit Marshall High, we are immediately witness to the striking differences between this public inner-city (mostly black) school and the private, suburban (mostly white) St. Joe's. These differences are seen in the forms of the security guards who walk the halls of Marshall to the identification badges that the students are required to wear around their necks. These institutionalized forms of control are in deep contrast to the free and clean movement we see at St. Joe's. We can imagine that William too would be walking these halls if it were not for his financial sponsor, Patricia Weir, director of Encyclopedia Britannica, who has paid his tuition and given him a job. Arthur's new coach at Marshall, Luther Bedford, recognizes the financial effects on Arthur's educational condition: "If he'd played like they thought [he should], he'd still be at St. Joe's. Economics would have had nothing to do with it. Somebody've made sure he'd still be there."

To add to the growing despair felt by Arthur and sympathetic viewers, Bo, Arthur's father, leaves the family after twenty years of marriage to Arthur's mother, Sheila. It is several months until we again see Bo Agee. When we do, we are on the same basketball court on which we first met Arthur. Again, he is playing ball, and his father, looking thin and changed, approaches the group. "Increasingly," we are told by narrative voice-over, "this playground court has become a place to buy and sell drugs." Suspiciously, Bo leaves the players on the court for another group of males who are standing around an abandoned storefront. Arthur hails his father repeatedly as Bo walks to the other group. As Arthur tentatively follows his father, in an effort to retrieve him, the camera moves behind Arthur so as to capture both father and son simultaneously in one frame. This shot gives the viewer a sense of the space that has obviously come between Arthur and his father. Moreover, as it is shot across the length of the dilapidated court, this scene further constitutes both Bo—as a father who is subject to the tide of drugs we have been told inhabit this playground—and Arthur—as a son who longs for his father to become once again a constructive role in the family. The camera operates as a direct constitutional device in the production of these two characters as bodies that move within its narrative.

In one review of the film, bell hooks writes that it "merely shows the failure of black male parents to sustain meaningful ties with their children. It does not critically interrogate the complex circumstances and conditions of that failure" (23). While I agree with hooks's claim about the lack of address of the specifics of Bo Agee's problems, I also think that the film does present us with a notion of how these types of behaviors, images, and actions get constructed as stereotypes in the first place. By shooting the scene in this manner, the film reveals how particular vantage points and angles constitute the creation of subjects. That is, by assuming a position supposedly outside the action it captures, the film can claim documentary laissez faire, since, in a documentary, "one works from social actuality but necessarily imposes form upon that actuality, turning it into what may be implied by the terms *art* or *fiction*" (Benson and Anderson 1). However, by understanding how bodies and subjects are created in rhetorical discourse, we are able to recognize not only their construction but also, and perhaps more importantly, we can understand the consequences of such constitution. Such consequences come in the form of stereotypes, like those hooks refers to of African-American men and inner-city youth, that become naturalized through their public usage. By reading and comprehending bodies and subjects as constituted temporally and rhetorically, we should better recognize how they are naturalized (made to look natural, real, actual, though they are not at all "natural") through repetition and reiteration.

As the film progresses through the years that each youth spends at his respective school, another aspect becomes clear in its strong and persuasive effects on the creation and constitution of Arthur and William. We have already made mention of the financial support that the school was able to offer William. As the film spends more time with these two characters, viewers learn more and more about the intricate working of something that comes to be known in the film as "the system." The system is not a single entity but rather a continuously moving and always referable institutional type of power-wielding being.

A System of Subjects

Near the beginning of his junior year, William severely tears a cartilage in his knee. Rather than being able to lead his varsity team "downstate" to the state basketball tournament, William is forced to miss most of the remaining season. But, his time is not spent away from athletics: he is taken to see a well-known knee specialist who deems surgery necessary to repair the tear. While William is in surgery, we listen to Emma Gates talk about her two sons: "I really thought that Curtis was going to make it. But he didn't, so I really wanted this one to make it." Basketball is once again referenced as *the way* to make it. In order to make it in basketball, William is going to need strong, healthy knees. To get these knees, William's school picks up the cost of his operation and subsequent rehabilitation. The (school's intricate) system is taking care of William because he is seen as a way for the school to make it.

Conversely, the system is failing Arthur. After Bo leaves the family, Sheila is forced onto welfare because of the limited financial resources available to her. The family apartment loses its power because Sheila misses an appointment with a financial adviser, and to this loss of power, she states: "The system is saying to me, they don't care." The sequence of scenes in which we learn of the Agees's financial troubles is cut in contrast to scenes of William's operation and rehabilitation at a contemporary medical clinic. This cinematic device of intercutting these two contrasting subjects highlights the corresponding manners in which the system, as a generic makeup of power and money, contributes to the constitution of Arthur and William. The system becomes a rhetorical device that influences the two in different ways. Thus, they must make decisions as a result of the burden placed on them from this system. Cut as these scenes are, they construct a tangible, visible system rather than an amorphous entity that exists somewhere "out there." This system is constructed as hidden, that is, it cannot be located in a place, person, or building. However, it is embodied in the form of results, consequences, and effects. Sheila, her financially struggling family— as subjects under the auspices of this system—and their material conditions of living are actual effects; thus, they are bodies produced, in part, by the system.

By the time the doctors tell William that he is cleared to practice, his team has made it to the state tournament. In a crucial game, William is playing point guard, and near the end has a shot at winning the game. In the closing minutes, William reinjures his knee. On the sidelines for only a minute, he reenters and is fouled, putting him on the free throw line. He hobbles to the line and misses both free throws: St. Joe's loses the game. In an interview after the game, William's brother-in-law, Alvin Bibbs, claims that "something's wrong with a system that finds winning that important. He shouldn't have been in there at all." Again, the system comes under scrutiny for causing an event. In this case, the system produces a reinjured body. However, Curtis, William's older brother, denies the effect of the injury: "That's no excuse. He got out there. As far as I'm concerned, there ain't nothing wrong with him. It's just an excuse." Our understanding of William comes, thus, from the system and from Curtis's dreams of making it. These two opposing views of the injured knee account for both a rhetorical constitution of our understanding of William—in Curtis's comment about excuse—and a nondiscursive construction of William as subject—as emerging (reinjured) from a faulty, misguided system. But, the system returns, though it is never absent in the sense of not-present, to take William to another knee doctor; this time though he is taken to see the Chicago Bulls team orthopedic surgeon. The system hurts but also mends those who are constructed in its care.

By this point in the documentary, we are beginning to get a fuller portrait of William and Arthur. Their actions within their particular worlds are attributable within the narrative the film has constructed. Their failures and successes, both on the court and off, are accounted for by this narrative, which is able to present a large picture of these two athletes. However, the production of a human subject—and this is particularly true of cinematically constituted rhetorical subjects—is always incomplete. Hence, we can view the rhetorical constitution of bodies as a rhetoric of becoming; indeed, rhetorical invocation is a becoming. In documentaries, if not in all films, we give our own practice of authority over to the film. Consideration of film from a rhetorical perspective is an important endeavor in this respect. It is through a recognition of rhetoric's role in the constitution of bodies and subjects that we can enlighten the moment(s) when identity (as subject or body) is guised as static and unchanging, even in film. Rhetorical criticism encourages us to recognize the multiauthored status of *all* subject positions and bodies.

A Voice from Above

Part of this authoring, this constitution of William and Arthur, comes through uses of voice-overs from the filmmakers. Rarely, but at points when the visual narrative cannot convey a full sense of story, the filmmakers interject small pieces of information to fill in for the viewer knowledge that helps drive the development of the film. One such instance came when we learned, from voice-over, that the playground had become a place for drug dealing. Another crucial voice-over comes during the summer between the boys' junior and senior years. Because he is such a nationally respected player, William is invited to attend the prestigious Nike basketball camp. Only the one hundred best players in the country are invited to attend this camp, which stresses academics as well as athletics. The group of young players hears speeches by Dick Vitale, a well-known college basketball commentator, and Spike Lee, a successful African-American filmmaker. Many of the nation's top college basketball coaches also attend the camp to scout star players to recruit for their programs. The youths are given clothing, shoes, and books from the camp organizers. As they play ball in front of a hundred or so onlookers, they appear to the film viewer as if they are on display for the spectators of the games being played. Their bodies are the signs of their abilities. How well their bodies perform here could get them into prominent college programs. Bob Gibbons, another independent scout, claims that "it's a meat market, and it's my job to serve professional meat" to the teams for which he recruits. This sort of bidding and selling of products (of meat, of bodies) continues as the youths listen to Spike Lee caution them about their futures as merchandise: "This whole thing is about money." Indeed, these young bodies are commodities to be bartered for.

As we realize how much special attention is given to these basketball hopefuls, the scene cuts to Arthur working in a restaurant kitchen. Here we hear the important voice-over that adds to our conceptions of Arthur as subject: "Arthur and [his friend] Shannon spend their summer at Pizza Hut, earning $3.35 an hour." Not only does the quick cut from the pleasant Nike camp to the kitchen of Pizza Hut make for narrative telling, but, also, the voice-over adds to viewer realization that Arthur and William are being constructed as subjects. That is, the rhetoric of *Hoop Dreams* produces as an effect of its discourse the very bodies, Arthur and William, that it simultaneously, as Judith Butler puts it, "claims to discover as that which precedes its action" (*Bodies* 30). In other words, the film is shot, as most documentaries are, as if it is somehow stumbling onto the narrative rather than admitting to its very constructive role in the subject it seeks to articulate: as opposed to "stumbling onto" Arthur and William, *Hoop Dreams* constitutes and produces them while claiming "to discover" (Butler 30). The camera is another constitutional device—with the system, family, schools, coaches, et cetera—that constructs Arthur and William as subjects throughout the film. As bodies moving in their worlds, William and Arthur do so by bouncing between, with, around, and through other bodies. They learn themselves and their roles through these exchanges. In discussing documentaries, Benson and Anderson recognize the slippery and "inevitable tension between social actuality and film form" (2). For viewers of the film, the camera adds additional constitutionality (in addition to that from the family, system, academia, et cetera) to these bodies. In the earlier description of cinematic laissez faire, we discovered how it is that the documentary camera can simultaneously (appear) separate from the action it films and be involved, for the audience, in creating the reality it presents. This is the "inevitable tension" to which Benson and Anderson refer.

Such inscription upon the body, from the camera or voice-over, creates mobile and shifting subjects. With voice-over, viewers are witness to a disembodied voice, a voice removed from its articulation. The fragmentary uses of voice-over, which aim to redouble narrative stress, reveal how it is that, from a rhetorical perspective, we can come to understand a subject and a body differently from one another. Previously, we stated that bodies are frequently the enemies of subjects. These uses of voice-over figure this alignment. Voice-over adds to the constitution of William and Arthur as subjects, subjects different from the bodies coached in basketball, trained in the classroom, and taught in their environments. We come to know William and Arthur as subjects through a cinematic narrative experience. Additionally, their bodies are the other vehicles through which we come to know them. And, as we have seen, the camera itself is a narrative apparatus that contributes to the constitution of subjects it films. In this sense, the body is the radical materiality of the subject. Visually, we can find the body and can even map its movements; but, the subject positioning is always a movement away and toward discourse simultaneously. This is why it is so difficult to talk about cinematic subjects: mapping is difficult work. Rhetoric is also a mapping, though. Through its enunciation, intent, and persuasion, rhetoric attempts to find and wrestle a body into compliance: "the body [. . .] becomes a location within various power-riddled discursive positions, but where the body is not a passive medium on which cultural meanings are merely inscribed" (Pile and Thrift 4).

And so it is with William, Arthur, or any other subject—they are prodded, disciplined, and ignored, and they are forgetful and transcendent. They receive, erase, delete, transfer, and employ the various rhetorical devices they encounter in the world, as the world. The senior year provides more instances for Arthur and William to be the vehicles of cultural rhetoric. William's experiences at the "meat market" basketball camp whittle down to a private recruiting visit from Marquette University coach Kevin O'Neill, who wants to "make [William] the best basketball player I can." On a visit to the university, William listens to a fictional recording of him winning the national championship for Marquette. Supplementing this invented scenario recording are fictionalized newspaper stories documenting the same victory. These documents are meant as enticement for William to imagine himself playing for Marquette. Additionally, they highlight for the rhetorical critic the ways in which William is continually being constructed by external rhetoric. He ends up signing a "National Letter of Intent" to play basketball at Marquette University, provided he earns high enough scores on his ACT. It is certainly not these fictitious accounts of William at the university that get him to commit to Marquette's program. The stylized rhetoric contained in these enticements, however, is symbolic of other ways that rhetorical constructions begin to have effects; and, as we have seen, bodies frequently emerge as effects of rhetorical discourse.

During his senior year, Arthur becomes a star on the varsity team. Marshall surprises many followers by not only beating their crosstown rival but also by winning the Chicago city championship. Arthur seals both of these important victories with clutch shooting in the waning minutes of the games. During the last few games of the season, many college recruiters come to watch Arthur play.

Most of these coaches, predominately from small or junior colleges, follow Arthur and his team to the state championship in Champaign, Illinois.

Although Arthur makes the all-tournament team, Marshall loses in the semifinals of the state championships. After a press conference following this loss, during which he deftly handles reporters' questions, the next time we see Arthur is during a recruiting visit to Mineral Valley Junior College in southern Missouri. Here, Arthur will have similar types of social, educational, and operational problems he had in high school; however, he once again succeeds in completing his education and earns a scholarship to Arkansas State University, where he helps the team win its first ever conference championship. As we leave him, he has faith that he will someday make it to the NBA, although he is not as myopic as he once was in his beliefs that basketball is the only future for him. William attends Marquette as planned but leaves school during his junior year; however, his team, school, and family successfully persuade him to return. Prior to the film credits, we read that, at the end of the filming of *Hoop Dreams,* both Arthur and William were beginning their senior years in college.

As Arthur and William are leaving their families to begin their college careers, we follow them through the ritualized movements as friends and family say their goodbyes. Prior to leaving his family, William sees Coach Pingatore for the last time. During this visit, the tension that seems to be emanating from William is clear as he tells Ping that he is "going into communications so that when you write me for a donation, I'll know the right way to turn you down." After William leaves his office, Ping claims that he never felt that William "bought into the system." Both William and his high school coach recognize the subtle but powerful workings and influences that this system can have on bodies and subjects. The system, as stated earlier, provides for William during his injury; but, William seems to recognize that the system also produces negative effects as consequences of its demands. Bodies and subjects shift even when involved in a continuous rhetorical flow like this invisible but powerful system. By recognizing more clearly, by listening to our bodies more thoughtfully, we, as community members, rhetoricians, or whatever, can better understand how to create productive affinities between one another rather than build obstacles, such as stereotypes and false generalities.

Temporary Conclusions

One thing that I have attempted to clarify is the nature of rhetorical construction of bodies and subjects orchestrated by cinematic narrative. This narrative, though, is not limited to its filmic presentation; it can be recognized in social and personal manifestations outside films as well. That is, although this essay has shown rhetoric's role in bodily formation in *Hoop Dreams,* the same appreciation can be made outside filmic presentations. Subjectivity and bodily formations are always relationships; they are not ontologically, prefigured categories of beings or things.

The cinema, as visualization, presents objects for viewers. However, as agents of engagement, we contribute to the subjectification of these filmic bodies. We should not, though, go so far as to say that visual practices, such as cinema, are regulatory. Cinematic presentation—the presenting of subjects and bodies—is an ambiguous and often contradictory screen of rhetorical construction. William and Arthur are presented in the film, but we continually contribute to their constitution as subjects. Thus, both in the film and through us, William and Arthur gain and shift in their subjective positions. In a manner of speaking, William and Arthur are mapped by the camera as if they are truth as subjects. As presentations, they are found by the camera in positions; however, through rhetorical analysis, we discover their very constitutionality is constructed by camera and by viewers.

In contrast to Dana Cloud's profitable conception of Marxist materialism as searching to "unmask the shared illusions of society" (145), this essay has sought to explore concretely how such materializations come into being, how specifically rhetorical discourse produces, defines, and constitutes bodies. Whereas it is certainly interesting and profitable work to examine rhetoric in specificity to texts such as *Hoop Dreams,* this theoretical groundwork can also provide us with the abilities not only to witness but also act and react to particular rhetorical investments outside of films, speeches, literature, or other texts.

Notes

1. For Ernesto Laclau and Chantal Mouffe, articulation is a way of understanding the struggle to temporarily fix meaning and define reality. In this essay, though, I want to use the same term to refer to the enunciation or invocation of rhetorical practices that seek to bring about a subjective positioning.

2. Two of Judith Butler's widely read books, *Gender Trouble* and *Bodies That Matter,* work through highly specific incarnations of feminist and gender legitimacy issues. These two books leave the reader with a clear understanding of the effects of discourse on issues of power, domination, and supremacy, particularly in terms of gender and race.

3. For more on nomadology as philosophy, see Deleuze and Guattari.

4. In *Hegemony and Socialist Strategy,* Laclau and Mouffe rely upon similar considerations of "subject positions rather than subject." However, they are not concerned directly with rhetorical influence on this constitution of positionality (as this essay is) as much as they are interested in the notion of the subject's inability to be the "origin of social relations" (115).

5. Again, the concepts of Judith Butler are helpful in the analysis. In *Gender Trouble,* Butler argues that gender is a "performance" that bodies play in order to participate. In *Hoop Dreams,* basketball is a performance that allows the bodies of Arthur and William to be recognized and taken seriously. It is often as if basketball is the dance they must perform if they want to achieve their dreams.

6. Wilhelm Dilthey elaborates a philosophy in which understanding comes from a discovery or rediscovery of the I in and through the Thou. To understand,

according to Dilthey, is to relive or reconstruct another's experience, to make another's experience one's own. For specific examples, see *Pattern and Meaning in History: Thoughts on History and Society.*

7. Much of Grosz's work concerns taking apart the body, examining it in this disassociation, and then putting it back together in new ways, with new points of association. In their introduction to *Sexy Bodies,* she and her coeditor, Elspeth Probyn, write, "[T]his collection is 'about' establishing new alliances, new connections between and among bodies, desires, pleasures, powers, cruising the borders of the obscene, the pleasurable, the desirable, the mundane and the hitherto unspoken" (xi).

8. Throughout this essay, I refer to things called "cinematic bodies." The specifics of this phrase will develop as the essay progresses. The phrase, cinematic bodies, is taken from Steven Shaviro's book, *The Cinematic Body.* Employing Deleuze and Guattari's thinking, Shaviro constructs arguments about the creation of bodies through spectatorship. Though his book is not concerned explicitly with rhetoric's role in the constitutional practice, Shaviro does focus on how bodies come to be and what they do cinematically.

Works Cited

Benson, Thomas W., and Carolyn Anderson. *Reality Fictions: The Films of Frederick Wiseman.* Carbondale: Southern Illinois UP, 1989.

Butler, Judith. *Bodies That Matter.* New York: Routledge, 1993.

———. *Gender Trouble.* New York: Routledge, 1990.

Cloud, Dana. "The Materiality of Discourse as Oxymoron: A Challenge to Critical Rhetoric." *Western Journal of Communication* 58 (Summer 1994): 141–63.

Deleuze, Gilles. *Logic of the Sense.* Trans. Mark Lester. New York: Columbia UP, 1990.

Deleuze, Gilles, and Felix Guattari. *A Thousand Plateaus.* Trans. Brian Massumi. Minneapolis: Minnesota UP, 1987.

Dilthey, Wilhelm. *Pattern and Meaning in History: Thoughts on History and Society.* New York: Harper, 1962.

Grosz, Elizabeth. *Sexual Subversions: Three Freudian Feminists.* London: Routledge, 1989.

Grosz, Elizabeth, and Elspeth Probyn. *Sexy Bodies: The Strange Carnalities of Feminism.* New York: Routledge, 1995.

Harre, Romano. *Physical Being.* Oxford: Blackwell, 1991.

hooks, bell. "Dreams of Conquest." *Sight and Sound* 5.4 (Apr. 1995): 22–23.

Hoop Dreams. Dir. Steve James. Feature Film Company, 1994.

Laclau, Ernesto, and Chantal Mouffe. *Hegemony and Socialist Strategy: Toward a Radical Democratic Politics.* New York: Verso, 1987.

Pile, Steve, and Nigel Thrift, eds. Introduction. *Mapping the Subject: Geographies of Cultural Transformation.* New York: Routledge, 1995. 1–12.

Shaviro, Steven. *The Cinematic Body.* Minneapolis: Minnesota UP, 1993.

Part Two

Rhetorical Perspectives on Film and Culture

In the wake of works such as Thomas Kuhn's *The Structure of Scientific Revolutions,* Richard Rorty's *Philosophy and the Mirror of Nature,* and David Bordwell's *Making Meaning: Inference and Rhetoric in the Interpretation of Cinema,* it has become somewhat of a truism to note that theory itself is subject to the same rhetorical forces that enable and contain other forms of narrative. While film studies has examined at great length the nature of its object as a semiotic system, as "like a language," there has not been much scrutiny of cultural and other problems posed by the slippage in signification as we shift attention from the verbal to the visual. Likewise, there has been only glancing attention to the ways in which the act of framing the object of perception, as well as viewing itself, positions both the filmmaker and the audience in a rhetorical and thus cultural dynamic. We can go back to Aristotle to see the origins of the conception of rhetoric as a form of ideological analysis. He defines rhetoric as the faculty of "discovering the possible means of persuasion in reference to any subject whatever" (1355b). The means of persuasion are not merely the devices of rhetoric but the storehouse of public opinion, in other words, what people generally believe to be true or can be made to believe is true.

Part two of *The Terministic Screen* casts yet a wider net than part one, looking at trends in cinematic treatment of cultural movements as indicative of ideological anxiety. Hollywood films reflect their times, of course, but they also shape the sentiments of the public who view them, functioning both as symptom and (proposed) cure, as ideology and hegemony. Thomas W. Benson's "Looking for the Public in the Popular: The Hollywood Blacklist and the Rhetoric of Collective Memory" analyzes films such as *The Front* (1976), *Fellow Traveller* (1990), *Guilty By Suspicion* (1991), and *Witch Hunt* (1994) to show a persistent refusal in American cinema "to accept fully a separation among public, private, and popular, and in doing so [these films] function not only as rhetorical appeals but also as a sort of implicit rhetorical theorizing about American society." Benson argues that the politics of this popular history of American anti-communism simultaneously denies the legitimacy of politics, even as it provides reassurance that the American spirit always redeems the balance of the society in the end.

Philip L. Simpson takes an equally expansive view of the functions of film as symptomatic of wider cultural trends. "*Copycat*, Serial Murder, and the De-(Terministic) Screen Narrative" analyzes the complex relationship between serial murder and representational narratives as well as the cultural milieu in which these narratives of serial murder have emerged. Simpson's essay focuses on one film in particular, *Copycat* (1995), a film that allows him to encapsulate the broader view of serial killer narratives he takes in *Psycho Paths: Tracking the Serial Killer through Contemporary American Film and Literature* (2000). Simpson reveals the ways in which terministic screens create fictions that would legitimate action and meaning.

The possibility that terministic screens not only rationalize but direct action is also explored in Davis W. Houck and Caroline J. S. Picart's "Opening the Text: Reading Gender, Christianity, and American Intervention in *Deliverance*," which draws its terminology from Umberto Eco's theoretical construct of the "open text." The authors show how director John Boorman constructs *Deliverance* as an interrogation of emergent cultural conceptions of masculinity and femininity, as a critique of Christian fundamentalism, and as an allegorical commentary on colonialism in the Vietnam era.

In "From 'World Conspiracy' to 'Cultural Imperialism': The History of Anti-Plutocratic Rhetoric in German Film," Friedemann Weidauer argues that it was the obsession with artistic integrity and the growing degree of self-reflexivity reflected in its films that ironically made the New German Film the true heir of the Weimar era, the films of which inspired the Nazi's use of film as one important dimension of its propaganda apparatus:

> The threat of a more successful competitor, Hollywood, created a kind of self-fulfilling paranoid prophecy. In the case of Weimar film, it created the horror scenarios of cultural domination by others on which the Nazis could build. Before long, the German film industry was dominated by something much worse. In the case of the New German Film, it led to such a degree of self-reflexivity that no one noticed (or cared to notice) that the audience had turned away in boredom.

Weidauer's essay demonstrates the utility of taking rhetorical perspectives on the politics of cultural change, in much the same way that Benson, Simpson, Houck, and Picart show how the very principle of the terministic screen—functioning as a way of seeing and not seeing—is inscribed within the ideology and the hegemonic structures that would foster group identification.

Work Cited

Aristotle. *The Art of Rhetoric.* 1926. Trans. J. H. Freese. Loeb Classical Library. Cambridge, MA: Harvard UP, 1982.

7

Looking for the Public in the Popular: The Hollywood Blacklist and the Rhetoric of Collective Memory

Thomas W. Benson

IN TWENTIETH-CENTURY INDUSTRIAL SOCIETIES, THE MASS MEDIA and popular arts often do the work theorized as the business of the public sphere. What are the rhetorical implications of conducting public business in the popular arts? This chapter is an examination of how television and film have remembered the Hollywood blacklist in fiction films.

The Cold War had profound effects on American motion pictures. One of the sharpest instruments prompting those effects was the blacklist, initiated in film, radio, and television as the result of anti-Communist hearings of the House Committee on Un-American Activities (HUAC) in 1947 and from 1951 to 1952. Several effects of the blacklist were, however profound, invisible to film audiences. Hundreds of suspected people lost their jobs in the industry. Films in general became more cautious about possible charges of insufficient patriotism. In a very few cases, films depicted HUAC or the blacklist itself. The first of these, *Big Jim McLain,* was produced by John Wayne in 1952; it features Wayne as a HUAC agent tracking down Communist spies in Hawaii. Much later, films critical of the blacklist began to appear. *The Front* (1976), written by the blacklisted Walter Bernstein and starring Woody Allen, describes blacklisting in television. *Fellow Traveller* (1990) and *Guilty By Suspicion* (1991) depict the blacklist in the film industry. *Witch Hunt* is a recent allegorical, made-for-cable film about the blacklist. Some of these films are more interesting as films than others; all of them are intriguing examples of the peculiar pressure that public themes impose on popular art, often with disappointing results both for popular art and for public deliberation. The films are characteristically American in proposing private or individualistic solutions to public problems, which is especially intriguing since this stance is both a form of self-censorship in the face of repression and a declaration of independence. Nevertheless, the very tensions that cause these films to seem problematic are instructive, and thus a contribution to contestation for the collective memory.

I propose to examine the rhetoric of these films, using two related senses of the term "rhetoric." I am interested in (1) what happens to the art of the fiction film when it is dealing with a controversial issue in the public sphere; and (2) what happens to the art of rhetoric as civic eloquence when it must find its outlet in fiction film rather than in something resembling an idealized or approximated public sphere in which a variety of voices have access to the forum and where public matters are resolved through public discussion and decision.

Although my frame is thus historical and theoretical, my approach will be primarily critical and interpretive. I propose a close reading of these films to discover the ways in which they combine popular form and public theme. The perspective of rhetorical criticism may help us to notice the ways in which these films theorize the domains of the public, the private, and the popular.

The Hollywood Blacklist, and the Cold War more generally, had such pervasive effects on American motion pictures that it is hard to know which films to include in a critical survey of the public implications of the popular since World War II. Even the seemingly most apolitical of Hollywood films might be seen as part of a general tendency to avoid controversial social themes, or to disguise them in layers of abasement, analogy, allusion, and allegory.

It might be hard to imagine a less political film than Gene Kelly's *Singin' in the Rain,* for example. And yet the film, released during the second round of HUAC's Hollywood hearings in 1952, was threatened by a campaign of harassment that had been directed at Kelly since at least 1947 by HUAC and its counterpart in the California Senate, the Tenney Committee.[1] The example of *Singin' in the Rain* repeated itself throughout the industry, where the direct and indirect effects of the blacklist continued to make themselves felt in the generic forms Hollywood developed to survive the Cold War. In writing of Hollywood in the 1950s, Peter Biskind observes that "every movie that was produced, no matter how trivial or escapist, was made in the shadow of the anti-Communist witch-hunt, subject to the strictures of the House Committee on Un-American Activities that dictated who worked and who didn't, which subjects were appropriate and which weren't, how plots could be resolved and how they couldn't" (4). It was not, as Biskind acknowledges, that HUAC directly monitored Hollywood production or issued explicit guidelines, but that the shock of the repeated investigations contributed to a culture of conformity and caution. Hollywood had often cooperated with the federal government in times of war or crisis.[2] Paul Vanderwood writes that in the early Cold War period,

> the Producer's Association promised the federal government that the industry would not release movies which did not accurately portray American life and institutions, a deliberately vague catchall that permitted arbi-

trary control of picture content and production. . . . Hollywood had always engaged in assertive self-censorship in order to avoid outright federal government restriction. (187–88)

From fairly early in the Cold War, some films analogized the McCarthy era through strategies of displacement and allegory. The western *High Noon* (1952), the science fiction films *The Thing* (1951) and *Invasion of the Body Snatchers* (1956), Elia Kazan's *On the Waterfront* (1954), and other films alluded to the threat of infiltration, the ethics of informing, or the dangers of conformist hysteria. In a few cases, Hollywood looked directly at HUAC and the blacklist, with peculiar results.[3]

Big Jim McLain

By 1952, when he produced *Big Jim McLain*, John Wayne, who had started acting in the 1920s, had achieved major stardom with such films as *Stagecoach* (1939), *The Long Voyage Home* (1940), *Red River* (1946), *Fort Apache* (1948), *She Wore a Yellow Ribbon* (1949), *Sands of Iwo Jima* (1949), and *Rio Grande* (1950). John Wayne and Robert Fellows produced *Big Jim McLain* for a Warner Brothers release.[4]

Wayne casts himself as Big Jim McLain, a HUAC investigator who with his sidekick Mal Baxter goes to Hawaii to break up a Communist spy network. Mal Baxter is played by James Arness, who had starred in *The Thing* and would later go on to star in the *Gunsmoke* TV series.

The film is anti-Communist agitprop at the height of the McCarthy period and seems highly peculiar today. The film's Communists are goons, thugs, weirdoes, or creepy foreigners. In contrast, Jim McLain, Mal Baxter, and Nancy Vallon (actress Nancy Olson) are all-American characters. But the casting is not so simple as this. Some of the minor, sympathetic, roles are played as comic vaudeville stereotypes. Veda Ann Borg, for example, plays the landlady of Namaka, a suspected Communist spy. She is loud, comical, sexy, and drunkenly seductive and makes a play for Wayne despite the jealousy of her comically loutish boyfriend. Hans Conried appears in one scene as a lunatic anti-Communist would-be informer who wants to share his secrets with McLain; the episode is inserted in the film as an isolated comic turn in no way connected to the plot and connected to the larger form of the film only by the way it hits some of the zany notes struck by Madge (Veda Ann Borg) and by its comical mirroring of other, more "serious" scenes of informers passing along vital information to McLain. The issue of casting in *Big Jim McLain* is further complicated by the film's use of nonactors. Honolulu police chief Dan Liu plays himself in the film, and members of HUAC also appear.

The casting of the film may be a clue to its form. Veda Ann Borg (1915–73) was married to Andrew McLaglen, who worked as an assistant director on Ford's *The Quiet Man* the same year *Big Jim McLain* was made. McLaglen was also an assistant director on *Big Jim McLain* and on Wayne's Cold War propaganda tale *Blood Alley* (1955) and himself directed the Wayne films *McLintock!* (1963), *The*

Undefeated (1969), *Chisum* (1970), and *Cahill* (1973). Andrew was the son of Victor McLaglen, who was often a supporting player to Wayne and, like Wayne, a part of the circle of drinking pals around John Ford. The practice of drawing on friends and relations, who evidently shared or were willing to subordinate themselves to Wayne's simpleminded anti-Communism in making *Big Jim McLain,* may explain in part the film's peculiar lack of narrative and artistic discipline. It does seem striking that when Wayne had achieved the clout to control his own films, he grew increasingly mediocre, political (*The Alamo* [1960], *The Green Berets* [1968]) or preachy (the films he later made with Andrew McLaglen). But it is not clear whether the confusions of *Big Jim McLain* are the result of its politics or the lack of an artistic talent that could coordinate the production. Screenwriting credit for *Big Jim McLain* went to James Edward Grant, who often worked with Wayne and who, writes, Garry Wills, "had more to do with Wayne's blustery style of superpatriotism than anyone else" (200). Victor Navasky reports that other collaborators on the script were Richard English, "who specialized in writing anti-Communist movies," and William Wheeler, a HUAC investigator who drew on his own "HUAC experiences in Hawaii" to write the script (42n).

The film drew mixed reactions in its own day. Virtually all the reviewers noted the film's anomalous form. *Newsweek* found *Big Jim McLain* "just another spy melodrama saved from being merely that by a certain amount of adroit comedy playing" by Veda Ann Borg and Hans Conried (104). In the *National Parent-Teacher,* Mrs. Louis L. Bucklin conceded that the film "entertains and arouses emotions," but warned that it "oversimplifies a very important problem" while at the same time adding "extraneous romance [. . .] as well as scenes of violence based on a seemingly incurable belief that fisticuffs solve all problems" (37). A reviewer in *Variety* noted the technical and artistic flaws in the film but apparently admired its topicality in showing "the story of the patriotic work going on to expose Communist activities endangering this country and its possessions" (6). *Time* found that the film "has some pleasingly authentic Hawaiian background, but the action in the foreground is implausible and fumblingly filmed" (93). William Whitebait, writing in the British journal *New Statesman and Nation,* found that the film's treatment of "the seamier side of freedom" did not "even with John Wayne, quite make a film" (509). Bosley Crowther derides the film as a travesty of its political premise, arguing that "the over-all mixing of cheap fiction with a contemporary crisis in American life is irresponsible and unforgivable. No one deserves credit for this film" (35). Since the film was so transparently inept even in the midst of the anti-Communist hysteria of 1952, we cannot assume that its rhetoric was particularly effective. Nevertheless, the rhetoric of the film is characteristic and has something to show us about Hollywood's attempt to treat public issues through popular genres.

In form, the film is in some ways merely a ho-hum B thriller about spies who happen to be Communist agents, to which is added the obligatory love story. But a number of burdens and diversions are added to the basic formula, challenging the coherence of the film experience. In one direction, the film reaches toward a documentary flavor that would have been familiar to viewers of contemporary crime thrillers. The propagandistic anti-Communism would also have been familiar in the world of McCarthyite hysteria and in the context of a number of other anti-Communist quickies thrown out by Hollywood in the period largely as insurance against further government intrusion into their otherwise studiedly apolitical industry. In another direction, the film reaches toward a tradition of performative, vaudevillian comedy that appears in the scenes with Veda Ann Borg and Hans Conried. The mix seems anomalous today, and to some of its reviewers at the time, but it seems important to note from a rhetorical perspective that the mix did not seem incoherent to all of its contemporary viewers, perhaps because the combination of patriotism, documentary, comedy, romance, and thriller were all so familiar and appealed in substance to a seemingly unified wellspring of common, popular/populist feeling and tradition. Indeed, though it may be important for a critic to "expose" and debunk the film's clumsily brutish superpatriotism, it is equally important to try to re-imagine the film from the point of view of an appreciative spectator.

As potentially confusing as its mix of styles is the film's political appeal. *Big Jim McLain* is about politics in the sense that its whole reason for being is to define Communism as the enemy and to warn against its subversive appeal. But in the world of the film, Communism is not political, and therefore our response to it requires not politics but police measures. The film justifies extremes of suspicion and commitment in a world where anyone—even a relative—might be a Communist. For this reason, it seems to me that Thomas Doherty misses part of the rhetoric of the film when he argues that "the anti-communist films of 1948–1954 set priorities, preclude alternatives, and force exclusive commitments. They demand choice" (16). Doherty is correct, I think, to claim that the films "preclude alternatives," but in doing this, at the very same time they demand choice, they make choice irrelevant—there really is no choice. Doherty's analysis is rightly derived from the work of Robert Ray, who argued that a primary ideological function of Hollywood films was to conceal the necessity for choice between independence from and commitment to community.[5] *Big Jim McLain* is different from the films Ray identifies in *A Certain Tendency of the Hollywood Cinema, 1930–1980,* but not because it makes choice possible. In the world of *Big Jim McLain,* this problem never arises. Big Jim is in a different world from Humphrey Bogart's Rick Blaine in *Casablanca.* Rick's problem, argues Ray, is to evade the choice between autonomy and community, and the film's problem is to allow him to act on behalf of the community without having to sacrifice his romantic, masculine independence. But this is never Big Jim's problem. Big Jim is an eager spy-chaser from the outset, never for a moment having to overcome any reluctance to serve his community, as do the heroes identified in Ray's "certain tendency." Hence, *Big Jim McLain* conceals the "necessity for choice" between autonomy and community by never allowing it to become a problem in the first place.

The only choice in *Big Jim McLain* is the choice between Communism and Americanism, and that, too, proves not to be a political choice. It is on this point that the film encounters another rhetorical anomaly (anomalous, at least, to the rhetorical theorist), since at the same time it takes patriotism off the list of those things subject to political choice, the film makes choosing patriotism the central organizing force of its didactic structure. The film attempts to persuade us about matters that are outside the realm of choice. To put it another way, the film implicitly regards its audience as in need of salvation by persuasion, but it regards its diegetic subjects—the characters in the film itself—as more or less innately virtuous or corrupt, and hence, as immune to persuasion.

If the film were consistent, it might openly engage in political persuasion about a matter regarded as subject to doubt. This is precisely what Aristotle observes in defining the art of persuasion as dealing with those matters that are not necessary or demonstrable.

> Since few of the premises from which rhetorical syllogisms are formed are necessarily true (most of the matters with which judgment and examination are concerned can be other than they are; for people deliberate and examine what they are doing, and [human] actions are all of this kind, and none of them [are], so to speak necessary) [. . .] it is evident that [the premises] from which enthymemes are spoken are sometimes necessarily true but mostly true [only] for the most part. (42–43)

The film achieves its unity, resolving the potential contradiction between its simultaneous appeal to and denial of choice, partly through its appeal to two surrogate arguments. The first argument is the premise that Communism is a defect of character in the individual Communist. The second surrogate argument is that Communism itself is at war with the free world, and that this state of war places Communism outside the sphere of politics.[6] But if these are surrogate arguments, what are they surrogates for? The apparent answer, given both the text of the film and the political context in which it emerged, is that the suppressed argument of the film lies in its attack on the political wing of American Communism, on the subjects of the blacklist and the McCarthy investigations, and, by extension, on the bleeding-heart liberalism that serves the cause of the Communist enemy. The necessities of character and the extremities required by a state of war are stand-ins for what might otherwise have to be acknowledged as the contingencies of a political debate raging between liberalism and conservatism at the outset of the Cold War.

David Zarefsky has described surrogate arguments in the Lincoln-Douglas debates of 1858. Zarefsky argues that both debaters employed the surrogate argumentative themes of law, history, and political conspiracy as a way of suggesting orientations to the theme—mostly avoided—of the morality of slavery itself. According to Zarefsky, the surrogate arguments allowed the discussion to continue, whereas an immediate and exclusive attention to the issue of the morality of slavery would have stopped the discussion in its tracks and made both debate and the hope of resolution impossible. But if surrogate arguments helped to make continued talk possible in the case of the Lincoln-Douglas debates, the surrogate arguments in *Big Jim McLain* suggest, on the contrary, that debate is pointless or dangerous. In *Big Jim McLain,* the surrogate argument *is* the moral argument, and it is not subject to debate.

The film's appeal to necessity and extremity in its surrogate arguments provides both unity and persuasive force to what might otherwise seem a self-contradictory and disorganized adventure.

In turning its back on public debate and choice, the film does not, however, elevate the private and the personal. Though the film spends most of its time and attention on the romance between Jim McLain and Nancy Vallon, it otherwise explicitly subordinates personal values to public interests. In two separate subplots, the film recommends betrayal of personal and family loyalties for the good of the country. In one scene, a nurse at a leper colony tells how she left her former husband because he remained loyal to the Communist Party. In another scene, an immigrant father and mother inform on their son, who was seduced by Communism during a high school student exchange visit to Russia. But in a peculiar way, though the personal is subordinate to the needs of the group, it appears that personal character determines political destiny.

John Wayne's on-screen persona lends a unifying structure to the otherwise strange assortment of characters in the film. All of them find their places in the film in relation to Wayne's character, who provides a center of interest and normality that anchors the film's structure and at the same time constitutes its central rhetorical argument. The appeal to patriotism in *Big Jim McLain* is finally an appeal to character, and it is this appeal that provides unity to a structure that might otherwise seem self-contradictory. The appeal to character centers on Big Jim McLain, who is presented as the icon of American patriotism. Though *Big Jim McLain* is not in the same class with Wayne's best films, it shares with those films the appeal to character. Garry Wills argues that Wayne's conservative Americanism was expressed not so much in his actual political activities, in his personal accomplishments (he avoided service in World War II to protect his acting career), or in his articulation of political sentiments, but rather in his screen persona. "Wayne did not just have political opinions. He embodied a politics; or his screen image did. It was a politics of large meanings, not of little policies— a politics of gender (masculine), ideology (patriotism), character (self-reliance), and responsibility. It was a matter of basic orientation. Its dogmas were (usually) implicit" (29).[7]

Half an hour into the film, Wayne and Olson's characters sit in a convertible on a windy hillside overlooking the Pacific. Without preamble, Olson starts a conversation about her boss, Dr. Gelster, whom we know from an omniscient narrator to be a Communist agent. In the brief conversation that follows, the film's central contradictions and their bids for resolution are set forth.

Vallon (Olson): I've been thinking.

McLain (Wayne): That's a good idea. A girl studying to be a psychiatrist should think.

Vallon: Has anything come up in your investigation to prove one way or another about Gelster being a Communist?

McLain: Not so far.

Vallon: Well, if he is, why?

McLain: I don't know.

Vallon: I've been trying to analyze. I think he has a frustration.

McLain: Oh?

Vallon: He's a good boss, but you never have the feeling that you'd like to do something for him, outside of the line of duty.

McLain: You do and I'll beat his brains out.

Vallon: Don't be an ape. I mean he doesn't draw affection from people.

McLain: In your case he'd better not.

Vallon: Stop that! You know what I mean. If he asked me to do a favor, the only reason I'd do it is because I don't want to lose my job. He doesn't attract people. In fact he doesn't even have the quality of repelling people—that at least is an act of emotion between individuals. He just is a neuter of a personality. I think he had to try and search for a cult of some kind, something to make himself—

McLain: Look, baby. I don't know the why. I've heard all the jive. This one's a commie because momma won't tuck him in at night, that one because girls wouldn't welcome him with open arms. I don't know why. The what I do know. Like when I was wearing the uniform, I shot at the guy on the other side of the perimeter because he was the enemy. Hey! We'd better get out of here or I'll start talking politics.

This brief scene distills the thematic line of the film, its contradictions, and its resolution of those contradictions. *Big Jim McLain* wants to have it both ways—to insinuate psychology as a way of stigmatizing the Communist villains and to deny any interest in psychology from Wayne's matter-of-fact perspective. The psychological theorizing about the Communist psychiatrist, who is presumed to be depraved because he's desexualized, is supported by the film as a whole; that is, we are meant to believe it. But at the same time, we are meant to admire and accept Wayne's rejection of all psychology in favor of an unquestioning patriotism. What makes some people susceptible to Communism—a weakness of character, a psychological flaw—is mirrored in Wayne's resistance to Communism, which clearly derives from his inherent masculinity, his normality. Wayne's teasing machismo makes psychological theorizing a woman's game, but it's a game the audience plays, too. So, we are to believe the Communists are sexual misfits and social perverts, and that Wayne's eager heterosexuality is the ideal, but we are also to believe that reflection on these matters is pointless, that analysis is inferior to the principle of action. In the end, the common denominators are

Wayne's iconic character and his assurance that political talk is dangerous. "'We'd better get out of here.'"

The Front

Hollywood's cycle of propaganda films about the dangers of American Communism more or less ended with the McCarthy period, after which anti-Communism became a nonpolitical staple of Cold War entertainment. Russians were villains, and the threat of war was always present, but internal political subversion was seldom a primary topic. For many years the effects of the blacklist kept Hollywood writers and artists out of the industry; some came back only late in the 1960s, and some never came back. Others, even while blacklisted, managed to find work behind the cover of pseudonyms or "fronts" whose names were put in the credits. Well into the 1990s, Hollywood craft unions were still debating how to restore proper credit to blacklisted artists whose work had been disguised and uncredited.

Walter Bernstein was a Hollywood writer and a Communist who was blacklisted for many years. He found work writing for television by using a number of other people as fronts. Bernstein wrote the script for *The Front*, which was released in 1976, nearly thirty years after the first wave of HUAC hearings that initiated the blacklist.

As a political exercise, *The Front* is partly a long-postponed rebalancing of the scales, in which Bernstein and others involved in the film can thumb their noses at HUAC and its allies. But though it is clearly a political film, *The Front* is structured in such a way as to avoid the central political issues it raises. Bernstein writes in his memoirs that the only way he could get studio approval for the film was to write it as a comedy (278).[8] In the film, three blacklisted television writers hire Woody Allen, a part-time bookmaker and cashier in a bar, to front for them. In a gesture of political candor, the three are acknowledged to be committed Communists, but because of the shift of the film's center of attention to Woody Allen, the actual politics of these writers is never examined—it's a convenient move, since to try to follow and justify the party line through the period described by the film might risk losing the sympathetic adherence of the centrist and liberal audience at whom the film's rhetoric is addressed.

What might be called the political economy of *The Front*—that is, the system of production that made a comic treatment the necessary condition for financing and distributing the film—could be seen, as Bernstein himself seems to describe it, as a continuing intrusion from the Right on popular treatments of the blacklist. But other forces seem to contribute to overdetermining the somewhat callow treatment of politics in the film. That the film is in many ways satisfying as an entertainment (through which it exerts whatever political appeal it may exercise) is testimony to the ways in which popular generic conventions swallow up the political, usually reducing political contingency to a we-they morality tale. But even as Bernstein testifies in his memoirs against the controlling effects of the production system in warping his film script, he gives implicit evidence of the contributing effects of a traditional popular front tactic of disguising Stalinist politics in a liberal fleece, since his memoir, while detailing the effects of the blacklist, is mostly silent on his own political activities while he was a Communist. He is entitled to his politics, to his reticence, and to his reasons, but his effacement of the political seems to suit his own ends as much as those of the Hollywood establishment.

The Front tells the story of the blacklist from the point of view of the Left, but without making the politics of the Left much clearer. That this should be so is not necessarily a cause for lament, but it should remind us what happens when the popular meets the political. The solution is not to wish, as cultural critics sometimes seem implicitly to do, that the popular would become more explicitly political. Popular art is not merely a form of public address by other means.

Fellow Traveller

Fellow Traveller (1990) is a U.S.–U.K. made-for-television movie produced by the BBC in cooperation with HBO. Ron Silver plays Asa Kaufman, a Hollywood scriptwriter who has fled to England to avoid the blacklist and its choice between naming names and losing his job. While in England, he writes scripts for the TV series *The Adventures of Robin Hood,* remembers his earlier years, and tries to work through his conflicts over guilt and betrayal in political and family life.

Asa Kaufman is caught between Marx and Freud, a dilemma made explicit in the plot of the film. At one point, shown in a series of flashbacks, Asa tells a party psychotherapist (Daniel Travanti) that the studios and HUAC suspect him of trying to insert Red propaganda into his scripts while his comrades, reading his scripts on the party literary committee, accuse him of Freudian mystification.

Asa's boyhood friend Cliff becomes a movie star for whom Asa writes heroic scripts. At the beginning of the film, after Asa has left the United States just one step ahead of a subpoena from HUAC, Cliff commits suicide in his swimming pool. Asa finally realizes that the psychotherapist has been betraying his party clients, encouraging them to testify before the Committee, and passing along tapes of their therapy sessions to the investigators. When confronted by Asa at a political meeting in London, the therapist argues that he acted to advance the cause of world socialism, since the sacrifice of a few Hollywood Reds undermined the legitimacy of the U.S. system in world opinion, making it seem no better than the Stalinist system of purges and show trials.

The film ends with Asa reunited with his wife and children, but still in exile in England. The family is the only refuge in a world where politics is a labyrinth of betrayals and bad dreams, lost somewhere in its impossible choice between the determinism of vulgar Marxism and the mysteries of the Freudian psyche.

The rhetoric of film style is used both to provide some distance and to convey the challenge that the blacklist years posed to the imagination. The "present" of the film is Asa's time in London, living in a rooming house; writing *The Ad-*

ventures of Robin Hood; learning of Cliff's suicide; getting involved with Cliff's former lover Sarah; coming to realize the role of the psychotherapist and confronting him; and finally reassembling his family. The gloomy, cold, dark settings of England are contrasted with flashbacks to sunny Hollywood and to sessions, also in Hollywood, with the psychotherapist, which are in turn interrupted by dream sequences in which Asa observes a primal scene between his mother and an FBI agent.

The filmmakers manage to evoke the imaginative world of the time, so that instead of seeming didactic or "symbolic"—a rhetorical code by which the filmmaker insinuates an authorized filmic "meaning"—the film's Marxism and Freudianism appear to be part of the characters' ways of making sense of their world. For example, Asa and Cliff, who have been lifelong friends, are both portrayed as energetically heterosexual, and yet there is a strong and unresolved suggestion of homoerotic attachment between them. When Asa leaves Hollywood for England, he kisses his wife perfunctorily, but Cliff—who has just betrayed him to HUAC—clings to him in a desperate embrace. After Cliff's suicide, Asa and Cliff's former lover Sarah attempt to make love, but Asa, looking into Sarah's eyes, remembers a recurring scene of tumbling on a sunny beach with Cliff and becomes impotent. Throughout the film, Asa sucks hungrily on one cigarette after another; in this context of heightened symbolic signification, the cigarette smoking seems to echo Cliff's suicidal moment of putting a revolver into his mouth.

The stylization of the English scenes suggests Asa's sense of the oddness of the place, as do the casting and acting styles of the English supporting players—his landlady, various policemen, the television workers—who are presented as 1950s comic stereotypes. As in all of these films about the blacklist, stylization is part of the political interpretation, suggesting a world that is beyond our capacity to understand in everyday terms. This makes for compelling drama, and for a satisfying sense of the complexity and weirdness of the anti-Communist purges of the early Cold War. The thriller climax, in which Daniel Travanti appears as a double-double agent, who has betrayed his clients to the FBI and HUAC in order to advance the cause of Stalinism, conveys the sense that there is simply no safe, central place to stand in the political world of the time. Asa's return to a united (but exiled) family hence stands as a repudiation of the public world, and as a conventional melodramatic turn, but one achieved by a complex imagining of the interplay of Marxist and Freudian perspectives and of the competing conventions of the public, private, and popular. The film's psychologizing of the political and its expressionistic style make a comparison with *The Cabinet of Caligari* (1919) and with Siegfried Kracauer's interpretation seem inevitable. Kracauer argued that the film, in which Dr. Caligari, a seeming mass murderer, turns out instead to be a psychiatrist treating the deluded hero from whose point of view the story has been told, undermined the possibility of dissent from authority and ushered in a cycle of films that reconciled the German audience to fascism by suggesting that all politics came down to a choice between chaos and tyranny.[9]

The parallel with *Fellow Traveller* is not precise, but it is perhaps suggestive. Confused by the interaction of political and psychological forces, Asa Kaufman discovers that the political world leads to betrayal and death; loyalty to family provides a refuge. In contemplating the political world, popular art seems to discover political motivations in the private and to be able to resolve its narrative convincingly only by a retreat from the public to the private. To suggest this is not necessarily to complain about *Fellow Traveller* in particular or (even if this probably too sweeping generalization is accurate) about popular art in general. When films on political themes do celebrate the public over the private, or when they seem to recommend collective action, at least in the films about domestic Communism early in the Cold War, whether from the Left or Right, it is hard for them, whatever their merits, not to seem preachy and didactic.

Guilty By Suspicion

Guilty By Suspicion (1991) was written and directed by Irwin Winkler, whose early credits as a producer included Sylvester Stallone's *Rocky* (1976) and Martin Scorsese's *Raging Bull* (1980). In the film, a Hollywood director, David Merrill (Robert DeNiro) is named in a HUAC hearing as a Communist and finds himself blacklisted. The film traces Merrill's descent into the blacklist and his attempt to decide whether to cooperate with the committee to get himself off the blacklist. The film makes it clear that Merrill, though briefly a member of the Communist Party, is basically a nonpolitical liberal, rejected even by the party because he was too ornery and independent, in the spirit of the lone wolf individualistic hero described by Robert Ray in *A Certain Tendency of the Hollywood Cinema*.

Guilty By Suspicion, though it follows a realistic film style, nevertheless depicts HUAC as a grotesque gang of bullies who abuse witnesses and gavel down all opposition. The film's agenda is openly didactic, and yet, paradoxically, nonpolitical. HUAC is described as looking for power and publicity, rather than setting any sort of political goal. David Merrill has no political connections and no political convictions that go beyond high-school civics. As in *Big Jim McLain, The Front,* and *Fellow Traveller,* the hero of *Guilty By Suspicion* resolves his problems by dint of personal courage and good old American character.[10]

Witch Hunt

Witch Hunt (1994) is a made-for-cable feature film, produced by HBO, that re-creates the McCarthy period in Hollywood by displacing it into a world of science fiction, special effects, and comic noir. This is a re-imagined Hollywood of 1953, where licensed and amateur magicians are transforming technology and culture. Magic has introduced the wonders of TV dinners and modernist home design, but a few practitioners may be using magic for criminal ends. Hollywood private investigator H. Phillip Lovecraft (Dennis Hopper) is hired by movie star Kim Hudson (Penelope Ann Miller) to investigate first her husband, producer N. J. Gottlieb, and then her husband's murder-by-magic. In a converging plotline,

Senator Larson Crockett, chairman of the Senate Subcommittee on Un-Natural Activities, is in town looking for witches to burn at a public rally. The senator, in a subplot borrowed from *The Godfather, Part II,* is implicated in the murder of Gottlieb and fails in his attempt to burn Lovecraft's partner, licensed witch Hypolita Kropotkin, at the stake.[11] In a newsreel that opens the film, Ronald Reagan is shown being sworn in as a friendly witness at a hearing of the Subcommittee on Un-Natural Activities.

Witch Hunt was directed by Paul Schrader, who went on to film school after majoring in philosophy and theology at Calvin College. As a young film critic, Schrader wrote a well received book, *Transcendental Style in Film: Ozu, Bresson, Dreyer,* and then went on to work as a screenwriter—*Obsession* (1976); *Taxi Driver* (1976); *Raging Bull* (1980); *Mosquito Coast* (1986); and *The Last Temptation of Christ* (1988). Schrader directed *Cat People* (1982). He was screenwriter and director of *Blue Collar* (1978) and *Mishima* (1985). *Witch Hunt*'s considerable success owes much to its music score, written by Angelo Badalamenti, who also wrote the music for David Lynch's *Blue Velvet;* its production design by Curtis A. Schnell, who was set designer for *Cat People* and *Blade Runner;* and its script, by Joseph Dougherty, who had been a producer, writer, and director for the TV series *thirtysomething.*

Witch Hunt is saturated with references to other movies and to the politics of America in the 1950s. The film's confident light-heartedness and the way it seamlessly weaves into its own fantastic plot the language of 1950s anti-Communism allow it a direct contempt for the witch-hunters that, instead of assuming a burden of accuracy in its depiction, challenges the audience to discern what is the difference, if any, between the everyday craziness of its hypothetical world where a senator is tracking down witches for a public burning and the actual Hollywood of the early Cold War where ambitious politicians hunted down Hollywood subversives to get their names in the paper.[12]

The Popular and the Public

Our culture's notions of the public, the popular, and the private are in some ways historically contingent, derived from situated practices and material circumstances. They are also, at least as they seem to present themselves to us, idealized abstractions, which may suggest that they are transcendent ideals. Particular instances of the public, the popular, and the private may seem to appeal to or operate under the authorization of a (possibly counterfactual) ideal. There is probably no way of settling, by argument or observation, the proper balance between circumstantial and ideal, and in any case, the rhetorical critic is after a different sort of game. Our methods cannot settle the larger philosophical issue, but they can examine the ways in which particular texts appeal to us to understand these issues in the context of a grounded narrative. These film texts refuse to accept fully a separation among public, private, and popular, and in doing so they function not only as rhetorical appeals but also as a sort of implicit rhetorical theorizing about American society.[13]

Big Jim McLain appears to support a narrative of orthodoxy, which could come from either the Left or the Right, but in the conditions of 1952 in the United States, the narrative of orthodoxy comes from the Right. Under this conservative orthodoxy, the personal must be subordinate to the values of the political, but the politically loyal are granted a wide range of personal freedom—that is, the unquestioningly loyal person may feel and act as if he or she has complete freedom. It is peculiar that in none of these films about American Communism do we have a frank depiction of life inside the party, of its political ambitions, its range of action, or the mechanisms by which it exerted its own orthodoxy. *Big Jim McLain* is content to reduce Communism to a group of deviant, robotic conspirators at war with America. The other films depict Communists as liberals who operate under pretty much the same code of honor that John Wayne invokes in *Big Jim McLain*—a code that owes as much to Hollywood genres as to political ideals of the Left or the Right.

In a peculiar way, the films agree, too, in their depiction of anti-Communism, which in all of these films is apart from politics.

Similarly, each of the films bids for a definition of our collective memory of the blacklist. It is a memory that asserts the continuity of the American character and the appeal of nostalgia, while at the same time it disavows history, contingency, choice, and collective political action.

Most of the anti-HUAC films discussed in this essay came after the end of the Cold War, when Communism (and therefore, perhaps, anti-Communism) could be regarded as safely dead. Beginning with *The Front,* the anti-HUAC films do take a sort of revenge on the blacklisters, but only by turning them into villains and buffoons. They opt out of the political debates that were part of the early days of the Cold War. In no sense are these films defending leftist visions, except perhaps in sketching faintly the appeal of progressive social values to the individualistic idealists who in this vision became the victims of the blacklist. Taking the films one at a time or as a group, a contemporary critic might be concerned that every one of these films is in flight from politics. Is this a cautious avoidance of a subject still too dangerous to bring into the political arena? Is it a sort of tact that refuses to turn American movies into mere political didacticism? Or is it, perhaps, a form of resistance—a politics that attacks the excesses of anti-Communism by refusing to take it too seriously? It seems clear that the anti-HUAC films present themselves as enacting a code of resistance to political excess. In doing so, they may be reinforcing a popular American story of resisting political excess by resisting politics altogether. The politics of this popular history of American anti-Communism is a denial of the legitimacy of politics, and at the same time, a reassurance that the American spirit always redeems the balance of the society in the end.

Notes

1. For an account of the art and politics of *Singin' in the Rain* and the campaign against Gene Kelly, see Wollen, *Singin' in the Rain.* On the blacklisting of

Kelly's wife, Betsy Blair, see McGilligan, "Betsy Blair Reisz," *Tender Comrades*. On the rhetoric of personal memoirs and biographies of the blacklist, see Benson, "Looking for the Public in the Private."

2. See, for example, Koppes and Black in *Hollywood Goes to War*. In a recent article, Worland has shown how the Office of War Information took an interest even in war-era horror films; see his "OWI Meets the Monsters: Hollywood Horror Films and War Propaganda, 1942 to 1945."

3. After his exile from the United States, Charles Chaplin made a film that includes a critique of HUAC and the McCarthy period. *A King in New York* (1957) was not shown in the United States until 1973; it is generally regarded by critics as the least successful of all Chaplin's work. In *The Way We Were* (1973), the romance of Barbra Streisand and Robert Redford is damaged by her politics, which include opposition to HUAC. An extended sequence on the blacklist was apparently cut from the film before its release. Walter Bernstein wrote the script for *The House on Carroll Street* (1988), which indirectly invokes the menace of the blacklist period as the corrupt staff of a congressional committee conspire to infiltrate former Nazis in the United States. A list of other films warning of the dangers of anticommunist enthusiasms would include *The Boy with Green Hair* (1948); *We Were Strangers* (1949); *Dr. Strangelove* (1964); *Seven Days in May* (1964); *Daniel* (1983). Stanley Kubrick's *Dr. Strangelove* was a U.K. release. Arthur Miller's play, *The Crucible*, was filmed in France in 1957. Tim Robbins's *Cradle Will Rock* (1999) depicts the harassment of the Federal Theatre Project by the Dies Committee, the precursor of HUAC. See also Neve, "Fellow Traveller."

4. Other films about American Communism in the early blacklist period include *The Red Menace* (1949); *Conspirator* (1949); *I Married a Communist* (1950); *I Was a Communist for the FBI* (1951); *My Son John* (1952); *Red Planet Mars* (1952); *Pickup on South Street* (1953); *Security Risk* (1954); *Trial* (1955); *The Fearmakers* (1958).

5. For more about Ray's thesis, see *A Certain Tendency of the Hollywood Cinema, 1930–1980*. For further discussion of Ray's thesis, see Benson and Anderson, "The Ultimate Technology"; and Benson, "Respecting the Reader."

6. Navasky describes "a general national failure to distinguish between the Communist as theoretical Marxist and the Communist as espionage agent" (112).

7. On the relation of gender and politics in early Cold War America, see Corber.

8. Bernstein reports that Columbia Pictures "has also insisted on a star and suggested Robert Redford or Warren Beatty but has agreed to our choice of Woody [Allen]."

9. For an analysis of film culture, politics, psychology, and history in Italian film, see Angela Dalle Vacche, *The Body in the Mirror*.

10. For a more extended analysis of the rhetoric of *Guilty By Suspicion*, see Benson, "Thinking through Film: Hollywood Remembers the Blacklist."

11. Prince Peter Alekseyevich Kropotkin (1842–1921) was a Russian anarchist, philosopher, and revolutionary. Hippolyta was a queen of the Amazons and wife

to the mythical Athenian king Theseus. H. Phillips Lovecraft (1890–1937) was an American writer of Gothic terror tales, said to have influenced the work of Robert A. Bloch, author of *Psycho* (1959), on which Alfred Hitchcock's film *Psycho* (1960) was based. These and other borrowed names, like the filmic allusions, do not appear to be required to read the narrative or the politics of *Witch Hunt,* but they do create a web of associations and in-jokes that help draw the viewer into the spirit of self-creation that inhabits the film.

12. On Joseph McCarthy's depiction of himself as a figure of fantasy, see Darsey.

13. On implicit rhetorical theory, see Benson, "Implicit Communication Theory in Campaign Coverage."

Works Cited

Aristotle. *On Rhetoric: A Theory of Civic Discourse.* Trans. George A. Kennedy. New York: Oxford UP, 1991.

Benson, Thomas W. "Implicit Communication Theory in Campaign Coverage." *Television Coverage of the 1980 Presidential Campaign.* Ed. William J. Adams. Norwood: Ablex, 1983. 103–16.

———. "Looking for the Public in the Private." *Rhetoric and Public Affairs* 1 (1998): 117–29.

———. "Respecting the Reader." *Quarterly Journal of Speech* 72 (1986): 197–204.

———. "Thinking through Film: Hollywood Remembers the Blacklist." *Rhetoric and Community.* Ed. J. Michael Hogan. Columbia: U of South Carolina P, 1998. 217–55.

Benson, Thomas W., and Carolyn Anderson. "The Ultimate Technology: Frederick Wiseman's *Missile.*" *Communication and the Culture of Technology.* Ed. Martin J. Medhurst, Alberto Gonzalez, and Tarla Rai Peterson. Pullman: Washington State UP, 1990. 257–83.

Bernstein, Walter. *Inside Out.* New York: Knopf, 1996.

"Big Jim McLain." *Newsweek* 3 Nov. 1952: 104.

"Big Jim McLain." *Time* 29 Sept. 1952: 93.

"Big Jim McLain." *Variety* 27 Aug. 1952: 6.

Biskind, Peter. *Seeing Is Believing.* New York: Pantheon, 1983.

Bucklin, Louis L. "*Big Jim McLain.*" *National Parent-Teacher* Nov. 1952: 37.

Corber, Robert J. *In the Name of National Security: Hitchcock, Homophobia, and the Political Construction of Gender in Post War America.* Durham: Duke UP, 1993.

Crowther, Bosley. "The Screen in Review." *New York Times* 18 Sept. 1952: 35.

Darsey, James. "Joe McCarthy's Fantastic Moment." *Communication Monographs* 62 (1995): 65–86.

Doherty, Thomas. "Hollywood Agit-Prop: The Anti-Communist Cycle, 1948–1954." *Journal of Film and Video* 40.4 (1988): 16.

Koppes, Clayton B., and Gregory D. Black. *Hollywood Goes to War: How Politics, Profits, and Propaganda Shaped World War II Movies.* New York: Free Press, 1987.

Kracauer, Siegfried. *From Caligari to Hitler.* Princeton: Princeton UP, 1947.

McGilligan, Patrick. "Betsy Blair Reisz." *Tender Comrades: A Backstory of the Hollywood Blacklist.* Ed. Patrick McGilligan and Paul Buhle. New York: St. Martin's, 1997. 540–55.

Navasky, Victor S. *Naming Names.* New York: Viking, 1980.

Neve, Brian. "Fellow Traveller." *Sight and Sound* 59.2 (1990): 117–19.

Ray, Robert B. *A Certain Tendency of the Hollywood Cinema, 1930–1980.* Princeton: Princeton UP, 1985.

Vacche, Angela Dalle. *The Body in the Mirror.* Princeton: Princeton UP, 1992.

Vanderwood, Paul J. "An American Cold Warrior: *Viva Zapata!*" *American History/American Film.* Ed. John E. O'Connor and Martin A. Jackson. Expanded ed. New York: Continuum, 1988.

Whitebait, William. "The Movies." *New Statesman and Nation* 1 Nov. 1952: 509.

Wills, Garry. *John Wayne's America.* New York: Simon, 1997.

Wollen, Peter. *Singin' in the Rain.* London: British Film Institute, 1992.

Worland, Rick. "OWI Meets the Monsters: Hollywood Horror Films and War Propaganda, 1942 to 1945." *Cinema Journal* 37.1 (1997): 47–65.

Zarefsky, David. *Lincoln, Douglas, and Slavery: In the Crucible of Public Debate.* Chicago: U of Chicago P, 1990.

8

Copycat, Serial Murder, and the (De)Terministic Screen Narrative

Philip L. Simpson

THE 1995 JON AMIEL FILM *COPYCAT* DEPICTS ITS RECLUSIVE PROTAGONIST, Dr. Helen Hudson, under siege from a serial killer who invades her home in a number of ways, at first through a computer virus. The techno-virus that violates the sanctity of Hudson's apartment serves as apt metaphor for the contagion of serial murder, at least as it has proliferated in American media instruments, including genre cinema. Like a replicating virus, the serial killer film, a small but financially lucrative subgenre of thriller and horror cinema, is endlessly derivative of its predecessors. Also, the subgenre tends to depict its serial killers as suffering from an infection or disease of the soul, sometimes caused by the "viruses" of demonic influence, bad parenting,[1] and/or violent media. While the virus metaphor is not completely inappropriate in this context, the subgenre falters when it eschews complex sociopolitical criticism and instead blames one or perhaps two "viral" agents for the perpetuation of violence. *Copycat,* with its titular serial killer depicted as the victim of media corruption and bad parenting, is a prime example of one of these overly simplified narratives of serial murder. For a film such as this to venture further into the complex intellectual territory of causation and motive would distract from the narrative's primary purpose, which is to thrill (or titillate) an audience at once desensitized and hyperconscious of the fictional and factual images of spectacular criminal violence transmitted daily through other media venues. This cultural obsession with real and imagined murder infiltrates the individual psyche like a particularly hardy strain of virus—the very point that *Copycat* argues from a particularly reactionary position.

Regardless of its intellectual shortcomings, *Copycat,* by presenting a fictional serial killer who imitates real-life serial killers, is nevertheless a valuable text for illustrating that serial murder as a narrative subject consistently blurs the categories of fact and fiction and elides the differences between historic serial killers and fictional ones. The news reports of serial murder frequently adopt the conventions of horror fiction,[2] while television and theatrical films on the subject routinely employ the conventions of documentary reporting. Most fictional serial killers are blatantly or subtly based on real-life precedents: Jack the Ripper, Ed Gein, Ted Bundy, Henry Lee Lucas. These killers initiate their murderous agendas within the context of a virtually real culture that, with its excesses of "reality TV" and public discourse that labels the Jeffrey Dahmer case a "real-life *Silence of the Lambs*," collapses together, as Robert Conrath suggests, "traditional epistemological categories of fact and fiction, veracity, and verisimilitude" (149). Annalee Newitz likewise argues that "Because fictional representations of serial killers are often based on biographies of actual killers, one might say the serial killer narrative spans both fictional and non-fictional genres" (39). These critics suggest that there is no easy distinction to be drawn between the fact and the fiction of serial murder as it is culturally defined. The serial killer has become a media obsession precisely because a series of murders translates so well into the representational sine waves of mimetic fictional narrative. Note, for example, how the Wisconsin murders of Ed Gein during the 1950s found fictional expression during the 1960s (Alfred Hitchcock's film *Psycho,* based on Robert Bloch's novel *Psycho*), 1970s (Tobe Hooper's film *The Texas Chainsaw Massacre*), and 1980s (Thomas Harris's novel *The Silence of the Lambs*).[3] Once a series of murders (like Gein's) has been "written" about and disseminated into cultural consciousness, another serial killer will provide source material for the next generation of fiction. In other words, a "rhetoric" of serial killing, wherein real killers and their inevitable chroniclers communicate with a voyeuristic audience, has been developed.

As symbol makers, human beings (including serial killers) reconstruct reality into the narratives through which they make sense of the world. But how does a given storyteller decide what is important to tell? According to Kenneth Burke, a narrative's final form depends on the storyteller's terministic screen—Burke's term for the perceptual filter through which an individual receives and interprets external events.

As symbol makers dependent on idiosyncratic terministic screens, we as human beings necessarily interpret the flux of events as fictions that include some possibilities of meaning and action and exclude others. Burke argues it this way: "Even if any given terminology is a *reflection* of reality, by its very nature as a terminology it must be a *selection* of reality; and to this extent it must function also as a *deflection* of reality" (45). We also tend to conceive of our individual biological trajectories through existence as "stories." We divide our lives into distinct stages and thus create more or less orderly but highly selective and ideologically colored "autobiographies" out of the chaos of countless possibilities. We self-dramatize our miseries and triumphs, endlessly cast ourselves as the protagonists in important events that may or may not have much to do with us, and do our best to sanctify our own versions of events as the Truth. Occasionally, given an undefinable mix of chance, zeitgeist, self-promotion, and proper publicity, our private actions, or "stories," will appeal to the larger society's vested interest in producing commercially appealing stories for mass consumption. Out of such raw stuff, factually based human drama can be created in many different narrative structures and genres. These diverse stories can encode any number of ideological messages that, as Burke would say, deflect attention from other possible selections of reality. In particular, private events that involve sensational murders, such as the random serial killings of strangers, provide endless grist for the public storytelling mills of mass culture, much to the consternation of critics who lament our increasingly desensitized culture of spectacle. But again, in a culture driven by capitalistic market forces, how does the storyteller decide what is important or profitable to tell?

In the case of the serial murder film, the storyteller is inevitably drawn again and again to the symbolic connection between narrative craft and violence. The connection is made explicit in the term "serial murder" itself. Mark Seltzer, noticing the conceptual link between serial murder and literary craft, claims that most of the sociological definitions of the phenomenon equate murder-as-adventure serial killing with "an addiction to representations" and hence "a pathological addiction to representation as the cause of violence" (94). Perhaps, then, the cinematic creator of a serial murder narrative recognizes something of his/her own addiction to aesthetics in the real-life criminal phenomenon and re-creates that obsession in the fictional protagonist's baroque crimes. Given the complex but gripping identification strategies by which narrative-based cinema thrives, it is not surprising that, reciprocally, some members of the film-consuming audience may forge an at-least subconsciously sympathetic link with the artist-murderer's aesthetic practices. It stands to reason, then, that an actual serial murderer, existing within a culture that consumes and thus to some extent implicitly condones sensational murders as acceptable subjects for narrative treatments, may pose as a particularly dark form of the socially shunned "starving artist."[4] All of these diverse terministic screens find convergence, satisfaction, and pleasure in the spectacular narratives of serial murder.

It is tempting, at this point, to follow the lead of cultural critics who accuse the popular media of creating an imagistic environment in which media consumers inclined toward violence can find precedent, however fictional, for their worst imaginings, and thus some tacit justification or even acceptance for their deeds. Additionally, some cultural critics fear that these narratives are how-to primers for creative murder techniques and avoidance of capture. For example, in a 1984 documentary entitled *Murder: No Apparent Motive,* convicted killer Edmund Kemper claims to have learned most of his evasive techniques from watching television "cop shows" during the 1960s and 1970s. Another infamous serial murderer, Ted Bundy, told a number of interviewers, most famously the politically conservative family-advocate James Dobson, of his early obsessions with lurid detective magazines and bloody pornography. Such "confessions" give ammunition to those who fear that the media plays a significant role both in inciting potential criminals to act and in training them. Typical is a comment by New York City police detective Ray Pierce: "Every other day, when you turn on the television, there's a story on it about serial murder. . . . You can be sure the killers are watching, too, and that they're adjusting their behavior accordingly" (qtd. in Davis 21). Similarly, reacting to the presentation of night-vision goggles as an effective aid in the stalking of victims in the 1991 film *The Silence of the Lambs,* psychiatrist Park Dietz says, "Hollywood has done much to pave the way for serial killers" (qtd. in Davids 150).

On a more academic level, Deborah Cameron, exploring the possible links between pornography and sexually motivated murder, argues that serial killers, in a nonverbal and roughly conceived manner, are extremely conscious of and motivated by cultural narrative conventions of violence, since they choose an inherently literary structure (the series) for striking out against real or imagined personal wrongs (7). In other words, according to these diverse critics of the sensational media, violent images often provoke and/or guide the violent actions of copycats. These copycats, who presumably would have lived essentially blameless lives were it not for the corruptive influence of external forces, are mimetically inspired to ever-more flamboyant acts of brutality and murder by the "viral" contagions of dehumanizing pornography and fictional portrayals of mayhem.

According to this theory, the serial killer who copycats the hegemonic cultural narratives of sensational murder available to him consciously or unconsciously selects and frames his most personally significant social interaction in terms of the narrative conventions of pornography and/or horror melodrama, as do the inevitable secondary chroniclers of his murders. These chroniclers are the unindicted coconspirators in the media's perpetuation of the murder cycle. Within serial murder's complex and cyclic transformation from fact to fiction back to fact, the demarcation between the facts of a given case and the "true crime" and fictional narratives that derive from the events blurs. We receive the media images of a Jeffrey Dahmer as if he were a character in a horror film because the framers of his story have made him into one. Thus, the cycle of historical-murder-cum-fiction narrative continues, and the self-referentiality that such a cycle represents best suits that particular strain of postmodernism that celebrates the hollowly parodic even as it relocates modernism's lost God within the simulacratic constructs of humankind. The murdering copycat of fact and fiction, then, stands as a particularly apt symbol of the postmodern age's supposed aesthetic bankruptcy and the collapse of all historical periods into one imagistic stew.

There is, however, a significant problem with the theoretical underpinnings of the copycat theory, which in turn limits the theory's usefulness as an explanation of social deviancy. The copycat theory's selection-and-deflection strategies, in Burke's terminology, are flawed at best and disingenuous at worst. For example, Joseph Grixti, on the basis of his exhaustive survey of popular claims about the alleged pernicious effect of violent media images and narratives upon the masses, concludes that those who promote the copycat theory by railing against the media are typically proceeding on rather simplistic and largely discredited behaviorist and neobehaviorist theories. In effect, such theories claim that human psychology—an elaborate web of terministic screens—is determined almost exclusively by environmental influences. As a result of this problematic behaviorist foundation, Grixti concludes that the copycat theory is too limited to be of much intellectual use. Such limitation complicates our reading of those cinematic texts that rely upon the copycat theory to provide convincing character motivation. Nevertheless, since many filmmakers and media critics uncritically accept and act upon the theory's postulates as convincing explanations for human behavior, it is important to explore further why the copycat theory persists.

Perhaps the theory persists in America in particular because of the widespread cultural bias toward quantification, which complements behaviorist science. According to its critics, classical behaviorism and its intellectual descendants appropriate the methodology and rhetoric of the physical sciences and thus consider only those mechanistic or conditioned aspects of human psychology that can be measured, tested, or quantified. Intangibles such as motivation and context are disregarded; or, as Burke would have it, behaviorism as rhetoric deflects attention away from the unquantifiable. Ideologically, behaviorism implies that personal responsibility or free will is an illusion, in spite of a surface rhetorical emphasis on the individual. In such a deterministic conceptual framework, what Grixti calls a kind of "magical thinking" dominates, wherein "The explanatory role once performed by concepts and abstractions like 'chance,' 'fate,' 'destiny,' 'the divine will,' 'heavenly bodies,' and 'the stars' has been passed on to a suitably mathematized and 'scientifically' perceived conditioning environment" (122). For behaviorists, then, the process of social learning means that the individual must be conditioned by an objective norm, which itself is inevitably determined by the social status quo. The values or morality of the norm itself are beyond criticism and taken for granted. Individual deviancy becomes the focus of investigation and "correction," not the norm itself. Reconditioning strategies tend to focus not on the larger status quo but on a more local and "controllable" social force, which of course leaves intact the cultural values that constitute the norm itself. Grixti claims that those who link deviancy to one primary agent or precipitating cause and deflect attention away from the larger social context in which deviant and agent coexist are, in actuality, "conservative guardians and reinforcers of the very structures and interactive processes which they claim to observe and explain dispassionately" (135). Thus, a given factual or fictional narrative in which a copycat's problems are blamed exclusively on one or two precipitating and immediate agents is constructed from a reactionary terministic screen.

In terms of the debate over media portrayals of violence, then, the many critics from both the left and right sides of the political spectrum who so earnestly accuse the media of creating the conditions for social deviancy or copycatting are thinking locally and not globally and tend to be champions (in some cases, *unwitting* champions) of the status quo. The keenest irony here is that the media instruments themselves, driven by profit and ratings in the capitalistic culture of the United States, usually promulgate, although timidly because of the need for survival in a ruthless marketplace, the same values that critics accuse them of defaming. The conservative tendencies of the large media companies lead to many delicious paradoxes, such as extremely violent movies blaming extremely violent media for creating criminals *(Natural Born Killers, Copycat)*. The violent and at-times subversive content of the media narratives blinds the offended critics to the fact that, time after time, the narratives also uphold—even venerate—status-quo American values and conventions. The narratives' tendency to champion the status quo is often forgotten in light of the transgressive or radical nature of the textual incidents of explicit and graphic violence and violations of sexual taboo. Of course, it can then be argued that the text's inherent radicalism undermines its own conservatism—but the status quo is most definitely invoked in order to be undermined in the first place. In any event, regardless of one's politics, the copycat theory appeals because it reduces complexity to simplicity.

However, while it is important not to blame violent movies for creating violent people, a simplification often made by politicians campaigning for office via the sound bite, it is equally important to note that identification strategies inherent in narrative cinema do implicate the viewer by proxy in the happenings *on-screen*. If those happenings include murder, it is not surprising that some audience members may feel an immediate visceral attraction to the fictional murderers and then a retrospective intellectual self-repulsion toward this attraction. The resulting audience unease may indeed compel unsettled viewers to denounce a violent film as a contributor to violence in America, since it is easier to denounce a film than to address real issues of social injustice, poverty, racism, sexism, et cetera. Viewer unease is further provoked because, deliberately or incidentally, the maker of violent films is giving voice to the deepest reactionary fears of his/her audience, a cinematic trend firmly established during the decades of the 1980s and 1990s by films such as *Copycat*.

Peter Foley and Daryll Lee Cullum are the central serial killers in *Copycat*. The film they inhabit eschews historical and political complexity in favor of simplicity. For example, Foley is brainwashed by the media and Cullum is a religious fanatic. As "copycats" of inherited narratives that catch in their private terministic screens, Foley and Cullum are next-generation copies of other, more renowned killers. For example, Foley renames himself Peter Kurten after an infamous German serial killer. The film itself takes the forms and elements of other recognizable genre films, melts them down and re-coalesces them into a derivative, hybrid narrative in which the serial killer subgenre's creative bankruptcy is suddenly touted as an ironic strength. As Jonathan Romany puts it, *in his praise of the film,* "everything [in the movie] seems to have been assembled piece by piece from a genre kit" (35). The film doesn't content itself with plundering the storylines of its cinematic predecessors, however. It also recycles the specific MOs and "signatures" of notorious real-life serial murderers into its fictional narrative. History matters only insofar that it provides a template or inherited narrative for a copy-cat to slavishly follow. *Copycat* as a film superbly illustrates the catching and sifting process of the terministic screen. The title of the film alone tells the viewer to expect endless recycling, or viruslike replicating, of earlier precedents.

Copycat, being a film first, delights in recycling earlier noteworthy films within the same serial killer subgenre or other related genres. The film's opening se-quence, wherein Dr. Helen Hudson is captured, tormented, and nearly killed by one of the breed of psychopaths she has until now studied only at a safe distance, imitates the famous opening of Alfred Hitchcock's 1959 psychological thriller *Vertigo.* In the latter film, Detective Scottie Ferguson, taking part in a San Fran-cisco rooftop chase after a criminal, slides down one angled roof and barely catches himself from falling off. Hanging by his hands from the edge of the building's roof, he watches helplessly as a fellow policeman, attempting to save Scottie, loses his footing and falls to his death. The scene then fades to black, and the viewer never knows exactly how Scottie extricated himself from this precarious situa-tion—only that he somehow did, but at a cost. Scottie now suffers from a profes-sionally and personally paralyzing fear of heights, which he must attempt to overcome throughout the rest of the narrative. Similarly, *Copycat's* Dr. Hudson, as a professional pursuer of criminals (though a more academic one than Scot-tie), finds the tables alarmingly turned upon herself following a college lecture on serial murder attended by, unbeknownst to her initially, both a practicing serial killer and a serial killer to-be. (What are the odds?) The practicing serial killer, Daryll Lee Cullum, has stalked and set up Hudson in spite of her scrupulous use of police protection. When Hudson enters a bathroom stall in what she believes to be a safely guarded women's room after the lecture, Cullum, who occupies an adjacent stall, loops a cable over her throat and hangs her from an overhead pipe. As she dangles from the ceiling, she watches helplessly as Cullum kills her police escort and then advances on her. At this point, she is in as much danger of im-minent death as a similarly hanging Scottie Ferguson. Outside the bathroom, another police officer runs down the hallway, presumably in response to the scuffle, but as in *Vertigo,* the scene ends without the viewer ever knowing pre-cisely how Hudson's miraculous return from the brink of death is accomplished.

Nor do the similarities between the two films end there. As does Scottie Ferguson, Helen Hudson appears psychologically crippled in the aftermath of the near-death experience.[5] Already inclined toward paranoia of her surround-ings (as evidenced in the opening scene by her desire for police escort and her laying-down of strips of toilet paper on the seat to prevent contact with other people's germs), she becomes a full-blown agoraphobic after Cullum's assault. She refuses to leave her safely controlled, steel-shuttered apartment for thirteen months following, communicating with the outside world only by telephone and computer and medicating herself with generous doses of alcohol and pills. When-ever she does have to open her apartment door, whether to retrieve a newspaper or escape a nocturnal intruder at a later point in the narrative, her slightest venture into the hallway outside causes a full-scale panic attack, represented on-screen by horizontally distorted point-of-view shots of the hallway that strongly resemble Hitchcock's famous vertiginous point-of-view shots of the abysses and stairwells in *Vertigo*. Finally, just like Scottie, who hopes to resolve his fear of heights by scaling the stairs to the top of a mission bell tower, Hudson conquers her agoraphobia by mounting a stairwell to the top of a tall building, where she escapes into the night air from the second pursuing serial killer, Peter Kurten, who has slavishly reenacted her primal trauma (the hanging by Cullum) for her.

In addition to *Vertigo*, any number of films from other genres have been mined for plot elements of *Copycat*. Sometimes these borrowings are of major importance. At other times, they seem merely perfunctory, such as the obligatory scene between Peter and his bedridden, overly solicitous mother, whose interest in Peter seems more than motherly in the fashion of Mrs. Bates's incestuous relationship with serial killer Norman in Hitchcock's 1960 *Psycho*.[6] Peter calls his mother "darling," and she by turns scolds him ("naughty little boy") and arouses him (demanding a romantic bedtime kiss). As is common in the contemporary serial killer subgenre, of which *Psycho* is the prototype, the implication is that the sexualized mother of the serial killer is to blame for arousing and twisting the son's normal sexual desires. Thus, the male killer remains curiously innocent and wounded, while the demonic mother assumes the lion's share of textual blame for the mayhem.[7]

Another serial killer subgenre borrowing, which is also meaningful in relation to the film's political subtext, is from Don Siegel's 1970 film *Dirty Harry*. *Copycat* is set in San Francisco, as is *Dirty Harry*. The professional name of the title character from Siegel's film is Inspector Callahan. The professional name of the lead law-enforcement figure in *Copycat* is Inspector Monahan—surely not a coincidental similarity. The two inspectors are alike in other significant ways. Callahan and Monahan are both mavericks, outside the mainstream of law enforcement—Callahan because of his stubborn refusal to follow proper police procedure in the "liberal" era of Miranda rights, and Monahan because she is a woman in a masculine profession who refuses to follow the spoken and unspoken "male" rules, such as using lethal force indiscriminately. Like Inspector Callahan, Inspector Monahan is breaking in a likeable new partner, Ruben Goetz, who will come to grief as a result of Monahan's tactics. Nor do the similarities between *Dirty Harry* and *Copycat* end with the protagonists. *Dirty Harry*'s villain, who calls himself "Scorpio" to the cops and media, is based on the "Zodiac Killer," who murdered several people in the San Francisco area during the late 1960s and 1970s and boasted of his deeds in coded letters to the newspapers. The Zodiac Killer is briefly mentioned in *Copycat* as one of the cases Inspector Monahan's boss, Lt. Quinn, worked on and failed to resolve. All of these borrowings from one of the more infamously reactionary films in cinema history convey, via the symbolic shorthand of genre conventions, some indication of *Copycat*'s political orientation.

The other major recognizable genre film that *Copycat* has generously helped itself to is Jonathan Demme's 1991 popular and critical hit *The Silence of the Lambs*. As the defining film of the 1990s wave of serial killer cinema, *The Silence of the Lambs* has inspired numerous imitations, all of which seek to replicate its Gothic atmosphere, somber tone, haunted characters, and superficial feminism. In *Copycat,* there is the elegiac, haunting soundtrack music; the horrifying but usually off-screen violence; the distinctive series of murders; the jail-cell interview with the uber-criminal who can provide valuable insights into the psyche of the at-large serial killer; the murderer who disguises himself in the uniform of a murdered cop; the gender-switching murderer; the "surprise" ending that promises yet another cycle of serial murder on the way. Clarice Starling also reappears in *Copycat,* this time as seasoned detective M. J. Monahan, working within the San Francisco police department rather than as an FBI trainee—a teacher of men rather than a student of them. However, the distinction is minimal. Such thinly disguised borrowings from other serial killer subgenre films typify *Copycat's* approach to storytelling.

Copycat's effectiveness relies not only upon an audience's knowledge of genre cinema but also upon their awareness of specific real-life serial killers—those who have received the most media exposure—and their "styles." The infamous murderers central to *Copycat's* narrative are Albert DeSalvo, the self-confessed but never-convicted "Boston Strangler"; Kenneth Bianchi and Angelo Buono, "the Hillside Strangler"; David Berkowitz, "the Son of Sam"; Jeffrey Dahmer; and Ted Bundy. The fictional Dr. Hudson mentions these six real individuals as part of the lecture that opens the film and sets the stage for Hudson's primal trauma at the hands of first Cullum and then Kurten. The order in which she mentions the killers—DeSalvo, Bianchi/Buono, Berkowitz, Dahmer, Bundy—establishes a rigid narrative formula that Kurten adopts as his own for the murder series whose climactic target is Hudson. These killers as catalogued by Dr. Hudson have fixed themselves irrevocably in Kurten's terministic screen.

Kurten first emulates the Boston Strangler crimes by strangling three women and posting their bodies postmortem. The *Copycat* audience sees one of these dead women, strangled by ligature and left on gruesome, spread-eagle display in a bathtub with a large, loopy bow tied around her neck. The San Francisco cops don't recognize the "allusion" to the Boston crimes in this murder and the two others, but Hudson does upon her inspection of the assorted crime scene photos, as Kurten knows she will. Hudson, as the film's primary sign-reader, accurately diagnoses or profiles Kurten by referring to his "major interest in golden oldies."

Kurten reaffirms his interest in golden oldies by next recreating one of the Hillside Strangler's murders. As did Bianchi and Buono, Kurten tortures a bound woman by nearly suffocating her with a plastic bag over the head and then injecting her with window cleaner before murdering her. Kurten then tosses her nude body onto the side of a San Francisco hill, where her violated body is shockingly visible to the city below. Again, consultant Hudson recognizes the signature as an homage to earlier serial murders, in this case the Hillside stranglings, and sardonically appreciates the in-joke: "Very witty, our guy."[8]

Next, shooting a woman in a parked car, Kurten replicates one of the Son of Sam's random shootings in New York City during the 1970s. Hudson, in radio communication with Monahan, who is at the crime scene, quickly recognizes Kurten's intertextual play this time as well, right down to knowing that the 1970s cassette tape (cued to the Partridge Family song "I Think I Love You") that will be found in the car's tape deck has been left there by the killer. (Kurten has chosen his primary audience well.) Hudson also knows that the killer, in his imitation of Berkowitz, will have left a note for investigators in a nearby phone booth, so she successfully directs her surrogate Monahan to the message, ominously addressed to Hudson and quoting from the Police song "Murder by Numbers." With each successful recognition of Kurten's various copycat phases, Hudson draws closer to understanding him, even as he narrows his noose around her throat by sending her notes and emails and sneaking into her apartment at night.

Kurten's next murder, even closer to home, targets Hudson's gay secretary and assistant, Andy, whom she has employed in an effort to keep a reassuringly masculine but nonheterosexual (and hence nonthreatening) presence near her. Andy and his companion, celebrating San Francisco's Festival of Love (a nostalgic revisiting of the vanished 1960s and another textual instance of copycatting) at a gay bar, are stalked and set up by Kurten in a fashion similar to Jeffrey Dahmer's predations upon gay men in Milwaukee. Kurten, following Dahmer's widely publicized strategy, flirts and talks with Andy long enough to drug his drink. Once Andy is drugged and disoriented, Kurten leads Andy outside to an alley, clubs him to death, and saws off his head—a distillation of all of Dahmer's outrages into one crime. In conjunction with this murder, Kurten phones Hudson and plays a tape recording of her fateful lecture—a clue that leads Hudson to the epiphany that the killer has been using her own long-ago, casual recitation of the names of infamous murderers as a structuring principle for his own murders. Next on the list, then, is Ted Bundy, which compels Hudson to assume that Kurten will finish his series by recreating in a San Francisco setting Bundy's nocturnal attack on the Chi Omega sorority house in which two women (not three, as the movie erroneously insists) died. However, Kurten departs from his private script in his one real moment of unpredictability, so that he may instead climax his murder series with the slaughter of Hudson while the rest of the city is looking for a young man driving a tan Volkswagen Bug—Bundy's trademark vehicle. Nevertheless, Kurten's last planned murder is no more original, since he intends to kill Hudson according to the parameters of the initial crime as defined by progenitor Cullum.[9]

Copycat thus presents to its audience a serial killer even more literally programmed and robotic than the usual. Kurten renames himself after a prolific German serial killer of the 1930s, apes the distinctive "signatures" of four more contemporary American killers, and unswervingly proceeds according to the schema unwittingly laid out for him by Dr. Hudson, with an end goal of successfully completing the murder that Cullum failed to and in exactly the same fashion that the original killer had planned. Thus, Hudson is only half-correct when she characterizes Kurten's breed: "These guys are like viruses. . . . there's always some new mutation."[10] Kurten's replication of murderous precedent is indeed viruslike, but there's nothing new about it. Instead, he mechanically reproduces the crimes of others and seems helpless to innovate (with the sole exception of his use of the Bundy red herring). There is no thinking human being to be found in Kurten's character—only a murdering machine that confirms the worst reactionary fears of film viewers who lament the corruption of American youth by a pervasive and violent media, the supposed incubator of the serial-killing virus.[11]

As the current reactionary fear of media influence is often directed at the Internet, particularly regarding its alleged suitability as a cyberspace playground for pornographers looking to victimize women and children, *Copycat* doesn't waste any time giving that fear its full paranoid expression. Director Amiel, apparently having heard of Internet predators who solicit victims online (Stack C1), portrays Kurten as a hi-tech computer whiz completely at home in cyberspace. He can even stalk Hudson through the Net, sending to her computer ghoulish and mocking messages designed to unnerve her. But since the vast Internet is too difficult and novel a narrative subject to sustain the film, *Copycat* reserves its worst narrative condemnation for the two women representatives of the more traditional media: the irresponsible female television reporter Susan Schiffer[12] and Dr. Hudson, who writes popular books and gives canned lectures on serial murder.

Hudson receives most of the narrative apportionment of blame: by giving academic respectability as well as media legitimacy to the subject of violent crime, she attracts those serial murderers who crave a popular following to her orbit and enables them to succeed in their projects. Hudson realizes her value to her murderous following: "I'm their damned pin-up girl. . . . I'm the fucking muse of serial killers." Neither is the point lost upon Monahan, the narrative's representative of postfeminist law and order. At a later point in the narrative, after Hudson informs Monahan that the killer must be caught first in order to be famous, Monahan chides her: "So you can write a book about him." The young Kurten, dreaming of notoriety and his psyche infected by overexposure to the lethal viruses of media accounts of serial murder,[13] including the reporter's sensational broadcasts and the chronicler Hudson's books, attempts to exact a terrible revenge upon Hudson. In so doing, he acts as a surrogate for the audience in their desire to punish Hudson for her intellectual arrogance. As a secondhand transmitter of forbidden knowledge to the easily corrupted youth of America, she must be punished by a murderous representative of the very youth so infected. Hudson temporarily survives, but the film's ending, wherein Cullum is literally setting another psychopath named Conrad upon Hudson's scent via jailhouse correspondence, makes it clear that Hudson's trials are only beginning. The film's anti-media message, another product of the reactionary age, could not be clearer.

Indeed, one narrative agenda in *Copycat* and other 1990s films like it *(Seven, Natural Born Killers)* is to give full voice to reactionary fears about crime, the poor and the lower classes, and the "liberal bias" of media, academia, and feminism.[14] The film takes many gratuitous swipes at the usual liberal suspects, not the least of which is the supposed leftist nostalgia for the entire decade of the 1960s—a specious idea usually advocated by those who fail to recognize that the political violence of the late 1960s actually marked a breakdown of the moderate/liberal consensus that had dominated American politics since Franklin Delano Roosevelt's presidency and signaled the long, inexorable shift of American politics toward the right. For example, the serial murders take place against the backdrop of the city's Festival of Love: a made-for-TV celebration of simplistic media caricatures of the complex politics of the 1960s.[15] Kurten selects one female victim, dressed in retro-hippie garb, after she appears on the local news broadcast where Kurten can capture and manipulate her image with his computer software before doing the same to her in real life. He chooses another victim, Andy, who, in addition to being employed by Kurten's primary target, makes the fatal mistake of attending the festival as an openly gay, alternate-lifestyle practitioner. It is only fitting that Kurten, a savage product of the reactionary 1980s and 1990s, chooses to draw his most brutalized victims (one injected with poisonous window cleaner, another beaten to death and decapitated) from this quaint, atavistic festival. He targets this event because he, like the culture that has commodified the violent 1960s into a patronizing and clichéd "celebration" of love, mindlessly stereotypes the decade as a "liberal" one. The memory of that decade must either be expunged from the collective consciousness or, lacking that, lampooned and safely contained through transformation into yet another product to be sold and purchased. *Copycat* as a film sells serial murder in the same antiseptic way.

Not content to invoke caricatures of liberalism, *Copycat* relentlessly stereotypes other sociopolitical demographics as well. The film's other serial killer is Daryll Lee Cullum, who represents a distorted view of the disadvantaged class of impoverished, uneducated, rural, white Southern males. One could argue that Cullum's character, who resorts to high-profile murder because he is denied opportunities for any other socially meaningful work, actually betokens the presence of a class-conscious narrative sensibility, perhaps like the one that guides the fictional *Henry: Portrait of a Serial Killer.* Certainly, there is the implication that disempowerment generates murder, but *Copycat's* narrative is clearly not concerned with a complex sociology so much as the exaggeration of already overblown audience stereotypes of the poor, rural, and white laboring classes for the purpose of neo-Gothic melodrama. As portrayed by an over-the-top Harry Connick Jr., Daryll Lee Cullum evokes the cartoonish image of Henry Lee Lucas in more ways than just the name similarity—the semi-illiterate and heavily accented colloquialisms ("Hot potato, you bloodied up my knife, you dawg"), the leering and rape-oriented perversity ("Whattya say you 'n' me have a little fun"), the frightening physical appearance (pock-marked face, bad teeth), and the animalistic habits (licking the blood from the knife used to kill Hudson's guard). Through such caricaturing, the film assures the members of the middle-class audience that their discomfort with visible representatives of the white-trash culture is not borne out of irrational prejudice but rather judicious discretion. Cullum's grandiose religious beliefs, which he professes from his jail cell, further reinforce his stereotypical status as an ignorant fundamentalist from the deep South.[16]

However, the nature of his religious statements, later validated by the narrative's resolution, also transform Cullum into a demonic, anti-Christ figure able to target Hudson in pseudosupernatural fashion from his prison cell. For example, during his satellite interview with Hudson from his cell, he tells her: "I'm just like Jesus. I got disciples too. And they're just dying to do whatever I ask 'em to do as long as I say the word. I'm death and life to you, doc. Death and life." Cullum then manipulates Hudson into sending him an autographed pair of her panties, which she believes he wants only for his own perverse ends but in actuality Cullum will use to incite another murderer to pursue Hudson. The last scene of the film shows Cullum, in a state of mystic transport, sending a letter (Hudson's death warrant) to his second disciple Conrad with the words: "Peter [Kurten] strayed from the path and the Lord smote him good. So keep it simple. Then glory is yours and vengeance is mine, as the Good Book says." Cullum, then, has the film's last word. Even though he shares Kurten's obsession with Hudson and his copycat pathology,[17] Cullum accurately diagnoses the flawed composition of Kurten's plan—too elaborate, too flashy, too derivative. His loosing of another monster upon Hudson promises her eventual death and hence proper punishment for her sins, so he is an instrument of not only his God's vengeance but that of an audience presumed by the filmmakers to be sick of the social and media violence promulgated by people like Hudson. So, beneath the cartoonish surface of Cullum, there is a primitive, blameless innocent who seeks revenge on the media culprits that turned him into a monster and yet another mouthpiece for the kind of simple determinism that underlies the copycat theory of deviancy.

It is significant that Cullum chooses a professional, academic, and apparently wealthy (note her steel-shuttered, computerized apartment and her personal manservant) female for the target of his vendetta against what he perceives to be evil social forces. Feminism receives acidic treatment in *Copycat*'s narrative arc. As portrayed by Holly Hunter doing her best Jodie Foster impersonation, Monahan is the pretty-but-vulnerable individualist[18] fighting the worst the big city has to offer: not only savage murderers but a largely ineffectual patriarchal law enforcement apparatus. She is a cheerful, optimistic, benignly spacey outsider within this brutal cadre of practical-minded males—a woman who speaks of "good karma" and "intuitive" policework when teaching her overzealous male partner and rookie Goetz not to take a human life but rather to disable criminals by shooting their brachial nerves. She is a woman who proudly calls a vibrator "a tool of survival" in a world of men who cannot sexually satisfy their partners. She is a woman who, most importantly, recognizes that fellow female outsider Helen Hudson, in spite of her anxiety attacks and her rivalry for Goetz's affection, can contribute to the investigation. There are moments of female empowerment, such as when Hudson turns the tables on her largely male, voyeuristic audience in the opening scene by making them stand, uncomfortable and exposed, before the unflinching scopophilic eye of the lecture hall cameras. All of these elements would seem to affirm *Copycat* as a feminist film, or at least a film that feminists can tolerate.

However, as Christopher Sharrett notes, recent "feminist" horror films (such as *The Silence of the Lambs,* which *Copycat* clearly—well—copies) tend to rely upon an essentially neoconservative ideological foundation, in that these films' relentless demonizing of both the lower and the upper classes and redemption of the state law-enforcement apparatus through the plucky efforts of its individualistic hero contradicts its surface gloss of progressive feminism. Much of the same agenda is played out in *Copycat.* The fact that Hudson and Monahan, two otherwise very professional and career-oriented women, allow themselves to descend into a schoolgirl rivalry over the possible romantic attentions of the handsome Goetz is the least egregious textual instance of *Copycat*'s consistent subversion of feminism.[19] Monahan as a female law-enforcement figure implicitly redeems big-city police departments by her very willingness to be a part of the patriarchal system, however flawed it may be. The extent of Monahan's reform efforts is limited to snide verbal digs at her male superior, Lt. Quinn, whom she reminds, for example, that his methods failed to catch the Zodiac Killer. In every other significant way, she conforms to and thus sanctions Quinn's methodology, including his unauthorized solo removal of evidence from a murder scene (a stocking tied around a strangled woman's neck) in order to keep details from the hated news media, as exemplified in the shrewish and panic-mongering ("Is there a serial killer stalking the streets of San Francisco?") persona of Susan Schiffer, "the Mouth." Monahan interrogates Quinn about why he committed evidence tampering but then admits she would have done the same thing. After this capitulation, the victorious Quinn calls her, in gruff-but-lovable grand patriarch style, "one pushy broad." She acknowledges the "compliment" with a smile and leaves. The legitimacy of Quinn's actions, and his blaming of the female-coded media instead of, say, leaks from within his own department is never textually questioned.

Finally, Monahan's attempts to bring a more "feminist" perspective to the SFPD, such as her well-meaning advice to Goetz about reining in his trigger-happy instincts so that he may disable suspects rather than kill them, are definitively repudiated when she fails to kill the Asian-American suspect who has taken Goetz hostage. She wounds the suspect in the shoulder, which apparently resolves the situation happily enough and initially vindicates her karmic approach. However, the suspect recovers just long enough to kill Goetz and prove to the horrified and grief-stricken Monahan, once and for all, the folly of humanism within a crime-ridden society. And so Monahan is finally free to kill Kurten, not only saving Hudson where Monahan could not save Goetz before (hampered as she was by mercy) but also avoiding the uncertain outcomes of the criminal courts. *Copycat* thus confirms its status as one of the more reactionary films in a notoriously reactionary cinematic subgenre.

In conclusion, according to the subtext of a film such as *Copycat,* the American 1980s and 1990s has seen the culture-wide transmission of the serial killer "virus" by a sensationalizing and violent media that supposedly "celebrates" deviancy and programs impressionable youth in antisocial behavior. However, as this essay has argued, the reality is that the (de)terministic screen from which media agencies must construct their narratives generally leads the resulting subtexts to champion contemporary policy and values at the same time it questions state ideology. The boundaries between the fact and the fiction of sensational crime have been neatly elided, contributing to a social atmosphere in which horror-film clichés dictate a reactionary policy designed to counter hyperinflated menaces such as serial murder. These menaces are necessary as justification for the maintenance of control institutions and their dogma. Strangely missing from films such as *Copycat,* which dramatize cultural debate over America's undeniable social ills, is any acknowledgment that the system itself may be flawed in fundamental ways. Instead, blame is assigned to various subfactions or, in many cases, specific "mad" individuals within the society. Such blaming is a political strategy that allows public wrath a focus while sheltering the overall socioeconomic structure from meaningful criticism. In particular, serial killers, both in reality and fiction, direct attention away from the social milieu in which they operate and onto intriguing but ultimately fruitless deterministic explications of their supposed lunacy. *Copycat,* while perhaps valuable as a text that deliberately demonstrates the intellectual bankruptcy of oversimplified deterministic philosophy, stands as one of the most problematic of the 1990s serial killer films.

Notes

1. See, for example, Tony Williams's discussion of the theme in chapter 12 of his *Hearths of Darkness: The Family in the American Horror Film.*

2. For an example, see my analysis of the media coverage of the "Gainesville Student Murders" in 1990 in the film journal *Cineaction,* no. 38.

3. For a detailed analysis of how media accounts of Gein's murders influenced novelist Robert Bloch to write *Psycho,* which director Alfred Hitchcock then purchased the rights for a screenplay adaptation, see Stephen Rebello's *Alfred Hitchcock and the Making of Psycho.* For information about other Gein-influenced films, see Paul Anthony Woods's fascinating *Ed Gein—Psycho.*

4. Certainly, the fictional serial killer usually sees himself as an artist. Note, for example, Thomas Harris's character Hannibal Lecter, who whiles away his time in the asylum by sketching crucifixions and architecture.

5. This is a point also made by Barbara Shulgasser, "Serial Thriller Has Snap, Crackle."

6. The hatred of a serial killer for his mother is also a strong theme in *Henry: Portrait of a Serial Killer.*

7. This is an antifeminist and conservative tendency in the genre that Jane Caputi has explored at length in her book *The Age of Sex Crime.*

8. These and other morbidly humorous lines make it clear that Hudson, though psychologically traumatized by her experiences, nevertheless takes predatory zest in the pursuit of serial killers: a dark edge to her personality that makes her in some ways a third partner in a lethal Trinity consisting of her, Cullum, and Kurten.

9. Kurten is so deterministically programmed by his fetish to emulate his predecessor that he tries to pose the body of Hudson's murdered police escort in exactly the same fashion as Cullum left the first police officer. Kurten is frustrated by real life's messy inability to conform to his (de)terministic screen: "This is wrong. . . . Everything has to be just so."

10. Kurten's status as human virus carrier is confirmed by an email that he sends to Hudson; the taunting message contains an electronic virus that destroys the message after it has been read. Hudson is angry as well as terrified by Kurten's contamination of her self-enclosed world, but the film implies that she too spreads the contaminatory virus as a result of her contact with and cultural transmission of serial murder.

11. As Jonathan Romney writes, "The film's conservative thrust is to suggest that we have become too interested in slaughter and should perhaps have a moratorium on depicting it fictionally" (35).

12. Lt. Quinn, Monahan's boss, calls Schiffer "the Mouth" in a sequence that is followed by Kurten cropping on his computer screen the image of a future female victim into that of a disembodied, screaming mouth—a clear expression of *Copycat*'s narrative desire to punish Schiffer (and the media in general) for speaking.

13. Kurten knows, for example, that "more books have been written about Jack the Ripper than Abraham Lincoln."

14. For a full analysis of *Seven* and *Natural Born Killers,* as well as other films and novels in the serial killer subgenre, refer to my book *Psycho Paths: Tracking the Serial Killer Through Contemporary American Film and Fiction.*

15. The San Francisco setting, the "birthplace" of the countercultural movement, reinforces the theme.

16. This is a stereotype also exploited in Martin Scorsese's remake of *Cape Fear.*

17. Cullum, initially drawn to Hudson's status as the "muse of serial killers," is compelled to kill her, as is Kurten. After his capture, Cullum then writes a book, entitled *My Life with a Knife,* an imitation of Hudson's literary efforts.

18. Monahan is the "good hick" to offset Cullum's "evil hick."

19. Goetz has his own rival in the film. He engages in verbal and ultimately physical sparring rounds with Detective Nicoletti, who is a former lover of Monahan's eager to reclaim their intimacy. Nicoletti's careless handling of the Asian-American suspect allows the latter to grab the gun that will be used to kill Goetz. The removal of Goetz from the narrative by the indirect agency of Monahan's paternalistic ex-lover finally allows Hudson and Monahan, the romantic distraction now dispensed with, to form an effective female partnership and successfully resolve the investigation in classic vigilante fashion.

Works Cited

Burke, Kenneth. *Language As Symbolic Action.* Berkeley: U of California P, 1966.

Cameron, Deborah. "Pornography: What Is the Problem?" *Critical Quarterly* 34.2 (Summer 1992): 3–11.

Caputi, Jane. *The Age of Sex Crime.* Bowling Green: Bowling Green State U Popular P, 1987.

Conrath, Robert. "The Guys Who Shoot to Thrill: Serial Killers and the American Popular Unconscious." *Francaise d'Etudes Americaines* 60 (May 1994): 143–52.

Davids, Diana. "The Serial Murderer As Superstar." *McCall's* Feb. 1992: 85+.

Davis, Joe. "Killer Catcher." *The New Yorker* 2 Aug. 1993: 21–22.

Grixti, Joseph. *Terrors of Uncertainty: The Cultural Contexts of Horror Fiction.* London: Routledge, 1989.

Newitz, Annalee. "Serial Killers, True Crime, and Economic Performance Anxiety." *Cineaction* 38 (Sept. 1995): 38–46.

Rebello, Stephen. *Alfred Hitchcock and the Making of Psycho.* New York: Harper-Perennial, 1990.

Romney, Jonathan. "The Last Word on Serial Killing." *New Statesman & Society* (May 3, 1996): 35.

Seltzer, Mark. "Serial Killers (1)." *differences: A Journal of Feminist Cultural Studies* 5.1 (1993): 92–128.

Sharrett, Christopher. "The Horror Film in Neoconservative Culture." *Journal of Popular Film and Television* 21.3 (Fall 1993): 100–10.

Shulgasser, Barbara. "Serial Thriller Has Snap, Crackle." *San Francisco Examiner* 27 Oct. 1995: C1.

Simpson, Philip L. "Mystery Rider: The Cultural Construction of a Serial Killer." *Cineaction* 38 (Sept. 1995): 47–55.

———. *Psycho Paths: Tracking the Serial Killer Through Contemporary American Film and Fiction.* Carbondale: Southern Illinois UP, 2000.

Stack, Peter. "*Copycat* Is Razor Sharp: Serial Murderer Stalks S. F. in Smart Thriller." *San Francisco Chronicle* 27 Oct. 1995: C1.

Williams, Tony. *Hearths of Darkness: The Family in the American Horror Film.* Cranbury, NJ: Associated University Presses, 1996.

Woods, Paul Anthony. *Ed Gein—Psycho.* New York: St. Martin's Press, 1995.

9

Opening the Text: Reading Gender, Christianity, and American Intervention in *Deliverance*

Davis W. Houck and Caroline J. S. Picart

VERY FEW FILMS ACHIEVE THE STATUS OF CULTURAL MONUMENTS—films that help shape the culture even as they are produced by it. Some films attain this status largely because they are the first of a certain type or genre. Such films, for example, as *Birth of a Nation, Psycho, Jaws,* and *Deep Throat* opened up a filmic space for future filmmakers. Other films have embedded themselves into the culture's collective consciousness through a memorable scene. Several such scenes come to mind: the shower scene in *Psycho,* Marilyn Monroe's levitating dress in *The Seven Year Itch,* Burt Lancaster and Deborah Kerr's passionate, prostrate beach embrace in *From Here to Eternity,* Clint Eastwood's queries to Scorpio as to whether he felt "lucky" in *Dirty Harry,* and Linda Blair's demonically inspired neck gyrations in *The Exorcist.* Perhaps none of these scenes, though, caused such a visceral public reaction as the graphic and protracted rape scene in John Boorman's *Deliverance.* We contend, though, that *Deliverance* is not simply "about" a brutal rape and its consequences on the male psyche, as some have proffered (Mellen 317–21). Perhaps because of the rape scene and the response it engendered, the possible meanings and rhetorical importance of the film have not been carefully investigated by film critics.[1] Even during the filming, one observer sensed the overwhelming weight of the scene: "the rape scene was becoming what the movie was about; it was the thing everybody was going to remember" (C. Dickey 45). Or, in the vernacular of rhetorical studies, the scene became a shorthand filter for interpreting the film, thus overdetermining its possible meanings.

This essay relates directly to both the journalistic and scholarly critiques of the film. More specifically, by treating the film as a unified or "closed text," in which meaning is bound by its temporal unfolding, critics have been predisposed to interpret the film's rhetoric as ambiguous, uncertain, and ultimately meaningless. Taking the critical consensus on both method of treatment and the film's meaning as our starting point, we argue that the film's thematic meanings hinge upon resisting a rhetorical strategy that treats the film's text as "finished." Borrowing from Umberto Eco's *Role of the Reader,* our critical project is to "open" the film's text. Our project is thus one that simultaneously affirms each reading as rhetorical and interpretive, while recognizing its structure as a dynamic, organic whole (Eco 49). By adopting Eco's critical position, we hope to illustrate both the utility of such an approach and to comment on an important film whose meaning has been largely missed and dismissed by nearly all critics.

Our "open" reading of *Deliverance* foregrounds issues of gender, religion, and domestic American politics; as such, our reading is rhetorical in Blakesley's fourfold sense of that term (see the introduction). First, in terms of film as language, our reading calls attention to how the film undercuts stable categories of identity. Such undercutting also functions rhetorically and simultaneously to critique them—thus film functions as ideology. Third, in terms of film as interpretation, by calling attention to a closed versus open act of viewing, Boorman asks the reader/viewer to choose: either treat the film within its diegetic narrative and risk uncertainty and confusion or treat the film as open text, in need of finishing given the hints/clues/evidences that the director provides. Finally, and in keeping with Kenneth Burke's sense of identification (19–29), from the very outset of *Deliverance,* unity and division propel much of the filmic action (e.g., man versus nature; urban versus rural; sacred versus profane) as well as provide boundaries for our open reading.

We will proceed by (1) discussing briefly the background of the film; (2) reviewing the representative commentary on the film and its relevance to our method; (3) analyzing the film; and (4) offering concluding remarks.

Deliverance was shot on location along the southern stretches of the Chattanooga River in Rabun County, north Georgia, during the spring of 1971; the film opened in movie theaters in August 1972. The film was a commercial and a critical success as it was nominated by the Academy for three Academy Awards, including Best Director, Best Editing, and Best Picture. The film, starring Jon Voight, Ned Beatty, Burt Reynolds, and Ronny Cox, also featured extras recruited from a nearby local jail (C. Dickey 42). Englishman John Boorman directed the film; the screenplay was adapted from novelist and poet James Dickey's best-selling 1970 novel by the same name. Dickey himself wrote the screenplay, which he later claimed that Boorman had misinterpreted and misunderstood. Dickey notes in the afterword to the screenplay that "the movie, enormously successful as it was and with a longevity given to few films to achieve, is not the film as I would have it. [. . .] For anyone who wishes to imagine or 'see' the film as the author wished it to be experienced, it is here, in words, and in the imagination" (156–57). Dickey's animosity for both Boorman and his directing was reciprocal as Boorman eventually banished Dickey from the set because of his tips to the actors during breaks in filming.

The only aspect of the film that Dickey approved was cinematographer Vilmos Zsigmond's filming of the river scenes. Zsigmond's cinematography won critical acclaim not only from Dickey but also from most of the film's reviewers. The object of their praise was not the river scenes as much as Zsigmond's "sepia-tone" photographic techniques, which had a "monochromatic" effect (Gilliatt 52). In the words of *New York Times* critic Vincent Canby, such techniques projected "a kind of bleached color that denies any thoughts of romantic sentimentality" (21). The technique, known in film circles as "saturation," involves "combining a black-and-white print with a color print" (Boggs 153). Both Boorman and Zsigmond wanted to mute the brightness of the colors—which were "too happy and cheerful looking"—in order to create a more somber mood (153).

The journalistic and scholarly responses to *Deliverance* mirror the film's emotional highs and lows. The critics share, to varying degrees, a visceral reaction to the film's often graphic depiction of human interaction with nature. Despite their claims that the film's meaning is ambiguous, critics are, nonetheless, polarized in their evaluative comments. The extremes range from Stanley Kauffman's minimalist critique—"no performance deserves comment" (35)—to Gene Siskel's assessment that the film "may be the most exciting motion picture in my experience" (sec. 2: 14). That these polarized views are not idiosyncratic is illustrated by Robert F. Willson and Arthur Knight. Willson claims that the film is a "hardly thought-provoking adventure story" (52). In direct contrast, Knight argues that the true achievement of *Deliverance* lies precisely in its ability to engage the imagination: "After the fade-out, the mind takes over" (21).

The film's critics also disagree as to what *Deliverance* is about. Whereas the film's evaluations are split, are bipolar in nature, little agreement exists regarding the film's meaning. Paul D. Zimmerman claims that the film is a "parable of survival and original sin" (61). Penelope Gilliatt says that *Deliverance* is "a ragbag of all the myths about maleness" (52). Richard Schickel argues that *Deliverance* is about "man's need to try himself by placing his life on the line" (8). For Jay Cocks, the film is about the need to "capitulate" to nature's forces (76). Hal Aigner states that the main themes are the blessings of both nature and civilization and man's survival abilities (39). Charles Thomas Samuels views the film as representative of civilization's inherent tendency to "emasculate" maleness via technological progress (154). Robert Armour emphasizes the religious meaning of the film, arguing that each character embodies a different version of Edenic Adam (280–85). Stephen Farber claims that the film is both a "devastating critique of machismo" and a "serious and meaningful challenge to the belief in rites of manhood" (sec. 2: 9). Gary Arnold posits that *Deliverance* concerns itself with eliminating "signs of normalcy" (B1). Charles Champlin contends that the film is "about whether man in his natural state is benign or savage" (Cal 1). Michael Dempsey alleges the film to be "a study of how people dissatisfied with ordinary life plunge into alluring fantasy worlds" (10). Joan Mellen argues that the film is concerned principally with sexual repression and latent homosexuality (317–21).

And finally, Carol Clover treats the film as symptomatic of the bifurcation between urban and rural life (126–34).

While each critic asserts that the film contains a single meaning, many of these same critics equivocate and even contradict such thematic claims by emphasizing *Deliverance*'s ambiguous content. As a result, ambiguity becomes the film's de facto meaning. For instance, Samuels's frustration with the film stems from his uncertainty as a viewer: "We can't tell whether the tenderfeet have been improved or brutalized by their experiences" (154). He adds that "Instead of clearing up such contradictions or ambiguities, the film emphasizes them" (154). Like Samuels, Willson cannot identify with Jon Voight's character—Ed Gentry—largely because of the ambiguities surrounding his actions: "Would they have received a fair trial for the first man's murder? Was Drew really shot? Did Ed bag the right man after his tortuous climb up the hill? Will he ever be the same?" (52). Moreover, Willson directs his anger at Boorman for "ignoring" these dilemmas and for "complicating" Ed's murder of the mountain man (52, 58). Joy Gould Boyum expresses similar sentiments: none of the "fine performances excuse the film of its failure to provide satisfactory answers" (8). What Gould Boyum "demands" from *Deliverance* is that the viewer "be furnished with clues sufficient for their [problems'] resolution" (8). Arnold is equally bothered by Boorman's obfuscation of *Deliverance*'s cinematic meaning: his interpretation of James Dickey's story is "always murky" (B1). Like Gould Boyum, Arnold's wrath also extends to Voight's character. According to Arnold, Voight's performance is "one of the most incomprehensible I've ever seen" (B1). Winfred Blevins agrees with his fellow critics: "Added to the deliberate and evocative ambiguities of *Deliverance*'s script, the lack of coherence is confusing and frustrating" (B9).

Whereas Samuels, Willson, Gould Boyum, Arnold and Blevins see the film's ambiguity as a weakness, several critics label it as a strength. "*Deliverance* doesn't attempt to answer questions," argues Knight; instead, rights or wrongs "are left unresolved.[. . .] It is this unresolved, open-ended quality that leaves the viewer haunted and unresolved in his own mind" (21). This "open-ended quality" makes Farber uneasy since *Deliverance* "would be more comforting" if the viewer "could be sure" Ed's violence was in self-defense (sec. 2: 9). Furthermore, Boorman's refusal "to dispel the questions and ambiguities [. . .] robs the outcome of any sense of triumph" (sec. 2: 9). In a similar vein, Champlin states that the film's events are "anything but clear cut" (Cal 1). Moreover, the film "is not clear enough soon enough that the events are in fact fatefully ambiguous" (Cal 1). According to at least one critic, though, thematic ambiguity is a staple of Boorman's moviemaking in that his "rites of passage are always ambiguous" (Dempsey 13). Michael Dempsey notes further that "Boorman responds most fervently to images of absurdity and meaninglessness" (13). Such is the case with *Deliverance*, claims Dempsey, since it "leaves us with what Herzog's film refers to as a 'landscape without any possible meaning'" (17).

Despite the critical consensus regarding the film's ambiguity and meaninglessness, all of its critics argue for a particular reading of the film—a reading that asserts, however tentatively, a single meaning. More importantly, though, all of the critics assume an identical critical posture: each critic treats the film as an organic whole, or what Blair, Jeppeson, and Pucci term a "material unity" (282). Eco, in his discussion of the critic's role in aesthetic theory, refers to such a treatment as "closed" in *The Role of the Reader* (8, 49). Treating the film as "closed" essentially forces the critic to "make sense" of the film's narrative as it unfolds from beginning to end since, according to Eco, the critic brings a set of expectations to bear on a text—a set of expectations informed by previous experiences viewing films (8). The critic, by re-authorizing a pre-existing text, makes a significant evaluation of the film before even viewing it. In the case of *Deliverance,* nearly every critic's expectation of narrative closure was violated, resulting in an interpretive reading that simply does not yield informed, or even logically possible, evaluations.

What other positions might a critic adopt? Eco argues for a critical posture that positions the critic as a "performer" in which texts are treated not as linear, chronological unfoldings but as complex amalgams of textual inference and intertextual competence. Such a view veers radically from the notion that to incite the interpretative cooperation of the reader is to pollute the structural integrity of the text. Rather, it assumes that the reader, as an active principle of interpretation, is part of the generative process of the text.

Nevertheless, a text that seems so immoderately open to every possible interpretation is inevitably a closed one: "An open text, however 'open' it be, cannot afford whatever interpretation," reminds Eco (9). Ultimately, then, his favored interpretive position is one that attempts to wrestle with the tense, ricocheting motion between open and closed—a motion best seen in his brilliant analyses of the multiple polarity of serial composition in music. Thus, a seemingly finished discourse is actually a dense reconstruction of all the bits of other discourses from which it was woven. Texts, as such, are always "unfinished" (50). This position flows from the idea that although a work of art is "a complete and closed form in its uniqueness as a balanced organic whole," any reception of a work of art is also an interpretation and a performance of it as well (49).

Perhaps it is best to draw out the implications of this position by elaborating how Eco studies musical pieces such as Stockhausen's *Klavierstuck,* Berio's *Sequence for the Solo Flute,* and Pousseur's *Scambi.* For Eco, such pieces are unlike classical compositions like a Bach fugue or Verdi's *Aida,* which oblige the performer merely to reproduce the format devised by the composer. Conversely, "multipolar" pieces appeal to the initiative of the individual performer, and hence "offer themselves not as finite works which prescribe specific repetition along given structural coordinates but as 'open' works, which are brought to their conclusion by the performer at the same time as he experiences them on an aesthetic plane" (49)

Similarly, Eco uses Allais's *Drame,* a hybrid of what appears to be a mere literary joke and verbal *trompe-l'oeil* or "something half-way between the engravings of Escher and a pastiche a la Borges" (204–5), to illustrate the notion of a metatext simultaneously speaking of and inviting the cooperative principle in narrativity, while challenging the reader's yearning for cooperation by punishing such intrusiveness by ultimately remaining a cipher. *Drame* works precisely because it explores the conditions of possibility within which a reader, in interpreting a text, may resort to "intertextual frames"—to interpretative moves that are not the result simply of the reader's whims or fancies, but are "elicited by discursive structures and foreseen by the whole textual strategy as indispensable components of the construction of the fabula" (32).

By using chapter 2 of *Drame* as a reduced model of the whole work, one arrives at the difference between a "discursive" structure and a "narrative" one. Hence, when Raoul pursues Marguerite and raises his hand, the reader, resorting to the frame, "conjugal quarrel," realizes that Raoul intends to beat his wife. In doing so, the reader performs a double inferential movement: s/he realizes that Raoul wants to beat Marguerite (a "discursive" inference); and s/he expects Raoul actually to beat Marguerite (a "narrative" inference). The discursive inference is true, but the narrative inference (which is arrived at through taking "inferential walks" among various intertextual frames) is proven false. Margeurite cleverly prevents Raoul from beating her by throwing herself in his arms and asking him to save her. Nevertheless, what this illustrates, for Eco, is that "every text, even though not specifically narrative, is in some way making the addressee expect (and foresee) the fulfillment of every unaccomplished sentence" (214).

How then does Eco's theoretical construct inform our rhetorical reading of *Deliverance*? First, it invites us to treat the text as always and fundamentally "open," as "a work to be completed," since a text is incomplete, always in need of interpretation or "text formation" (62). This, naturally, amounts to an act of improvised creation—an act that simultaneously affirms a work of art as a complete and closed form in its uniqueness as an organic whole while portraying how such a work is infinitely open to "countless interpretations which do not impinge on its unadulterable specificity" (49). Second, Eco urges the critic to search for clues to a text's meaning from within the matrices that comprise the ostensibly finished text. A text, as such, "is not an amorphous invitation to indiscriminate participation" (62). In other words, each part of a text can represent one piece of a larger puzzle. The text, then, invites its own close reading that "make[s] the work together with the author" (63). Eco extends his musical analogy to illustrate his point: "The multiple polarity of a serial composition in music, where the listener is not faced by an absolute conditioning center of reference, requires him to constitute his own system of auditory relationships. He must allow such a center to emerge from the sound continuum" (61).

A potential problem with applying Eco's framework involves the filmic medium. Eco's frame of reference ricochets among the narrative, discursive, visual, and musical. In conjunction with this, the critical parameters that we employ are informed by several visual, musical, and discursive cues that coalesce into the categorical unit of themes. Our method of arriving at such themes is not informed by a desire to close or "totalize" the text, but to explore the conditions of possibility within which a text is simultaneously interpreted and performed, thereby affirming its "openness" and "closedness."

Drawing from Eco's framework then, we posit that *Deliverance's* rhetoric is not ambiguous or meaningless, as critics contend. Rather, we argue that the film engages three themes: gender, Christianity, and American intervention in Vietnam. Further, within each theme, Boorman interrogates and challenges traditional conceptions of masculinity and femininity, some "foundational" tenets of the Christian religion, and American intervention abroad. As such, Boorman's rhetorical strategies deployed throughout *Deliverance* function to radically question three staples of American life, circa the early 1970s.

Perhaps the film's most obvious theme involves masculinity, or what it means to be masculine and what are its consequences. Boorman calls into question several ostensibly distinct versions of masculinity through four main character representations. We are introduced to these versions of masculinity (and our preexisting expectations about them) as the four men arrive in the town of Oree to purchase gas and seek out some locals to drive their cars downriver to Aintry, where they plan to disembark from the Cahulawassee River. Lewis Medlock (Burt Reynolds) is clearly the leader of the expedition. As he emerges from his car, he declares, "I never been lost in my life." With a cigar in hand, Lewis takes charge by speaking with one of the mountain people. He instructs the attendant, a frail old man, to fill up the cars with gas and then asks him where he can find some drivers. As he questions the attendant, Boorman induces further use of intertextual frames to depict Lewis's leadership. A patch directly above a skydiving patch on Lewis's vest reads "co-captain" (see fig. 9.1). Lewis clearly embodies male machismo, through his chiseled physique, his outward self-confidence, his own self-fashioning and his assertive behavior with strangers.

The other three masculine "types" are more subtly introduced. Bobby Trippe (Ned Beatty), a short, portly character donning a porkpie hat, comes across as the unreflective, carefree jokester, eager to elicit a laugh. Bobby also feigns assertiveness by eagerly investigating the cluttered grounds surrounding the gas station. However, Boorman cues the viewer to see Bobby's self-confidence as fraudulent when he backs down from his assertive posture. Confronted with a stranger, he defers to Lewis: "Lewis, we got a live one over here." Only after Lewis has interrogated the stranger does Bobby talk with him. We are also invited to see Bobby as the malicious jokester as he mockingly tells the attendant, "I love the way you wear that hat," to which the attendant replies: "You don't know nothin'." Bobby, having aroused the desired response, whispers to Lewis, "Lewis, ask him about his hat."

Drew Ballinger (Ronny Cox), a tall, lean, bespeckled man with a sunny disposition, represents the innocent/naive man-child. Drew's naivete is emphasized

Figure 9.1

as he emerges from the station wagon with his guitar—an instrument incongru-
ous with the harsh realities of white-water rafting and a canoe's limited space.
Drew's innocence is underscored through his brief dialogue with Bobby upon
arriving in Oree:

> *Bobby:* Christ, Drew. Drew, look here. I think this is where everything
> finishes up. We just may be at the end of the line.
> *Drew:* Not so loud, Bobby. We don't want to upset these people.

In this environment, far removed from the hostilities of the water, Drew's naivete and innocence are rewarded as he engages in a memorable musical duel with
an apparently inbred and unnamed young boy. Despite the boy's obvious physical otherness, Drew eagerly responds to his musical challenges and offers his own.
As the pace quickens, both Drew and the boy respond with wide grins, indicative of the joy and spontaneity of the musical communication; as such, Drew is
the only one to communicate successfully, albeit somewhat agonistically, with
the mountain people.

Yet duels typically have winners and losers—fatally so. That Drew will eventually "lose" is foreshadowed by a subtle yet very important visual clue. From
behind the boy, the camera frames his banjo's neck cutting diagonally across
Drew's neck (see fig. 9.2). In a manner reminiscent of Allais's *Drame,* the apparent success of Drew's musical communion with the mountain people bears within
it an ambiguous structure that resists closure. Following the music and Drew's
exuberant declaration—"I could play with him all day"—we see that Drew's
success at communication is only partial as the boy looks away when Drew at-

Figure 9.2

Figure 9.3

tempts to shake his hand (see fig. 9.3). This duel scene is of paramount importance in interpreting the film since it establishes the musical leitmotif of battle
(which ironically appears as "musical communication")—with its dark, fascinating portents of danger and death—as well as Drew's eventual death.

Carefully observing this scene is Ed Gentry (Jon Voight), a fair-haired man
with an average build, whose thoughtfulness is emphasized by his slowness to
speak and his pipe smoking. Ed's masculine type is not readily forthcoming because the other three characters dominate the scene. Ed appears sympathetic to
each of the other three types: he is willing to entertain Bobby's jokes; he gladly
allows Lewis to take charge and offer advice; and he looks on with amused interest as Drew and the boy "duel." Perhaps because of this adaptability and uncertainty, again, via an inferential walk that attempts to "gather intertextual support (a quest for analogous 'topoi,' themes or motives)," the viewer is subtly cued
to the possibility that Ed will be confronted with a choice of which type of masculinity he will emulate when he is confronted with a crisis.

Boorman questions each of the masculine types at various points in the film.
First, Bobby's masculinity is savagely repudiated by a mountain man. In a manner
recalling his first meeting with the natives, Bobby ventures without trepidation into
the woods as he and Ed take a break from rafting. He spots two mountain men
while Ed looks on cautiously from a few yards behind. Bobby's greeting—"How
goes it?"—is firmly rebuffed: "What the hell ya think yur doin'?" Not only is Bobby's
assertiveness repudiated but his physical appearance incites the bestial mountain
man to exclaim, "Boy, you look just like a hog," and "Looks like we got us a sow
here instead of a boar." During the infamous rape scene Bobby's assertive masculinity is reduced to passive "femininity" as he quickly acquiesces to the rapist's
last commands: "Get them britches down." Bobby's masculinity is figuratively
castrated by both the rapist and by Boorman. More importantly, however, the
audience vicariously participates in Bobby's emasculation as we are led to believe
that his masculinity has been firmly and violently rebuked.

Following Bobby's rape, Boorman questions the masculine types represented
by both Drew and Lewis. After Lewis kills the rapist with an arrow to the heart,
he and Drew, with Ed and Bobby listening intently, argue over what to do with
the dead body. Lewis wants to bury the body since a fair trial among the mountain people would be impossible. Drew advocates taking the body to the police
in Aintry. While Lewis argues in a very cold, calculated manner, Drew's appeals
are fraught with heaving hysterical sobs. Lewis eventually wins out as Bobby and
Ed vote to bury the body. This violation of Drew's moral code sends him "over
the edge," as is evidenced by the burial scene. Digging without any equipment,
Drew furiously excavates the damp earth with both hands. His sobs and cries
punctuate each up-and-down movement, ironically analogous to the movements
and sounds associated with acts of sexual intercourse—the rape is still fresh in
the viewer's mind. After burying the corpse, the men sprint back to their canoes
with Lewis leading the way. Ed is the only one to stop to wash his hands. As Drew

jumps into the canoe with Ed, and with the sound of white water looming ominously in the background, Drew refuses Ed's request to put on a life jacket. Ed
repeatedly shouts his instructions to an incoherent Drew, who continues to paddle
despite his glazed-over look. As the river's current quickens, Drew falls overboard
and is immediately engulfed in the raging waters. Both canoes then capsize and
the men are hurled violently down a steep falls, eventually ending up in a protected cove. While we do not know how Drew died, Boorman leads the viewer
to question, if not repudiate, Drew's masculinity by depicting his innocence and
moral code as being too weak to cope with a crisis.

Boorman also undermines Lewis's machismo, but does so in a subtler manner. Though Lewis's body looks invincible, Boorman offers clues that his interior might be far different. For example, despite his preparedness to lead the
excursion, Lewis is unable initially to find the river (recall Lewis's earlier boast
that he had never been lost). A few scenes later, when Lewis bow hunts for sup-
per while Ed gently steadies the canoe, Lewis initially misses badly as he attempts
to hit a motionless fish. Another visual *trompe l'oeil* is subtly revealed: as viewers, our expectations are violated since, so far, we have been led to see Lewis as
an adroit outdoorsman. Moreover, when Lewis does finally shoot a fish, he lets
out several loud, childlike shouts, as if it were his very first catch. And, following the rape scene in which Lewis heroically rescues Ed and Bobby, he momen-
tarily loses his cold, detached persona. In response to Drew's question as to where
they would bury the body, Lewis responds, "Everywhere, [pause] anywhere
[pause], nowhere." Lewis has lapsed into a trancelike state that competes with
his logical exterior.

While each of these examples subtly calls into question Lewis's masculinity,
the decisive event occurs after the canoes capsize. In the process of being hurled
down the falls, Lewis suffers a compound fracture of his right leg, causing him
to lapse in and out of consciousness for the remainder of the film. Lewis, who
declared earlier that he looked forward to the day when survival of the fittest
would be the "game," has his manhood taken away precisely at the defining hour.
Lewis's mental powers have slipped as well, since he cannot even offer advice to
Ed or Bobby; he can only mutter to Ed: "Now you've got to play the game."

It is difficult to fit Ed Gentry into a distinct masculine category. Though Ed
gets along with Bobby and Drew, it is clear that he has an affinity for Lewis. This
admiration, which some describe as having a "homosexual overtone" (Buckley
46), manifests itself at several points: Ed and Lewis go on weekend trips frequently; Ed admires Lewis for not carrying life insurance; the two travel to Oree
in the same automobile; Ed clearly admires Lewis for not backing down in his
negotiations with one of the Griner brothers—a giant man who dwarfs even
Lewis; Ed confesses his failure to shoot a deer at point-blank range only to Lewis;
Lewis saves Ed from experiencing sexual humiliation; and after the murder of
the rapist, Ed agrees with Lewis that they should bury the body, despite Drew's
appeals to law and order.

This relationship between Lewis and Ed changes, though, once Lewis is badly injured, Drew is presumed drowned, Bobby suffers the indignities of rape, and the second mountain man threatens to exact more revenge from high above the cliff directly above them. Ed is confronted with a choice: either become like Lewis and courageously tackle the obstacles confronting the party or passively accept the fate that awaits—a passivity that led to Bobby's rape and his near rape. Ed opts for direct intervention. During the last third of the movie, Ed scales a vertical cliff with his bare hands; shoots and kills the rapist's presumed accomplice with his bow and arrow; pulls an arrow through his side after impaling himself on it upon shooting the accomplice; survives a treacherous fall when his rope snaps against the sharp precipice at the top of the cliff; skillfully guides the canoe through extremely rough white water; maintains emotional stability as he buries his friend Drew; quickly invents a plausible story that accounts for all of the events of the previous two days; safely guides the canoe to Aintry; secures the help of the locals; helps invent a "new" story to account for the second canoe being found upriver; brings Lewis back to consciousness while he's lying in a hospital bed in order to inform him of the revised story; and keeps the local sheriff at arm's length by artfully lying his way through many complicated details. Not only does Ed become Lewis in performing such heroic deeds but he actually takes on his physical appearance. Substituting a life vest for Lewis's sleeveless wetsuit, and with his biceps bulging from overuse, Ed takes on Lewis's physical persona.

On the surface Boorman praises Ed's (and Lewis's) masculinity; after all, by becoming like Lewis, Ed not only saves his own life but also the lives of Lewis and Bobby. However, in the last scene of the film, Boorman reveals that Ed's transformation is not necessarily an improvement. Like *Drame*'s ambiguous "resolution," Boorman shows that becoming like Lewis merely results in Ed suffering a nightmare in which his sins are made manifest; Ed's rebirth into "real" manhood causes anguish and psychosis, not redemption.

Having questioned the masculinity represented by each of the characters, what are we to make of Boorman's challenges to manhood? Drew is dead. Bobby's psychic wounds may never heal. Lewis's physical wounds may heal, but his psychic scars are also profound, and Ed presumably will be forever haunted by his own doubts: Should he have sided with Drew? Did he shoot the right man? Will the incriminating evidence ever turn up? With few, if any, answers forthcoming, Boorman's rhetorical tactics compel viewers to rethink traditional views of what masculinity entails.

A second, albeit less "visible," gender issue involves femininity. Whereas masculinity is overtly contested throughout the film, we are given precious few clues that Boorman may also be challenging what constitutes femininity. One could plausibly argue, as some have, that the film is a "buddy film," concerned exclusively with the masculine condition (Mellen 317–21). This conclusion overlooks the fact that by "ignoring" females the film would, nonetheless, be making a statement about females and femininity. By making femininity an osten-

sible "nonissue," one has either knowingly or unknowingly made it an important issue.

Where does this feminine text reside and, more importantly, what might it
say? The text is discernible in the characters of Bobby and Drew. While Bobby
and Drew are clearly male characters whose masculinity gets challenged, Boorman
hints that both characters can simultaneously be read as feminine representations.
Our first, and perhaps most obvious clue, involves the characters' names: Bobby
and Drew are both gender neutral names, suitable for either males or females.
Moreover, their actions in the film corroborate many "traditional" views of
women. The two men, for example, are never allowed to navigate the river in
the same boat, as Lewis and Ed direct and instruct them from the stern of the
canoe. Also, in two of the film's crucial sequences, Bobby's and Drew's "feminine
traits" appear to cause extreme maladies. As he is about to be raped, Bobby is
told, "Looks like we got us a sow here instead of a boar"—a clear rejection of
Bobby's masculinity. Bobby is also told to "drop" his "panties," another explicitly induced intertextual reference to his effeminate nature. Bobby also plays the
role of caregiver on two occasions: while Ed scales the vertical cliffs following
the capsizing of the canoes and when Ed goes for help after they arrive in Aintry.

In addition, by evoking an intertextual frame, Boorman transforms Drew, after
the murder of the rapist, into the virtual embodiment of the hysterical woman.
Drew loses his rational faculties following the rejection of his plan to take the
body to Aintry. Drew's hysteria is manifested in both his furious digging of the
grave and his failure to heed Ed's advice to wear his life jacket.

Such "feminized" readings of Bobby and Drew have additional critical warrant in the archetypal conflict between man and sea. As Michael Osborn argues,
a "vital point of similarity between river and sea life is that the river [like the sea]
gives manliness to its men, while the land effeminates them" (360). Bobby and
Drew are both "land lovers," men made soft by their urban existence in Atlanta,
and out of touch physically and emotionally with the harsh realities of the river.
Additionally, the film illustrates that both men "lose" their masculinity on land
(Bobby is raped; Drew becomes hysterical).

What, then, does the film seem to tell us about femininity? At one level, the
answers are largely negative, apparently reinforcing traditional stereotypes: rape
accompanies a woman's feminine appearance; opportunities to lead are firmly
rebuked, if raised at all; women cannot act rationally in a crisis situation; and
given a chance to perform heroic deeds, women will (and should) defer to men.

Boorman, though, allows for a different interpretation. For instance, Drew
is the only member of the group to communicate successfully with the mountain people. Drew would not let his principles be compromised by Lewis; as such,
he is the only character to "survive" with his principles intact. Bobby temporarily
overcomes the psychological trauma of rape to care for Lewis and skillfully guides
the canoe through extremely rough white water, despite having only a broken
paddle. Additionally, when he is confronted with evidence that contradicts their

alibi, Bobby does not give in, but quickly offers a new version that effectively keeps the "innocence" of the survivors intact. By presenting both interpretations as tenable, Boorman forces the viewer to decide. Importantly, though, whereas the film leaves little if any room for a positive view of masculinity, Boorman does leave us with an option to view traditionally feminine attributes with favor—an option that adds ironic fodder to the indictment of masculinity.

While several scenes cue the viewer to issues of gender, the film, as the title not-so-subtly suggests, also engages the Christian religion. Boorman, however, goes beyond commenting on Christianity to questioning some of its fundamental assumptions. Boorman achieves this effect principally by evoking and subverting the meaning of traditional symbols associated with Christianity. These symbols include the purificatory powers associated with water, the Lord's Prayer, the salvation offered by Christ's crucifixion, and the permanence of the church.

In the New Testament, water functions as a cleansing or purifying agent; it typically functions to "wash away" the sins of the "unclean." Water's cleansing, hence purifying, power is best illustrated in the ritual of baptism in which the sinner is cleansed of his/her sinfulness via the agency of water. Both John the Baptist and Christ frequently anointed new souls in the rivers and lakes surrounding Jerusalem and Galilee. Water, as represented in the New Testament, thus provides a vehicle for rebirth and salvation.

In *Deliverance,* however, water functions in the opposite manner: the river is the site of murder, rape, and perhaps even suicide—each act an anathema to Christianity. Moreover, the water functions to hide sins (burying two bodies) rather than uncovering and confessing them, thereby preventing cleansing. In an act reminiscent of the serpent in the Garden of Eden, the river also functions to deceive the men as its initial serenity and calm hide its truly destructive nature. That this initial serenity is a malevolent deception is underscored by the imagery of a black snake as it forebodingly slithers its way ahead of Ed's and Bobby's canoe as they first begin to head downriver. The river also destroys rather than heals: Lewis's leg is badly broken; one of the canoes is split in two; and Drew may have drowned in its currents. The river does indeed cause a transformation in each of the survivors, but their "rebirth" is antithetical to the salvation associated with that provided by water in the New Testament.

Boorman also evokes and subverts Christian prayer, both as a means of communication with God and as a way for God to fulfill the sender's requests. Boorman cues the viewer to the issue of prayer in the rape scene. After he has tied Ed to a sapling, the rapist admonishes Bobby: "Just you drop them pants." As Bobby concedes, the rapist then states, "'Dem panties, tak'em off." Boorman's camera follows the rapist's command back to Bobby, who is reciting part of the Lord's Prayer: "Deliver us from evil." In the sixth chapter of the Book of Matthew, Christ promises the sender of the Lord's Prayer that the Father "will reward you." However, shortly after Bobby's prayer, he is raped—ostensibly God's "answer" to his request.

After the rapist has finished with Bobby, he and the other mountain man approach Ed, who is still tied to the sapling. Once Ed is freed from the tree the following dialogue ensues:

Rapist: Whaddaya wanna do with him?
Second man: He got a real pretty mouth, ain't he?
Rapist: That's the truth.
Second man: Boy, yur gonna do some prayin' for me and you better pray good.

"Prayin'" in this context is a euphemism for oral sex. Luckily for Ed, Lewis's intervention saves him from this act. Boorman thus subverts the traditionally "closed" reading of communicating with God by associating it with homosexuality, rape, and sodomy. Moreover, Boorman implicitly depicts God not only as a liar but as a being complicitous with the godless.

A third Christian symbol that Boorman simultaneously evokes and subverts is the crucifixion of Christ, whose death on the cross and resurrection hold the promise of eternal salvation to believers. Boorman parodies this imagery when Ed and Bobby come across Drew's body, which is elevated out of the water (see fig. 9.4). On what looks like a broken cross, Drew's arms are not both outstretched as if crucified; rather, his left arm is badly mangled, wrapped behind his head with his left hand facing outward and resting below his right shoulder. Such a

Figure 9.4

distortion invokes the symmetry of the cross while at the same time subverting, perhaps even mocking, its universal message. In addition, a closer look at Drew's left palm reveals a puncture mark—another overt intertextual reference to Christ's crucifixion (see fig. 9.5). Thus, despite Drew's innocence, purity, concern for the mountain people, and eagerness to commune with the Other (certainly among Christlike characteristics), Boorman's parody or mockery of his crucifixion calls into question the Christlike life: Is Christianity a historical relic in need of some modernist revisions? Is Christianity possible in the presence of sinners? Is Christianity simply a cruel hoax, discernible only at the moment of death? If, as Ed claims while eulogizing him, Drew was "the best of us," should the viewer favor situational exigencies over both Divine Law and juridical law? Boorman leaves the viewer to ponder these questions as his camera pulls back from the scene to reveal a massive black rock casting its shadow on the survivors (see fig. 9.6). The all-encompassing blackness provides a visual reminder of the black skies following Christ's death on the cross.

Figure 9.5

At various points in both the New and Old Testaments, God and/or Christ emphasize the permanence (hence eternal nature) and immutability of both His message and His institution (the Church) by employing the metaphor of the rock. In the Gospel of Matthew, for example, Christ tells His disciples that "on this

Figure 9.6

rock I will build my church, and the gates of Hades will not overcome it" (1466). Boorman, though, challenges this metaphor that connotes permanence and sta- bility. As Ed, Bobby, and Lewis finally reach land in Aintry, Ed emerges from the river. To his right is a pristine, white church with a small steeple (see fig. 9.7). Each character's "deliverance" is visibly associated with God's divine power as it is manifested in the Church. Yet Boorman subverts this imagery by undermin- ing the stability and permanence associated with the Christian church. Follow- ing their arrival in Aintry and police interrogation, Bobby and Ed are driven back to their hotel by a local cab driver. As the driver attempts to turn left into the parking lot, we see the same church, the Church of Christ, being towed out of town on a small trailer (see figs. 9.8 and 9.9). Not only does this scene call into question the survivors' "divine" deliverance but it also explicitly subverts the "rock" imagery, the metaphorical permanence represented by the church. Instead of being immutable and eternal, the Church is depicted as malleable and tran- sient—the antithesis of Christ's account in Matthew. The permanence of the Church is merely an illusion, or even worse, perhaps, a hallucination that the viewers share with the survivors as they arrive in Aintry. Thus, in literally "un- dermining" God's House, Boorman subverts one of the fundamental tenets of Christianity—the permanence of God's Church.

A final means by which Boorman parodies Christianity is by employing a Judeo-Christian concept as the film's title.[2] "Deliverance," as it is employed in

Figure 9.7

Figure 9.8

Figure 9.9

the Bible, typically means to be "delivered" from evil (as in the Lord's Prayer) into the heavenly Kingdom of God.[3] Additionally, God or Christ provides the vehicle through which "deliverance" is attained; in other words, He is the "Deliverer." How does this concept of "deliverance" function in the film? The "deliverance" we are exposed to in the film is far from the peaceful "rest" promised by God. Having been "delivered" from the seemingly "demonic" forces of the Cahulawassee River—an occurrence visually emphasized by the Church of Christ—each survivor enters into his own personal Hell rather than salvific Heaven.[4] Bobby will be forever haunted by the rape and the ensuing murders of the mountain men. Lewis's visual scars will always be a reminder of the trip and the fact that when the "game" needed to be played, he was castrated of his manhood. Boorman, though, emphasizes the personal Hell into which Ed has been "delivered." Ed's sleep—sleep being perhaps a spiritual equivalent of God's promise of "rest"—is plagued by nightmares in which his sins are visible for all to see. Thus, Ed's "rest" is haunted by the sins he committed on the river, hardly the "deliverance" promised by God.

In scanning the profound interplay between textual inference and intertextual competence, we should not overlook the historical and social context in which the film took place. The film was shot in the spring of 1971, a time when America was still heavily involved in the Vietnam War. Though Richard Nixon's "Vietnamization" program had been in place for over two years, such significant events as the bombing of Cambodia, the mining of Haiphong Harbor, and the bombing of Hanoi were yet to occur (Dittmar and Michaud 326). In 1971, the Vietnam War was very much a part of the social and political landscape.

On the surface, *Deliverance* does not seem to reference American involvement in Vietnam: a canoe trip in north Georgia is far removed from a war being fought in the jungles of Southeast Asia. Yet upon closer inspection, Boorman gives us visual and discursive prompts that not only evoke visions of the Vietnam War but also function to question American interventionism generally. First, Drew, Bobby, Lewis, and Ed are portrayed as outsiders who are intervening in the business-as-usual existence of the mountain people. The mountain people treat the four men as fundamentally different—so different in fact that they are unwilling even to shake hands with the "strangers." The banjo player does not acknowledge Drew's outstretched hand; one of the Griner brothers refuses Ed's help after smashing his finger on an anvil; and the rapist answers Bobby's "How goes it?" with "What the Hell ya think yur doin'?" Except for Drew's musical duel, all of their friendly overtures are firmly rebuffed. That our four adventurers have arrived in a fundamentally different world is also intertextually underscored by the physical landscape: the houses are small wooden shacks; the gas pumps are ancient; old cars litter the grounds; and the Griner brothers travel in a 1940s-era tow truck.

Not only does the physical environment appear hostile to the "outsiders" but the inhabitants also warn them not to "interfere" with the river. The gas station attendant tells Lewis: "Hell, you crazy." One of the Griner brothers asks Lewis, "What the hell you wanna go fuckin' around with that river fur?" and later adds, "You get in there and can't get out, you gunna wish it [the river] wadn't [there]." Thus, despite initial warnings of the impending perils by the natives (the Vietnamese), the outsiders (Americans) do not heed their warnings.

Boorman offers further clues as the "interventionists" head downriver. The thick foliage surrounding the river recalls the dense jungles of Vietnam, as do the snakes, the oppressive heat and humidity, the mosquitoes (Bobby states that he has "bites on top of my bites."), and the sense of being lost (Bobby's reply to the rapist: "Yur right, we're lost."). Also, as night falls and Bobby, Drew, and Ed head to their sleeping bags, the camera focuses on Lewis who, despite being prostrate, stays "on guard" since he thinks he has heard someone in the woods.

Boorman's clues are more explicit, however, following Bobby's rape, the rapist's death, and Drew's disappearance. Because of the sepiatone techniques, the clothing worn by the characters resembles the olive green and sandy brown colors typical of combat fatigues. Furthermore, after Ed's exhausting trek up the face of a nearly vertical cliff, he collapses into a small ravine at the summit of the cliff. He awakens to see a menacing silhouette in the near distance: a person with a gun looks out over the river. Given Ed's ostensibly "correct" intuition that "If he knows where we are, then we know where he's gonna be," the viewer is encouraged to assume that Ed has the enemy at point-blank range. Following several tense moments in which Ed releases his arrow, then pierces his side with his remaining arrow, and the wounded man staggers forward toward Ed with gun in hand only to collapse before shooting him, Ed lies next to the slain mountain man attempting to compose himself. Looking curiously at the mountain man, Ed exclaims, "No, oh no." Furiously, Ed examines the mountain man for his one very discernible feature: his missing front teeth (see fig. 9.10). Ed opens the man's mouth only to find a mouthful of teeth; however, Ed tugs at his dental work and finds, to his relief, that the dead man's two front teeth are in fact dentures. Following this apparent "confirmation," Ed carefully lowers the body over the cliff both to act as an anchor for his descent and to have Bobby identify the body. Despite his rope breaking, which causes him to slide bare-chested down the jagged face of the cliff and to plunge into the river with the corpse, Ed finally meets up with Bobby and an unconscious Lewis. The following dialogue ensues between Bobby and Ed:

> *Bobby:* I don't believe it. You did it, Ed. You killed him. . . . You sure it's him? That's the guy with the gun, huh?
> *Ed:* I think so.
> *Bobby:* "It wasn't just some guy up there . . . up there huntin' or somethin'?
> *Ed:* You tell me. [Ed thrusts up the dead man's face to Bobby.]

Figure 9.10

Once again, as an overt subversion of viewer expectations, Bobby's response is never heard as Boorman cuts to an overhead shot of Ed sinking the body.

The scene intertextually recalls a major obstacle many American GI's encountered in Vietnam: the problem of identity.[5] Given the physical similarities between the North and South Vietnamese, were American soldiers killing the "right" people? Similarly, is Ed's victim a victim of "friendly fire," a not uncommon occurrence in the jungles of Vietnam (Hackworth and Sherman 465)? Like Ed Gentry, many soldiers killed simply because the Other carried a weapon and looked like the enemy. These seemingly random acts of killing in both *Deliverance* and in Vietnam entail similar questions: Who is the "real" enemy? Is it Ed/the American soldier for shooting first and asking questions later, in addition to the "invasion" of a foreign territory they were warned to stay away from? Or should we blame Lewis/the commanding officer for blindly leading his unprepared "troops" into the hostile environs simply because "it's [the river] there"? Regardless of where the blame falls, we know that Ed is forced to suffer the same maladies that would haunt many Vietnam veterans: nightmares in which their crimes are laid bare.

One of the main frustrations expressed by the film's critics is its ambiguity; specifically, the uncertainty as to whether Drew was shot and whether Ed killed the right man. One viewing of the film will not clear up these ambiguities. However, by closely examining and replaying several key scenes, some of the ambiguities concerning Drew's death and Ed's killing of the mountain man may be clarified. This clarification, moreover, also recalls some of the tragedies of the Vietnam War.

With regard to Drew's death, Lewis claims that "Drew was shot." "Proof" for his claim resides in Lewis's repeated glances toward the top of the cliff just prior to Drew's falling overboard (see fig. 9.11). Though the camera does not focus on the object of Lewis's gaze, Lewis clearly sees something or someone. Moreover, Lewis would surely not be distracted by something unimportant given that he was in very rough white water. The viewer, though, never hears the sound of a gunshot before Drew's plunge into the river. Also, Drew's body does not react violently as if shot; he appears to simply fall over the side, as if willfully bringing about his own death. Further proof that Drew was not shot is that neither Ed nor Bobby—after finding his body—can locate a gunshot wound.

Regardless of the cause of Drew's death, we must still inquire as to whether Ed shot and killed the rapist's accomplice, who, as Ed thinks, is plotting their demise. Despite the dental evidence, Boorman provides a very subtle clue that Ed shot the wrong man. That is, the rapist's toothless companion is clearly right-handed in that he aims his rifle at Bobby with the butt of the gun on his right shoulder (see fig. 9.12). However, as he stumbles toward Ed after being pierced by the arrow, the mountain man fires the gun left-handed—an unnatural act if one is right-handed (see fig. 9.13). On this admittedly thin evidence, we can ten-

Figure 9.11

Figure 9.12

tatively conclude that Ed most likely shot the wrong man. Ed's willingness to "avenge" Drew's death by shooting first and asking questions later is not dissimilar from many of the atrocities committed by American soldiers in Vietnam. Such a shoot-first-and-ask-questions-later mentality resulted in several massacres of innocent South Vietnamese villagers, most notably the 1968 My Lai massacre.

Figure 9.13

Boorman's critique of American intervention in Vietnam is unequivocally devastating. Boorman explodes the myth of the conquering frontiersman (interventionist) by emphasizing an unwillingness to listen and an ignorance of the challenges that await. Our "heroic warriors" return home not triumphantly but badly scarred, both psychically and physically. Rape, death, physical and mental suffering, and uncertainty about the future are the tangible "rewards" for their intervention. Perhaps the most telling indictment and repudiation of American interventionism occurs near the end of the film. As they are about to depart from Aintry, the Sheriff arrives to ask Bobby and Ed a few more questions. Having answered the questions to his satisfaction, the Sheriff (played by James Dickey) tells Ed: "Don't never do nothin' like this again. Don't come back up here. . . . I'd kinda like to see this town die peacefully." Bobby responds, "You don't have to worry about that Sheriff." Thus, the film invites the interpretation that not only has American interventionism been firmly repudiated by the natives but also that the Americans have voiced their assent in staying away.

Methodological choices have consequences. Read as a linear, material unity, *Deliverance* resists thematic interpretation in that the viewer is left with ambiguities that are largely unresolvable. A linear, unified narrative creates its own interpretative demands on the critic, which in the case of *Deliverance* are ultimately frustrated, as evidenced by its reviewers in a manner which may be seen as analogous to Eco's "naive" reading of Allais's *Drame.*

At issue here is a very important methodological choice between what we would term "critical time" versus "filmic time." Moreover, as we have illustrated in this essay, the choice that the critic makes will predispose the critic to "read" the film in a particular manner. By "filmic time" (otherwise called "diegetics" by various critics), we are referring to the actual temporal progression of the film: what follows what. On this "traditional" view, films have a beginning, middle, and ending within which characters are introduced, a conflict emerges, and a resolution occurs. By accepting the film's "time," the critic passively spectates on a series of events whose "meaning" is largely fixed or predetermined within the sequential matrix. "Critical time," on the other hand, involves the critic's suspension of "filmic time" in order to construct a text based on its fragments— fragments whose meaning is not necessarily influenced by *where* and *when* they occur in the film, but that they occur at all. Such a critical repositioning enables the critic to become "an interventionist rather than a deferential, if expert, spectator" (Blair, Jeppeson, and Pucci 283).

By reading above and beyond "filmic time," we have illustrated that *Deliverance* does in fact "mean" and that its meaning is not simply "meaninglessness" (Dempsey 17). By problematizing gender, the Christian religion, and American interventionism, Boorman's film functions as a critique of early 1970s American culture. Text performance, though, is a very speculative endeavor, especially given the medium under consideration. Without knowing the author's intent, the critic must find meaning in visual, musical, and discursive cues—cues which rarely appear as univocal or uncontested. Such an approach views the text as "a form, namely a movement . . . an infinite contained within finiteness" (Eco 63). In keeping with Eco's framework, we do not hope to "prove" that our reading is "right" or "correct." What is of paramount importance to us is that the text that we have constructed is not the text only as we would have it, but that Boorman's text has succeeded in exacting its own demands on the critic.

Notes

An earlier version of this essay was presented at the 1995 Literature and Popular Culture Conference in Binghamton, New York. We would like to thank Tom Benson of Pennsylvania State University for his helpful reading of and suggestions on an earlier draft.

All illustrations in this essay are from *Deliverance,* © 1972, by Warner Brothers, Inc.

1. That *Deliverance* has been largely ignored by film and rhetoric scholars is

attested to by the amount of critical dialogue on the film. Aside from film reviews, only three scholarly essays have been devoted to it. See Armour, "Four Variations of the American Adam" (1973), Dempsey, "*Deliverance*/Boorman: Dickey in the Woods" (1973), and Robinson, "'Emotional Constipation' and the Power of Masculinity" (2001).

2. Boorman's intent in keeping Dickey's title may have been motivated by strictly pecuniary prospects since the novel *Deliverance* was a best-seller.

3. For other examples of "Godly" deliverance, see Psalms 34.4, Psalms 107.6, Psalms 116.8, Romans 4.25, Obadiah 1.17, and Matthew 6.13.

4. Novelist James Dickey claims that the river scenes in the book were inspired by Satan's voyage through Chaos in Milton's "Paradise Lost." See Endel, "Dickey, Dante, and the Demonic" (1988).

5. For an excellent discussion of the problems American GI's had in correctly identifying the enemy, see Hackworth and Sherman, *About Face* (1989).

Works Cited

Aigner, Hal. *Deliverance. Film Quarterly* 26.2 (1972–73): 39–41.

Armour, Robert. "Four Variations of the American Adam." *Literature/Film Quarterly* 1 (1973): 280–85.

Arnold, Gary. "*Deliverance:* A Gripping Piece of Work." *Washington Post* 5 Oct. 1972: B1.

Blair, Carole, Marsch Jeppeson, and Enrico Pucci. "Public Memorializing in Postmodernity: The Vietnam Veterans Memorial as Prototype." *Quarterly Journal of Speech* 77 (1991): 263–88.

Bledsoe. J. "What Will Save Us from Boredom?" *Esquire* Dec. 1973: 227–33.

Blevins, Winfred. "'*Deliverance*': Fascinating, Stunning Film." *Los Angeles Herald-Examiner* 17 Aug. 1972: B9.

Boggs, Joseph M. *The Art of Watching Films.* 2d ed. Palo Alto, CA: Mayfield, 1985.

Buckley, Peter. "*Deliverance.*" *Films & Filming* Oct. 1972: 46.

Burke, Kenneth. *A Rhetoric of Motives.* Berkeley: U of California P, 1969.

Canby, Vincent. "The Screen: James Dickey's 'Deliverance' Arrives." *New York Times* 31 July 1972: 21.

Champlin, Charles. "Men Against River—of Life?—in *Deliverance. Los Angeles Times* 13 Aug. 1972: Cal: 1.

Clover, Carol. *Men, Women, and Chain Saws: Gender in the Modern Horror Film.* Princeton: Princeton UP, 1992.

Cocks, Jay. "Rites of Passage." *Time* Aug. 1972: 75–76.

Dempsey, Michael. "*Deliverance*/Boorman: Dickey in the Woods." *Cinema* 8 (1973): 10–17.

Dickey, Christopher. "Summer of Deliverance." *The New Yorker* 13 July 1998: 38–51.

Dickey, James. *Deliverance.* Carbondale: Southern Illinois UP, 1982.

Dittmar, Linda, and Gene Michaud, eds. *From Hanoi to Hollywood: The Vietnam War in American Film*. New Brunswick: Rutgers UP, 1990.

Eco, Umberto. *The Role of the Reader*. Bloomington: Indiana UP, 1979.

Endel, P. G. "Dickey, Dante, and the Demonic: Reassessing *Deliverance*." *American Literature* 60 (1988): 611–24.

Farber, Stephen. *"Deliverance*—How It Delivers." *New York Times* 20 Aug. 1972: 2: 9.

Gilliatt, Penelope. "The Current Cinema." *The New Yorker* Aug. 1972: 52–53.

Gould Boyum, Joy. "Uncharted Paths in an Ugly World." *Wall Street Journal* 8 Oct. 1972: 8.

Hackworth, David, and J. Sherman. *About Face*. New York: Simon, 1989.

Kauffman, Stanley. "Fair to Meddling." *New Republic* Aug. 1972: 24, 35.

Knight, Arthur. *"Deliverance* . . . and Deliver Us from Evil." *Film 72/73*. Ed. David Denby. Indianapolis: Bobbs-Merrill, 1973. 19–21.

Mellen, Joan. *Big Bad Wolves: Masculinity in the American Film*. New York: Pantheon, 1977.

The New International Version Study Bible. Grand Rapids, MI: Zondervan, 1985.

Osborn, Michael. "The Evolution of the Archetypal Sea in Rhetoric and Poetic." *Quarterly Journal of Speech* 63 (1977): 347–63.

Robinson, Sally. "'Emotional Constipation' and the Power of Damned Masculinity: *Deliverance* and the Paradoxes of Male Liberation." *Masculinity: Bodies, Movies, Culture*. Ed. Peter Lehman. New York: Routledge, 2001. 133–47.

Samuels, Charles Thomas. "How Not to Film a Novel." *American Scholar* 42 (1972–73): 148–54.

Schickel, Richard. "White Water, Black Doings." *Life* Aug. 1972: 8.

Siskel, Gene. *"Deliverance." Chicago Tribune* 5 Oct. 1972: 2: 14.

Willson, Robert F. *"Deliverance* from Novel to Film: Where Is Our Hero?" *Literature/Film Quarterly* 2 (1974): 52–58.

Zimmerman, Paul D. Review of *Deliverance*, dir. John Boorman. *Newsweek* Aug. 1972: 61.

10

From "World Conspiracy" to "Cultural Imperialism": The History of Anti-Plutocratic Rhetoric in German Film

Friedemann Weidauer

THE READER FAMILIAR WITH JOSEPH GOEBBEL'S SPEECHES WILL immediately be reminded of them by the title of this essay. It was he who in 1941 reminded the Germans that propaganda in film is the most important means of leading the people "in the fight against plutocracy" (qtd. in Wollenberg 37). It is typical of the Nazi rhetoric to use terms such as *plutocracy* that are devoid of any concrete sociohistoric context, terms that name enemies, but don't exactly tell you who they are, a textual device perfectly suited to create a general feeling of paranoia that in turn can be given content and direction as the situation at hand demands. Also in tune with the thrust of Nazi rhetoric is the fact that such nebulous terms do not point at any specific social class so as not to alienate any sector of the *Volksgemeinschaft* that still might turn out to be of use to those in power. If the Nazis had been true to the misnomer in their party's name (national *socialist*), the word of choice would have been *capitalism*. It is of course obvious to anyone familiar with the Nazis' anti-Semitic rhetoric that the term *plutocracy* is used to make a distinction between the "good, honest Aryan leaders of industry" and the "bad, cheating Jewish plutocrats," a dichotomy established in Germany's archive of cultural stereotypes that can be traced back to the beginning of the industrial revolution and that has been realized most insidiously as a compositional device in Gustav Freytag's best-selling novel *Credit and Debit*.

Given this history of the term *plutocracy,* it must appear like a horrible insult to German film to attempt to argue that the use of this term as rhetorical device is one of the constants in the history of German film. However, this seems like an aspect in the scholarship on German film that has been neglected, in particular since histories of German film seem to suggest that there were distinct periods that, since they can be delineated and charted off against each other so neatly with the help of historic events, appear to have not much in common in terms of their ideological backdrop: Weimar Film, Nazi Film, Postwar Film, the New German Cinema. In fact, as if to make the breaks between periods tangible, it is difficult to find histories of all four periods within the confines of one book. Of course we know that early on scholars like Siegfried Kracauer tried to establish that the ideological roots of Nazi film lead us back to some of the films of the Weimar period. Similarly, the escapist phantasies embodied in the bulk of movies produced during the Nazi period (the majority of films produced in those years cannot be linked directly to propagandistic purposes) find their continuation in similar phantasies of the postwar period. But otherwise, the Weimar period and the New German Cinema are usually set off against the other two periods on the basis of stylistic and content-related arguments. On the one hand, Weimar Film and New German Film have in common the impetus to create a style at least partially in opposition to Hollywood film (and this intention is reflected in the organizational style preferred by the New German Cinema, the *Autorenfilm*). The New German Cinema, on the other hand, mainly seemed to deserve this name because it cut off any connections to the problematic ideological tenants of the previous two periods while claiming as its ancestor the "progressive" tradition present in the Weimar period: "A gap of a quarter century opened. In literature and other areas this was by no means as dramatically apparent. We, the new generation of film directors, are a generation without fathers. We are orphans. We only have grandfathers, like Murnau, Lang, Pabst, the generation of the twenties" (Herzog; qtd. in Rentschler 116). This self-stylization of the New German Filmmakers as orphans and as the true heirs of the Weimar directors has been accepted as a true statement about their ideological innocence. This however creates a paradox: Siegfried Kracauer has tried to show how Weimar film represents aspects of tyranny that prefigure historic realities. At the same time, in a programmatic statement at the beginning of his book, he states: "The films of a nation reflect its mentality" (5). At the same time, representatives of the New German Film like Volker Schlöndorff are in general agreement with Kracauer's theses. If then a number of films of the Weimar period display an at best equivocal fascination with tyrants (more on this in the analyses of Weimar films below), according to Kracauer this reflects the mentality of the German nation at this point in time. In turn, the directors form part of this nation, so the films are reflecting their own mentality as well. According to Kracauer, it is a mentality which made the Germans particularly susceptible to the lures of a dictatorship. So if one claims to be the true heir of these Weimar grandparents, how can one be at the same time immune to their susceptibility to authoritarian tendencies?

I would like to show therefore two things: Some of the Weimar films in fact do display susceptibility to authoritarian tendencies beyond those discussed in Kracauer's programmatic statement that has already been quoted. For the analyses of the Weimar films, I would actually like to enhance Kracauer's approach by also using a more differentiated one that was formulated at pretty much the exact same time as Kracauer's:

> Between the film and public there exist effect and counter-effect. Many films are made with the intention of creating certain effects. Alternatively, changes in taste influence the selection of film subjects. . . . The political history of the Cinema in Germany has many interesting examples of these effects and counter-effects. (Wollenberg 29)

The next step then logically follows: Are the New German filmmakers heirs to their Weimar forefathers in this regard as well? If this kind of continuity can be demonstrated, the continuity promised in the title can be established for the entire history of German film.

The films analyzed in this essay lend themselves to a rhetorical approach as they contain both a rhetoric to aesthetic ends, "a fiction's suasion that its unfolding form be accepted," and a rhetoric to ideological ends, a "message beyond" (Chatman 188). Each aspect here affirms the other. A successful narrative helps get the ideological message across, and the recalling and reshaping of ideologies in circulation among the intended audiences make the narrative appear to follow a more stringent logic. At the level of their ideological message and rhetoric, the films discussed here occupy "the mid ground of rhetoric—between the unconscious response and blatant manipulation" (Harrington 4). For their aesthetic "suasion," the films rely on and reshape images that have come to form the repertoire of the filmmaking tradition of which they aspire to be heirs. For their ideological "suasion," they select, transform, and exploit "ideologemes" (the building blocks of large-scale ideologies in Louis Althusser's definition) from all levels of the culture in which they perform this rhetoric, everything from medieval folk legends to contemporary political events. As I hope will become clear in the course of my argument, it is this repertoire of ideologemes that can be seen as the building blocks of a national (German) language of film. In this language of film, the metonymic connections between images as they change over time make possible the argument for a continuous history of German film, in contrast to the traditional claim that the history of German film is marked by discontinuity. As the title of my essay already suggests, there is a metonymic connection even between the "large-scale" ideologies of a (Jewish) "world conspiracy" against Germany and the "cultural imperialism" supposedly directed at German film (and German culture in general) by Hollywood (and by U.S. culture in general). The "fabula" of each film discussed here contains at its core a tale of evil forces conspiring against the soul of German culture, and in each film, "the fabula world stands for a set of abstract propositions whose validity the film at once presupposed and reasserts" (Bordwell 235) as well as readjusts over time.

My argument for continuity relies on the ideologically vague link between plutocracy and tyranny. This link is intentionally vague and therefore dangerous because invectives against the rich could be directed against the rich representatives of a certain ethnic group and thereby, for example, be filled with anti-Semitic content as has been the case in Goebbels' speeches, in Nazi films, and in the precursory form in Weimar films. This tendency can be summarized in the paranoia about a "Jewish world conspiracy," the paranoia that a certain ethnic group that supposedly controls most of the world's financial assets is posed to take over the world. Invectives against the rich can also stem from the resentments of the "occupied" against the "occupiers," as was the case in postwar West Germany. In this case, the ideological link between plutocracy and tyranny is formed by anti-American sentiment as a result of the presence of this dominant (and wealthy) occupying force among the Allies on West German soil. As one can see, this connection can be made regardless of the political system that the "plutocrats" represent:

> And do we not find again the same submission (as the submission of the Germans to Nazi authority in the 30's; FW) directly after the Second World War, with the exception that here one submits to the democracy of the victors—here an American, there a Soviet one—but never truly emancipates oneself and establishes a republic of one's own? (Schlöndorff; trans. in Rentschler 11)

There are four remarkable points being made in this quotation. First, it implies that a democracy existed in the Soviet Union; second, that this democracy was only different from the Western one in terms of its national character; third, that one submits to a democracy just as one does to the terror of an authoritarian regime; and fourth, the statement gives the impression that this democracy was imposed over a people who had already thought about alternatives but were not given the chance to realize them. If one accepts the four assumptions contained in this statement, it becomes easy to conceive of the occupying forces as tyrannical or imperialist intruders. Thus we have arrived at the other term in the title of this essay, the phrase "cultural imperialism," coined by the German Left in the 1960s as the description of American activities on German soil that most of the representatives of the New German Cinema accepted as a given. The protagonist of Wim Wenders's *Kings of the Road* (1976) formulates it only slightly differently: "The Yanks have colonized our subconscious."

I hope it will become clear that I am not trying to equate the ideology of the German Left of the 1960s with that of the Right of the 1930s. What I want to show is that unqualified attacks on "the rich" as we find them in Weimar Film, Nazi Film, and the New German Cinema reflect and create a paranoia that can be put to the worst ideological purposes (for example, creating a kind of "preemptive tyranny" in the form of a tyranny by one person or by one class against the one we fear will be imposed on us by the "plutocratic" tyrants) and that can only be counteracted by an exact analysis of who "the rich" are at a given point. So this is the other big paradox that needs to be pointed out before we go into the analyses of specific films: As part of the student movement of the 1960s and as the professed heirs of the highly politicized cultural climate of the Weimar Republic, New German Filmmakers have created films which display an amazing and conspicuous absence of any analyses of the sociohistorical background of "the rich" that have come to colonize us and about which the films seem to warn us. It is this lack of sociohistoric analysis which turns criticism that might be justified into ideologically dangerous commonplaces.

The rhetoric against the plutocrats contains three elements that can be combined in a number of ways to form an almost infinite number of possible plots. As we will see, the plutocrats, apart from being rich, are usually also seductive in a sexual sense and have forces at their disposal that seem to originate from sources other than worldly powers. They are, in other words, Mephisto-like characters who seduce their victims with the promise of making them rich and, in the process, corrupt their environment morally. They do this in ways that often seem to rely on faculties that lie beyond the reach of the average mortal. Thus the encounter of characters in the films with the plutocrats often involves a Faustian kind of pact in which souls are being exchanged for rewards in the form of financial success or sexual adventures. It seems that this archaic conception of what it means to be rich is particularly well suited to serve a variety of ideological projects since it alludes to deep-seated fears about the magical powers of material wealth. In the case of German film, these ideological projects are at the same time overdetermined by another constant in German film history: the competition with and fear of the commercially more successful Hollywood film industry. The plutocrats that play with the souls of the Germans are also the Hollywood film directors that dazzle the German audiences through the opulence of the illusions they create. From Weimar to the New German Film, German directors who "have made it" in Hollywood are perceived of as having done so by selling their souls and their "German" way of filmmaking for the riches offered by this magical kingdom. To refuse the pact with the Hollywood devil meant the New German filmmakers simply refused one Faustian deal in favor of another: "That means we will have to maintain a definite *non-commercial* position within the framework of a free-market economy. For these reasons the Cultural Minister Conference has recommended the support of culturally significant films in the discussions about the 1963 budget" (Kluge; trans. in Rentschler 11). In other words, the pact with the commercially successful Hollywood Mephisto was replaced by one with the Beelzebub of state subsidies. One can only wonder incredulously at the naïveté of these filmmakers who seem to have forgotten that the entanglement of state subsidies with state censorship had not only never been disentangled in the history of German film but had in fact led to some of its worst ideological aberrations. In the following analyses of the depiction of Mephistophelean plutocrats, one should therefore also keep in mind that these plots at the same time form displaced discussions by the filmmakers of their ambiguous position within filmmaking as an industry.

Plutocrats in Weimar Film

Siegfried Kracauer has argued that the obsession with and fear of tyrants displayed in films of the Weimar period reflect an obsession with and fear of bolshevism (77). But even his own filmic analyses do not produce any evidence to support this claim. One of the common denominators of the tyrants that haunt German cinema of this time period—from Dr. Mabuse in the film with the same title to Haghi in Fritz Lang's film *Spione*—is that they are financial geniuses. The irony is that this type of tyrant thrives in those environments that can be called democratic. One could therefore argue that the German fear of tyrants as reflected or constructed in these films does not relate to a fear of tyranny as a political system, but to a fear of political systems that allow such monsters to thrive, in other words, laissez-faire Western democracies. Thus I would argue that Kracauer's line of argument—reflected in the title of his book, *From Caligari to Hitler*—has to be reformulated. The obsession and fascination with tyrants does not foreshadow the advent of Hitler as the embodiment of these artistic constructions. The type of tyrant populating Weimar cinema is a new and unfamiliar type of tyrant, one who is in control of the seemingly magical powers of the financial market. The political type of tyrants, one could argue, the Germans were thoroughly familiar with. One usually does not obsess with or irrationally fear what one has experienced firsthand for quite some time. Fear arises from what is unknown and other. What the Germans did not know much about at this time were the perils of the stock market, which made those who were able to play it masterfully appear like sorcerers. One of the sources of paranoid fear is reality, and as the crash of 1929 showed, paranoia about the stock market was at least partially justified. On the other hand, paranoia also arises when one does not exactly know what the danger is, and again, no one exactly knew what kind of catastrophes the stock market could produce. The increasing visibility and importance of the stock market therefore provided an ideal focal point of an as yet unfocused feeling of uncertainty in these economically less than secure years. The closer we get to the year 1929, the more concrete the image of the tyrant as financial magnate becomes in Weimar film. The more uncertain the economic situation becomes, the more magical power is attributed to these magnates. The tyrant Hitler should therefore not be seen as a continuation of this obsession, but as the expression of the hope to be relieved of this fear: A more familiar type of tyrant, a political one, was supposed to tame these unfamiliar monsters, and as we know, Hitler had included in his demagogy the promise to do so.

It is fairly easy to see a parallel to this process within the film industry of this time period. German cinema was in fierce competition with other movie producing countries, in particular, with the United States. The competition did not only concern commercial issues, but was just as fierce in the arena of technological innovation. If German directors then chose to construct images of tyrants who are not only financially successful but also in control of technologies that border on magic, this must be seen not just as a reflection of fears they perceived among the rest of the population but also as the projection of their own fears, their fears of being overrun by commercially more successful and technologically more advanced products from other nations. The more familiar tyrant in this case must therefore be the one who promises protection in the quiform of censorship of or quotas on foreign films in connection with hearty subsidies for the indigenous film industry. This tyrant came in the form of such agencies as the UFA, which among others controlled the first-run cinemas, or the TOBIS and the Klang Film Company, which was supposed to absorb the attack of the talkies on the German film market in 1929 (cf. Wollenberg 12, 24). The readiness to call in the more familiar tyrant to battle the magical powers of the unknown was established in this time period, in politics as well as in the film industry.

The financial magnate depicted in the film *Freudlose Gasse (Joyless Street)* (G. W. Pabst, 1925) is still a fairly realistic character, but he already shares a number of attributes with his more sinister successors in later films. Don Alfonso Canez, the "international speculator," has "ten thousand dollars in his pockets and no scruples." As the epithet "international" implies, his activities are neither limited to one country nor does he show concern for the specific country that he chooses as the staging ground. This of course is a precondition for being involved in a "world conspiracy" that ruins local economies exactly because it has no feeling of belonging, no roots, no *Heimat*. Though this character is not clearly constructed in anti-Semitic terms, it is clear however that the lack of a "fatherland" and the endless wandering form part of the complex of anti-Semitic stereotype. Apart from his name, Don Alfonso Canez is also clearly constructed as "non-Germanic" in terms of his physical features. In addition, he is surrounded by a lawyer and his wife who bears a Jewish name, Lia Leid.

Compared to the demonstration of desire to rule the world displayed by his successors in German film, Don Alfonso's scheme is still relatively limited: By spreading rumors of a strike the price of shares in the local coal company will be driven down, he will then buy a controlling majority of these shares and then make a remarkable profit as demand for heat and power will certainly drive up the price of the shares again. While Don Alfonso provides the financial assets that drive this scheme, he doesn't seem to be its mastermind. Rather, he is surrounded by locals (Austrians) who contribute to this plan in the hope of profiting from it as well.

One of the victims of this scheme is counselor Rumfort, who, in the hope of turning around his family's financial situation, has cashed in his pension fund to buy shares of this company. When he hears of the drop in price, he suffers what seems to be a heart attack. "Faced with the ghost of misery," this in turn induces his daughter Greta to accept a position at a disreputable nightclub. Her good middle-class reputation is restored, however, when it becomes known that the money she used to pay off her father's debts was not money earned at this club. She is rescued from the club before having to compromise her morals. Her

lower-class colleague Maria is not as lucky. This woman has fallen in love with
Don Alfonso's secretary, Egon, who in turn hopes to profit from the scheme of
his employer by playing the stock market but lacks the cash to do so. Maria hopes
to escape her misery at home with the help of Egon, so she plans to provide him
with money by accepting a position at the same club, which happens to be fre-
quented by such men as Don Alfonso himself. In fact, she becomes his paid escort. This involvement with evil for the sake of such nonaltruistic motives results in a downward movement that ends in her arrest: Recognizing the threat
to her plan, she kills Lia, who had also been having an affair with Egon.

Don Alfonso would not be able to pursue his schemes without the help of
the locals. They, however, through the contact with him, become corrupted themselves and are punished for this association with the foreign speculator in a variety of ways: Egon briefly goes to prison as the prime suspect in the murder of
Lia, and, obviously, Lia herself gets killed. The real victim however is the virtue
of the Austrian women.[1]

Don Alfonso does not have to rely on magical powers; he can rely on the
collaboration of unscrupulous locals and on the desperation of men like Rumfort.
So while the stock market was certainly not the main reason for the misery of
the average Austrian at this time, the setting in which Don Alfonso operates is
still fairly realistic. There is even an element of hope contained in how the film
ends: the women on the street stage an impromptu uprising against the local
manifestation of financial power, a butcher who had traded meat for access to
the meat market operated out of the nightclub. But Don Alfonso also already
represents a number of the trademarks of a long line of financial tyrants: he is
foreign, he corrupts the indigenous population morally, and he forces them into
Faustian pacts in which they give up their souls. Above all, his scheming happens at a level that is so far removed from the level of experience of the average
citizens that they must feel they are the victims of superior powers. At the same
time, the film makes it clear that the difference in having these powers or not is
simply a result of the uneven distribution of wealth. Thus, the tone of the film
vacillates between a realistic view of the social effects of drastic differences in the
material well-being within a class-conscious society and a less than realistic fascination with wealth as the instrument of moral corruption. The film is already
engaged in constructing the dichotomy between "good" and "corrupt" leaders
of industry, identities that will later allow the fascist leaders to include "Aryan"
capitalists in the *Volksgemeinschaft* while polemicizing against the Jewish financial "world conspiracy." Characteristic of the members of the latter group is that
their lifestyle includes a preoccupation with what later will be termed "degenerate" art: Whenever the rich are celebrating one of their orgies in this film, they
listen to jazz music.

Any change in the distribution of wealth is out of the question in the world
we enter in Fritz Lang's *Metropolis* (1926). The class system is written in stone,
in a literal sense, as the construction of the whole city constitutes its spatial equiva-

lent.[2] But the stubborn refusal of the ruler Frederson ("the brain") to give the workers ("the hands") their fair share nevertheless represents a source of conflict. The workers in turn engage in an effort at organizing themselves; the leader they have chosen, however, Maria, does not talk about redistributing the wealth of this empire, but rather about some vague notion of reconciliation that has to take place between "the hands" and "the brain." The workers are supposed to wait for a mediator who will serve as "the heart," the link between the hands and the brain.

But even this desire to soften the grip of tyranny on the inhabitants of Metropolis is more than Frederson is willing to tolerate. To crush the early manifestations of the workers' attempts to organize, he develops a plan that aims at expanding his power into totalitarian rule as it will allow him to intrude into areas of the lives of the workers to which he previously had no access. His accomplice, the inventor Rotwang, builds a robot, in the likeness of Maria, who will incite the workers into rising up against Frederson, which in turn will allow him to expand his control over them in the course of cracking down on this revolt.[3]

This plot allows Lang to distribute aspects of tyranny onto two different characters. Though a tyrant, Frederson's attributes will, if used right, allow him to become an authoritarian ruler under whose firm leadership all of society will prosper. Rotwang, on the other hand, is associated with the powers of evil that threaten to corrupt and destroy the order in Metropolis. He is at the same time a construct of aspects from the archives of anti-Semitic stereotypes. His residence resembles medieval architecture in this otherwise futuristic city, but he also has at his disposal the most advanced kind of technology, which he uses to build the robot; thus, he embodies the prejudice against the Jewish people of being "backward," while at the same time having the power to bring to life the Golem. Moreover, his name is Jewish and its German pronunciation invokes the incarnation of Jewish financial genius, the Rothschilds. He is the one who "corrupts" the Christian Maria and turns her likeness into a sexually seductive rabble-rouser. In the course of doing so there are several scenes that resemble a rape of Maria. To establish the link to anti-Semitic prejudice further, prominently displayed on the door of Rotwang's house is a pentagram that, as the German audience knows from the Faust legend, when drawn on a doorwell can either keep evil forces out or trap them inside. Though clearly visible in one shot, it is present on the screen only for such a brief moment that most people won't be able to discern whether they have just seen a pentagram or the Star of David.

In the scene of reconciliation between "the brain" and "the hands" in which Frederson's son Freder plays "the heart" and in which the arrangement relies heavily on pillaging motives from the New Testament, this construction of "evil" tyranny as the result of a collaboration between the representative of an ultimately beneficial autocracy and a demonic representative of corruptive and supernatural powers allows a quick and easy reformulation of the system into the shape of a *Volksgemeinschaft* as it will be put into practice by the Nazis: the forces of "evil" can be surgically removed. In this case, the evil Rotwang is thrown off the roof of, naturally, a Gothic cathedral by Freder in his attempt to rescue Maria, who has been taken hostage by Rotwang. This having been accomplished, Frederson and the representative of the workers shake hands, affirming Maria's earlier teachings that they are all "brothers," or *Volksgenossen,* the term the Nazis used. Even though Frederson himself didn't change much (Kracauer argues that in fact he has "outwitted" his son [163]), he now represents a cleansed and reformed form of tyranny in which everyone lives in brotherly harmony. While it is not clear whether Lang grasped the ideological implications of his film, the Nazis clearly understood them: The "good" ruler/"bad" tyrant dichotomy established in the characters of Freder and Rotwang/Rothschild served as a kind of blueprint for two Nazi movies, each one of them further elaborating on the two aspects of this dichotomy. The film *Der Herrscher* ("The Ruler," directed by Veit Harlan, 1937) gives us an example of the good plutocrat modeled after Krupp, while *Die Rothschilds—Aktien von Waterloo* ("The Rothschilds—Shares on Waterloo," directed by Erich Waschneck, 1940) traces the supposedly evil scheming of this family throughout European history. *Metropolis* also offers a version of the Faust plot, which could also serve as the model for the pact between Hitler and the Germans: by staging public spectacles during which "Mephisto" is "thrown off the roof," it is suggested that from now on whenever you sell your soul to anyone, you can be assured that the buyer cannot be this evil genius anymore.[4]

In terms of its overt ideological thrust, Lang's later movie *Spione* (1927) lags behind its famous predecessor. The political order that forms the backdrop of the plot of this film, Britain's constitutional monarchy, is not at stake in the fight between the forces of evil and the representatives of virtue. In fact, apart from the Japanese envoy who kills himself after he realizes that his moral weakness cost three of his agents their lives, there are no characters who seem to act in accordance with any moral imperatives. The protagonist representing the British system, the secret agent Donald Tremaine, is as committed to a set of political ideas as his famous successor Agent 007; that is, he probably wouldn't be able to tell you how government gets selected. He is surrounded by bumbling British state bureaucrats who are more concerned with securing a comfortable retirement than with defending their country's freedom and values. In other words, the system they serve does not seem to inspire any fervent commitment in the people who serve it. Thus the Japanese envoy, whose hara-kiri is preceded by visions of the imperial Japanese flag and of his countrymen dying in the line of duty, stands out as a shining example of patriotic devotion. One can only speculate whether or not the writer of the script, Thea von Harbou, meant to suggest that Japan should not risk any alliances other than the one with Germany, which in this regard seems to offer itself as an ally akin to the values presented by the Japanese character.

The laissez-faire political system depicted in this film provides the ideal climate for villains like Haghi, a bank director and financial genius as well as a master spy and circus clown. A somewhat pluralistic society seems to give too much freedom to criminals with multiple identities. A more orderly system, or in our vocabulary, a totalitarian one, would make this character stick out like a sore thumb on account of his otherness: His name and physical features (dark hair, goatee) mark him as different and group him with other villains of the type of Don Alfonso. He seems to be able to recruit his followers because he offers them the opportunity to commit themselves to a principle, that is to himself as their master, exactly because the political system in which they live does not encourage this type of unconditional devotion but rather creates its own enemies on account of its abstract judicial system: Haghi has recruited one of his most loyal followers by freeing him from prison; another one, the woman who is supposed to seduce the government agent Tremaine, works for Haghi because "the government" destroyed her father and brother.

In contrast to Frederson, Haghi combines the attributes of the financial genius and of the sorcerer in one person. Thus, he cannot be "reformed" by surgically removing his evil attributes. This is where we finally find a connection to the Bolsheviks as perhaps one of the focal points of (subconscious) German paranoia. Haghi's evil empire conjures up visions of Stalin's Soviet Union. The effort to destroy his empire takes the form of a large-scale military operation whose imagery evokes what at this point was simply called the "Great War": Poison gas is used to "flush" people out of Haghi's bank, and the train wreck that takes place just before this scene resembles a battlefield littered with bent metal and populated by medical orderlies rescuing the wounded. Though the existing political system is eventually able to defeat Haghi, this seems to occur more by chance than on the basis of the strength of this system. By implication, any future conflict of this type, the film seems to suggest, will have to be staged as a battle of ideologies between troops committed to the "right" and "wrong" kind of authoritarian figure.

Nevertheless, the link between the attributes of a plutocrat and a Soviet-type dictator in this film is still as weak as it was, and is, in reality. To establish the ideological link between these opposing principles was left to the Nazis via their version of anti-Semitic prejudice and hatred, the concept of a "Jewish world conspiracy." The film contains one element of which this ideology could take hold. Haghi is bound to a wheelchair, an element which forms a constant contrast to his omnipotence in all other aspects of life. One of the elements that overdetermines anti-Semitic ideology is the combination of paranoia about Jews as sorcerers who poison the water and bring to life the Golem and the phantasy about their inferiority in terms of physical strength. The construction of the character of Haghi seemed to have worked along parallel lines to create this form of double vision and makes the film susceptible to this interpretation. To top it all, the cunning of Haghi is further stressed by revealing that he has only faked his physical impairment.

The three films discussed here in chronological order represent a continuous development in two respects: As the real financial disaster of the crash of the stock market approaches, the films become less and less concrete in their analyses of how financial power can create misery. In turn, the responses to the plutocratic tyrants become increasingly a matter of ideology, and not of people's reactions to the economic conditions imposed onto their lives. *Freudlose Gasse (Joyless Street)* showed how playing the stock market can hurt the "little" people, and consequently showed them staging a small scale revolt. *Metropolis* showed how the stubbornness of a financial magnate can threaten an entire political system and suggested a solution of class reconciliation that relied on a purely ideological construction of what is good and evil. We never learn why the workers should be better off after they have shaken their tormentor's hand. Finally, in *Spione,* we don't even hear or see what kind of financial transactions Haghi undertakes, but we know that they are aimed at getting control of the entire world. As vague as the attack on the existing order is the response to it suggested in the film: a "world war" waged by the forces of virtue following the example of self-negating subordination under a higher principle as depicted in the hara-kiri of the Japanese character. The Faustian pact that ruined individual people in the first film is purged of its evil aspects in the second. The film shows that such a pact is possible without risking one's soul. The third, *Spione,* shows how alliance to the "right" pact for life pits the masses against those who signed the "wrong" one and will lead to the destruction of the latter. Once the Germans had signed their pact with Hitler, films didn't have to rely on complicated plots anymore to bring across their ideological message.

The Plutocrats of Nazi Film

In fact, one does not have to do anything beyond retelling the plot to bring out this message when it comes to Nazi films. This is of course no surprise, as Goebbels sometimes wrote parts of the scripts himself.[5] Some films seem intended to demonstrate how elements of earlier Weimar films can be made to congeal into the specific viciousness of Nazi ideology. For example, there is the film *G. P. U.* (directed by Karl Ritter, 1942) about the Soviet secret police: Jewish agents, Bolsheviks, seductive women, "degenerate" music, et cetera combine to show the Germans the true character of the "world conspiracy." In this sense, trying to relate the plots of some of these films in a coherent way already means improving on the original film.

Der Herrscher and *Die Rothschilds—Akten von Waterloo* are in a sense sequels to *Metropolis.* Thea von Harbou, who provided the script of *Metropolis,* contributed her "fortunate combination of receptivity and confusion" (Kracauer 162) also to the writing of the script of *Der Herrscher.* The two films show the two sides of the Frederson-Rotwang dichotomy in more detail. Clausen, the industrialist portrayed in *Der Herrscher* is the reformed leader of industry, the *Volksgenosse* who defines himself as the "first worker" in a society where everyone is a worker mirroring the all-encompassing "brotherhood" of the end tableau of *Metropolis.* The expression "first worker" also provides the link to legitimation in German history as Frederic the Great referred to himself as "the first servant of his state." But while Frederson's handshake with the rest of his brothers signified the end of the threat to the world of *Metropolis,* Clausen warns his fellow workers that "we exist to work for the community. . . . Everything else must be subordinated to this, even if it means the whole place going under with me." This new pact of the individual with the rest of the community turns the Faustian pact into a new version that is supposed to glue together the *Volksgemeinschaft* under Hitler, even if it means going to hell together.

Die Rothschilds is supposed to show what happens to a country when Frederson does not get rid of his Rotwang: The fall of the British into decadence is due to the prolonged and corrupting influence of the Jews on a people so as to turn them into "the Jews of the Aryans"[6] (Goebbels; qtd. in Leiser 78). The attempt to conquer Britain is interpreted as the somewhat belated effort to purge this island of its Rotwangs.

While *Der Herrscher* introduced the audience to the possibility that even the well-intentioned industrialist might have to run his ship aground, the film *Titanic* (initially directed by Herbert Selpin, later completed by Werner Klingler, 1943) provides another example of greed ruining the world of which the ship is a metaphor. As drowning for a good cause and drowning as the result of another stock market scheme look remarkably similar to the untrained eye, *Titanic* was not screened in Germany until after the end of World War II. It was felt that the scenes on the sinking ship would remind the German audience too much of the historic situation they faced. The Titanic collides with an iceberg because President Ismay of the White Star Line bribes its captain to take the more dangerous northern route so as to set a new speed record for crossing the Atlantic. This in turn will raise the stock of the company, which has been pushed artificially low, just as in Don Alfonso's scheme in *Freudlose Gasse (Joyless Street)*. As "the panic that breaks out on board shows each person in his true color" (qtd. in Hull, *Illustrierter* 231) and as there are British, German, and Jewish characters on board, not much more needs to be said about why this film was made: It is supposed to show the national character of each of these groups when they are faced with imminent death.

In contrast to the Weimar films, which all suggested solutions to the impending catastrophe, the three examples of Nazi films discussed here introduced the audience to the possibility of being faced with a lose-lose situation, perhaps suggesting to them that it might be better to go to ruins for a noble cause than for the greed of stock market players. This presents a striking parallel to the situation of the filmmakers under Nazi rule. Those who had refused to "sell out" to the magical kingdom of financial success in Hollywood and had stayed in Germany were forced to help the German film industry along on its downward slide under Nazi rule. If they didn't play along, they were executed. The director in charge of the *Titanic* project, Herbert Selpin, was killed by the Nazis after he had raged against a member of the German military who had proven his ineptitude in the course of making this film.[7]

The New Plutocrats of the New German Film

The tradition of blaming Germany's catastrophic situation on sinister conspiratorial powers, on some form of a "world conspiracy," was continued immediately after the war by one of those works that are supposedly proof of a German Zero Hour *(Stunde Null)* and a "clean slate" *(Kahlschlag)* in the area of cultural production. Wolfgang Borchert had written the script for a play *Ein Mann kommt nach Deutschland* ("A Man Returns to Germany," 1946) that was made into a radio show by Northwest German Radio. This story of a soldier returning from the war and from the POW camps presents an honest attempt at calling to task those groups within German society responsible for the war, but it underwent a somewhat astonishing metamorphosis as it was turned into a radio play, especially when one considers that this happened under the watchful eyes of the censors the Allies. First, it got a new title that robbed it of its sociogeographical specificity, probably in an attempt to give the suffering of the soldier a more existential dimension: *Draußen vor der Tür* ("Outside the Door"). But more importantly, the responsibility for the disaster that the soldier finds at home was at least partially shifted onto those who were to be assigned the role of subversive plutocrats in postwar Germany: the Allies themselves. In the original version, the soldier finds out that his parents have committed suicide because of their involvement with the Nazis. The radio play blames the death of the parents on the Allied bomb raids: As longtime workers in the shipyards of Hamburg, the parents couldn't stand the sight of them having been blown to shreds by the Allies. Vicious bombs have robbed the innocent shipyard workers of their livelihood. Before he ran into problems for his role in the film industry under the Nazis, Wolfgang Liebeneiner, the director of a film on euthanasia with the title "I accuse!" *(Ich klage an!* 1941), was allowed to turn the script into a less politically charged film with the title *Liebe 47* ("Love in 1947").

As the story of this script shows, continuity existed on the cultural scene in regard to themes as well. The radio play foreshadows the role of the Allies, and in particular the Americans, as the most defining other in German culture of the postwar era. Apart from attacks on the American "unculture" (a term used not only by Nazi functionaries but also more recently by Jean Baudrillard [*America*, 1986]), Nazi films were relatively free of anti-American sentiment, perhaps because they were seen as the natural enemies of the British (cf. Hull, *Film* 260). As the richest of the Allies, they were however assigned the role of scheming, decadent plutocrats in German postwar film. But the task of pointing out what the seemingly friendly Americans were up to (the colonization of the German subconscious) had to wait a little while, until they had revealed themselves, in the opinion of large portions of the public, to be morally depraved as well in the course of the Vietnam War. Up until the mid-1960s, those sitting in the glasshouse were still too afraid to throw stones.

In the course of the time period in German film history referred to as New German Film, the arsenal of cultural prejudice accumulated in the Weimar years was piece by piece revived and projected onto the Americans. While Rainer Werner Fassbinder's *Die Ehe der Maria Braun* ("The Marriage of Maria Braun," 1979) presents a fairly differentiated view of the American occupational forces, his earlier *Der Amerikanische Soldat* ("The American Soldier," 1970) reintroduces the fear of the other as a fear of sexual seductiveness that used to form part of the anti-Semitic paranoia: One of the German female characters explains that her attraction to the Americans is "because they are so good at fucking." The film also introduces a new element that will continue to serve as a way to construct and overdetermine the feeling of German moral superiority: American capitalism doesn't only destroy exotic countries but also wrecks the global environment. While Lang staged the consequences of reckless capitalism as a flood threatening Metropolis, the New German filmmakers will point to the same potential in American capitalism in the form of the threat it poses to world peace and the global ecology. As always, paranoia doesn't work without a link to socioeconomic realities. But to work its full effect, it must at the same time avoid a careful examination of these socioeconomic realities. The American soldier in Fassbinder's film tosses an empty (Coke?) can into the pristine German landscape while simultaneously proclaiming: "I love this country." The Americans are out to love this country to death.

  The Marriage of Maria Braun seems to present the American occupiers more objectively. The four American characters in this film each portray one of the roles Americans played in the postwar era: a judge who presides over a trial of Germans accused of murder, a situation resembling the Nuremberg trials; a GI who falls in love with a German woman and provides her family with luxury items like chocolate and cigarettes, just like in the familiar photographs of such wartime encounters; a drunk GI on a train who harasses the film's protagonist, representing the often maligned American soldiers stationed in Germany in the decades to come; and a business man who helps the German industry by ordering manufactured goods. But with each of these characters, Fassbinder also conjures up aspects of the complex of anti-American prejudice: The judge is not cultured enough to understand the difference between "to like" and "to love" (when Maria tries to explain her simultaneous relationships to the American GI and her husband), the first GI in a scene of gratuitous frontal nudity alludes to the fear of sexual inferiority vis-à-vis African Americans (while the pregnancy resulting from Maria's relationship with him results in a miscarriage, as if to say there is something unnatural about this relationship), the drunk GI becomes the subject of an outburst of swear words in English by Maria, showing him up as an ignorant monolingual brute. The business man, though first portrayed as tough, finally is no match for the seductive forces of Maria, implying that behind the matter-of-fact facade hides a lecher.[8]

  In addition, the various ways in which the Americans influence postwar German culture as represented in the character of Maria combine to create a new version of the Faustian pact.[9] In the course of her dealings with the Americans, Maria, who learns quickly, becomes tremendously successful in her business, but she loses her soul. The love of her husband, which she claims motivates her reckless behavior—she is just trying to make enough money for them to have a good life—is gone when they are finally together. The house they have bought goes up in flames, as the result of a gas explosion, before they can settle into their new postwar affluence.[10] It seems as if Fassbinder, under the fresh impression of a series of terrorist attacks in the mid-1970s, wanted to say that Germany's financial success was achieved at the price of neglecting its soul, for which it is going to be punished.

As *The Marriage of Maria Braun* revives the myth of the pact with Mephisto in the bodies of American plutocrats, two other films from the same time period concentrate on the "cultural imperialism" that comes with this pact as the representatives of "unculture" colonize what is left of German culture after the Nazis and the culturally boring years of the economic miracle. In doing so, these films, Werner Herzog's *Stroszek* (1977) and Wim Wenders's *Der amerikanische Freund* (1977), also reflect the attempts of German filmmakers to come to terms with their most vicious competitor, Hollywood.[11] Both films can be read as parables of the honest artist and how he is betrayed by the evil genius of "unculture."

The protagonist Bruno in Herzog's film earns his living by playing the accordion in the backyards of Berlin's old apartment houses. Music seems to be the only medium in which he can express himself. When he and his neighbor, Clemens, face insurmountable problems as they try to save a woman, Eva, from a couple of brutal pimps, they all decide to emigrate to the United States, where they hope a relative will help them find jobs. But things go from bad to worse: Until the pimps turned nasty, the paternalistic West German welfare state still allowed Bruno, Clemens, and Eva to live a relatively protected life irrespective of their contributions to the gross national product. At their destination, Railroad Flats in Wisconsin, the harsh winds of unfettered capitalism ruffle their feathers, in particular, because here in this new country, they cannot express themselves artistically anymore: Bruno's accordion, the neighbor's piano, and even their pet bird have all been left behind. They are forced to watch TV in a trailer home that is owned by the bank (and ultimately repossessed). The poetry of their backyard music is replaced by an auctioneer's sell, the poetry of late capitalism according to Herzog:

> In Western Europe there is such a strong domination of American culture and American films. And all of us who are working in filmmaking have to deal with this sort of domination. For me, it was particularly important to define my position about this country and its culture, and that's one of the major reasons I made *Stroszek*. (qtd. in Corrigan 128)

This position is defined *ex negativo* by Bruno's fate: He loses the woman he was determined to protect to some truck drivers passing through town.[12] As in so many other films, the catastrophe is initiated by the lure of sexual prowess. As he tries to follow her, his old truck fails him near the Wisconsin Dells, where

the final scenes serve to illustrate Herzog's vision of American "unculture":
Robbed of all meaning in life (love, art), Bruno, after a fairly unsuccessful bank
robbery that only nets a frozen turkey, ends up setting into motion an assortment of machines in an amusement arcade. One of them features a chicken that
is forced to dance as the floor of its exhibit is heated up. Compressed into this
image, Herzog's definition of his position about this country becomes a warning to other German filmmakers: they may become this type of chicken if they
leave the refuge of state-subsidized art in Germany.

The other parable of the German artist getting seduced by the shiny surfaces
of American culture, Wenders's *The American Friend* presents a new twist to the
plot of sexual seduction: In this film, the erotic attraction that sets matters into
motion does not take the detour via a woman. Seduction by the other culture,
one could argue, is not displaced onto women as supposedly more prone to such
diversions. The relationship between the two men, the German framemaker(!)
and the American con man/mafioso has clear homoerotic undertones, which
makes the jealous wife of the framemaker exclaim in disgust: "You and your
American friend!" Knowing the attraction Hollywood exerts upon him, Wenders
indirectly admits through this variation on the usual triangular relationship that
the involvement with the other culture can come about not just through being
pulled into it by others. The film portrays mutual attraction between the two
men and not simply the seduction of the German by the American. Nevertheless, the character attributes and how they are distributed between the two men
still relies on preconceived complexes of cultural stereotypes: The German is
honest, adheres to traditional family values, is not poor but definitely not wealthy,
and works as an accomplished artisan. The American is cunning, single, and plays
with lots of money, though not necessarily his own, which he makes by peddling
counterfeit works of art. The last term on these lists of attributes seems to represent Wenders's view of the respective strengths of both countries' cultural productivity. While the framemaker creates on a small scale nearly perfect, though
not economically viable, products, the American engages in large-scale schemes
of selling inauthentic art.[13] This film's version of the Faustian pact relies exactly
on the dichotomies set up between the two men: The framemaker agrees to work
as a hit-man for the American in order to gain the financial security of his family after his, as he is made to believe, imminent death due to a fatal disease. But
again, the framemaker is not just an innocent, morally upright victim of American scheming, he seems to enjoy at least some of the excitement that comes with
his new assignment. The end of the film, however, again contains a warning about
this kind of involvement with life in the fast lane, for framemakers as well as filmmakers: The framemaker dies of exhaustion.

More recent German films demonstrate that this involvement with Hollywood
does not necessarily lead to the death of a "German" way of making films, to the
end of German cultural life, or to total submission by Germans under the other,
American, culture: Since the early 1990s Germany has produced a series of eco-

nomically successful films that have not given up on tackling substantive issues and also do not show the complete absence of filmic artistry, as the earlier horror scenarios of "cultural imperialism" tried to suggest. But these films were, at least initially, not always greeted as achievements by the German film critics. They were viewed suspiciously exactly because they were commercially successful. This attitude of the critics reflects how the entire cultural apparatus in Germany (consisting of the artists themselves, the critics, the boards and agencies in charge of distributing the budgets for cultural productions, etc.), until very recently, still adhered to the concept of art in the tradition of the modernist avant-garde, which did not care much about popular appeal or commercial success. On the other hand, the changing commercial fortunes of German films and a growing chorus of critics who are starting to take these films seriously[14] seem to indicate, for better or worse, that the cultural logic of globalization is gaining a foothold on German soil. In turn, one can argue that it was exactly the obsession with artistic integrity (which, on the other hand, did not mind state sponsorship) and the ensuing growing degree of self-reflexivity reflected in the films that led the New German Film on its path into oblivion. In this sense, the New German Film is the true heir of the Weimar era: The threat of a more successful competitor, Hollywood, created a kind of self-fulfilling paranoid prophecy. In the case of Weimar film, it created the horror scenarios of cultural domination by others on which the Nazis could build. Before long, the German film industry was dominated by something much worse. In the case of the New German Film, it led to such a degree of self-reflexivity that no one noticed (or cared to notice) that the audience had turned away in boredom. While the Nazis made use of the careless ideological implications of some of the Weimar films and incorporated them into their own propaganda apparatus, the postwar West German public chose simply to ignore the paranoid scenarios of the New German filmmakers. Even the students' movement, which would seem to have offered itself as the natural ally of these filmmakers, had little use for their attempts to formulate artistic integrity. These attempts had taken the turn to an at times autistic self-reflexivity, an elitist endeavor without any mass appeal.

The filmmaker Herbert Achternbusch formulated the relationship of himself and his colleagues to America in very precise terms: "And America? If America is a dog, I said, then we have the dog shit" ("Amerika"; qtd. in Rentschler 211). The paranoid fear of becoming just that never allowed the New German Film to come out of its state-subsidized ghetto and prevented the formulation of a solution to the dilemma that dependency on public funds presents to independent filmmaking. But it looks like some representatives of this group have learned in the meantime, though one could say they represent that faction that already in the 1970s flirted with commercial success: Academy Award winner (for best foreign film *Die Blechtrommel,* "The Tindrum," 1979) Volker Schlöndorff recently made *Palmetto,* apparently simply for the enjoyment of indulging in Hollywood high gloss, and Wim Wenders, who always hovered at the fringes of the Hollywood scene, has watched his *Der Himmel über Berlin* (Wings of Desire, 1987) being made into a Hollywood spectacle as *City of Angels*, apparently much to his liking: "I was a little anxious when I got the script. But with every page, I felt Dana [Stevens] had done something intelligent and respectful, translating my 'poem' into an American 'story'" (qtd. in Mermelstein 29). Being at the top of the food chain of cultural materials is certainly one way to avoid the predicament formulated by Achternbusch.

Notes

This essay is reprinted courtesy of *Film & History* (www.filmandhistory.org).

1. For a thorough discussion of constructions of gender in this film, see Myers.

2. A discussion of *Metropolis* as an urban landscape can be found in Neumann.

3. On the interrelation of gender, sexuality, technology, and modernity, see Janet Lungstrum, "*Metropolis* and the Technosexual Woman of German Modernity," in *Women in the Metropolis: Gender and Modernity in Weimar Culture.*

4. A treatment of *Metropolis* as an example of "reactionary" modernism can be found in Rutsky's "The Mediation of Technology and Gender: Metropolis, Nazism, Modernism" and Hales's "Fritz Lang's *Metropolis* and Reactionary Modernism.

5. The way Goebbels interacted with film directors in shaping the films of this era is well documented in Hull's *Film in the Third Reich,* with quotations from passages in Goebbels's diaries in which he comments on film.

6. Koch provides a comparison between the American and German versions of a similar theme. The same volume contains studies of the treatment of the Rothschilds and in other media.

7. For more detail about Selpin's fate, see Hull's *Film in the Third Reich,* pages 226–30.

8. For a detailed discussion of the relationship between gender and economics in this film, see Haralovich.

9. Triggs sees a direct link between this film and Johann Wolfgang von Goethe's *Faust.*

10. Rheuban establishes the link between ideology and the use of melodrama, which is somewhat of a constant in Fassbinder's work.

11. Corrigan highlights this recurrent theme in New German Cinema as one of the displacements referred to in the title of his book.

12. This is where the title of the movie comes from: the episode forms a parallel to Georg Büchner's play *Woyzeck* whose protagonist runs amuck after his lover betrayed him.

13. Another dichotomy, that of German understatement versus American narcissism and its relationship to the theme of "cultural imperialism," is investigated by Mahoney.

14. How attitudes among film critics have changed can best be observed through the film reviews appearing in magazines such as *Der Spiegel* that cater to audiences representing the educational elites.

Works Cited

Achternbusch, Herbert. "Amerika: Bericht ans Goethe-Institute." *Es ist ein leichtes, beim Gehen den Boden zu berühren.* Frankfurt am Main: Suhrkamp, 1980. 143–49. Translated as "America" by Marc Silbermann in *semiotexte* 11 (1982): 8–15. Qtd. in Rentschler.

Bordwell, David. *Narration in the Fiction Film.* Madison: U of Wisconsin P, 1985.

Chatman, Seymour. *Coming to Terms: The Rhetoric of Narrative in Fiction and Film.* Ithaca: Cornell UP, 1990.

Corrigan, Timothy. *New German Film—The Displaced Image.* Bloomington: Indiana UP, 1994.

Frieden, Sandra, Richard McCormick, Vibeke R. Petersen, and Laurie Melissa Vogelsang, eds. *Gender and German Cinema: Feminist Interventions.* Providence, RI: Berg, 1993.

Hales, Barbara. "Fritz Lang's *Metropolis* and Reactionary Modernism." *New German Review* 8 (1992): 18–30.

Haralovich, Mary Beth. "The Sexual Politics of *The Marriage of Maria Braun.*" *Wide Angle* 12.1 (Jan. 1990): 6–16.

Harrington, John. *The Rhetoric of Film.* New York: Holt, 1973.

Herzog, Werner. "Die Eisnerin, wer ist das?" *Film Korrespondenz* 30 Mar. 1982: I–II. Rpt. in *West German Filmmakers on Film—Visions and Voices.* Ed. and trans. Eric Rentschler. New York: Holmes and Meier, 1988. 116.

Hull, David Steward. *Film in the Third Reich—A Study of the German Cinema 1933–1945.* Berkeley: U of California P, 1969.

———, trans. *Illustrierter Filmkurier* (Berlin) No. 3336. Rpt. in *Film in the Third Reich—A Study of the German Cinema 1933–1945.* Berkeley: U of California P, 1969. 231.

Kluge, Alexander. "Was wollen die Oberhausener?" *Kirche und Film* (Nov. 1962): 2–3.

Koch, Getrud. "Tauben oder Falken—Die Rothschild-Filme im Vergleich: *The House of Rothschild* (USA 1934, Alfred Werker) und *Die Rothschilds—Aktien auf Waterloo* (Deutschland 1940, Erich Washneck)." *Jüdische Figuren in Film und Karikatur: Die Rothschilds und Suss Oppenheimer.* Ed. Cilly Kugelmann and Fritz Backhaus. Sigmaringen: Thorbecke, 1995.

Kracauer, Siegfried. *From Caligari to Hitler—A Psychological History of the German Film.* Princeton: Princeton UP, 1947.

Leiser, Erwin. *Nazi Cinema.* Trans. Getrud Mander and David Wilson. New York: Macmillan, 1975.

Lungstrum, Janet. "Metropolis and the Technosexual Woman of German Modernity." *Women in the Metropolis: Gender and Modernity in Weimar Culture.* Ed. and introd. Katharina von Ankum. Berkeley: U of California P, 1997. 128–44.

Mahoney, Dennis F. "'What's Wrong with a Cowboy in Hamburg?' Narcissism as Cultural Imperialism in Wim Wenders's *The American Friend.*" *Journal of Educational Psychology* 7.1–2 (Mar. 1986): 106–16.

Mermelstein, David. "The Remake as a Risky Take on a Classic." *The New York Times* (5 Apr. 1998): 29.

Myers, Tracy. "History and Realism: Representations of Women in G. W. Pabst's *The Joyless Street*—German Film History/German History on Film." Frieden et al. 43–59.

Neumann, Dietrich. "The Urbanistic Vision in Fritz Lang's *Metropolis.*" *Dancing on the Volcano: Essays on the Culture of the Weimar Republic.* Ed. Thomas W. Kniesche and Stephen Brockmann. Columbia, SC: Camden House, 1994. 143–62.

Rentschler, Eric. *West German Filmmakers on Film—Visions and Voices.* New York: Holmes and Meier, 1988.

Rheuban, Joyce. "*The Marriage of Maria Braun:* History, Melodrama, Ideology." Frieden at al. 207–26.

Rutsky, R. L. "The Mediation of Technology and Gender: Metropolis, Nazism, Modernism." *New German Critique* 60 (Fall 1993): 3–32.

Schlöndorff, Volker. "Der Wille zur Unterwerfung: Siegfried Kracauers epochale Untersuchung *Von Caligari zu Hitler* neu gelesen." *Frankfurter Rundschau* (16 Feb. 1980).

Triggs, Jeffery Alan. "The Faustian Theme in Fassbinder's *The Marriage of Maria Braun.*" *Studies in the Humanities* 16.1 (June 1989): 24–32.

Wollenberg, H. H. *Fifty Years of German Film.* 1848. *The Literature of Cinema: Series II.* Ed. Martin S. Dworkin. New York: Arno Press and The New York Times, 1972.

Part Three

Perspectives on Films about Rhetoric

In *A Rhetoric of Motives*, BURKE DESCRIBES THE FUNCTION of identification in rhetoric, saying that "insofar as the individual is involved in conflict with other individuals or groups, the study of this same individual would fall under the head of *Rhetoric*" (23). While the aim of rhetoric may be identification (and by implication, a desire for what Burke calls *consubstantiality*), inscribed within identification we see the corresponding concept of *division*. To the extent that people are not consubstantial, where identification is either psychologically or socially problematic, there is division, and hence, the characteristic invitation to rhetoric. We expect, of course, that film will display rhetorical properties by virtue of its appeal to an audience using a recognizable symbol system. Some films make this process of appeal, of identification, the primary subject matter of the film narrative itself.

The essays in part three examine films that are self-reflexively rhetorical, or that specifically address the interrelations of identification and the making of meaning. In "Rhetorical Conditioning: *The Manchurian Candidate*," Bruce Krajewski asks fundamental questions about the utility of taking rhetorical perspectives on film: "What happens to rhetoric when juxtaposed to film? And concomitantly what happens to films analyzed rhetorically? What does rhetoric offer to the study of film that semiotics, phenomenology, deconstruction, psychoanalysis, Marxism, or other interpretive modes, do not?" His answers to these questions are in part driven by the rhetoric of *The Manchurian Candidate*, a film that stares back at us and the cultural rhetoric that it calls into question.

My essay, "Sophistry, Magic, and the Vilifying Rhetoric of *The Usual Suspects*," accepts director Bryan Singer's invitation to see the film as a self-reflexive narrative on the verbal and visual resources of rhetoric. While the film serves as an interesting exploration of sophistry and the construction of ethos, it vilifies rhetoric even as it exploits its "magical" powers of endowing the word and the visual representation on screen with presence. This essay shares with Harriet Malinowitz's "Textual Trouble in River City: Literacy, Rhetoric, and Consumerism in *The Music Man*" (chapter 13) a focus on how such films function as a cultural critique of rhetoric itself. As she puts it,

> [*The Music Man*] depicts empiricism and phenomenology, logic and sophistry, classical rationalism and romantic expressionism, highbrow aesthetics and popular culture, the Protestant work ethic and the capitalist pleasure fantasy, all vying for sovereignty in such quotidian sites as the local library, the schoolhouse, and the parlor music lesson.

In "Screen Play: *Ethos* and Dialectics in *A Time to Kill*," Granetta L. Richardson draws on classical conceptions of ethos as the creation of moral and ethical character to show how "filmmakers approximate *ethos* on-screen in the service of ideological imperatives," which in the case of *A Time to Kill* translates into a mixed message on racism and righteousness. In the book's last essay, "Postmodern Dialogics in *Pulp Fiction:* Jules, Ezekiel, and Double-Voiced Discourse," Kelly Ritter draws on Mikhail Bakhtin, Jean Baudrillard, and Kenneth Burke to show that in Tarantino's film "Jules's dialogue not only with Ezekiel's words but also with himself exemplifies the role language has in an age that no longer has a concept of the 'original' in any word, orator, or act. *Pulp Fiction* thus challenges us to see the seams between Jules's own speech and that which Jules appropriates for his own ends as cinematic agent." In foregrounding Jules's "set-speech," Tarantino forces us to examine the centrality of identification to the rhetorical act.

Each essay in part three is careful not to read rhetoric into the respective films, but takes the invitation to do so from the film directors. In *The Manchurian Candidate,* the theme of the film is Cold War rhetoric and "brainwashing." In *The Usual Suspects,* Keyser Söse turns out, after all, to be "Verbal." In *The Music Man,* Harold Hill is a con man and traveling salesman (perhaps the most familiar sort of rhetorician we can imagine). In *A Time to Kill,* the explicit subject of the film is the ethical character of Carl Lee Hailey and the rhetorical ability of his lawyer, Jake Brigance. In *Pulp Fiction,* Jules is the preacher teaching others and himself a lesson. In part three, we bring our understanding of rhetoric to bear on these films, concluding *The Terministic Screen* with discussions of films that represent the culture's understanding and use of the rhetorical arts in social life.

11

Rhetorical Conditioning:
The Manchurian Candidate

Bruce Krajewski

This Hollywood movie based on a commercial novel, from long ago,
or not so far away, is a fantasy of a life we could be living.
—Greil Marcus, "The Last American Dream:
The Manchurian Candidate"

THE TERMINISTIC SCREEN DEALS NECESSARILY WITH TERMINOLOGY, with the terms
of rhetoric, though rhetoric in the context of film studies usually means rhetoric as an instrument, employed by neutral analysts. Too often rhetoric becomes
unthoughtfully another method of analysis, or perhaps merely a set of tools that
set one at work on a filmic "text," treating "visual tropes" in much the same ways
one would tropes in a written text, with movies thereby reduced to the sludge of
syntagmas, to "cinematic *écriture*." The displacement of the visual, treating images as if they were no different from words, permits metalanguages like semiotics
(Metz), or narratology (Chatman), or even phenomenology (Sobchak), and these
metalanguages tend to function along similar lines to the film critics who wish
to throw rhetoric, not as a discipline, into the mix.

Rhetoric used to be the study of traditions about what had been said about
particular topics and ways in which those things were said to differing audiences.
The student of rhetoric became not so much a clever technician as one learned
in the ways of various discourses, a person with access to copiousness on all sorts
of matters, a person familiar with rhetoric's public and effective uses, knowing
what to say on what occasion before a particular audience and for what reason.
Thus, on this view, rhetoric does not look like an atemporal, conscienceless—
hence painless—science of tropes, visual or otherwise, but an art of situations,
as well as an art of contingencies and improvisation, such as when the situation

with which you are confronted turns out to be other than what you had imagined and for which you had prepared.

What happens to rhetoric when juxtaposed to film? And concomitantly what happens to films analyzed rhetorically? What does rhetoric offer to the study of film that semiotics, phenomenology, deconstruction, psychoanalysis, Marxism, or other interpretive modes, do not? Terminologically, rhetoric can help to introduce a vocabulary used infrequently by film critics and scholars, and it might be that such a vocabulary has effects on thinking, in the way Michael Baxandall describes the changes brought about by humanists' attention to Ciceronian Latin. "In 1300 a man [*sic*] could not think as tightly in words as he could by 1500; the difference is measurable in categories and constructions lost and found" (Baxandall 6). Though Baxandall addresses wholesale linguistic changes over centuries, I want to suggest merely that rhetorical categories and terms brought to bear on film studies might aid in thinking *differently* about film, though as yet no precise delineations of that new thinking seem available nor is it clear to what those differences in thinking are *committed,* if anything, other than generating further interpretations, further publications for academics. The presupposition seems to be that rhetorical taxonomies are cross-cultural, transhistorical, universal even, à la George Kennedy's *Comparative Rhetoric,* and thus a "rhetorical analysis" can be done on a Hollywood musical from the 1930s *in the same way* as on a film from China in the 1990s. Situations become almost irrelevant. In this scenario, rhetoric no longer functions as a living tradition, but as dead methodology. Furthermore, *persuasion tout court* is out of the question, banished from consideration, perhaps as too empirical for the high aims of "rhetorical analysis." "The practical effects of texts on public attitudes is more properly a subject for the social sciences" (Chatman 186). Apparently, disciplinary boundaries count at some stage, even in the face of rhetoric's, or narratology's, universal scope and "neutral gaze." What rhetoric *does* to people, to things, at particular times no longer matters. The only audience that matters is the one that will buy the rhetorical analyses.

This is not to say that all visual theorists who invoke rhetoric see their "objects" of study in the same way. Michael Ann Holly, for example, concerned with the "rhetoric of the image," wants to remind her colleagues that "works of art are forever looking back at us" (xiv); that is, the gaze is not unidirectional. Although Holly does not have film in mind, she wants to reverse the standard treatment of visual images as objects upon which interpreters work by positing, via Gadamer, that these visual works call the interpreters into question. (There is a confusing treatment of the issue when she cites Jonathan Culler as saying "it [the work] only answers" [Holly 26]). What these questions are, in any given instance, goes without saying, and that fairly sums up the limits of visual theories, even one as philosophically informed as Sobchack's, or ones naive enough to think that invocations of Jürgen Habermas's notions about transforming the public sphere will be engagement enough—one thinks here of W. J. T. Mitchell's comment: "[T]hough we probably cannot change the world, we can continue to describe it critically and interpret it accurately" (425). Practicing visual theory or rhetorical analysis of films becomes an ideological substitute for a lack, that lack being specific considerations of what the results of such practicing are, or ought to be. Change the world to what? What effects different forms of thinking take, even rhetorical ones, on the whole—call this whole global living conditions—*those* remain grossly underdetermined, untheorized, and ungrounded philosophically or politically, in the practical sense of *any* party politics.

Fantasia

> When political and military leaders went about designing the intelligence apparatuses of postwar government, their designs were often inflected by notions of detection and spying borrowed from literature and movies.
> —Shawn James Rosenheim, *The Cryptographic Imagination:*
> *Secret Writing from Edgar Poe to the Internet*

The Manchurian Candidate puts on display at least three major fantasies and several minor ones; it is in Slavoj Žižek's words, a film that exhibits a "plague of fantasies." The three major fantasies might be described as follows: (1) The American dream in the form of a Cold War nightmare, the nonmilitaristic, communist takeover of the United States; (2) The communist dream, or the Cold War fantasy from *the other side:* namely, the nonmilitaristic, communist takeover of the United States; and (3) The fantasy that we, the audience, are past, beyond, over the previous two fantasies, and thus living in a post-communist, post-ideological, postmodern world that is allegedly witnessing a triumph of capitalism and democracy, with the latter term the causal result of the continuing "triumph" of the first. Fantasies one and two seem incompatible, at first, to the extent that the film is seen as not taking sides, as giving "triumph" to neither capitalists nor communists. Greil Marcus reads the film in exactly that way: "And yet there is no message here, no point being made, not even any felt implication that Communists are bad and Americans are good, nothing like that at all—this is all, somehow, taking place in an atmosphere of moral neutrality [. . .]" (210). The "moral neutrality" here fits fantasy three, though not in any obvious way, almost as if Marcus would be more comfortable were his reading one that could see the film taking the side of the good Americans against the bad communists, the anticipated siding of many Hollywood films made during the Cold War and about the Cold War, with a few notable exceptions, such as *Dr. Strangelove, The Day the Earth Stood Still,* and *Fail Safe.* Marcus's fantasy seems to be a desire for American propaganda. Despite his complaints about the film, he found himself attracted to it, and attracted others to it.

I remember seeing it, alone, when it came out in the fall of 1962, at the Varsity Theater in Palo Alto. The first thing I did when it was over was call my best friend and tell him he had to see it, too. We went the next night; as we left the theater, I asked him what he thought. "Greatest movie I ever saw," he said flatly, as if he didn't want to talk about it, and he didn't. He said it stunned, with bitterness, as if he shouldn't have had to see this thing, as if what it told him was both true and false in a manner he could never untangle, as if it was both incomprehensible and all too clear, as if the whole experience had been, somehow, a gift, a gift of art, and also *unfair;* and that was how I felt, too. (214)

So, it's not so much neutral as *"unfair."* The unfairness lies with the film's breaking of the rules. For Marcus, he sees "too many rules broken" (214), as if film, not even a century old at the point of his viewing, had established an unquestionably firm set of rules, and that breakage certainly could not be part of the "gift of art," when one is surveying aesthetic pleasures in the form of surprises, the unexpected, "as if he shouldn't have had to see this thing." What is expressed by "he shouldn't have had to see this thing"? It is the sort of thought anyone could imagine being uttered by the main character in *A Clockwork Orange,* or by a witness to the primal scene. The sentence expresses a kind of negation of duty, as well as a sense that one should have known *this,* or one already knows *it,* but leaves the sentence in the perlocutionary mode. My suggestion will be that the response "I shouldn't have to see this thing" is symptomatic of fantasy three. That is, one shouldn't have to see the fantasy, because one is living it, supposedly seeing it all the time (in other words, Žižek's statement, "the Unconscious is outside" [3]), but, as with "brainwashing," it is exactly one's participation in the brainwashing, the fantasy, that is usually occluded from access. It is *unfair* at the site where unfair and horror meet.

Before exploring the sociopolitical dimensions of fantasy three further, I should make clear that brainwashing was, and likely is, a technique whose victims are still among us. Like the Internet, brainwashing developed in a military context, and experiments were carried out on all sorts of people other than "the enemy," some of the evidence for that can be found in John Marks's *The Search for the "Manchurian Candidate,"* a book that describes the means of brainwashing as quotidian rather than thaumaturgical.

> The team of Wolff and Hinkle became the chief brainwashing studiers for the U.S. government, although the Air Force and Army ran parallel programs. Their secret report to Allen Dulles, later published in a declassified version, was considered the definitive U.S. Government work on the subject. In fact, if allowances are made for the Cold War rhetoric of the fifties, the Wolff-Hinkle report still remains one of the better accounts of the massive political re-education programs in China and the Soviet Union. It stated flatly that neither the Soviets nor the Chinese had any magical weapons—no drugs, exotic mental ray-guns, or other fanciful machines. Instead, the report pictured communist interrogation methods resting on skillful, if brutal, application of police methods. (Marks 128)

As anyone might guess, the U.S. Government was not satisfied with this insight, but decided both before and after the Wolff-Hinkle report to "improve" the results of "standard procedures" for "re-education," or "brainwashing," by making soldiers and hospital patients victims of drug experiments. Marks's data on such experiments parallels similarly sanctioned U.S. Government actions in connection with exposing various populations, military and civilian, to radioactivity. The military attempted to maintain secrecy about these "experiments" by ensuring silence among military personnel by offering advanced forms of medical care in exchange for that silence. Many film scholars know part of the history of that story through the film *The Atomic Cafe*. In short, *The Manchurian Candidate*, while labeled a fictional film, registers all-too-real situations for victims of brainwashing experiments.

The Manchurian Candidate emerges from a particular political atmosphere of projected conspiracies and paranoia, even if such an atmosphere feels too familiar in North America in light of the Oklahoma City bombing and of television programming like the *X-Files* (an atmosphere also described by Mitchell 415–16). J. Hoberman reports that fantasy one is not peculiar to *The Manchurian Candidate*, which he sees as a "comic version of the John Birch Society's so-called 'Black Book'—a samizdat that had been circulating among the true believers since the summer of 1958—in which Birch Society founder Robert Welch identified President Eisenhower as the dedicated agent of a vast Communist conspiracy, who had been painstakingly manoeuvred by his Kremlin handlers into the White House" (12).

Phantom of the Opera

> Schizophrenic patients may also believe, for instance, that what appear to be other human beings are really phantoms or cleverly designed machines.
> —Louis Sass, *The Paradoxes of Delusion:*
> *Wittgenstein, Schreber, and the Schizophrenic Mind*

> [T]his gaze is the impossible neutral gaze of someone who falsely *exempts* himself from his concrete historical existence.
> —Slavoj Žižek, *The Plague of Fantasies*

The gaze of the "brainwashed" is an innocent, yet frightening, spectacle. Raymond Shaw's gaze when he is engaged as "the mechanism" contains a neutrality, an indifference, a calmness that almost anyone can recognize, perhaps especially in leftist literary and visual critics. From the workers in *Metropolis* to the eyes of zombies in *Night of the Living Dead*, most filmgoers will recognize this kind of detached gaze. It is also akin to the gaze of the hypnotized, a gaze familiar to film history as early as the accusations about what Valentino's "look" could do to women (e.g., *The Sheik*), though the kind of gaze I wish to point to here is not so much one that looks but one that has ceased looking and is likely closer to staring (at what?), the gaze as object, rather than the usual demeaning gaze. Raymond's glazed look upon hearing the phrase "Why don't you pass the time by playing a little solitaire" signals his transformation into "the mechanism" to be "operated." Here staring is a loss of self, superseded by another vision, the conditioned, implanted training. (A parallel case for the importance of eyes for detecting androids, for separating humans from "mechanisms," can be found in *Blade Runner.*) However, it is important to note that Raymond retains a vision of some sort, and the tasks he is told to perform are ones not unimaginable by the audience, for the audience is capable, à la Sass, of a version of schizophrenic projection, in other words, of taking another human for a machine, allowing that that taking could be tragic as well as comic. In fact, the foregrounding of Raymond's conditioning occurs somewhat humorously in one instance, when it is triggered accidentally at a bar. A man is telling a story, and utters the colloquialism "Go jump in the lake." The conditioning, wrapped tightly with symbolic and metaphoric bands nonetheless functions, at one level, *literally.* Upon hearing the sentence "Go jump in the lake," Raymond gets a cab, goes to Central Park, and carries out the imperative. The need for Raymond to operate effectively depends on his being able to carry out instructions without the introduction of ambiguity or special interpretation. The linkage between being programmed and literal-mindedness is overt. What is unimaginable for the audience, and thus humorous in its display, is someone performing the phrase "Go jump in the lake," as the audience is linguistically preprogrammed to know how to take that sentence. In Raymond's case, the taking of the nonliteral as literal becomes an important indicator in distinguishing the human from the automaton, the loyal soldier from "the mechanism" called Raymond. That is, the programmed subject/machine exists outside the hermeneutical realm; the programmed subject/machine lacks almost any interpretive, reflective element and is immune to pain, especially the searing pains of guilt. "[T]he scene of conscience is a scene of bearing witness and attestation. Conscience not only calls; it passes judgment, and it inflicts punishment. Conscience hurts, and if it doesn't, it's not conscience" (Lukacher 86). Raymond's handler mentions explicitly that pangs of conscience undermine the brainwashing.

Another triggering device for Raymond's conditioning is when he looks upon the queen of diamonds, the *red* queen, with the concomitant relationship of "red" to the "Red Scare," the communism from which the left in North America, with rare exceptions, still recoils. Raymond shuts down when he looks upon the queen of diamonds, and that card becomes linked, Oedipally and otherwise, to his mother (Angela Lansbury) and, late in the film, to his soon-to-be wife, Jocie, who arrives at a costume party outfitted as the queen of diamonds (see fig. 11.1). The Oedipal tension in the film seems to be one-sided, evidenced mainly by the kiss his mother gives Raymond toward the end of the film (this takes place moments after the frame in fig. 11.2). However, the novel leaves no doubt that the

Figure 11.1

mother has her own Oedipal fantasy working with her son and with her own absent father:

> Raymond looked right at her and, for the first time in many, many years, actually smiled at her, and she thought he looked positively beautiful. Why—why he looks like Poppa! Raymond, her own Raymond, looked exactly like her darling, darling Poppa! She clutched his hand as she led him out of the salon and along the two corridors to the library, causing one woman guest to tell another woman guest that they looked as though they were rushing off to get a little you-know-what. [. . .] (Condon 253)

Why this card, the queen of diamonds? The "experts" in the film suspect in Levinasian ways that this part of the triggering program must be a *face* card. Etymologically, it is the card of an *adamant* woman, his mother, someone Raymond would rather not face (see fig. 11.3). One should not also miss the implications of triggering paralysis in Raymond by his seeing a queen, when *queen* is slang for male homosexual, since Raymond's sexuality is questioned from the outset of the film, more so in the novel (Condon 20, 97, 105), where even his own mother tells Senator Jordon that her son is a homosexual. In another instance, Raymond is with a woman he has met for the first time: "[T]he door was flung open and a small but strapping red-headed girl with a figure that made him moan to himself stood in the doorway and stared at him accusingly [here a stare means something else]. 'What the hell is the matter with you, honey?' she asked solicitously. 'Are you queer?' [Raymond responds:] 'Queer? Me?'" (105). The argument against this reading would be to cite Ray-mond's interest in Jocie; how-

Figure 11.2

ever, this argument could be countered by appealing to the novel, to a passage in which Ben Marco tells Raymond, "They are inside your mind. Deep. Now. For eight years. One of their guys with a big sense of humor thought it would be a great gag to throw you a bone for all of the trouble they were going to put you to, and fix it up inside your head so that, all of a sudden, you'd get interested in girls, see?" (223). This can also be read as an antecedent to all the contemporary discussions of the social construction of sexualities, and simultaneously, if that's possible, as a claim that homosexuality is "all in someone's head," that is, it is a state that can be "fixed."

Ben Marco is depicted as a kind of libertine with women in the novel, and toward the end of the novel, he says to Raymond: "'You were twenty-two, going on twenty-three years old, when you left the Army, and you had never been laid. More than that. You had never even kissed a girl, had you, Raymond?' Marco leaned across the table, his eyes lambent with affection, and he said softly, 'You never even kissed Jocie, did you, Raymond?'" (212). It seems to me that this can be read in the light of the issue of "homosexual panic" that Cavell discusses in a postscript to his essay on *Now, Voyager*. Stephen Mulhall has seen the relevance of this postscript, for he concludes his book on Cavell with a discussion of that text and notes that while the issue of the closet is relevant for both homosexuality and philosophy (Raymond commits suicide in a booth), Mulhall also notes that Cavell connects "homosexual panic" to castration anxiety. Cavell writes:

When Freud introduces the threat of castration he notes at once that "usually it is from the woman that the threat emanates" [. . .] and he goes on

Figure 11.3

to specify the medium of that threat [. . .] as the woman's voice: it is the woman who says what "the father of the doctor" will do, and who says how the punishment may be mitigated; her overwhelming threat, accordingly, is to tell. However this division of legal labour—between telling and executing—gets encoded, it emerges that the one responsible for maintaining and affirming the child's existence is the one whose voice can negate it, mar it, give it away. Then the key to one's (male) preservation is to control the woman's voice, contradictorily to stop it from speaking (from reporting) and to make it speak (to promise a further mitigation or intercession). Some control. ("Postscript" 276)

Anyone would recognize that this description fits Raymond, whose mother is his "American operator" in the film, playing up Raymond's role as machine and his mother's role as the one controlling the machine, so that whichever voice wins out in the duel determines what happens to Raymond. Cavell would see the "opera" in "operator." In several instances in the film, Raymond attempts to shut down his mother's voice by putting his hands over his ears (see fig. 11.3). Early on in the novel, Raymond's ideas about silencing his mother turn violent and foreshadow the shooting at the end of the novel. The scene occurs when Raymond is at the White House about to receive the Medal of Honor. "All the cameras were strewn about in the grass while everybody waited for the President to arrive. Raymond wondered what would they do if he could find a sidearm some place and shoot her through the face—through that big, toothy, flapping mouth?" (59), the point being to stop up, at either end, (her) mouth or (his) ear, the circuit of sending and receiving. This is a sample of Raymond's skepticism, for as Cavell says, "[Skepticism] is the denial of having to hear" (Borradori 134). The novel reinforces this point early on in a description of Raymond: "Raymond also distrusted all other living people because they had not warned his father of his mother" (15). In this instance, skepticism emerges from what was not said, silent voices, subjunctive voices—were they not silent, not subjunctive, things might have been different.

Both novel and film (I treat both as sources of evidence, leaving within the realm of deniability the issue of whether, on some counts, the film necessarily offers a substantially different account) also portray Raymond as neutral, as cipherlike, a spectral figure, such as at the end of the novel when Ben attempts "listening for the sound of Raymond ever having lived, but there was none" (308). Compare this to a similar comment in *Double Indemnity,* the *film noir* in which Walter Neff, the main character, after having murdered Phyllis Dietrichson's husband, cannot hear his own footsteps, as if he walks but does not exist. Žižek frames it like this: "[T]he specter gives body to that which escapes (the symbolically structured) reality" ("I Hear You with My Eyes" 113). As a specter, Raymond exists in the gap between reality and the real, since he is the means, "the mechanism," by which any of the three fantasies comes into existence, and, of course, within the space of the film, Raymond is seen as the one who helps mediate between others' dream states and reality, so that it is Raymond who receives the letter from the soldier whose nightmares have placed him on a road to desperation. His status as mediator between this realm and another is re-emphasized at the film's conclusion, when Raymond is disguised as a priest at the party convention. Furthermore, the role as priest reinstates Raymond as sexually neutral and also links him religiously to a Christian tradition that allows him to occupy a place where he can be prophet, messiah, and martyr.

The Manchurian in *The Manchurian Candidate* brings East and West together etymologically, since the word comes from the Greek *manteuesthai,* "to prophesy." Finally, and I do not suggest that this list is exhaustive, Raymond also functions as the pivot between the two factions of the political party representing democracy in the film, the Iselin family as head of one faction, the Jordon family the other, both of which have key members absent, the Iselin family's father is missing, as is the Jordon family's mother, indicating a correspondence with the children; the male (Raymond) child's father is absent, as is the female (Jocie) child's mother.

The Usual Suspects

A discussion of the number of "card-carrying communists" in the government serves neither precision nor mathematics. The shifting numbers open up a space that pre-answers a question that hadn't been asked, so that all subsequent questions about how many communists there are presuppose the existence of *some* card-carrying communists. The work of the House Committee on Un-American Activities was less than a decade old at the time *The Manchurian Candidate* appeared, making the question of communists a rhetorical one in the usual sense of that term, meaning that the truth would be that there were some communists in the United States. Given that "enemies" (communists) had been found—covert activity was underway on behalf of communism, just as it was on behalf of democracy—some found that discovery the legitimation for all sorts of questionable actions (Navasky 426–27). Some used the specter of Marx to permit themselves to further nationalist, supposedly democratic, causes, exposing the instrumental, rather than substantive or mathematical, nature of the issue. To some extent this continues, though it causes a degree of chagrin: "It is the same in today's Eastern Europe. The 'spontaneous' presupposition was that what is 'repressed' there, what will burst forth once the lid of 'totalitarianism' is removed, will be *democratic desire* in all its forms, from political pluralism to a flourishing market economy. What we are getting instead, now that the lid *is* removed, are more and more ethnic conflicts [This analysis also applies, in part, to what took place after the breakup of the Soviet Union, in other words, the appearance of versions of virulent nationalisms.]." (Žižek, *Tarrying* 207). In short, the removal or eradication of "the usual suspects" in the dynamic dichotomy that pits democracy against communism, as if the two terms must be mutually exclusive, can have surprising, unpredictable results, and *The Manchurian Candidate* serves notice that calling up anxieties about closeted communists can further communists' ends as well as others. Whether that notice fuels skepticism, furthers understanding, cancels out the tactic's utilitarian value, or accomplishes or negates something else—it all depends (on what?). What to do when the usual suspects fail to function according to expectation, especially here in a film in which the inversion of expectations is foregrounded, such as the continual linkage of Senator Iselin to representations of Abraham Lincoln?

Some Like It Cold

> Well, we *are* at war. It's a Cold War but it will get worse and worse until every man and woman and child in this country will have to stand up and be counted to say whether or not he or she is on the side of right and freedom.
>
> —Raymond's mother, *The Manchurian Candidate*

The *cold* in Cold War means, for one, a bloodless war, where *bloodless* means without emotion or feeling, a war for automatons as well as for apathetics. *The Manchurian Candidate*'s focus on America, on the founding fathers (with Raymond's founding father conspicuously absent), on how one becomes an "American hero," on the beginning of a new America in a garden (the closing scene takes place during the Republican convention at Madison Square Garden, with Raymond as the machine in the garden) is certainly as strong as Stanley Cavell's focus on these same matters in *This New Yet Unapproachable America*. Cavell's written texts for thinking through these matters are often nineteenth-century ones, and I am attempting to move the discussion into the twenty-first century—not that Cavell doesn't have splendid things to say about these issues via twentieth-century films like *The Philadelphia Story;* in short, this isn't an attempt at supercession—by appealing to a novel and film that take into account the fact of television for America and the will, as Cavell puts it in his essay on television in *Themes Out of School,*" "to theatricalize ourselves" (262). As Raymond tells it, the key moment in his mother's plan at the convention will succeed in part because it will occur on television and in part because Senator Iselin is histrionic:

> [H]e will get to his feet gallantly amid the chaos that will have broken out at that time, and the way she wants him to do it for the best effect for the television cameras and the still photographers is to lift the nominee's body in his arms and stand in front of the microphones because that picture will symbolise more than anything else that it is Johnny's party which the Soviets fear most, and Johnny will offer the body of a great American on the altar of liberty. (280)

Raymond says, "Mother said this was the part Johnny was actually born to play because he overacts so much and we can certainly use plenty of that here." All this points up the fact of television for *The Manchurian Candidate,* that it too, like Raymond, is a device that can be used for America's downfall, and it is foregrounded in a number of scenes in the film, particularly the first time Senator Iselin makes his announcement that there are communists in the government and that the miasma has begun and must be eradicated, perhaps eventually irradiated. Television is a medium for catastrophe, because it renders the extraordinary ordinary, sufferable. Cavell writes, "Consider that the conquering of television began just after World War II, which means, for the purposes of the hypothesis I wish to offer here, after the discovery of concentration camps and of the atomic bomb; of, I take it, the discovery of the literal possibility that human life will destroy itself; that is to say, that it is *willing* to destroy itself" (266-67; see also Maurice Blanchot's *The Writing of the Disaster*). Cavell has more to say about the meaning of "the bomb" in an essay called "Hope against Hope" in *Conditions Handsome and Unhandsome,* where he writes, "[I]t is precisely a climate of despair that will ease the fulfillment of our worst fears" (130). Mrs. Iselin despairs in the novel, because her superiors used her son as a killing machine, but once her mission has ended, and she and her husband have taken power (after Raymond assassinates the man who would have been the Republican candidate for the presidency), she plans to take revenge on the world. Raymond reports,

> [S]he was really deeply upset and affected for the first time since I have known her [apparently bloodless to this point] when she discovered that they had chosen me to be their killer. She told me that they had lost the

world when they did that and that when she and Johnny got into the White House she was going to start and finish a holy war, without ten minutes' warning, that would wipe them off the face of the earth. (Condon 279)

My guess is that the phrase "without ten minutes' warning" indicates the use of nuclear weapons. This would be a form of destroying the world that would have been unimaginable for nineteenth-century writers, though both Emerson and Thoreau knew that those who are dead to the world are likely to make the world into a mirror image of that deadness. This is also true in the case of Mrs. Iselin and Raymond, both of whom are said to be mostly lifeless. As Raymond says above, there was but one time when his mother showed deep feelings for anything. As for Raymond, the novel ends with Marco "listening intently for a memory of Raymond, for the faintest rustle of his ever having lived, but there was none."

The Conversation

One of the strangest conversations ever recorded on film, between Ben Marco and Rosie Cheyney, goes like this:

Ben: Do you mind if I smoke?
Rosie: Not at all. Please do. [Marco gets up and goes to the space between two cars, where he has broken into a sweat, and has closed his eyes. Cheyney follows him out of the car, and then lights a cigarette for him. She sees that he has his eyes closed, so taps him on the shoulder. His eyes open, and she hands him the cigarette.] Maryland's a beautiful state.
Ben: This is Delaware.
Rosie: I know. I was one of the original Chinese workmen who laid the track on this straight. But, nonetheless, Maryland is a beautiful state. So is Ohio for that matter.
Ben: I guess so. Columbus is a tremendous football town. You in the railroad business?
Rosie: Not any more. However, if you will permit me to point out— when you ask that question, you really should say, 'Are you in a railroad *line?*' Where's your home?
Ben: I'm in the Army. I'm a Major. I've been in the Army most of my life. We move a good deal. I was born in New Hampshire.
Rosie: I went to a girls camp once on Lake Francis.
Ben: That's pretty far north. What's your name?
Rosie: Eugenie.
Ben: Pardon?
Rosie: No kidding. I really mean it. Crazy French pronunciation and all.
Ben: It's pretty.
Rosie: Well, thank you.
Ben: I guess your friends call you Ginny.

Rosie: Not yet they haven't, for which I am deeply grateful. But you may call me Ginny.

Ben: What do your friends call you?

Rosie: Rosie.

Ben: Why?

Rosie: My full name is Eugenie Rose. Of the two names, I've always favored Rosie, 'cause it smells of brown soap and beer. Eugenie is somehow more fragile.

Ben: Still, when I asked you what your name was, you said it was Eugenie.

Rosie: It's quite possible I was feeling more or less fragile at that instant.

Ben: I could never figure out what that phrase meant—"more or less." You Arabic?

Rosie: No.

Ben: My name is Ben. It's really Bennett. Was named after Arnold Bennett.

Rosie: The writer?

Ben: No, the Lieutenant Colonel. He was my father's commanding officer at the time.

Rosie: What's your last name?

Ben: Marco.

Rosie: Major Marco. Are you Arabic?

Ben: No.

Rosie: Let me put it another way. Are you married?

Ben: No. You?

Rosie: No.

Ben: What's your last name?

Rosie: Cheyney. I'm production assistant for a man named Justin, who had two hits last season. I live on Fifty-fourth Street, a few doors from the Modern Museum of Art, of which I'm a tea-privileges member—no cream. I live at Fifty-three West Fifty-fourth Street, Apartment 3B. Can you remember that? Eldorado 59970. Can you remember that?

Ben: Yes.

Rosie: Are you stationed in New York? Or is *stationed* the right word?

Ben: I'm not exactly stationed in New York. I was stationed in Washington, but I got sick, and now I'm on leave, and I'm gonna spend it in New York.

Rosie: Eldorado 59970.

Ben: I'm gonna look up an old friend of mine who's a newspaper man. We were in Korea together.

The non sequiturs, verbal gymnastics, and flying buttresses in this conversation would perhaps not be out of place in a Beckett play or in a Marx Brothers film. "Maryland's a beautiful state." "This is Delaware." Or: "Are you Arabic?" "No."

"Let me put it another way. Are you married?" *The Manchurian Candidate* follows a narrow bridge between hyperbole, exaggeration, chaos, tragedy, hysteria, comedy, and Oedipal angst. By almost no one's criterion could the film be seen to take itself as outright comedy. However, it does see itself as pointing from the beginning to the hypnotic effects—the "conditioning" of my essay's title—of the ordinary, such as in the scene in which the American soldiers are on display as subjects of communist brainwashing, subjects who have been "programmed" to see themselves as attending a women's garden club meeting. The repeated use of 360-degree shots demonstrates the wish to highlight the shifting perspectives in this scene between the ordinary women's meeting and the extraordinary scene of verifying before high-ranking communist officials the success of the soldiers' brainwashing.

One could also point to the sentence "Why don't you pass the time by playing a little solitaire?" as deliberately unobtrusive, unadorned expression, which, if intercepted, might not immediately attract anyone's attention. It is as if the entire methodology of brainwashing consists in establishing the commonplace as the medium by which "mechanisms" are programmed, a lesson pronounced in differing ways by Freud *(Civilization and Its Discontents),* by Althusser (on ideology), and by numerous poets and writers in the twentieth century, perhaps most famously beginning with T. S. Eliot's *Waste Land.* Vance Packard, in an important 1957 study of "depth manipulation" entitled *The Hidden Persuaders,* makes the case that brainwashing has been an ordinary, documented effort not of communism but of the most devoted capitalists, particularly advertisers.

Stanley Cavell, the philosopher most attuned to the effects and neglects of the ordinary, finds it pertinent that ordinary language philosophy addresses the states or moods produced by our habitual encounters with the ordinary. Ordinary language philosophy is the philosophical study of everyday language as spoken by the average individual. One neglects or shuns the ordinary at one's peril, Cavell is wont to say, with a potentially concomitant consequence that one will end up embracing not human existence, but something other, mechanical, automated, programmed. My aim here is to account somewhat more fully for what might be happening with Raymond as automaton. In Cavell's discussion of E. T. A. Hoffmann's "The Sandman," he uses it as a kind of proof-text for Freud's essay on the uncanny.

> Hoffmann's story features the beautiful automaton Olympia with whom the hero [Nathaniel] falls in love (precipitated by his viewing her through a magic spyglass constructed by one of her constructors). At first this love serves for the amusement of others who are certain they see right through the inanimateness of the machine; but then the memory of the love serves to feed their anxiety that they may be making the same error with their own beloveds. (*In Quest* 155)

Nathaniel forsakes his childhood sweetheart, Clara, for the automaton. However, Clara returns at the end of the tale—post-Olympiad. Nathaniel and Clara are at the top of a tower. "'Nathaniel [. . .] found Coppola's spy-glass and looked to one side. Clara was standing in front of the glass. There was a convulsive throbbing in his pulse. [. . .]' What we are, accordingly, climactically asked to think about is [. . .] why [. . .] a chance vision of Clara causes Nathaniel's reentry into madness" (*In Quest* 157). What interests me about this passage is not only Cavell's reading of the tale that evokes Nathaniel's horror at a projected *ordinary* future with Clara, as well as Nathaniel's fascination with an automaton, but also Cavell's pointing to rhetoric—"figuration"—as the means by which Nathaniel's madness comes about. Cavell writes:

> The glass [spy-glass] is a death-dealing rhetoric machine, producing or expressing the consciousness of life in one case (Olympia's) by figuration, in the other (Clara's) by literalization, or say defiguration. One might also think of it as a machine of incessant animation, the parody of a certain romantic writing; and surely not unconnectedly as an uncanny anticipation of a movie camera. The moral of the machine I would draw provisionally this way: There is a repetition necessary to what we call life, or the animate, necessary for example to the human; and a repetition necessary to what we call death, or the inanimate, necessary for example to the mechanical; and there are no marks or features or criteria or rhetoric by means of which to tell the difference between them. (*In Quest* 157–58)

The Manchurian Candidate adds a twist to Cavell's amazing commentary linking rhetoric and film, for the film is not about renouncing the mechanical, the automated, the programmed existence in favor of, let's call it, quotidian existence; rather, via the characters of Ben and Rosie, the film wants to say something about the possible redemption of the mechanical, the automated, the programmed by treating *"it,"* or *"the mechanism,"* as *human*, caring for "programmed" human beings, risking contact with them, undoing the programming. In the situation of the conversation between the strangers on a train, Ben and Rosie, the result is *the undoing of rhetoric,* the disfiguring of ordinary discourse, given that the medium of the programming is the ordinary itself. Rosie's breaking the usual links of language—puns, non sequiturs, uncalled for responses, bizarre repetitions— turns out to be parallel to Ben's efforts later in the film to break the chains of Raymond's programming by showing him an uninterrupted repetition, a stacked deck containing fifty-two queens of diamonds. Before accepting this as a final thesis, I want to say that Rosie's undoing of rhetoric isn't the whole of what's happening in the conversation. To say that it is would be a misreading, for she also makes use of Ben's programming for other purposes, such as to implant—if that's not too strong a word—her address and phone number into Ben. It's not clear to me if it's possible to say whether it matters if Rosie has an awareness of Ben's programming. Nonetheless, my reading of the alteration in Ben's voice after Rosie's twice-uttered question "Can you remember that?" would seem to indicate that a sentence like that might have been part of his programming sessions, though, again, the evidence for this is unavailable through the usual channels, except through attention to Ben's altered state in the context of these questions' utterance.

Let me leave undefended, since I wouldn't know how to prove it, a claim that Rosie helps Ben after witnessing his distress on the train. Ben is a self-described "sick" man who has reached a level of impotence that prevents him from lighting his own cigarette. That Rosie observes this and then follows Ben out of the train car and lights a cigarette for him—gets it going—those actions constitute concern of some sort, even if one wants to chalk it up to something as plain as that she seems to be interested romantically in him, wanting to know whether he is married ("Are you Arabic?" [!]), giving Ben her phone number, et cetera. The cigarettes constitute a form of communication. Many authors have understood the uses to which cigarettes are put as instruments of what is frequently called communication," writes Richard Klein.

> Smoking cigarettes bodies forth an implicit language of gestures and acts that we have all learned subliminally to translate and that movie directors have used with conscious cunning. [. . .] Careful viewers have long observed that in the movies, one can not only watch but read cigarettes like subtitles—translating the action on the screen into another language which the camera registers but barely foregrounds. (Klein 9)

We do not have a developed rhetoric of cigarettes, though *Cigarettes Are Sublime* might be the first textbook on the subject, even if it seems wholly deluded regarding the economic motives driving U.S. tobacco companies. Nonetheless, whatever the cigarettes speak in *The Manchurian Candidate,* they are not part of the undoing of rhetoric, for they work as familiarly as the cigarettes in *Now, Voyager,* even if *Now, Voyager's* cigarettes say more, almost becoming thematic, certainly unmissable.

The back and forth between Ben and Rosie contains a fragility—not clearly a fragility of goodness—perhaps visible only in Rosie's searching, puzzling eyes, as she looks continually at Ben, who often looks away or closes his eyes altogether, to gauge what is happening with their words and to *see* whether more words are necessary, as if Rosie cannot let the conversation wilt without risking losing Ben (to what?). And she wants to convey to Ben that despite her verbal dexterity, she is vulnerable to him, such as when Ben questions aggressively why a discrepancy exists in her being called both Rosie and Eugenie:

"Still, when I asked you what your name was, you said it was Eugenie." Rosie's hypothetical response is: "It's quite possible I was feeling more or less fragile at that instant," letting Ben know that her feelings are under sway, alterable, depending on the directions this conversation between them takes. That same response maps out a range of character for Eugenie/Rose/Ginny, at one end of the range the fragile Eugenie and at some other end the brown soap and beer Rosie, though in either case Eugenie/Rose/Ginny will carry out the Adamic task of deciding how she will be called, named: "You may call me Ginny."

Dark Victory

The film's conclusion opens up questions about party politics, the way in which democracy is prescripted—the speechwriting, the planning, the organization, the "party machine," the party convention functioning as a grand display of *deus ex machina*—so that one of the accepted *topoi* of freedom in democracy, improvisation, is as far removed as possible from what takes place during an election. The loss of spontaneity, of the unrehearsed, the nonprogrammed—all these take their place near the center of the film's concerns, with this aspect spotlighted through the particular trope of the Garden of Eden, first as the idyllic setting for Raymond and Jocie's summer of "lovableness" and at film's end as the site of politics in the Garden (Madison Square Garden). Perhaps too blatantly, the film insists on keeping our attention on the snakes in both Gardens.

However, one of the Garden narratives leaves the snake intact, as if its continued existence is required. *The Manchurian Candidate* seems to require the opposite, an (immediate) ridding of the snakes, and their killings are significant, in the way Nicole Loraux notes in *Tragic Ways of Killing a Woman* that deaths in the *Iliad* and in ancient dramas happen in very distinctive, telling ways. The film makes no less a point with the various methods and images of death, as is made all too visible, almost comical, in Senator Jordon's murder, a container of milk in hand and over his heart when he is shot. Given that this is a film about brainwashing, the head takes on a significant role. Both Jocie and her father are shot in the chest, not the head, whereas Raymond places his stepfather and mother's heads in his rifle's crosshairs, as if their heads are the locus of the problem and the solution. However, despite a cephalic emphasis in the killings at the film's end, one of the main differences in the shootings of Raymond's mother and stepfather is that their assassination takes place before an audience (at the party convention at the Garden, at a garden party), reminding us of Raymond's first programmed killings on stage (at a garden club meeting, he thinks) before the communist leaders gathered to be convinced of the brainwashing's success. In the latter instance, the audience knows what to expect from Raymond. The former diegetic audience's reactions depends on its distance from the esoteric, encrypted events, the causes of which they are not privileged to know. The film attempts to undo the viewer's adoption of the former diegetic audience's reactions. Some might say the film's point of view aligns itself with Ben Marco's position. For instance, only Ben witnesses Raymond's suicide, and the film's ending, at night with rain and thunder, gives Ben the last word, uttered with a mixture of anger and despair, amidst a kind of eulogy to Raymond that concludes with the word *hell*, as if the end of Raymond and his family, as well as the destruction of the communist plan, have not cleared the stage for a new dawn, but rather have opened the space of a lamentable, dark victory.

This brings me back to the incapacities of terminological labeling of the rhetorical variety, for the identification of tropes at work in *The Manchurian Candidate*, sophisticated as that task could become, leaves intact the plague of fantasies, and potentially leaves its recipients politically inert, deprived of refuge, housed still in Ben's "hell." "For rhetorical theory," as Charles Altieri has it, "meaning is not a central concern: what matters is how the control over meaning can be deployed, at times by wielding ambiguity rather than engaging it and at times by manipulating the other" (95). The construction of a framework in which everything has a place, every kind of language, including cinematic *écriture*, a category, is what some call representational-calculative thinking, and that kind of thinking seems to me incapable of opening up what is at stake, poetically and politically, with *The Manchurian Candidate*, a film that is, in part, if I understand correctly, about "the appearance of that which conceals itself . . . *as* that which conceals itself" (Bruns 185), about at least what Ben calls "the unspeakable," that is, the nonrhetorical, and thus unconnected to rhetorical tropes. The disaster in the film is what did not happen, a fantasy's failure to arrive: a dream of full control—where marshal law would look like anarchy—gone awry. To the extent that the film plays up rhetoric's histrionics, exposes its republican weaknesses, and points out the therapeutic usefulness of resisting, even undoing rhetoric (as in the conversation above), it remains antithetical to rhetoric's controls (say, over audiences; for example, Ben's last movement is to turn his back to the audience), including its methodological and terminological projects.

Note

All illustrations in this essay are from *The Manchurian Candidate*, © 1962, 1990, by MC Productions.

Works Cited

Altieri, Charles. "Toward a Hermeneutics Responsive to Rhetorical Theory." *Rhetoric and Hermeneutics: A Reader*. Ed. Walter Jost and Michael Hyde. New Haven: Yale UP, 1997. 90–107.

Baxandall, Michael. *Giotto and the Orators: Humanist Observers of Painting in Italy and the Discovery of Pictorial Composition 1350–1450*. Oxford: Clarendon, 1971.

Blanchot, Maurice. *The Writing of the Disaster*. Trans. Ann Smock. Lincoln: U of Nebraska P, 1986.

Borradori, Giovanna. *The American Philosopher: Conversations with Quine, Davidson, Putnam, Nozick, Danto, Rorty, Cavell, MacIntyre, and Kuhn*. Trans. Rosanna Crocitto. Chicago: U of Chicago P, 1994.

Bruns, Gerald L. *Heidegger's Estrangements: Language, Truth and Poetry in the Later Writings*. New Haven: Yale UP, 1989.

Cavell, Stanley. *Contesting Tears: The Hollywood Melodrama of the Unknown Woman*. Chicago: U of Chicago P, 1996.

———. "Hope Against Hope." *Conditions Handsome and Unhandsome: The Constitution of Emersonian Perfectionism*. Chicago: U of Chicago P, 1990.

———. *In Quest of the Ordinary: Lines of Scepticism and Romanticism*. Chicago: U of Chicago P, 1988.

————. "Postscript: To Whom It May Concern." *Critical Inquiry* 16 (1990): 248–89.

————. *Themes Out of School: Effects and Causes.* San Francisco: North Point P, 1984.

————. *This New Yet Unapproachable America: Lectures after Emerson after Wittgenstein.* Albuquerque: Living Batch, 1989.

Chatman, Seymour. *Coming to Terms: The Rhetoric of Narrative in Fiction and Film.* Ithaca: Cornell UP, 1990.

Condon, Richard. *The Manchurian Candidate.* London: Michael Joseph, 1959.

Hoberman, J. "When Dr. No Met Dr. Strangelove." *Sight and Sound* 3 (Dec. 1993): 17–21.

Holly, Michael Ann. *Past Looking: Historical Imagination and the Rhetoric of the Image.* Ithaca: Cornell UP, 1996.

Kennedy, George A. *Comparative Rhetoric: An Historical and Cross-Cultural Introduction.* New York: Oxford UP, 1998.

Klein, Richard. *Cigarettes Are Sublime.* Durham: Duke UP, 1993.

Krajewski, Bruce. *Traveling with Hermes: Hermeneutics and Rhetoric.* Amherst: U of Massachusetts P, 1992.

Lichtenstein, Jacqueline. *The Eloquence of Color: Rhetoric and Painting in the French Classical Age.* Berkeley: U of California P, 1993.

Loraux, Nicole. *Tragic Ways of Killing a Woman.* Cambridge, MA: Harvard UP, 1987.

Lukacher, Ned. *Daemonic Figures: Shakespeare and the Question of Conscience.* Ithaca: Cornell UP, 1994.

Marcus, Greil. "The Last American Dream: *The Manchurian Candidate.*" *Hiding in Plain Sight: Essays in Criticism and Autobiography.* Ed. Wendy Lesser. San Francisco: Mercury House, 1993. 208–18.

Marks, John D. *The Search for the "Manchurian Candidate": The CIA and Mind Control.* New York: Norton, 1991.

Mitchell, W. J. T. *Picture Theory: Essays on Verbal and Visual Representation.* Chicago: U of Chicago P, 1994.

Mulhall, Stephen. *Stanley Cavell: Philosophy's Recounting of the Ordinary.* Oxford: Clarendon, 1994.

Navasky, Victor. *Naming Names.* New York: Viking, 1980.

Packard, Vance. *The Hidden Persuaders.* New York: D. MacKay, 1957.

Rosenheim, Shawn James. *The Cryptographic Imagination: Secret Writing from Edgar Poe to the Internet.* Baltimore: Johns Hopkins UP, 1997.

Salecl, Renata, and Slavoj Žižek, eds. *Gaze and Voice as Love Objects.* Durham: Duke UP, 1996.

Sass, Louis A. *The Paradoxes of Delusion: Wittgenstein, Schreber, and the Schizophrenic Mind.* Ithaca: Cornell UP, 1994.

Sobchack, Vivian. *The Address of the Eye: A Phenomenology of Film Experience.* Princeton: Princeton UP, 1992.

Žižek, Slavoj. "'I Hear You with My Eyes'; or The Invisible Master." *Gaze and Voice as Love Objects*. Ed. Renata Salecl and Slavoj Žižek. Durham, NC: Duke UP, 1996.

———. *The Plague of Fantasies*. London: Verso, 1997.

———. *Tarrying with the Negative: Kant, Hegel, and the Critique of Ideology*. Durham: Duke UP, 1993.

12

Sophistry, Magic, and the Vilifying Rhetoric of *The Usual Suspects*

David Blakesley

> No art cultivated by man has suffered more in the revolutions of taste and opinion than the art of Rhetoric. There was a time when, by an undue extension of this term, it designated the whole cycle of accomplishments which prepared a man for public affairs. From that height it has descended to a level with the arts of alchemy and astrology, as holding out promises which consist in a mixed degree of impostures wherever its pretensions happened to be weighty, and of trifles wherever they happened to be true.
> —Thomas De Quincey, *Selected Essays on Rhetoric*

THE USUAL SUSPECTS (1995, DIR. BRYAN SINGER) PROVOKES closer examination of rhetoric's reputation because it is a film that is explicitly about rhetoric as a social and verbal art. At first glance, the film's usual suspects are thieves, mobsters, and murderers. But look a little deeper and we see that rhetoric is the evil essence; the power of speech to bend the will, the quintessential menace. Pure persuasion—the delight in persuasion for its own sake—is Roger "Verbal" Kint's (Kevin Spacey's) motive, as well as the primary symptom of his evil nature. Rhetoric becomes the art of deception (fraud), and Verbal, the liar extraordinaire, the snake in the Garden. In vilifying rhetoric as it does, *The Usual Suspects* invites us to question the broader cultural attitudes—the ideology—that would routinely separate the matter from the manner. In making its equation between rhetoric and evil, the film thus reflects an ideology of naïve representational realism—the belief that words and images are but conduits of meaning—and a fear that there are those among us who would capitalize on the power of rhetoric to distort the truth (which can be known) and to ornament the unadorned facts of experience. It is a familiar attitude that may also reveal our anxiety over the difficulty of separating fact from fiction. In *The Usual Suspects,* this anxiety is in the spotlight and thus may reveal an even deeper ambivalence about the power of the word and the image to represent the real.

Rhetoric's Reputation

De Quincey was writing in 1828, but he knew then what we know now: rhetoric's reputation as an art has long been suspect, despite efforts by many great thinkers to show its vital and prominent role in the transmission of culture, the conduct of social and political life, and, as Cicero's Crassus put it, "the general welfare of the state" (16). As popularly conceived, there is rhetoric and there is reality, the former having no bearing on or relation to the latter. People believe that rhetoric merely embellishes or distorts the truth—the real—with fanciful or disingenuous word-mongering. It is the (dis)grace atop nature, in other words. Such a conception of rhetoric rests on age-old distinctions between the symbolic and the real—between the manner and the matter. These distinctions have certainly been put to the test in the wake of the rhetorical (or linguistic) and visual turns in critical theory, but nevertheless they continue to inform the popular understanding that rhetoric simply distorts or embellishes the real with an elaborated fiction. In retrospect and for good or ill, rhetoric's popular reputation seems to have been fated long ago by Socrates's condemnation of sophistic rhetoric in many of Plato's dialogues, where rhetoric's machinations are but fluttering shadows on a cave wall, far removed from the light of truth. Its pretensions, as De Quincey put it, are still seen as "impostures"; its revelations, "trifles."

This distrust of rhetoric and its capacity for rendering truth has deep roots, for a long time having been entangled also in ideological conceptions of identity and identification. In his famous speech "Encomium to Helen" (427? BCE), the sophist Gorgias admitted that "by entering into the opinion of the soul the force of incantation is wont to beguile and persuade and alter it by witchcraft" (286). "The power of speech," he said, "has the same effect on the condition of the soul as the application of drugs [*pharmaka*] to the state of bodies" (287).[1] Further complicating matters, at least according to Gorgias, were these three governing postulates:

1. Nothing exists.
2. Even if something did exist, it would be incomprehensible to human beings.
3. Even if someone could comprehend what exists, it could not be explained or communicated to anyone else.[2]

The central paradox of sophistic philosophy was that while our words function semiotically in a system of signs, they either signify nothing or, perhaps even worse, delude us into endowing referents with a presence that is both magical and ephemeral. The negative, or nothingness, is a rhetorical construction, one which humans rely on to assert presence where there is (nothing) but absence.

It is not hard to see why, in a world that values certainty, such a sophistical contention is dangerous, and the sophist, a menace.

Plato's Socrates criticized the sophists, of course, for accepting the paradox of nonexistence as a given because doing so only apparently legitimized speaking on both sides of an issue without regard for the truth. Sophists "pursue probability while speaking and let truth go to hell and stay there" (*Phaedrus* 272). Aristotle later admitted that rhetoric was not concerned with certainties or transcendent ideas, but rather with probabilities, with that which people believe to be true. As such, rhetoric for Aristotle (and later, Cicero) functioned both as a practical art (like politics and ethics) and a productive art (like dialectic) because it could build community, by fostering identification with widely held beliefs or by inquiring into the basis of belief itself. More recently, Kenneth Burke substitutes identification for persuasion in his formulation of rhetoric, saying, "[P]ut identification and division ambiguously together, so that you cannot know for certain just where one ends and the other begins, and you have the characteristic invitation to rhetoric" (*Rhetoric* 25). In other words, where there is ambiguity and uncertainty, when the best course of action is uncertain or knowledge at best probable—when people disagree—rhetoric comes to the fore, and people contest meaning. As the aim of rhetoric, identification for Burke is predicated on our desire for consubstantiality (sharing of substance), which makes rhetoric an ethic of identities. In reaching consensus, we desire to become "one" with the "other." Identity becomes the "subject of semiotics," to use Kaja Silverman's phrasing.

These days, it is a truism to say that rhetoric shapes attitudes toward and thus perceptions of the external world and the beliefs that give it form and coherence. Believing is seeing. And thus when we believe something, we use words to tell stories that make our beliefs credible to others, as if verisimilitude depended solely on our ability to give form to images and to put meaning into words. As readers, auditors, and spectators, we seek verbal explanations that confirm what we already know, or think we know, about the past and present state of things. In the absence of such confirmation, the meaning of subjective experience or the character of material reality remains ambiguous, creating the space in which we might project the self or the subject's desire. The ambiguous becomes the probable or the certain once the world of words and images in the mind jibes with expectations of how things are or ought to be. In other words, people need to believe to see.

Rhetoric as the Usual Suspect

In *The Usual Suspects*, "Verbal" plays the malicious sophist whose motives are ambiguous and whose entire delivery, including his construction of himself as an ethical subject, is a carefully orchestrated fabrication. In the final analysis, it is not only Keyser Söse's powerful will that makes him a fearsome figure—his "willingness to do what the other guy wouldn't"—but also his eloquence, his ability both to use words to self-fashion an identity that is inscrutably menacing and to assert his will on whomever he pleases.[3] Verbal's explicit association with language and its magical powers thus suggests an implicit cultural association between evil and rhetoric; rhetoric does, after all, perpetuate falsehoods. In *The Usual Suspects,* the main suspect is rhetoric.

Director Bryan Singer and writer Christopher McQuarrie, however, do more than just show that Keyser Söse's evil is manifest in his eloquence. Although eloquence can be the handmaiden of evil, it can also be used, when it suits the purpose, to surprise and entertain the audience. Because much of the film unfolds as an imaginative reconstruction in Kujan's mind as he hears Verbal's mostly fabricated story, Singer exploits our capacity, our desire, to convert word to image and to project upon the words of others our own fantasies and expectations. This power of the image to instill belief makes distinguishing between perception and reality impossible. Once we discover at the end of the film that Verbal is really the mysterious phantom and evildoer, Keyser Söse, and is not, as Agent David Kujan (Chazz Palminteri) believes, a stupid, two-bit crook, we realize that the entire narrative has been fraudulent. Like Kujan, Verbal's chief interrogator, we have been played the fool. The flashback that has replayed in his imagination and on the screen as he hears Verbal's story is not really a flashback at all, but an intricately constructed fantasy with indeterminate veracity.

I need to pause here to explain just what happens in *The Usual Suspects* and contrast it with what people tend to think has happened after an initial viewing. As you know, the film's ending is bewildering, a point made rather simply by Leonard Maltin, who says, with an exclamation mark, "If you think about it, the final twist negates the entire film!" (1503). In order for me to prove otherwise, I need to explain for a moment some important distinctions between *story* and *plot,* as well as introduce a term from film theory: *diegesis* (from the Greek word for "recounted story").

The "total story," or diegesis, of *The Usual Suspects* includes all of the explicitly presented events (including the so-called flashbacks) as well as all the inferred and tangled events that we construct as we watch and that help us make sense of the total narrative (Bordwell and Thompson 92). (One of the images tied to Verbal throughout the film is that of the tangled ropes and rigging we see at the scene of Keaton's death.) The diegesis is "the content of the narrative, the fictional world as described inside the story" (Hayward 84). In brief, the story of this film, up until the ending, is this: after the opening scene, we learn about a drug deal gone bad on a ship in the San Pedro harbor and that one of the survivors of the deadly mayhem that resulted, Verbal, was one of the crooks involved. He has made a deal of immunity with the DA, so he's under compulsion, but somewhat reluctant, to provide his account of these events. From this point on, the bulk of the film emanates from Kujan's interrogation of Verbal. After several twists and turns, we're led to believe with Kujan that Keaton (Gabriel Byrne) is really Keyser Söse, the mastermind of the drug deal, who himself has also perished in the explosion. (This version of the story, however, presents problems for us because we see Keaton shot by Söse in the film's opening sequence.) As Verbal walks to freedom, we get a montage of shots suggesting that all the details of Verbal's story have been taken from cues around Kujan's office, especially ones on the bulletin board. It turns out that Verbal is Keyser Söse after-all, which is first confirmed when a fax comes in showing a sketch of Verbal, one drawn from an eyewitness's description of Söse, and then again as Verbal's disguised limp turns into a confident stride after exiting the police station. Verbal, it seems, has made everything up. Hence, we tend to think initially, with Maltin, that the ending negates the entire film. It has all been a fantasy.

The *plot* of *The Usual Suspects,* however, consists not only of all the explicitly presented events (thus overlapping with its story) but also all of nondiegetic material, those aspects of the narrative that seem to be extraneous to the world of the story (Bordwell and Thompson 92), such as the words that we see on screen as certain flashbacks begin and that help us form a time frame for the events. Film editor John Ottman's fascinating verbal and visual montage sequence at the end of the film is also nondiegetic, to the extent that it reassembles elements of the surface story into another, entirely different one, and thus consists of Singers's manipulation of the story by means outside the story itself. (For example, we could not have otherwise inferred that Söse's imaginary henchman, Kobayashi, got his name from the manufacturer of the coffee cups that Verbal and Kujan hold.) The nondiegetic material in this film impresses upon us early on that we should view the unfolding story as a flashback, and since we are led to believe that Verbal is the one telling the story, we presume that it represents his version of events. The film's most powerful moment comes when we discover who Verbal really is and that he has constructed the story using words and images from around the interrogation office as well as "facts" that Kujan has himself disclosed. Once we have seen this concluding montage, however, we need to reassemble all of the inferences we made in constructing the story so that it becomes a very different story, one that on a second viewing makes perfect sense. Ironically, the nondiegetic material in the end forces a new diegesis, one which brings to the fore problems of language and perception.

But what is the story the second time around? I want to suggest that it is really Kujan's story, not Verbal's, that animates the entire film, or at least all that we see after the opening sequence. From this view, Verbal becomes not simply a despicable liar. Instead, he functions as the occasion for Kujan's own impulse to construct the "real" story from what he believes about drug deals, and especially about Keaton. The flashbacks, then, are not really flashbacks at all, but Kujan's imaginative reconstructions of the events at the moment of Verbal's retelling. They happen in the present. As viewers, we don't see them as subjective reconstructions the first time through because we're conditioned by conventional narrative devices to believe that when someone retells a story via a flashback, we are "seeing" what the storyteller imagines, not what the listener imagines. We actually do not hear much of Verbal's story. Instead, we see it as a fully formed visual experience and thus accept it as "what happened" more readily than had we simply heard Verbal telling it. We cannot, in other words, help but be fooled, since the visual experience is Kujan's, who has already been fooled by what Detective Rabin (Dan Hedaya) calls Kujan's "host of wild theories to answer all these questions."

At the same time that he associates eloquence with evil, then, Singer uses the reconstructed, fantasized images to make the film's climax all the more striking and thus to perform his own magic. We have no choice but to accept what we see, since the unreliable narrator's will has already been worked at the point we see and hear the tale. While the film ultimately condemns rhetoric by association, it simultaneously exploits the power of images to instill belief. To his credit, Singer draws attention to the rhetorical nature of the image by the end of the film, but by then the surprise so overwhelms our attention that we might forget that the whole flashback is the product of Kujan's imagination, not Verbal's, and only secondarily, the viewer's.

Verbal recognizes from the beginning of the interrogation that Kujan believes Keaton was the chief culprit, so he capitalizes on that expectation to tell a story that, with some fortuitous facts injected by Kujan, would lead to the association of Keaton with Söse. Each new "fact" that Kujan reveals to Verbal is integrated into the narrative seamlessly, so that by the end of Verbal's interrogation, the story neatly fits Kujan's version of it. His "wild theories" have indeed provided the answers he was looking for, but he fails to recognize that because Verbal, seeing that Kujan was uncertain, told him a story that would simply confirm what he already expected it to confirm, making the probably appear certain. Verbal discerns what story Kujan wants to hear, then gives it to him. Doing so without alerting Kujan is possible because Verbal knows that most of what Kujan knows is based on conjecture or prior expectations that also prompt the police to round up the usual suspects in the first place, the so-called rush-to-judgment or profiling that undermines the illusion of objectivity.

Verbal has the rhetorician's skill of extemporaneous topical invention, which we learn from the concluding montage that pairs elements of Verbal's story with words and images found in the interrogation room. The shots alternate between Verbal, who is leaving the police station, and Kujan, who scans the bulletin board and sees the bits of information (cues like "Redfoot," the "Kobayashi" coffee cup, the bulletin board made in Skokie, Illinois, by a company named "Quartet") that Verbal has used to fill the gaps in the story. Verbal's words replay in Kujan's head, connecting word to image directly, in a way that was not readily perceivable during the original telling. For Verbal, these connections were explicit. For Kujan, they were phantasms, the material that animated his imagination and charmed him into envisioning the whole story. Having endowed these cues with presence, Kujan makes Verbal's story confirm what he had suspected about Keaton all along. For his part, Verbal understands this desire to invest the word with phantastic properties, so he directs Kujan's attention to the protean, and thus probable, beliefs that, when combined with concrete details, essentially bring his suspicions to life.

The words and images that Kujan spots on the bulletin board and the "Kobayashi" coffee cup supply the concrete details of the narrative and the bulk of the pre-interrogation banter. The narrative's central story, however, comes from Kujan. Using the detective's inductive logic and his own assessment of Keaton's character, Kujan has supplied Verbal with all of the essential ingredients of the narrative, a narrative that unfolds in Kujan's imagination and thus on-screen. Had Verbal used details not readily found on the bulletin board, the result would still be the same. He has simply embellished a story that we now know to be false. Yet his evil is equated with this capacity for embellishing, while Kujan's phantastic imagination and the authorized conclusions of his inductive logic are what generate most of the deception. Kujan's mind is a sympathetic universe in which Verbal's inventions are free to work their magic.

Rhetoric and Magic

I want to digress a moment from this story of *The Usual Suspect*'s magic to situate the film's vilification of rhetoric in the broader history of rhetoric and its alignment with magic and, ultimately, evil. My premise is that a rhetorical approach to the film, which is itself explicitly about rhetoric, should establish the contexts that ambiguate the meaning of the film. These contexts force us to conclude that our fear and distrust of rhetoric are but rationalizations of our conflicted desire for deception and identity or of the inevitability of rhetorical fabrication with every utterance.

In *Magic, Rhetoric, and Literacy,* William A. Covino allies rhetoric and literacy with magic "because all three entail generation, production, and transformation" (29). Magic is, essentially, "a social act whose medium is persuasive discourse" (11). Literacy is "the alertness to linguistic ambiguity" (31); and rhetoric "the performance of literacy" (31). According to Covino, there are two species of magic, both operative in contemporary culture: arresting magic-rhetoric is a program of "spells" for foreclosing discourse, for disallowing alternatives to authorized knowledge (8). Generative magic-rhetoric, by contrast, is a "(re)sorcery of spells for *generating* multiple perspectives" (9), a "dialogical critique [of consensual systems of power] that seeks novelty, originating at a remove from the mass culture it would interrogate" (9).

The interanimation of word and image in discourse was not only a chief concern of sophists like Gorgias, as Covino notes. Plato, Aristotle, Cicero, and especially Quintilian have commented on what the Greeks called *phantasiai* and the Romans *visions.* Phantasy for the Greeks was the mind's recombinatory power, acting upon *phantasmata* (images) during reflection, invention, and interpretation. Phantasms for Aristotle were like sense data but without matter (Covino 32). Generally speaking, phantasms are sensory traces that form the basis for human language, cues for recalling and interpreting sensory data, and principles for organizing expression (32). "As a process for determining and producing human language; for mystical contemplation and philosophical explanation; and for generating vivid speech," Covino explains, "phantasy is closely and explicitly connected with both magic and rhetoric. It is always under suspicion, from Plato forward, as a tool of rhetorical deception; phantasy can create illusions that 'charm' audiences" (33). Rhetoric and magic, acting similarly on phantasms, invoke "invisible powers within a sympathetic universe of widely shared signifiers" (19).

Persuasion involves more than just stating a position and proving a case; it requires an ability to help an audience imagine situations in which the improbable may be probable, to enliven shared perceptions with the force of familiar images, or to elaborate ambiguity and multiply perspectives in the interest of finding common ground. Magic, acting upon the material world with *spells* and ritualized incantations, aims to reconstitute reality. Effective rhetoric is like magic in that it creates in the mind the illusion of some prelinguistic experience, a supernumenal reality prior to but reconstituting experience. Knowing the mind's desire to invest the word with phantastic properties (with presence), the sophist/magician/rhetorician directs the attention to those protean experiences and beliefs that can be remolded into newly formed perceptions of the external world. The sophistic evocation of phantasy as a means to express possible or alternative realities was condemned, of course, in the philosophical tradition that attempted to articulate a stable reality. Phantasy, essential to sophistic rhetoric because of its protean nature, has the potential to deceive as well as enlighten.

From its beginning, Kujan's interrogation sets up a Platonic ideal of dialectical investigation, which as Thomas Conley in "Plato's *Phaedrus*" argues, is essentially invention in reverse, working backwards from that which is presumed to be true . Kujan wants to ascertain the truth surrounding the incidents on the boat in San Pedro. But he doesn't want to explore all the possibilities in the interest of truth. He already has his suspicions, having once before acted on them in his initial arrest of "the usual suspects" early in the film, prior to their involvement in the drug deal gone bad. Kujan's suspicions function as arrestive magic, disallowing alternatives to (his) authorized knowledge, sanctioned as it is by his status as a DEA agent. As Kujan says to Verbal early on, "Let me get right to the point. I'm smarter than you. And I'm gonna find out what you know whether you like it or not."

The contest between Kujan and Verbal ultimately is not over the truth, which is predetermined and simply verified by Verbal's magic; it becomes a battle of wills, a struggle between two ethical lives, one sanctioned by the law (Kujan's) and the other sanctioned by the power of speech (Verbal's). From the beginning of the interrogation, we identify with Kujan, an identification stabilized by our presence in his imagination as Verbal's story unfolds. As a representative of the law, his character is, initially at least, assumed to be honest and fair, even if he does use verbal threats and fabrications of his own to get at (his) truth. Kujan's legal authority places his rhetorical method, which also includes physical threats and leading questions, above reproach and beyond question, overwhelmed as we are by the shock of learning Söse's identity. Kujan's is a sanctioned rhetoric and verbal magic in its own right. A well-known interrogation technique consists of this invention of scenarios that the unwitting suspect is asked to "imagine," and then with leading questions, the interrogator hopes to trick the suspect into revealing details of the crime that only the perpetrator could know. Even by the end of *The Usual Suspects,* however, we simply don't see Kujan as a sorcerer, a weaver of spells. Rhetorically speaking, however, neither Kujan's nor Verbal's rhetoric is ethically sound. While Verbal's rhetoric emerges as the more effective, it is still morally reprehensible. Although both Kujan and Verbal deploy the rhetorician's tricks for creating consensus, it is Verbal's rhetoric that we notice. Kujan's efforts to affirm what he already knows, verbally and imaginatively, are not presented as rhetorical, even though language, acting as the vehicle of phantasy, corrupts that knowledge. Verbal's sophistry exposes how the primary mode of inquiry for the police—the pseudodialectical interrogation and inductive logic—is in its enactment the agency of ideological maintenance, of confirmation not inquiry. Kujan sets out to prove what he already believes. He wants to know what Verbal knows only if it confirms what he himself already suspects.

The Greatest Trick the Devil Ever Pulled

Verbal recalls the sophists of old who challenged essentialist philosophy on this same predisposition to adopt methods of inquiry that stabilized preexistent knowledge. This status quo has great momentum, so Verbal becomes the devil, and his manipulation of Kujan, rather than being seen as a legitimate philosophical challenge to epistemology, is rationalized as a form of sorcery. Measuring method by ideological criteria (judging means in terms of ends) can generate the sort of wholesale distrust of eloquence we see in *The Usual Suspects,* even though the story Verbal tells is essentially the one that Kujan has determined by other means less maligned but every bit as rhetorical.

In any rhetorical act, ethos is the speaker's presentation of character. In *The Usual Suspects,* ethos becomes the principle means of deception, and it is fitting that a film near the end of the century in which identification replaced persuasion as the primary aim of rhetoric would show how character and identity—false appearances—are the primary instruments of deception (as opposed to simple falsehoods). Verbal understands the importance of character, so he constructs an ethos that Kujan will trust, an ethos suggesting that Verbal is too stupid and cowardly to lie. But Singer also provides the audience and Kujan with hints regarding the nature of Verbal's character, the character that lies hidden behind his self-fashioning. In telling the myth of Keyser Söse, Verbal says, paraphrasing from Baudelaire's short story "The Generous Gambler," "The greatest trick the devil ever pulled was making the world believe he didn't exist." The true character of the devil compromises the devil's ability to persuade, and therefore in adopting an absent presence, the devil can effectively manipulate opinion.

Verbal invents himself as timid and crippled in an effort to conceal his true identity and can thus leave Söse's disembodied ethos to cast its spell. Kujan never imagines that Verbal (in character) could possibly be Söse. Verbal also allows himself to be a victim (Keaton's pawn) in his own fiction, further separating himself from the fictitiously constructed crime, so when Kujan insists Verbal was duped by Keaton, Verbal is willing to play the fool.

In a world of probabilities, Jasper Neel writes,

> [s]ophistry is a way to make choices. [. . .] The process of choice-making occurs both privately, as one uses the power of rhetoric and writing to persuade oneself, and publicly, as one attempts to persuade others. In other words, sophistry, in conjunction with rhetoric and writing, is the process whereby the individual develops an ethical self. (207)

Verbal/Söse entangles himself in an elaborate act of self-mythologizing so that he can work his will, the primary aim of all rhetorical acts, on whomever he pleases. When Kujan asks Verbal about Söse during the interrogation, Verbal tells him the story of how Söse "showed these men of will what will really is." As it unfolds in Kujan's imagination, Söse's murder of his family is shot with a yellow filter, giving the scene a surreal quality that makes Söse appear even more menacing. Verbal then says that Söse can disappear on a whim: "And like that . . . he's gone. Underground. Nobody's ever seen him since. He becomes a myth, a spook story. . . ." In order for Söse's power to work, however, he can disappear in physical presence only. His name, his extended ethos, has to last. So Söse always leaves a witness, someone to perpetuate the myth so that it can continue its influence. And he enjoys having played the trickster. (He urinates on the fire in the opening scene so that he can reveal himself to and then kill Keaton.) Verbal works this magic on Kujan during the interrogation by flaunting Söse's conspicuous absence: "You think a guy like that comes this close to getting caught and sticks his head out?" Shot from a low angle with his head sticking out, Verbal taunts Kujan, knowing both that his ruse will be discovered after he leaves the police station and that having taken such a risk, the ethos of Keyser Söse will be all the more powerful in its work. In the end, Söse's self-fashioned identity has far more sway than Kujan's, which is legally defined and sanctioned but ultimately powerless.

Singer's Magic

The Usual Suspects condemns the magical powers of rhetoric by associating Verbal/Söse explicitly with literacy and evil. At the same time, Singer capitalizes on the beguiling (and rhetorical) power of the image to instill belief, fooling us into thinking that what we see is worth believing. The film, of course, draws attention to this process of constructing an image that can easily be mistaken for the real. In his interview with Andy Spletzer, Singer explains how film manufactures appearances that are inescapably deceptive:

It's the nature of film as a medium. When you look at a movie, what do you see? You see an image. That's what you perceive, but that's not what you're looking at. You're looking at 60% bright, 40% blackness. I'm always fascinated by that. I believe under everything that we see there's so much that we don't see, that we don't perceive. We don't live in the world of reality, we live in the world of how we perceive reality.

In one sense, literacy is alertness to the underworld of the imagination, to the inherent ambiguity in our representations of the world (visual or verbal). The word-image—the phantasm, in the classical sense—stabilizes perceptions and thus suppresses their nature as secondary representations of reality. We act—and believe—on the assumption that what we perceive is real, whether the perception comes straight from sensation of the physical world or comes filtered into the imagination via language or (re)presented images.

Literacy is alertness to ambiguity, and rhetoric is the performance of literacy. Both are possible because, as Covino writes, "meaning is always plural, always susceptible to transformation" (31). Certainly Verbal is literate according to this definition, throughout the film magically transforming Kujan's cloudy suspicions into a logical, neatly constructed narrative. Almost everything that Verbal says is a presentation of phantasy. (According to Quintilian, the ability to make absent things present, a function of phantasy, creates impressions that the audience cannot help but accept [Covino 36].) Kujan accepts Verbal's rhetorical phantasy, while the audience is further swayed by the visualization of Verbal's phantasy projected on the screen, in images separated from the verbal traces that generated them. Christian Metz theorizes that "the spectator is absent from the screen *as perceived,* but also [. . .] present there and even 'all-present' as *perceiver.* At every moment, I am in the film by my look's caress" (54). It is Singer's sleight of hand that encourages us to "caress" the narrative through Kujan. The inherent ambiguity in the verbal and visual representations of the world only reveals itself at the end of the film, when we "unwrite" the narrative we had constructed, when nondiegetic material forces a new diegesis.

The rhetor is a magician because he has the ability to make something so, simply by saying it (Covino 22). Everything Verbal says becomes an on-screen "reality" for the viewer. Of course, this magic has been concocted by the director. So Singer practices a deceptive form of rhetoric as well, but as he has admitted, the screen-image is always already a deception of sorts because the phantastic imagination animates it with verisimilitude. The power of the image to instill belief functions in much the same way that a sophist's manipulation of the word-image (the phantasm) does to make the uncertain appear probable. *The Usual Suspects,* while it reiterates the vilification of rhetoric, enacts visually the sort of eloquence for which rhetoric has been maligned through the ages: the embellishment of words and images to create charming illusions. The film capitalizes on our predisposition to name the power of evil: it is "rhetoric." It is the power of *The Usual Suspects* as well, evil or not.

Notes

I would like to thank Jeff Townsend for contributing perceptive observations about *The Usual Suspects* in the early development of this essay. This essay also extends and elaborates the discussion of *The Usual Suspects* in my book, *The Elements of Dramatism*.

1. Jacques Derrida examines the duality implicit in the rhetoric/medicine analogy in *Dissemination*.

2. Many of Gorgias's works come to us only in fragments. Some of them have been collected in Kerferd's *The Sophistic Movement*.

3. According to screenwriter Christopher McQuarrie, he chose Söse because it was the word for "verbal" in Turkish.

Works Cited

Blakesley, David. *The Elements of Dramatism*. Boston: Longman, 2002.

Bordwell, David, and Kristen Thompson. *Film Art: An Introduction*. 5th ed. New York: McGraw, 1997.

Burke, Kenneth. *Language as Symbolic Action*. Berkeley: U of California P, 1966.

———. *A Rhetoric of Motives*. 1950. Berkeley: U of California P, 1969.

Conley, Thomas. "Plato's Phaedrus." *The Writing Instructor* 8.1 (Fall 1988): 23–28.

Covino, William A. *Magic, Rhetoric, and Literacy: An Eccentric History of the Composing Imagination*. Albany: SUNY P, 1994.

De Quincey, Thomas. *Selected Essays on Rhetoric*. Ed. Frederick Burwick. Foreword by David Potter. Carbondale: Southern Illinois UP, 1967.

Derrida, Jacques. *Dissemination*. Trans. Barbara Johnson. Chicago: U of Chicago P, 1981.

Gorgias. "Encomium to Helen." Appendix I. *On Rhetoric: A Theory of Civil Discourse*. Aristotle. Trans. and ed. George A. Kennedy. New York: Oxford UP, 1991.

Hayward, Susan. *Cinema Studies: The Key Concepts*. 2nd ed. London: Routledge, 2000.

Kerferd, G. B. *The Sophistic Movement*. Cambridge: Cambridge UP, 1981.

Maltin, Leonard, ed. *Leonard Maltin's 2001 Movie and Video and Guide*. New York: Signet, 2000.

McQuarrie, Christopher. Interview by Todd Lippy. *Scenario* 3 (1996).

Metz, Christian. *The Imaginary Signifier: Psychoanalysis and the Cinema*. 1977. Trans. Celia Britton, Annwyl Williams, Ben Brewster, and Alfred Guzzetti. Bloomington: Indiana UP, 1982.

Neel, Jasper. *Plato, Derrida, and Writing*. Carbondale: Southern Illinois UP, 1988.

Silverman, Kaja. *The Subject of Semiotics*. New York: Oxford UP, 1983.

Singer, Bryan, dir. *The Usual Suspects*. Gramercy Pictures, 1995.

Spletzer, Andy. "Talking with Bryan Singer: Director of *The Usual Suspects*." *Film.com*. 13 Aug. 1996. <http://www.film.com/industry/interviews/singer.interview.stranger.html>. 8 July 1999.

13

Textual Trouble in River City: Literacy, Rhetoric, and Consumerism in *The Music Man*

Harriet Malinowitz

M ORTON DA COSTA'S 1962 FILM *THE MUSIC MAN,* adapted from Meredith Willson's hit 1957 Broadway musical, has been widely popular as a piece of cornball Americana; it has been called a "celebration of old-fashioned American virtues" and a "loving comic valentine to pre–World War I America" (Sennett 317). Willson himself reinforced—or perhaps more accurately, generated—this attitude in a note to the director of his stage script (ii). However, I would like to offer a reading of *The Music Man* that traces the ways its charm and humor are undergirded by a parodic stance toward American values as rooted in turn-of-the-century discourses of literacy, education, and morality and in the simultaneously burgeoning national obsession with buying and selling. An ingenious cultural critique that is very much *about* rhetoric itself—particularly in its showcasing of the rhetorics of salesmanship and consumption that, after 1890, transformed American culture—the film depicts empiricism and phenomenology, logic and sophistry, classical rationalism and romantic expressionism, highbrow aesthetics and popular culture, the Protestant work ethic and the capitalist pleasure fantasy, all vying for sovereignty in such quotidian sites as the local library, the schoolhouse, and the parlor music lesson.

Sexual and Textual Anxieties in the Progressive Era

In *The Music Man,* Robert Preston stars as con man/traveling salesman "Professor" Harold Hill, who works small towns across the country posing as a conductor and musical scholar and promising to create local marching boys' bands. He arrives in River City, Iowa, in 1912 with fabricated academic credentials; in reality, he is unable to read music or even distinguish one note from another. The person who threatens to unmask and undo him is Marian the Librarian (played by Shirley Jones), the anomalously intellectual "old maid" who, as the only person in town with proclivities toward research and critical reflection, has procured textual evidence that proves him to be a fake. Marian also moonlights as a piano teacher, favoring a no-nonsense pedagogy of practice and exercises.

John Trimbur has pointed out that beginning in late nineteenth-century America, when textual materials became affordable and widely circulated, there was an upsurge of cultural anxiety about literacy that focused particularly on those "professionals" who were simultaneously entrusted to disseminate and to police it: "Vice societies, social hygienists, and educators warned the public about the dangers of unregulated reading material, and increasingly librarians, teachers, and public spokespersons were expected to help middle-class Americans distinguish wholesome from degenerate reading material" (291). Readers, meanwhile, were considered to be "clients whose primary obligation was to trust the judgment of experts and professionals" (291). In *The Music Man,* a town benefactor, Henry ("Old Miser") Madison, has bequeathed the library to the people of River City, but all the books in it to Marian; we are told that the library has been a province entrusted to her for the purpose of improving River City's cultural level, though the citizens continually ignore her advice. In fact, the virginal, asexual Marian is ironically constructed by the townsfolk as something of a siren because she is a purveyor of "smut" such as Chaucer, Rabelais, and Balzac; her inheritance is likewise construed as payment for sexual favors rather than as transferred custodianship of intellectual property and a means of economic self-sufficiency ensured by an old friend of the family.

Significantly, Marian is situated within the epoch of the American New Woman, which according to feminist historian Carroll Smith-Rosenberg existed from 1870 to 1936. The New Women were born between 1850 and the early 1900s to middle- and upper-class families; were educated, economically independent, and most often single; frequently worked toward social reform; and "signaled the symbolic death of that earlier female subject, the refined and confined Victorian lady" (265). Many women college graduates formed intense alliances with other women, known as "Boston marriages," "devoted companionships," or, earlier in the nineteenth century, "romantic friendships."[1] By the turn of the century, male sexologists, along with educators and physicians, had sought to discredit these women as deviant by claiming that "the educated woman's brain would be overstimulated" and that she would "become morbidly introspective" and would manifest hysteria and insanity (267). While there is no suggestion in *The Music Man* that Marian has had even close friendships with women, she would nevertheless suffer to the onus of the single, intellectual, professional woman at a historical moment when these traits in women were being systematically demonized and linked to perversion.

Meanwhile, Harold Hill—who in fact has exploitive designs on Marian—stirs up the townsfolk's interest in a boys' band through a circuitous appeal to endangerment and deliverance that plays off the same fears Marian inadvertently arouses. In a remarkable display of rhetorical prowess, he convinces the town that the newly acquired pool table in their billiard parlor—which he links with popular novels and new forms of slang—is a sign of moral decay and youthful depravity, which can yet be offset by the wholesome alternative channeling of energies into the formation of a uniformed band. Amassing a summer evening crowd of stoic Iowans in the town square and inciting them to a revivalist frenzy of call and response, he leads them in singing:

> Trouble (oh we've got Trouble)
> Right here in River City! (Right here in River City!)
> With a capital T and that rhymes with P
> and that stands for Pool (That stands for Pool)
> We've surely got Trouble! (We've surely got Trouble!)
> Right here in River City! (Right here!)
> Gotta figure out a way t' keep the young ones moral after school!

("Ya Got Trouble," from Meredith Willson's The Music Man.
By Meredith Willson. 1957, 1958, 1966 [renewed] Frank Music Corp.
and Meredith Willson Music. All rights reserved.)

Hill plays not only with the townspeople's anxieties but also with their lack of literacy, both critical and textual. Aside from managing to invoke a pool table as a viper in their midst, he is able to persuade them that an arbitrary phonetic similarity—that is, the rhyming of P and T—actually constitutes a meaningful linguistic sign. And by inducing them, through his own example, to wave their hands in the air and heave their bodies in ecstatic righteousness as they sing, he creates at once a holy spectacle evocative (though distinctly outside) of the church and a civic spectacle evocative of a communal oneness that directly refutes the self-description of the Iowans upon Hill's arrival several hours earlier, when they soberly intoned:

> We can be cold as our falling thermometers in December
> If you ask about our weather in July
> And we're so by God stubborn we can stand touchin' noses
> For a week at a time and never see eye-to-eye.

("Iowa Stubborn," from Meredith Willson's The Music Man.
Words and music by Meredith Willson. 1957 [renewed] Frank Music Corp.
and Meredith Willson Music. All rights reserved.)

Rick Altman has, in fact, contended that "[t]he shared hands-in-the-air posture surfaces throughout the musical tradition as a reminder of the community religious fervor that lies at the root of much American popular music" (293). In The Music Man, the scene of Protestant virtue appears to be everywhere except in church—an institution that is surprisingly absent from both the film's imagery and its discourse. When glimpsed at all, the church lies in the background; with its strangely truncated steeple, the edifice may be discerned centrally planted within a frame, yet mostly hidden behind more prominent objects. It looms in the distance behind a public monument or, in one case, behind an incarnation of Grant Wood's *American Gothic* farm couple, who are seen in a medium close-up singing a brief interlude, their figures framed, as if in the stasis of the painting from which they escaped, by the packing crate that had been used to transport the pool table.

Religious passion, severed from the worship of God, finds expression in a sustained, if confused, moral linkage between literacy, prudery, and civic-mindedness; the secular is the sacred. Hill's evangelism and his flock's conversion take place in the town square, the high school, and the library. Much of the action takes place during the Fourth of July weekend; red, white, and blue festoons bedeck the sets, and citizens can be seen fastening flags in prominent places as Hill makes his way through town. The pompous, malapropism-spewing Mayor Shinn is first seen emerging from the town hall where a portrait of Theodore Roosevelt—ignored by the townsfolk and always at least partly visually eclipsed by them in the camera's eye—adorns the entrance. (It happens that the year in which the story is set, 1912, was the election year in which Roosevelt organized the Progressive Party, whose reform-oriented ideology was echoed in the spheres of education and librarianship and is misleadingly appropriated in Hill's appeal to social improvement.) In the concluding moment of the "Trouble" number, Hill climbs atop the pedestal supporting the statue of Henry Madison that dominates the town square and poses precisely as Madison does, one arm raised high with a finger pointing, church spirelike, toward heaven. And while most of the citizens warble and squeal their numbers in atonal cadences—underscoring the fact that they are plain folk, artistically untrained, culturally unsophisticated, and impervious to transcendent experience—Hill is able to unite the long-warring members of the school board by converting them into a barbershop quartet, their earnest folk harmonies and beatific visages suggesting the sweetness of a church choir.

Hill uses language impressively and persuasively, though expressly to deceive and manipulate. In fact, a central irony in *The Music Man* is that while Marian's literary appreciation of "classics" and the value she places on knowledge make her suspect in the eyes of the citizenry—that is, she fails to perform her duties, as an "expert," of policing literacy and is thus a potential danger to the town's youth—Hill gains the people's trust by professing "expertise," though he is in fact illiterate in his own medium. He gets away with this by avoiding contact with written musical scores altogether and by persuading the people of the town that musical literacy is not required for technical proficiency. ("Someday reading music is going to be absolutely obsolete," he avers.) Instead, he peddles a spurious "Think System" whereby one intuitively projects music from one's mind into an instrument. (It is as "natural" a process, he claims, as whistling.) When one boy asks how to hold his French horn, Hill assures him that the correct position will become apparent to him when he has developed a deeper relationship with his instrument. (Of course, this could be perceived as a romantic expressionist approach to music pedagogy—a variation on what nowadays in composition classes is called "freewriting.")

Though Marian is initially infuriated by Hill's success in duping her neighbors and family, she is won over when it becomes apparent that Hill, legitimately or not, has generated unprecedented excitement in River City. She is particularly moved when her little brother, a painfully shy and withdrawn child who is habitually silent due to a combination of grief for his dead father and shame over a lisp, bursts uninhibitedly into song as the band instruments are delivered by the Wells Fargo Wagon. At this point, she rips out a page from a reference book she has been carrying with her that furnishes evidence that Hill's conservatory "degree" is bogus, and she herself falls under his magical spell. ("Spellbinder!" Mayor Shinn repeatedly accuses him.) The music, the camera, and the lighting melt her into a new, "softer" Marian. No longer to be confused with the strident New Woman, the Marian who succumbs to Hill's charms is heterosexually vulnerable and willing to inhabit a world defined by emotion as much as—perhaps even more than—by reason. However, unlike the other townspeople, whose belief in Hill and the reality he purveys is truly naive, Marian has made an informed choice to suspend disbelief. She is working as a sort of double agent: Her mission has been to present the truth about Hill, but now she has come to see that "truth" as a rhetorical effect. If his words produce desirable results—in other words, induce happiness in other people—then she will abet his process of falsifying reality by suppressing the evidence that could be used to indict him. Yet he continues to believe that his seduction is enacted by virtue of an ingenuousness that he has cleverly produced in her, a special coup because she (presumably unlike other women he has known) is ordinarily so shrewd and skeptical.

As he continues to view her as prey, and she continues to conceal from him her knowledge and her power of disclosure, the romantic tension between them sustains itself partly because they are the only two in the town who can use language effectively, each the only one with sufficient wits to verbally joust with the other. But, ultimately, Hill's exploitation of Marian is aborted when he discovers that she has known the truth about him for some time and has been protecting him. He is converted to decent behavior by the knowledge that she has believed in him even while knowing him to be a liar; she understands the power of his rhetoric better than he does, the "reality" of the illusion he has wrought. (This sort of reality is very much like that of the Hollywood musical itself.) It is Marian who sees that Hill's scam, even qua scam, has produced all its promised effects—a wholesome outlet for young boys' energies; a newborn vibrancy of spirit in the stolid town; social cohesion, order, and stability; civic pride and responsibility; and new (musical) knowledge that, with its patriotic and militaristic iconography, is the very antithesis of the sort of knowledge that could conceivably be implicated in prurience and moral laxity.

Moved by Marian's fully cognizant sincerity to humbly manifest sincerity himself (as the school board has crooned earlier, "How can there be any 'sin' in *sincere?*"), Hill refuses to run even when the people of the town find him out and Marian encourages him to flee from the furious mob. He is brought into the high school, where he faces a tribunal of parents enraged and eager to see him brought to justice. However, Marian seizes the podium from the mayor and reminds her audience of how Hill has transformed their lives. It is now she, rather than Hill, who has assumed the authority of moral leadership and whose mastery of rhetoric is essential to swaying the tide of public opinion. One by one, the members of the crowd rise in agreement with her portrayal of the summer's events until the mayor jolts them back to the literal "reality" that there isn't any band. But literal reality has never had much grip on the popular imagination of River City. In the penultimate scene of the film, the boys march into the school assembly room in their just-arrived uniforms, wielding their instruments, and Marian induces Hill to lead them in a rendition of Beethoven's "Minuet in G," the piece they have been faithfully "thinking" for weeks. As a final act of enablement, she snatches the pointer from the chalkboard and breaks it in half over her knee, transfiguring a rigid instrument of rote learning into a makeshift conductor's baton. Hill, too savvy in the art of conning to believe in miracles, assumes that his moment of defeat is at hand, but his audience is bewitched in an act of reader response that would dazzle even Wolfgang Iser. In this audience's eyes, the town's children are rigged out in flashing regalia, and in its ears, the wretched strains of the "Minuet in G" morph into the rousing fanfare of "76 Trombones." Hill, with Marian on his arm, triumphantly leads a hallucinating parade of townspeople out of the schoolhouse and into the streets.

"The Sadder-but-Wiser Girl": The Repressed/Repressive Librarian

In *The American Film Musical,* Rick Altman's groundbreaking investigation into the defining qualities of the Hollywood musical genre, a number of oppositional elements in the musical are identified that establish its place in the world of entertainment and, correspondingly, of ideology. Altman argues that the musical is characterized neither by its plot, nor by its music per se, nor by the objectives of a single protagonist, but rather by a system of "constitutive dualities" that are most flagrantly embodied in two protagonists, one male and one female. The musical functions as a "cultural problem-solving device" by pitting against each other these two characters—who are presented via contrasting modes of symbolization, who embrace contrasting value systems, and who represent contrasting cultural or ideological spheres (for example, wilderness/civilization, travel/stability, freedom/order, big city/small town, work ethic/pleasure principle). When they become reconciled with one another (which involves relinquishing their polarized attributes and accepting hybridity—that is, each must acknowledge the qualities of the other as the repressed parts of him- or herself), there is a parallel reconciliation of the community and the opposing forces that had undermined it.

The effects on the community are particularly relevant to the "folk musical," the subgenre to which Altman assigns *The Music Man,* and the Marian Paroo vs.

Harold Hill duality encompasses characteristics similar to those Altman finds in other folk musicals as well. As the town librarian, Marian represents organization and order, sexual prudery coupled with unfocused romantic longing, a force of silence (it is the librarian's job to admonish people to be quiet—though Marian herself is silenced when she tries to speak out about Hill's fakery), a Platonic notion of truth that is experienced via a solitary relationship to print discourse, a sedentary life within a small geographic scope, a view of art as elevating and ennobling, a belief that hard and methodical work will produce a quality product, and educational values rooted in Arnoldian humanism. As a traveling salesman and con artist, Harold Hill represents a threatened disruption of the economic and social order, the sexual exploitation of virginal music teachers, the free expression of noise—indeed, cacophony (though he himself cries "Shhh!," finger on lips, when an old pal in town calls him by a name that is different from his current alias), a sophistic notion of truth purveyed through spectacular public acts of oral discourse, a nomadic life in which (through the constant recreation of himself in a new town with a new identity and a new set of victims) he may effect the same trickery again and again, a commodified view of art as essentially entertainment, a belief in the power of cunning to turn over a quick deal, and educational values rooted in American pragmatism.

What Marian and Hill have in common is intelligence and an acute awareness of others' lack of it. However, while she laments the citizens' philistinism and attempts to "sell" them on the idea of great literature and high culture, she is unable to inculcate in them an appetite for the intellectual merchandise of civilization. He, on the other hand, glories in their gullibility and uses it to sell them products, easily producing the desire for manufactured goods and the notion of consumption as a means of redemption. While her intellect is damningly linked to her spinsterhood, his dazzling ability to spin nonsense into the appearance of fact makes him all the more attractive, an American hero of ingenuity and entrepreneurship. Marian's mother is captivated by Hill's charming pseudo-erudition and fantasizes that he will become her son-in-law, but to her daughter, she talks/sings:

> Darling, when a woman's got a husband
> And you've got none
> Why should she take
> Advice from you
> Even if you can quote
> Balzac and Shakespeare
> And all them other hifalutin' Greeks.

It was, in fact, around the turn of the century that the "image problem" of the librarian—that is, the image of the fastidious, shushing old maid with a bun and glasses—began to take effect, and the image has persisted throughout the twentieth century (Radford and Radford; Sapp; Newmyer; Garrison). Film viewers will recall, for instance, that when the protagonist of Frank Capra's *It's a Wonderful Life* contemplates what the world would have been like if he had not been born, he envisions his wife as a spinster librarian—garbed, coiffed, and dour-faced in accordance with the stereotype. In "The Librarian as Main Character: A Professional Sampler," Gregg Sapp catalogues forty-six twentieth-century short stories that present the same basic idea.

According to Jody Newmyer, "the prevailing assumption prior to the 1870s [was] that the librarian was grim, grouchy, eccentric, and *male*" (44). And, in truth, even before 1876—the watershed year in which the American Library Association was created, the *American Library Journal* commenced publication, and Melvil Dewey produced the first edition of his classification system and subject index (Holley 175–76)—libraries and librarianship were governed by the minds and ideologies of upper-class men. Later on, when the field became flooded with women, male librarians still commanded the choice and elite positions, while women were herded into rank-and-file jobs involving children's literature and decisions regarding its "standards" (Garrison 180). There was little complaint about this because, as Garrison has pointed out, "[w]omen librarians who had given up hope of marriage were also less apt to strain for advancement, since they realized that society would further censure them for a display of 'male' aggressiveness" (184). Thus "most of these women merely left the home, not woman's sphere" and "became segregated in the woman-dominated service professions, where femininity was newly defined on a vocational basis" (184).

Harris and Spiegler suggest something of the genesis of the early male librarian stereotype in an essay about the founding of the Boston Public Library in 1854 and the concomitant development of the American public library movement. They argue that within the speciously unified category of "liberal reformers" have been lumped such disparate types as, on the one hand, transcendentalists, abolitionists, and other radical intellectuals (who valued individual creativity and tended to oppose formal institutions such as libraries, which they viewed as attempting to "control" society) and, on the other hand, "authoritarian-elitists" (who were upper-class, rigidly conventional men, condemnatory and punitive toward those who would violate social conventions and convinced that an aristocracy must lead the inferior and disruptive lower classes). It was the latter group that, seeking to contain social instability at a time when the forces of women's rights, abolition, suffrage, populism, and industrialization waxed and the moral, civilizing influence of the family and the church waned, sponsored and promoted the development of voluntary associations and organizations such as libraries. Later on, in the years before and after 1900, steel industrialist Andrew Carnegie donated approximately fifty million dollars to construct 1,463 libraries across the United States (Seavy 521; Helms 188). Other wealthy industrialists followed his example of strategic philanthropy, so that "no state was without public library service by 1920" (Seavy 521). Carnegie believed that "the result of knowledge [. . .] is to make men not violent revolutionists, but cautious evolutionists; not destroyers, but careful improvers" (qtd. in Newmyer 49). Under terms remarkably like Old Miser Madison's in his legacy to River City, the Carnegie Foundation supplied the library buildings while the local towns or municipalities had to pay for books, workers' salaries, and building maintenance (Seavy 521). Carnegie Libraries proliferated once again during the Depression years, a project that Newmyer convincingly attributes to the threat of worker rebellion and Carnegie's sense that libraries, like asylums, reformatories, public schools, and the social welfare system, could be effective agents of social control. Thus the fact that the soldiers in the trenches of the library movement were mostly women—who ultimately bore the brunt of the public's resentment against the libraries' repressive moralism and were lampooned as the libraries' founding fathers never were—does nothing to mitigate the fact that the hegemonic forces pulling the strings of the library apparatus were located in the bastions of male power and privilege. *The Music Man* portrays a gendered war between Marian as moralist and cultural guardian and Hill as freethinker and libertine. As Altman contends, this sort of male-female dichotomy of values and objectives is always at the thematic center of the musical, but more important, it is here illustrative of the fact that women librarians constituted the human, despised face of a powerful machine, even though the backstage ideological battle of the library movement was really one of brother against brother.

By 1910 women's faces *were* the ones naturally associated with librarianship, as 78.5% of U.S. librarians were now female (Garrison 173). The number of women enrolled in college had tripled since 1890 (175), and as one of the few professions that allowed women entry, librarianship could get away with paying its workers little while requiring long hours, extreme precision, detail orientation, and wide-ranging academic expertise; thus it produced its own increasing feminization (182). Sapp has pointed out that "[v]ery often, the same librarian who possesses all of the cliché foibles also embodies several positive attributes, such as honesty, candor, industriousness, and open-mindedness" (29). These are, indeed, attributes of Marian, for whom her neighbors' "narrow-mindedness" is a continual source of hurt and frustration. But they are still scant compensation for a scorned, de-eroticized social identity. In any case, as members of a genteel profession that transposed the Victorian ideal of the spiritually elevating "angel in the house" into a public worker serving the public good, librarians were expected to work essentially for love, to uplift the morals of the populace, and particularly to serve as guardians against immoral literature falling into the hands of the young.

From the earliest days of the profession, librarians often zealously embraced this mission. "The public library would serve as a direct rival to the saloon and would help to prevent crime and social rebellion," explains library historian Dee Garrison (36). But librarians' dedication to social reform was enmeshed with elitist notions of cultivation, so that they "continued to label mass culture as lowbrow and worker protest as dangerous" (60). In effect, their mission was to save the masses from themselves. An address entitled "The Moral and Intellectual Influence of Libraries upon Social Progress," delivered in 1865 to the New York Historical Society by its president, Frederic de Peyster, included this testimonial to the library's influence:

> It substitutes a salutary pleasure for gross and vicious indulgences, and confers a moral benefit by proposing intellectual instead of sensual gratification. Scarcely anything is more calculated to confer pleasure, and at the same time to elevate the soul, than familiarity with the works of the great writers of the world. [. . .] Books bring to bear upon us the example of the great and good. The record of their virtues, achievements and sacrifices, in all ages, impresses the imagination, excites emulation and rouses action. (de Peyster 800–81)

Once touched by literature, even the plebeian mind would be capable of distinguishing between the wheat of righteousness and the chaff of charlatanry. As another early library leader wrote, "To the [. . .] [free library] we may hopefully look for the gradual deliverance of the people from the wiles of the rhetorician and stump orator, with their distorted fancies and one-sided collection of facts" (qtd. in Garrison 36).

With the growth of urbanization, industrialization, and immigration, the site perceived to be the most threatened by social decay and corruption—and in need of salvation—was of course the city. Harold Hill therefore had to import the threat of metropolitan dangers to the agrarian hinterlands. The rural "wily rhetorician" would surely be an itinerant one, most likely a traveling salesman, whose rhetoric would bear the promises of patent medicine ("the Sarsaparilla Belt" is how Hill describes the environs of River City), manufactured goods, mind cures, and positive thinking. Hill's tactic—frightening the townsfolk into buying products as a bulwark against moral turpitude—both highlights the need for Marian to emerge as a guardian of culture and at the same time illuminates her failures, for the very culture with which she hopes to save the town is that which its denizens fear will destroy it. "This Ruby Hat of Omar Kay-ay-ay-" sputters Mrs. Shinn, the mayor's wife, her oversized Gilded Age confection bobbing on her head as she indignantly slams the book on the librarian's desk. "It's beautiful Persian poetry!" protests Marian. "It's *dirty* Persian poetry," Mrs. Shinn corrects her, to which Marian can offer no better argument than the lame, "But it's a classic!"

By the late Victorian era, a backlash against repressive moral crusaders and the emergence of mass culture—including wide-circulation popular magazines and dime novels—made fun, putatively "trashy" reading far more available and its readership far more unrepentant. In response, volumes with titles like *Books, Culture and Character; The Abuse of Reading;* and *The Reading of Books: Its Pleasures, Profits and Perils* were disseminated to provide guidance in the selection of reading material (Garrison 68). In a 1916 *English Journal* essay, a teacher named James Cloyd Bowman argued that only classics should be taught in school because "they cure us of a lot of our cheap materialistic and humanitarian optimism; they lift us above the mere emotional clatter of a multitude of opinions," whereas magazines are "likely to dissipate the power of prolonged attention" and "relax the mind from hard severe, effort" (qtd. in Reynolds 6–7). From reading magazines, claimed Bowman (who had actually experimented with them in his classes), "the student is likely to become fundamentally interested in a lot of clever small talk about many really unimportant matters" (qtd. in Reynolds 6–7).[2] Thus not only sexual depravity but the depravity that accrues from exposure to consumerist culture, opening our national gates to the barbarians and letting slip the reins of the Protestant work ethic, was in store for the reader who succumbed to the pleasures of popular literature.

The decades around the turn of the century were a time when librarians had to confront a basic conflict: They could continue to hawk their canon of ennobling tomes that nobody wanted, or they could actually lure readers into the library by offering the new popular fiction, which was in great demand. During those decades, their sense of their own mission gradually changed from one of moral uplift, to one of education, to one that allowed that recreational and educational purposes of reading had to negotiate a delicate relationship, to, finally, a more "democratic" position that held that readers must be the arbiters of their own reading material. According to Garrison, by 1920, librarians had reached an acceptance of this last view (89), though, she says, "Catering to the popular passion for suspect fiction was originally justified only as a means of creating a love for reading that would eventually lead the public to higher literary levels" (90). "Thus," she writes, "[a]s late as 1912, when the New York Public Library allowed patrons to check out four books at once, it was stipulated that only one could be fiction" (91 fn.).

By that year, then, when "the library as an institution [had] lost much of its former pretension to intellectual authority" (Garrison 89), there was a clear opening for a new kind of moral authority and leadership that could come from someone like Harold Hill, whose rhetoric linked decency to pleasure and expression rather than to discipline and self-denial, and whose concept of literate practice itself emphasized personal idiosyncrasy and emotion rather than the medicinal aims of rote learning. When Marian laments that the citizens of River City are insensible to aesthetic quality and devoid of good taste, she is, in 1912, sounding the librarian's last hurrah. Though librarians' humanistic ideals are by then increasingly submerged in the discourse of efficiency and mechanization (in other words, the rise of "library science"), and though Hill, too, declaims convincingly (if absurdly) about the "scientific" bases of his musical theories, one thing is clear: The "Think System" is a natural magnet for hearts and minds that were never captured by the Dewey decimal system.

The very ease with which the rogue Hill can incite the townsfolk's latent enthusiasm for profaning the sacred order of the library is marvelously illustrated in the famous song and dance number "Marian the Librarian." As Martin Sutton has pointed out, the scene in which a musical's dance number occurs is usually an open space associated with play and exuberance—in the case of *The Music Man*, that tends to be the town park or the school gym, though in other films it may be a ship deck, farmyard, theater stage, or dance floor. "Open space in the musical is the most expressive of media—it gives the body room to move and, through this, the mind room to expand" (Sutton 192). By breaking the filmic rules and staging a wildly choreographed number in the cluttered, claustrophobic atmosphere of a library, Da Costa invests the spectator with a visceral experience of transgression. The body moves here where it *doesn't* have room, or permission, to move; music roars rebelliously through the realm of compulsory silence. Though the library's physical and aural constraints are ostensibly designed to facilitate enlightenment, we get the message that constrained bodies have produced constrained minds, and that, conversely, by turning the library into a scene of revelry, its patrons have finally unleashed its ability to produce vital knowledge.

In discussing this scene, it is worth first considering an essay by Marie L. Radford and Gary P. Radford in which the authors analyze the stereotype of the female librarian through a Foucauldian lens, looking particularly at the ways that order, knowledge, and madness are perceived to function in the world of the library. Radford and Radford see the library operating in the Western literary tradition as a "metaphor for rationality" (254) in that it is an institution that orders unique texts in much the same way that positivist science attempts to order and catalogue the unique artifacts of nature. Libraries are "segregated places of intellectual activity" in which "social space loses its grip"; they work against and supply an alternative to "the breakdown of systematicity and the unconstrained production of discourse" that is madness. "[S]tructured by the values of order, control, and suppression" (255), the library assumes its ideal identity when its collection is complete, the volumes intact and arranged in their proper places. This means, of course, that these volumes are not in the hands of library users, for the sake of whose edification the library claims to exist. Thus a tension exists between the librarian, whose job it is—via devices such as cataloguing systems, date stamps, indexes—to conserve this order and completeness, and the library user, "a person who has the capacity to disrupt and ultimately prevent the ideal of the complete library" (257) simply by enjoying the privileges of book circulation.

If the library and the order it protects is—as the authors, following Foucault, suggest—socially necessary as a defense against a "fundamental fear of *discourse* and the dangers that *uncontrolled discourse* may give rise to" (260), then the stereotypical image of the female librarian

> can be thought of as a strategy in which this fundamental fear can be managed, defused, and disguised. [. . .] Female librarians are not gods who create and control the overpowering rationality of the library's space of knowledge. The stereotype is a front that defuses the power and fear of this rationality. Indeed, the relationship between rationality and the librarian is reversed in the female stereotype: it is the rationality that creates and

controls the librarian. The stereotype portrays people who are possessed: obsessed with the order that rationality demands of them. [. . .] Such figures are to be pitied rather than revered or admired. (261)

Within this scheme, there is no constitutive difference between disrupting the library and disrupting the librarian. As Harold Hill, who frequently demonstrates a Pied Piper–like ability to draw others in his wake, invades the library, it is clear that its otherwise intimidated occupants are happy to ride on the coattails of his bravery and effrontery. The theme of the number, order versus chaos, is reinforced on multiple levels. The scene begins with a shot of the library in its normal state of use. All is quiet. Marian, wearing glasses and with her hair tucked in a bun, is smiling as she carries an armful of books to a dumbwaiter. The camera comes in for a close-up of one leather-bound volume, its title fleetingly legible. It is the reference book in which Marian will later find the proof that Hill has invented his credentials, the book that later still, in an unprecedented act of treason against the rational world, she will desecrate in order to protect him. Now, unaware of the book's importance, she smiles vaguely at it and sends it up with the others to the mezzanine. The low, unobtrusive plunk of a bass establishes a faintly insinuating undercurrent, a beat that will build and swell throughout the scene.

Marian turns, looks past the camera in consternation. Patrons are entering the library, disturbing its order. Though Marian presumably wants people to use the library, she doesn't appear happy that they've come. The beat intensifies as she rhythmically stamps a series of books; a musical phrase concludes comically when the last "book" she stamps is Hill's hand, proffered to trick her. The song and the action build. Hill's professed seduction is really a blatant act of mimicry and, consequently, harassment. Singing of hopeless love, his intent is actually to frazzle her, to pry her—for his amusement—from the rational casing in which she is sheathed, so that, for instance, at one moment, in the midst of his "romantic" maneuvers, he threatens to unloose a bag of marbles and enjoys her ensuing panic. He trespasses upon the inner sanctum of her desk—only one of many violations that link the assault on her domain with a sexual assault. Rather than usurping the rhythm of the song/her world, he assumes control of it; he "sets" the beat with an improvised metronome, and the library's users robotically move to it in lockstep, caricaturing the library's militaristic regimentation. As the dancing heats up, teenagers turn cartwheels and swing from the mezzanine railing, heedlessly debasing the literature and information all around them in an explosion of the carnivalesque. In fact, it is the merging of these two forms of movement—military march and riotous cavorting—within the same dance number that gives the spectacle its potency. The "76 Trombones" theme—always associated with Hill's id-releasing power—sounds briefly as the horrified and distraught Marian loses control, though the theme abruptly ceases as she regains enough composure to utter the librarian's characteristic "Shhh!" Soon, however, she herself starts to become drunk with the carnival atmosphere. As a group of young men sweeps her off in a mad dance, she flings off her glasses, her hair comes undone, and it is not until others mimic an alarmed "Shhh!" at her that she again regains her senses—and her anger. By the end of the number, both library and librarian are in disarray, a triumphant Hill (who has brazenly sung every note of the song himself, reducing the librarian to utter silence in her pillaged domain) exits, and a vanquished Marian collapses—though in quite an orderly way—on the mezzanine railing on the final note.

In his fabulistic/allegorical essay "The Library of Babel," Jorge Luis Borges plays with the notion of the library as the repository of totality—"the universe"— a notion he portrays as reassuring to humankind: "All men felt themselves to be masters of an intact and secret treasure. [. . .] The universe was justified, the universe suddenly usurped the unlimited dimensions of hope" (55). For Borges, too, the library is a manageably rational, indexable universe, and therein lies its existential consolation: "In truth, the Library includes all verbal structures, all variations permitted by the twenty-five orthographical symbols, but not a single example of absolute nonsense" (57). It satisfies a longing for a permanence that will outlast nature:

> I expect that the human species—the unique species—is about to be extinguished, but the Library will endure: illuminated, solitary, infinite, perfectly motionless, equipped with precious volumes, useless, incorruptible, secret. . . . If an eternal traveler were to cross it in any direction, after centuries he would see that the same volumes were repeated in the same disorder (which, thus repeated, would be an order: the Order). My solitude is gladdened by this elegant hope. (58)

Clearly, Marian's solitude is also gladdened by this elegant hope, and it is not coincidental that through his project of imposing nonsense Hill divests her simultaneously of her dream of a perfect Order *and* of her solitude. As Altman has said, it is through the reconciliation of apparent binaries, realized through the male/female dyad, that the musical achieves its objectives. In *The Music Man,* Hill's musical numbers usually involve instances of "selling" the citizenry on a fantasy, and they usually place him at the center of a throng that he has roused to a state of excitement. Marian, on the other hand—first seen at the end of the "Trouble" song hurrying haughtily home from the library, far from the madding crowd—is always alone, both physically and mentally in her citadel of the mind. Hill's is a populist knowledge, available to all through the sheer desire to have it; Marian's is a thoroughly mystifying, specialized, and concealed sort that can be accessed only via arcane procedures of information retrieval. If he hawks content without form—and might thus be seen as an incarnation of "expressionist" rhetoric—she is all form without content—an embodiment of what compositionists call "current-traditional" rhetoric, best exemplified in the five-paragraph theme whose success is evidenced by its presentation of formulaic thesis, topic statements, introduction, and conclusion. Hill conjures a vivid picture of a band marching in the sunshine, playing stirring music without any technical knowledge of musical notation or the handling of instruments; Marian, framed by a window and backlit, ardently sings the love song "Goodnight, My Someone" to no one in particular. ("76 Trombones" and "Goodnight, My Someone" are rather obviously two manifestations of the same basic melody, reflecting the contrasting natures, ideologies, and social effects of the characters who sing them.) Hill rides the new wave of consumer capitalism, which is able to create and dictate costly tastes and needs; she, offering goods of the soul for free, can't find a market for her product. His notion of musical production involves synergetic expression of spontaneous energy; hers involves isolated dedication to tedious scales and exercises. (Interestingly, her piano student, Amaryllis, evinces no more virtuosity than do Hill's boys, despite her enforced rigor.) Hill's songs are always heard by a diegetic audience—that is, they are rhetorically oriented toward actual participants in the drama—while Marian's songs cast us, the film's real audience, as eavesdroppers on a private rumination. It is only at the end that the two protagonists achieve a synthesis, each admitting a kind of musical failure: Though love had surrounded them, they had never heard it "singing."

"A Logical Ekthplanathyun": Consumerist Rhetoric

Marian and Harold also dramatize the dismantling of another important binary that Altman asserts is fundamental to the American film musical. Situated as Hollywood is, at "the very junction of business and entertainment," erasing the impression of conflict between these two spheres of value is crucial to the film industry. It is here that the musical's "self-reflexivity" becomes so useful. Says Altman, "No doubt the world's most complex and expensive business scheme, the American film musical serves as Hollywood's own self-justification" (344). In a country where the Protestant work ethic so profoundly influences secular life, any activity that does not result in productivity (and that, furthermore, saps valuable time and energy that could have been devoted to noble toil) must afford a guilty pleasure. But like sports—which can be rationalized for their health benefits and thus their service to the interests of production—entertainment can be recast and revalued, so that it is

> not recreation in the modern sense of a pause from work, an opportunity for activities totally unrelated to work, but re-creation, like sleep a necessary break in the interest of higher overall productivity. The worker must, like a battery, be recharged in order to deliver a full measure of work. Entertainment is thus allowable, but only because it fits into an overall scheme of guaranteeing a sufficient labor force for an increasingly industrialized world. (338)

Like a pool table ("Friends," warns Hill in "Trouble," "the idle brain is the devil's playground" and "that game with the fifteen numbered balls is the devil's tool!"), entertainment is perceived as "the very type of leisure activity that leads to dissolution rather than re-creation" (339). Therefore, in order to sustain the status of film musical production and consumption as worthwhile activities, the genre has an investment in dissolving the work-entertainment polarity. It accomplishes this, once again, via its dual protagonists, one of whom represents "the thoroughly cultural values identified with work and a stable family structure, the other embodying the counter-cultural values associated with entertainment" (339). Through them, the film will demonstrate that "these two categories are not in fact mutually exclusive: working or raising a family can be fun, just as dancing is hard work" (49).

In *The Music Man,* both of the protagonists earn a living by teaching (or claiming to teach) music, and Marian also derives a portion of her income from working with literature. Her involvement, of course, is with "high" art, and his is with "low" entertainment. Running a library and giving piano lessons are seen by the townspeople as dry, if not downright grim, matters, though music and poetry are precisely what Marian loves. Hill's band, conversely, draws crowds with its sheer glitter and promise of pleasure, and Hill himself appears to enjoy a free-wheeling life—though secretly he must sweat through anxious moments and constantly strain to preserve the appearance of his legitimacy. But by the end of the film, love has transformed Marian into someone who asserts that fun and joy have conferred civic advantages on River City, just as it has transformed Hill into someone ready to settle down and pay his debt to society. It is through their joint talents and efforts—his creation of the myth of a boys' band and her construction of a new interpretive framework wherein that myth may become reality (and dreary reality, for its part, may achieve a spectacular sheen)—that a functioning band is actually produced and the community is restored.

Hill is seen in the last moments of the film in full bandleader garb prancing at the head of an exuberant march, which simultaneously suggests the triumph of a commercial job well done, an artistic triumph, and the triumph of a patriotic and emancipatory spirit. (As the final credits virtually enter the scene and identify the proud marchers one by one, we are also reminded that this is a triumph of the Hollywood film industry, both materially and in its role as representative par excellence of national ideologies. The opening credits, for that matter, are even less subtle: A parade of little toy soldiers is led by two marchers who carry a banner that says "Warner Brothers Pictures.") Hill marches (as he insinuates at one point) in the footsteps of the great bandmaster John Philip Sousa, who was "hailed as a leader and commonly compared to a general, a figure he certainly resembled in his smart military uniform," and who furthermore "depict[ed] himself as a force for disciplined order," boasting that "every single member of my band is doing exactly what I make him do" (Levine 178). Hill, too, is "an apostle of order in an unstable universe" (177), one who deploys goods and images in the service of culture and democracy. As Houston Baker has pointed out, even Martin Luther King Jr.—another twentieth-century American icon of freedom (and one who, in Baker's words, had the ingenuity to transform the "moral scandal" of Birmingham in 1963 into the "national media *spec-*

tacle" of the March on Washington)—was apparently inspired by marching band imagery and asked to be eulogized as a "drum major for justice" (17).

In the process of demonstrating that work and play are indivisible in the performance of good citizenship, the film has successfully assimilated the ethics of consumer capitalist culture into our nostalgic memories of a kinder, gentler, virtuous, Edenic past. Hill is posited as a deviant salesman who is rehabilitated into an authentic and reputable one. He is a con artist with (deep down) a heart of gold. When he atones for his sins and delivers the goods, he becomes, at last, a credit to an honorable profession and a liberator of Puritan superegos that would deny the felicities of market culture. There is nothing strange, finally, about Marian's unswerving virtue being enlisted to certify the utilitarian integrity of Hill's entire project. We are reassured that salesmen are not really scoundrels, consumers are not really dupes, advertising is not really deceitful, and the acquisition of goods is a perfectly sound and respectable way to achieve happiness.

There are two show numbers in *The Music Man* that are specifically concerned with the subject of buying and selling. Both of them are conceived in a style that Altman says is common in the folk musical: They are "onomatopoeic tunes" that "imitat[e] the rhythm and sounds of modes of transportation" (286). Willson, however, used onomatopoeia in particularly distinctive ways, impressionistically depicting salesmen's talk and women's gossip in his songs through clusters of words and other uttered sounds that often comprise a syntax of mood rather than of literal meaning. The first piece in the musical, "Rock Island," is performed by a group of salesmen traveling through the Midwest on a train. It is in this scene that we meet Hill and first learn, from his own peers (and in his presence, though that is not fully revealed to us or them until the end of the number), of his cheating ways. The number is spoken rather than sung—or perhaps it would be more accurate to say it is "talk-sung"—in a manner that seems to anticipate rap, though it is characterized by mad verbal repetition rather than rap's more discursive quality. As with "Marian the Librarian," a beat controls the movements of the participants. However, whereas in "Marian" the beat is infectious and summons one to dance along, in this case the passengers are simply jerked and jounced around by the movement of the train and spew forth their message with fidgety compulsivity. A few jump cuts to the exterior of the train punctuate the scene, shots that focus on the train's wheels, axles, and smokestack clacking, yanking, and venting, so that the jiggling men blowing off steam inside and the large piece of machinery that conveys them are brought into blatantly comical, rather than subliminal, association. Like Marian in her library, these men are trapped in a mechanical rhythm they can't break out of.

At first they exchange observations about their customers' persistent requests for credit, which the salesmen agree is "old-fashioned"; it is smart to accept only cash. (*"Cash,"* they chant to the relentless thump of the train, *"cash* for the merchandise, *cash* for the button-hooks, *cash* for the cotton goods. . . .") They lament the new merchandising trends that have made selling the old products so much harder: biscuits sold in airtight packages (no more need for cracker barrels), Model-T Fords and department stores that take customers away from small local stores and their wares. Then one of the men announces that he has just been chased out of a town because a swindler named Harold Hill has been "giving every one of us a black eye." (Much later in the film, this same man comes to blow the whistle on Hill in River City in order, he says, "to protect the good name of the traveling fraternity.") He outlines Hill's scam, but ultimately the worst thing he can say about him is, "He's just a bang beat bell-ringin' big haul, great go, neck-or-nothin', rip-roarin', ever time-a-bull's-eye sales man." (About as damning, really, as complaining that Bill Clinton is a *politician*.)

A pivotal point comes more than halfway into the film with the song "The Wells Fargo Wagon."[3] As the locals anticipate from the moment they spot the horse-drawn painted wagon with the familiar logo, it is coming to deliver the band instruments. However, almost greater than the thrill of this delivery is the citizens' excitement as they reflect upon the goods they have received, will receive, and hope to receive. In this paean to consumer products, luxury agricultural items (such as raisins from Fresno and grapefruit from Tampa),[4] hardware from Montgomery Ward, and ready-to-wear clothes are among the bounty reverently recounted. Significantly, they are recounted in excruciatingly awful singing voices, and the accompanying choreography consists of little more than the townsfolk lining up along the street and looking joyful. In addition to raising the possibility (which would give credence to the finale) that the whole town is tone deaf, the number establishes a benevolent, life-affirming relationship between manufactured products and the simple, grateful people who purchase them. As William Leach has pointed out, the "simple-life movement," whose foremost patrons included Theodore Roosevelt and department store magnate John Wanamaker (widely hailed as "the greatest merchant in America"), became popular in the early years of the twentieth century, and numerous goods were manufactured that catered to this taste. Simple-life proponents censured "'materialists' who had turned against the past to take up the 'new' and the 'modern'" (32). Yet their back-to-basics ideology was nurtured into practice through interior decorators and numerous merchants who could create "rustic" environments and a "simple" aesthetic for the well-to-do (32; 202–4). "The Wells Fargo Wagon" musical number can in this sense be seen as an advertisement that displays the residents of River City in an American primitivist tableau, an exemplum of simple folks' affectionate, homespun attitudes toward shopping. Within this scheme, Harold Hill is simply a man of his time employing the benign rhetoric of consumer culture, not an aberration and a crook, for, as the film shows us, the fulfillment that merchants assure us will come with consumption is real—once we come to understand that that "reality" is located in the eye of the beholder/consumer.

Read in this way, *The Music Man*, like the advertising industry, seduces us by delighting us, except that in this case the products being sold are the ideology of mercantilism and the practice that most essentially sustains it—advertising itself. In other words, if (as the noble Marian finally insists) Hill's integrity is to be measured by the ends he produces, not by his means—if little lies (such as his claims to a conservatory degree, the title "professor," and his ability to teach music) give birth to far greater truths (a reinvigorated town, a sense of pride and purpose among the young)—and if that is what really counts, then the whole new way of life taking shape in early twentieth-century America has a moral justification after all.

When Hill calls the region in which the story takes place the "Sarsaparilla Belt," he is referring to its receptivity to bogus claims, and hence its attraction for con artists. But what exactly constitutes a "bogus" claim? Where does one draw the line when it comes to hoodwinking the public? Numerous healing qualities were ascribed to sarsaparilla root that made it popular during those years. For example, "editorial" copy in what was actually a promotional booklet published by C. I. Hood and Company in 1888 claimed that Hood's Sarsaparilla would cure, among other things, "Sores, Boils, Pimples, all Humors, Dyspepsia, Biliousness, Sick Headache, Indigestion, General Debility, Catarrh, Rheumatism, Kidney and Liver Complaints." Furthermore, it said, the product "overcomes that Extreme Tired Feeling caused by change of climate, season or life, creates an appetite and builds up and strengthens the whole system." An attentive viewer of the train scene might notice that in some shots, the salesmen's stowed suitcases can be glimpsed on the luggage rack just beneath the top of the frame; lettering identifies their owners with enterprises such as "Apothecary Company" and "Humor Cure." Quite probably, a number of this "traveling fraternity" are hawking sarsaparilla or other counterfeit remedies. Wherein is Hill a blight upon their probity? But farfetched claims also came from the bastions of the respectable publishing and merchandising worlds. An 1894 ad in *Ladies' Home Journal* assured the reader that Chocolat-Menier was "as nourishing as meat." And when people became sick with "La Grippe" in 1890, a *New York Times* ad informed them that "physicians are prescribing, all over the country, the use of BLOOKER'S DUTCH COCOA by their patients, as the best possible food and tonic during this epidemic." Was Hill's proffered panacea more nefarious than these? When Marian says angrily to Hill, "As for your musical tricks—why don't you go into business with some nice carnival man who sells gold-painted watches and glass diamond rings?" she is invoking a corrupt, sideshow shadow world outside of civilization as we know it. But to what scrupulous world might Hill be restored?

Did Harold Hill manipulate the public's fears more than did the American toy business during World War I, when it "reviled the Germans as 'butchers' and their toys as 'blood toys'" in order to eliminate German competition (Leach 85)? Did he put music to crasser purposes than did John Wanamaker, who by 1915 had organized his army of department store workers into drum and bugle corps, choruses, an orchestra, and a Scottish bagpipe band in order to serenade customers and imbue them with the "family spirit" of Wanamaker's (118)? ("Store family" had by then replaced "employees" in the mass retailing lexicon [120–21]).

When Hill denied the hard work it really takes to play an instrument, was he acting more egregiously than were the retail stores that at a certain point decided to make manufacturing invisible to their customers and "worked systematically to remove all traces of hard work from the selling floor" and replace it with a carefully crafted aura of magic (147)? Was his marshaling of virtue-versus-vice rhetoric to create a socially redemptive role for consumption substantially different from that of Macy's management, which in 1913 invited a vigilante group working to "clean up" Manhattan's commercial districts to inspect the store in order to establish it as "the most decent store in New York" (117)? Didn't his delivery of quality instruments and uniforms signal a fairer deal than that offered by the booming turn-of-the-century garment industry, which flourished partly due to its practice of "dynamiting," a process that deliberately shortened fabrics' life and durability (94)?

Because Hill is, finally, a quintessentially American "salesman"—one who came to town on the Fourth of July—it is important that throughout the film he remain a sympathetic villain with the potential for heroism. This is accomplished by making his tricksterism apparent to the spectator from the very beginning. His ballyhoo is never meant to snow us. We are not the audience/object of his rhetoric and salesmanship; we are spectators in an act of deception in which the provincial River City citizens, who are always portrayed at a gently ironic distance, are the target audience. We get to see him wipe his brow, raise his eyes briefly in supplication to the heavens before launching into his pitch, perform quick mental searches for plausible and persuasive responses to his interlocutors. We are "backstage" with him; we know from the first what his designs are on Marian and their pecuniary (as well as sexual) roots. We see how bad he is, but we also see for ourselves that he is no worse than that. We see how he understands the people better than they understand themselves, how he senses and fulfills what each wants. Because we never feel personally betrayed by him—he hasn't tried to pull one over on us—we can feel relief about his reprieve once it turns out that no harm is really done to anyone. As in the wider national landscape, only goodness and improvement have been brought to River City by consumerism, after all, so that it really doesn't matter that they have been produced via a "benign" delusion. What's the harm? The people are deluded in so many other ways anyway.

Meredith Willson—who was born in 1902 in the small town of Mason City, Iowa—wrote in his prefatory "Note" to the director of the stage script of his play:

> THE MUSIC MAN was intended to be a Valentine and not a caricature. Please do not let the actors—particularly [those actors portraying the characters of] Zaneeta, Mayor Shinn and Mrs. Shinn, who takes herself quite seriously—mug or reach for comedy effect. . . . The humor of this piece depends upon its technical faithfulness to the real small-town Iowans of 1912 who certainly did not think they were funny at all.

Willson's message seems paradoxical at first. He says that the characters should not reach "for comedy effect," yet he acknowledges the play's humor. This humor is apparent to us and, obviously, to him, though not to them. As a highly entertaining portrait of people who cannot see themselves—and yet who, in their climactic jubilance, invite us to identify with them and share in the fun—*The Music Man* asks us to do precisely what the citizens of River City did. It asks us to suspend our own critical judgments about reality; only in this way can we participate in the pleasure of the delusion that is the Hollywood musical. The "old-fashioned American virtues" that we celebrate are not the ones that Marian the Librarian promoted, for we have not been elevated above the rest of the multitude through any contact with high culture, and neither are they related to the rectitude that Harold Hill the wily rhetorician claimed to advocate, for the two-and-a-half hours we've just spent in abandonment of all worthwhile pursuits surely proves our indolence. The "virtues" we celebrate are as American as McDonald's hot apple pies: They are sweetened, artificially flavored, packaged, mass-produced, and we buy them because we deserve a break. Looking for meaning in our nostalgic journey to yesteryear, we find it—though as Dorothy Gale, who came from the neighboring midwestern state of Kansas, put it, we needn't have looked any further than our own backyard.

As William Leach has brilliantly shown, the entire cultural apparatus of the United States participated in the creation of the twentieth-century commodity ethic. Art schools developed curricula in new subjects such as display advertising, product design, interior decoration, and commercial illustration; museums cultivated an intimate relationship with industry, bringing to professional designers and factory managers a knowledge of "how to relate 'primitive decorative art' to 'machine processes'"; universities, federal agencies, and municipal authorities, who gladly sanctioned enabling devices such as product-showcasing city pageants and transportation systems that converged near department stores, were all part of the "circuits of power" that shifted social priorities toward commercial ends (153–90). At the same time, business and industry developed a new service ideology that cloaked the quest for profit in an attitude of goodwill and demonstrated the "benevolent side" of capitalism. Service was introduced as an act of munificence for the public good, variously established in the molds of Christianity, populism, compassion, decency, wholesome family values, *gemütlichkeit,* neighborliness, charity, and the "promise of America" (112–50).

"Somethin' Special Just for Me"

To say that *The Music Man* portrays a classic slice of Americana is, then, to speak the truth. Though the film ghettoizes the mores of the nation in the rural Midwest—a place where moralizing librarians, slimy hucksters, and sorry chumps all exist at a quaint remove—it adroitly illustrates in a microcosm the felicity with which cultural and educational institutions capitulated to the rhetoric of consumerism in the early years of this century. Scene after scene hilariously illustrates that Marian's dream of an ennobling role for literacy in River City is not to be. Mayor Shinn keeps trying to make a speech, but the paper in his hand is mutilated and he can't read his notes. A roll of sheet music suddenly flies out of control in the player piano, rattling in circles and drowning out the mayor's words. The mayor tries to invoke the "Gettysburg Address," but he can't remember more than the first phrase. The newspaper is predictably wrong in its weather prediction. After the stout matrons of the Lady's Dance Committee, dressed in gym bloomers and led by Mrs. Shinn, have practiced walking gracefully with books on their heads, they join hands in a circle to rehearse their representation of a Grecian urn for the ice cream sociable; tilting their heads back, their books crash to the floor. Even Marian herself, once she has fallen for Hill, can live with the defilement of beloved quotations. "As the poets say," recites Hill, "a coward dies a thousand deaths—a brave man only five hundred." "Something like that," she smiles wanly.

Literacy has failed to save the town, because, as it turns out, it stifles the spirit (which is surprising, since that is what vulgar, materialist worldly pursuits are often said to do). In fact, the whole realm of literacy now constitutes a defunct battleground, since neither Marian's religious veneration of literacy, nor Hill's ersatz formula for technical literacy, nor the townsfolk's concern about literacy's ability to entice the young toward virtue or vice seems to matter to anyone any longer. But consumerism *has* rescued the town, because it liberates the spirit (which is also surprising, since that is precisely what art and culture have always promised to do). In that capacity, consumerism affords a common meeting ground where aesthetics, mercenary interests, the pleasures of acquisition, the blessings of community, and the value of a regulating ethos may be conjointly celebrated.

An old conning chum (played by Buddy Hackett) had counseled Hill early on that his boys' band scam wouldn't work in this spartan region ("Anything these Iowa folks don't already have, they do without."); but he was, apparently, behind the times. A revolution in the production of desire has swept the country, and among the "means of persuasion" now available to sellers is a simple invocation of the all-encompassing Pavlovian association of merchandise with bliss. The revolution has also relocated the techniques previously associated with con artistry from the margins to the center of American society. Within this new order, Marian can embrace Hill as a law-abiding, lovable sort of trickster who contributes meaningfully to public culture (as opposed to the crass, anarchic, self-seeking sort who raids and depletes it). And she can now regard Hill's aerobic verbal performances and slick literary allusiveness as estimable, marketable skills that further the respectable goals of social progress and career advancement. For his part, Hill has found a partner who will nurture and complement his talents and intelligence, and whose conception of moral agency is, conveniently, unimpeachable and flexible all at once. He can embrace Marian as a creative thinker whose inventiveness enhances the truth by opening it up to new perspectives (as opposed to rigidly enforcing some static, overdetermined version of it). In the brave new world of consumerism, Marian and Hill may collaborate and legitimize, rather than impugn, each other.

As ad expert Katherine Fisher wrote in 1899, "[t]he advertiser's problem [. . .] may be considered the controlling of other people's imaginations for his own advantage. It is a certain state of mind, and *not the real condition of things which is essential to the advertiser's success*" (qtd. in Leach, 403 fn.; italics in Leach). And Leach, describing a 1909 book called *Product and Climax* by Simon Patten— whom he calls "America's most influential economist of capitalist abundance and consumption" (233)—explains that in it, the author compares

> two sets of institutions, one, traditional (churches, libraries, and schools) and the other, "new" and "urban" (retail stores, theaters, nickelodeons, ice-cream parlors, penny arcades, etc.). His description makes plain which side of the street is better; in a radical switch, he put the new institutions on the "right side" (his term) and the older ones on the "wrong side." The older ones are literally in darkness and bolted shut, indicating their connection to the "barren" world of "prohibitory moral agencies." [. . .] The new institutions on the commercial street, on the other hand, are "festooned with lights and cheap decorations," and "the doors of shops" are "wide open." (qtd. in Leach 241)

And indeed the people of River City have been sold, along with the band paraphernalia, a new "state of mind"—one in which the shop doors of their imaginations are flung open, and their critical faculties (hadn't Marian always bemoaned their barrenness anyway?) are at last permitted—no, let's make that *encouraged*— to be bolted pleasantly shut. Clinching the deal is a new economy of truth and value that will serve retail and mail order empires well in the decades to come. And the band plays on.[5]

Notes

This essay is reprinted with permission. Copyright © 1999 by the National Council of Teachers of English.

1. According to lesbian historian Lillian Faderman, in the early twentieth century, women's colleges such as Vassar and Smith even held "romantic all-women dances" with ritualized forms of courtship (20). Smith-Rosenberg adds that sexologists at the time determined that the New Woman was "a secretly and dangerously sexualized figure. Her social liminality was rooted in sexual inversion. She belonged to an 'intermediate sex.' She embodied the unnatural and the monstrous. She was a 'Mannish Lesbian'" (268).

2. Reynolds makes the interesting observation that "Bowman [. . .] prefigures Allan Bloom's assessment of students, whose 'petty desires' figure largely into his dismissal of popular texts" (7).

3. I would refer serious fans of *The Music Man,* as well as others interested in its consumerist implications, to Wells Fargo's current literature, obtainable

through the company. In its periodically revised brochure, it attempts to sustain—through reproductions of period photographs, artwork, and advertisements, and through a lengthy, documentary-style narrative emphasizing the company's roots in the gold rush and the expanding frontier of the nineteenth century—a metonymic sense of its own historical identity as that of the United States. That is, the "story" of the growing nation here becomes symbolized by this icon of commercial transport.

4. Fans of the film may also find interesting a reproduced ad in the 1988 edition of the Wells Fargo and Company's brochure (19) that features an image of a bonneted girl (who seems to be half grape picker, half picnicker) set against a California sky on which is written, "California Raisin Days, April 28th and 29th, Ship by Wells Fargo." A caption for today's reader explains, "A 1918 wagon banner proclaiming Fresno's "Raisin Day" was one of many ways Wells Fargo promoted California's agriculture." This is just one sign, among numerous others, of the play/film's wonderful incorporation of actual cultural detail.

5. I would like to give many thanks to Lou Timmons, Sherri Barnes (aka "Madam Librarian"), Jane Dusselier, Tobie Matava, David Blakesley, Stacy Wolf, Sara Cytron, the Research Released Time Committee, and the Trustees of Long Island University. My colleague Wally Glickman (a professor of physics who played Harold Hill many years ago in summer stock) made the important comment upon reading this paper that it's not clear whether I *like The Music Man* or simply find it an interesting film to *analyze*. I'd like to clear that up right now: I totally *love The Music Man*. I would also like to thank my two *College English* manuscript readers for their helpful suggestions (one remains anonymous; the other is Donald Lazere, who turns out to be an Iowan and long-time fan of *The Music Man*). In addition, I want to express appreciation to Linda Adler-Kassner, Shawn Gillen, and Thomas Reynolds for their 1995 CCCC panel in Washington, D.C., on Progressive Era literacies, which helped me in thinking through this piece.

Works Cited

Altman, Rick. *The American Film Musical.* Bloomington: Indiana UP, 1987.

Baker, Houston A., Jr. "Critical Memory and the Black Public Sphere." *Public Culture* 7 (1994): 3–33.

Blooker's Dutch Cocoa. Advertisement. *New York Times* 16 Jan. 1890: 3.

Borges, Jorge Luis. "The Library of Babel." *Labyrinths: Selected Stories and Other Writings.* New York: New Directions, 1962. 51–58.

Bowman, James Cloyd. "The Use of the Magazine in English." *English Journal* 14 (1916): 332–40.

Chocolat-Menier. Advertisement. *Ladies' Home Journal* Feb. 1894: 27.

de Peyster, Frederic. "The Moral and Intellectual Influence of Libraries upon Social Progress." Address. New York Historical Society. 21 Nov. 1865. New York: New York Historical Society, 1866.

Faderman, Lillian. *Odd Girls and Twilight Lovers: A History of Lesbian Life in Twentieth-Century America*. New York: Columbia UP, 1991.

Garrison, Dee. *Apostles of Culture: The Public Librarian and American Society, 1876–1920*. New York: Free, 1979.

Harris, Michael H., and Gerard Spiegler. "Everett, Ticknore and the Common Man: The Fear of Social Instability as the Motivation for the Founding of the Boston Public Library." *Libri* 24.4 (1974): 249–76.

Helms, Claxton. "The Development of Library Services in Allegan County, Michigan." *Contributions to Mid-West Library History*. Ed. Thelma Eaton. Champaign: Illini Union Bookstore, 1964. 106–29.

Holley, Edward. "Raking the Historical Coals: The American Library Association Beginnings." *Reader in American Library History*. Ed. Michael H. Harris. Washington: Microcard Editions, National Cash Register, 1971. 175–76.

Hood's Sarsaparilla. Advertisement. *Hood's Book of Homemade Candies*. Lowell: Hood, 1888.

Leach, William. *Land of Desire: Merchants, Power, and the Rise of a New American Culture*. New York: Vintage, 1993.

Levine, Lawrence W. *Highbrow/Lowbrow: The Emergence of Cultural Hierarchy in America*. Cambridge: Harvard UP, 1988.

The Music Man. Dir. Morton Da Costa. Perf. Robert Preston, Shirley Jones. Warner Brothers, 1962.

Newmyer, Jody. "The Image Problem of the Librarian: Femininity and Social Control." *Journal of Library History* 11.1 (1976): 44–67.

Radford, Marie L., and Gary P. Radford. "Power, Knowledge, and Fear: Feminism, Foucault, and the Stereotype of the Female Librarian." *Library Quarterly* 67.3 (1997): 250–66.

Reynolds, Thomas. "Extracurricular Literacy: Magazines and Composition in the Progressive Era." Paper. Conf. on Coll. Composition and Communication Convention. Washington. 1995.

Sapp, Gregg. "The Librarian as Main Character: A Professional Sampler." *Wilson Library Bulletin* 62.5 (1987): 29–33.

Seavy, Charles A. "Public Libraries." *Encyclopedia of Library History*. Ed. W. A. Wiganel and D. G. Davis, Jr. New York: Garbanel, 1994. 518–28.

Sennett, Ted. *Hollywood Musicals*. New York: Abrams, 1981.

Smith-Rosenberg, Carroll. "Discourses of Sexuality and Subjectivity: The New Woman, 1870–1936." *Hidden from History: Reclaiming the Gay and Lesbian Past*. Ed. Martin Duberman, Martha Vicinus, and George Chauncey Jr. New York: Penguin/Meridian, 1990. 264–80.

Sutton, Martin. "Patterns of Meaning in the Musical." *Genre: The Musical*. Ed. Rick Altman. London: Routledge, 1981. 190–96.

Trimbur, John. "Literacy and the Discourse of Crisis." *The Politics of Writing Instruction: Postsecondary*. Ed. Richard Bullock, John Trimbur, and Charles Schuster. Portsmouth: Heinemann, 1991. 277–95.

Wells Fargo Since 1852. Brochures. San Francisco: Wells Fargo and Company, 1988, 1996.

Willson, Meredith. "Musical Synopses of Scenes." *The Music Man.* Stage script, 1957.

14

Screen Play: *Ethos* and Dialectics in *A Time to Kill*

Granetta L. Richardson

IN TODAY'S TECHNOLOGICAL AND ELECTRONIC AGE, AUDIENCES ARE inundated with images on screens as a primary communicative mode, be they the computer screen with the Internet, the television screen with advertisements, or the large screen of motion pictures, with its entrancing images. The rhetorical methods used on these screens are not that far removed from those methods used by ancient Greek rhetoricians teaching the art of persuasion on their blue shores thousands of years ago. Aristotle, in particular, argues that, for rhetorical methods to work most effectively, the rhetor must be able to convey a sense of *ethos,* that is, moral and ethical character, to an audience. The focus of this essay will be the ways in which filmmakers approximate *ethos* on-screen in the service of ideological imperatives. Because film can be defined as a type of perlocutionary act (a form of communication designed to convince, persuade, or mislead), it is possible to examine its ethical nature and ways that it adapts classical strategies of ethical appeal to the unique conditions of film spectatorship. Filmmakers "persuade" audiences to react in ways that correspond to distinctly political and ethical stances, rather than necessarily moral positions, because a spectator's response to film need not be positive, even if a film does coax a change of attitude and thus, potentially, a predisposition to act. Filmmakers encourage roughly equivalent responses from viewers by interanimating image, dialogue, and sound. The dialectic amongst these cinematic elements can, by virtue of their accumulation, deletion, repetition, and interrelation in strategic ways, allow filmmakers to structure interpretation more precisely toward the desired audience response. The aesthetics of the cinema provide a conduit through which ideological meaning is conveyed to the audience.

Film language and film style are the approximations of *ethos* in cinema. For Aristotle, style is ornament, used for embellishment of the orator's argument; in cinema, spectacle serves as ornament, freeing style for other uses. When cinematic choices such as editing, montage, mise-en-scène, framing, camera shots, focus, sound, color, music, et cetera interact within a given film, the resulting dialectic can more specifically trigger audience members to adopt the ideological argument of the filmmaker. According to narrative theorist Seymour Chatman, filmic narrative techniques such as the aforementioned not only support an aesthetic end but may also "urge some proposition or resonate thematically about the real world" (53). Filmmakers put these techniques together to create meaningful combinations that contribute to a given audience's understanding of the film-maker's world, that is, the filmmaker's "terministic screen." Kenneth Burke defines a "terministic screen" as a monitoring device that uses terms to direct "the attention to one field rather than another," and he further adds that, within a given field, several screens exist, "each with its ways of directing the attention and shaping the range of observations implicit in the given terminology" (50). In film that range is limited by stylistic choices, the given terminology to which Burke refers. An example might be Eisensteinian "intellectual montage," where the editing of certain images is crucial to the interpretation of those images. In Eisenstein's *Potemkin* (1925), the shot of a horrified woman wearing a pince-nez is juxtaposed with a shot of the same woman with her right eye bleeding and injured. The observation shaped by spectators in this instance is that the woman has been struck in the eye by some kind of object.

For purposes of illustrating ways in which a particular director creates dialectic combinations for political motives, I will discuss Joel Schumacher's *A Time to Kill*. Although the film seems to purport that the American justice system is fair and workable, in actuality it serves as an example of how suasion is used to pardon acts, which by the justice system's own standards would be punishable, acts such as Carl Lee Hailey's vigilantism, the KKK's rhetoric, and violence by blacks in the face of long-standing oppression. As Brian D. Johnson notes, by "fudging moral dilemmas, confusing sentiment with truth, and suggesting that violent retribution is divine right, *A Time to Kill* sanctifies everything that is alarming about the American justice system" (50). Even though the film itself is morally ambivalent, the political agenda/*ethos* of the film remains undisturbed because the meanings conveyed by the dialectic combinations of film style and film language continue to remind the viewer that revenge, especially when one is driven to it by racism and heinous crime, can be perfectly justifiable and even heroic, as in the scene where detective DeWayne Looney, who loses his leg due to Carl Lee's revenge, exclaims, on the witness stand, "He's a hero—you turn him loose! Turn him loose!" The visual element of the anguished facial expression of Looney—interacting with the verbal element of the dialogue quoted above, the murmuring and supportive sounds of the courtroom spectators, all within the characteristic tight close-up framing of the figures in the film—guides viewers to join in the chorus of "Free Carl Lee!" and to embrace the idea that vigilantism, for purposes of "righteous" revenge, is socially acceptable.

The *ethos* of film is inextricably linked to the political agendas of filmmakers and is determined by ways they creatively construct aesthetic techniques to foster consensus about those agendas within the viewing audience. By cleverly employing film *ethos,* filmmakers can screen out rival ideologies and screen in their own political predilections.

This study will begin with a brief definition of the perlocutionary act, follow with an analysis of Aristotelian principles of rhetoric, and conclude with a discussion of narration and of constructivist theory, all of which will address ways spectators are actively cued to understand narrative through specific stylistic devices of film, in particular, the film *A Time to Kill.* As such, this study is concerned with ways that narrative is received by a spectator along with ways style shapes that reception. Film theorist David Bordwell asserts that a film's "formal systems both *cue* and *constrain* the viewer's construction of a story" (49). However, he remarks that this system cannot predict any actual response or interpretation but rather can only reflect the most logical permissible responses based upon a medium's conventions. Narrative cues, then, can further restrict viewers' interpretations, to varying degrees, so that they align with the filmmaker's vision of reality, his or her terministic screen, which sheds light upon the filmmaker's *ethos.* These same narrative cues determine epistemological boundaries for ways a text can be read. Edward Branigan, in his *Narrative Comprehension and Film,* states that film is a medium with distinct techniques for representing time, space, and causality (for example, mise-en-scène, camera movement, sound, editing, etc.) and that these techniques do not convey meaning in and of themselves but constitute "instructions" that relate to the procedures and rules used by spectators to construct meaning (117). Spectators may also use these procedures and rules to adopt a stance or a specific frame of reference, often along political lines. Branigan warns that the procedures and rules must be measured in terms of success or failure with respect to the goal to be achieved, that is, if a desired response from spectators is obtained or not obtained.

With regard to speech act theory, a perlocutionary act also works to elicit action or to produce a state within a hearer that will move that hearer. The perlocutionary act is the most important of the four types of speech acts rhetorically, because it is the situation in which a hearer is engaged by the utterance, and, by extension, in film, a spectator would be engaged. This utterance can be imbued with ideology as it interacts with a person's terministic screen or with ways the spectator conceives of reality. The suasive nature of perlocutionary acts is evident in its promotion to act or to affect the spectator's state of mind; the result of "saying something" is either to convince, persuade, deter, surprise, or mislead (Austin 109). Because perlocutionary acts can also be nonverbal ones (such as a person throwing a punch), it can be argued that image systems in films are also perlocutionary in nature and can elicit action or produce a state of mind within viewers. For this reason, a filmmaker can select appropriate combinations of images and/or film style to imbue a scene or sequence with ideological intent.

However, the suasive nature of these speech acts might also give rise to unintended readings of these same acts. According to linguist J. L. Austin, what a speaker intends to produce in his utterance may not actually result; conversely, when a certain effect is not intended, it might still occur nonetheless (106). A distinction between attempt and achievement becomes most evident with perlocutionary acts, as Branigan argues, with regard to the complexity involved in obtaining desired responses. It must be stressed that Austin refers to speech acts in terms of words uttered, and words are often inexact. But film, with its use of images that take precedence over words, bypasses the ambiguity of words, which are easily misconstrued. Images more precisely screen out associations that may obfuscate intent. By way of illustration, if a person utters the words, "She's thin," it is unclear to the hearer whether this comment is a compliment or a critique, but, in film, the utterance accompanied by a visual image of either a slender woman or an anorexic makes the meaning much more precise as to the intent of the utterance. So, if a filmmaker selects appropriate images and devices, the probability of confused readings among spectators will be less likely. Even the most capable filmmaker obviously risks some degree of ambiguous or alternative readings, but there would still exist, because of the control the devices of film allow, a more privileged reading.

Convention, argues John R. Searle in *Speech Acts,* provides another means of shaping intent; he writes, "Meaning is more than a matter of intention, it is also at least sometimes a matter of convention" (45). Film follows conventions, and its subgenres also follow their own conventions; these conventions provide additional cues whereby spectators can construct meaning. Bordwell argues that this construction of meaning from narrative signals and conventions is a set of inferences that he terms "fabula" (51). Construction of meaning, a process of testing, selecting, and rejecting hypotheses by spectators, is an ongoing, interpretive activity, simultaneous with the viewing of a film and similar to Bordwell's discussion of the creation of fabula.

The oration sequence in *A Time to Kill* serves as an instance of a perlocutionary act within the larger perlocutionary act of a film, because the filmmaker, Joel Schumacher, endeavors to convince his spectators to reconsider racial inequities in America within the context of the courtroom drama convention. The protagonist, Jake Brigance (Matthew McConaughey), must deal with the stony-faced jurors, bent upon convicting his client, Carl Lee Hailey (Samuel L. Jackson). The jurors serve as the ostensible hearers of Jake's perlocutionary act, but the spectators, although not so predisposed to blame Carl Lee, due to events that have endeared him to them, as a result of their rejecting the hypothesis of Carl Lee as guilty while they construct meaning (fabula), are also the object of Jake's argument that Carl Lee's vigilantism is justified.

Jake's powerful dialogue concentrates upon the search for truth as it accentuates the fragility and the metaphorical death of the girl's (Tonya's) spirit. He states initially, "In all this legal maneuvering, something has gotten lost—that something is the truth." Then he asks the jurors, "What is it in us that seeks the truth? Is it our minds, or is it our hearts?" These queries also resonate with the spectators, as Schumacher, through this perlocutionary act, attempts to touch upon the spectators' sense of justice for all and tries to move the spectators towards being more fair and equitable in judging others, especially those of other races. As Jake notes, "The eyes of the law are human eyes," therefore making a supposition that justice is flawed and not color-blind. By extension, spectators are suaded to concede that justice is unfair when it comes to race. Spectators are further guided to this assumption by the interanimation of the shot selection with Jake's dialogue, for, while statements are being made, close-ups and extreme close-ups are provided of the courtroom audience, the jurors, and the pitiable, tearful face of Tonya's mother; nothing is more sorrow-inducing than a mother's tears and anguish. The facial expressions that the close-ups reveal show very human people grappling with the difficult issues that Jake discusses.

At the peroration of the oration, Jake asks the jurors to close their eyes and to visualize the events of Tonya's rape, while he recounts the painful details, like the shattering of the child's womb and the tearing of her flesh from her tiny bones. Since the spectator has been privy to the horrifying rape sequence, with its rapid cutting, swish pans, tilts, and rolls that Schumacher uses to heighten the terror of the events while also subtly avoiding graphic, disgusting details, the spectators are even more revolted than are the jurors and are moved to desire the liberation of Carl Lee. After detailing the rape of Tonya, Jake asks, "Can you see her? Can you see her? I want you to picture that little girl. Now imagine she's white." Immediately following are a series of close-ups of characters opening their eyes, beginning with Carl Lee, and progressing through Jake's mentor, Lucien Wilbanks (Donald Sutherland), the jurors, the DA Rufus Buckley (Kevin Spacey), Judge Omar Noose (Patrick McGoohan), and concluding with Jake and a weeping, white female juror. These close-ups represent the epiphany, the literal eye-opening of these characters to racism in America. And Schumacher, with the way he drives the scene, hopes to produce a similar effect of eye-opening awareness of racism in his spectators. Following these wrenching realizations is a cut to the silent, anxious, racially mixed crowd outside the courthouse, who await the verdict. A little boy shouts, "Innocent, he's innocent!," and then trumpets of jubilation burst forth on the sound track and continue to blare as Jake emerges from the courthouse like an ancient Roman triumphator. He is hailed because he can overcome racial boundaries and see a black man as an equal.

This oration sequence is imbued with Schumacher's ideological stance that racism should not be tolerated in the courts and in our lives. The spectators are promoted to act by giving up racial prejudices, and their state of mind is influenced to regard people of other races as equals, as Jake has been successful in doing.

Because of their ideological intent, films have a sense of ethics, as witnessed by Schumacher's challenge to eschew racism in *A Time to Kill*. Schumacher's harsh judgment of racial intolerance provides the means by which his political views can be made manifest. In this respect, one can argue that Schumacher expresses Aristotelian *ethos* through his dialectic of film technique. By urging spectators to divest themselves of racism, Schumacher demonstrates concern for the spectators' benefit, a classical rhetorical device, which Aristotle recommends as a foundation block for the building of *ethos*. To be truly convincing, says Aristotle, the rhetor must show that he or she has the audience's happiness or best interest in mind (5); surely the eradication of racism, one of Schumacher's cherished goals, would be for the spectators' benefit. Although some might quibble with Schumacher's suggestion that eye-for-an-eye justice is for the common good, since the judicial system does not always act on behalf of its public, few would disagree that something must be done so that the races can live in harmony. The ending of *A Time to Kill*, which focuses upon images of the daughters of Jake Brigance and Carl Lee Hailey, juxtaposed with the two sets of parents picnicking together, reminds the spectators that the state of racial relations in America rests upon individual efforts, suggests Schumacher. Through depicting racial tolerance in his interanimation of film style, Schumacher builds credibility with his audience. *Ethos,* as defined by Aristotle, depends upon the credibility of the speaker and is achieved "by what the speaker says, not by what people think of this character before he begins to speak" (25). So, while spectators view a film, not only are they assembling a fabula or a storyline, they are also piecing together a sense of the filmmaker's *ethos* as well as his political stance. Since *ethos,* as Aristotle notes, rests within the words of a speaker, as well as with images, in a film, and not within the person himself or herself, film, then approximates *ethos* through its paradigmatic choices (its categories of film options). Filmmakers achieve *ethos* by their selection of artistic options and then reinforce those ideas through the construction of images, through film's syntagmatic choices (its categories of construction, i.e., editing).

For critics of *ethos,* ethics do not connote morality. When discussing ethical criticism, Wayne Booth writes that such criticism

> looks both at the *ethos* implied by or discerned in any human construction and the *ethos* of the person who receives or recreated that construction, and then tries to find language first to describe and then perhaps to evaluate the ethical relation between them. Thus the parallel term for "ethical" here would be "political" rather than moral. In this usage criticism and the effects it treats will be "ethical" whether or not the critic finds the ethical relation admirable or contemptible, and whether or not the language in which it is expressed includes terms ordinarily employed to make moral judgments. (58–59)

For Booth, "ethical" and "political" are synonymous, and the ethical relation subsumes both the admirable and the deplorable. For this reason, whether spectators agree or disagree that vigilantism in Schumacher's film is morally sound is not the issue; rather, Schumacher's discussion of a complex issue is ethical (or political) in Booth's definition, not to be confused with moral issues. Seymour Chatman supports this same assertion when he notes, while discussing the two types of rhetoric (one which works to suade to aesthetic ends and one which works to suade to ideological ends), that the latter, the ideological rhetoric, suades an audience "to something outside the text, something about the world at large" (52). Even though Chatman suggests that aesthetic rhetoric has as its goal to convince an audience about something interior to the text and ideological to something outside of the text, the two can converge whenever the audience is convinced not only that a text is aesthetically successful but also resonates meaningfully about their lives. And, since, states Chatman, the success of either aesthetic or ideological rhetoric depends upon "the set of narrative tools available to the author" (53), a given rhetorical stance will be as good as the aesthetic and paradigmatic choices that a filmmaker makes, with the ideological import, then, resulting essentially from the artistic choices selected.

In book 3, chapters 1–12, of the *Rhetoric,* Aristotle feels that style does not serve such a lofty rhetorical purpose, but rather gives grace and ornament to a persuasive argument. Style as ornamentation for Aristotle includes the proper use of connecting words and their arrangement, use of concrete language, avoidance of ambiguity unless the intent is to confuse, et cetera, and he views style as "unworthy" when compared to other means of persuasion (165). In film, stylistic choices are of utmost importance, for it is through style that the filmmaker articulates his ethical purpose. Without style, the cinema could not "mean"; it is much more than mere trappings, for, according to Bordwell, "the didactic ends often make film style operate as compositionally justified ornamentation" (239). Similar to Aristotle, Bordwell believes that film style is ornamental, yet he cannot help but see its purposefulness, rhetorically speaking, and implies that the filmmaker's stylistic choices can be crucial for shaping audience responses.

Classical rhetorician Edward P. J. Corbett defends Aristotle's notion about style, arguing that Aristotle never intended to suggest that style is merely ornament or embellishment; instead, says Corbett, Aristotle preached the "integral and reciprocal relationship between matter and form. [. . .] [that is,] matter must be fitted to the form, and form to the matter" (415). Despite the reasonableness of this assertion, Aristotle suggests a subservient position for style when compared to argument. Admitting that style can be ornamental, and that it provides a vehicle for thought, Corbett later argues that style is another available means of persuasion, another means of arousing the appropriate emotional response in an audience, and another means of establishing credibility (415). Thus style serves *ethos,* according to Corbett, and his definition of style translates well to cinema, for film style achieves a similar function—it too conveys *ethos,* arouses an emotional response within an audience (i.e., through the terministic screen), and is a potent means for the filmmaker to persuade. Further, cinema has its own form of ornament, which would be spectacle. Unlike Aristotle's definition of spectacle, which he says is the "stage-appearance of the actors" used to arouse pity and fear

(230), in cinema, spectacle can likewise produce pity and fear, but it can also convey deeper messages when part of the filmmaker's dialectic. Film spectacle encompasses special effects, pyrotechnics, mise-en-scène, as in *A Time to Kill,* when Pete Willard sports a shirt with the motto, "Mississippi Serpent" (costuming is a form of mise-en-scène); this motto reinforces the idea of Willard as predatory, satanic, and venomous and fills the audience with pity for Tonya and fear of Willard. Though spectacle arrests and maintains the interest of the spectators, in film it can also be tinged with ideology.

The revenge/vigilantism sequence of *A Time to Kill* illustrates the manner in which Schumacher frames his ethical argument stylistically. Beginning with the outraged faces of black prison inmates staring angrily at the two white rapists, the popular funeral dirge "Take My Hand, Precious Lord" (commentative, offscreen sound) plays on the sound track and continues throughout the sequence of Carl Lee's slaughter and revenge. The lyrics, with such words as "take my hand," "lead me on to the light," let me stand," convey Schumacher's intent to vindicate Carl Lee and to make Carl Lee's murder of the rapists justified and even holy. The song suggests God's condoning and participation in the support of Carl Lee, thereby showing that Schumacher feels that he can justify the ways of God to spectators; if God approves, how can the spectators not do so? Spectators then see shadowy shots of Carl Lee behind bars, a visual trope suggesting punishment for a crime that the music sanctions as well as Carl Lee's imprisonment in his own hatred of the rapists. Canted, low-angle shots of the courtroom audience, including shots of a rapist's (Billy Ray Cobb's) family, follow; such shots suggest a world out of kilter, "out of joint," where the scales of justice attempt to regain equilibrium through Carl Lee's massacre of the rapists. As soon as the two men proceed up the stairs of the courtroom, Carl Lee's red eye, crazed with fury, is revealed in an extreme close-up; this type of shot of a glance, Branigan writes, "bristles with implications about space, time and causality," suggests a character's intentions and motives, and "is an important measure of the *acquisition of knowledge* by character and spectator" (53). In the case of *A Time to Kill,* the glance shot is causal because it indicates the rationale behind Carl Lee's killing of the rapists—his hate, his disgust, his anger, his revenge. Spectators are cued by this shot to share Carl Lee's feelings and to understand his motivation for the crime. Next, Carl Lee bursts forth blasting his enemies, riddling them with bullets, and even striking the innocent Deputy Looney. Carl Lee executes the men while both he and they stand upon the state seal of Mississippi, which bears the state motto, a piece of mise-en-scène, "Virtute et armis," meaning "Manhood and Arms." This motto implies that, in bearing arms and using them, Carl Lee has become a man in doing what he feels is justified; thus, the state seal becomes a literal seal of approval of Carl Lee's revenge. Schumacher, through a variety of devices, has turned a hideous crime into a familial crusade. Granted, spectators with a higher degree of filmic critical literacy will more greatly appreciate Schumacher's use of the state motto, but all spectators are guided to feel that Carl Lee's actions should be forgiven. Schumacher's support of Carl Lee is so partisan that the rapists are given virtually no positive traits (they are unkempt, overweight, loud, stupid, vile). Through a dialectic of film style, Schumacher builds credibility both for Carl Lee and for his own idea that murder is suitable revenge under certain circumstances. Once again, the ethical nature of this sequence is not necessarily linked to morality because, despite the seeming appropriateness of Carl Lee's behavior, he still commits murder, though Schumacher would have spectators believe otherwise.

Spectators can come to realizations like the one about Carl Lee's supposed innocence because filmmakers expect that spectators have the cognitive ability to unify and to discern the patterns and arrangements of film style and of film language so as to assemble a perception of the film's connotative meaning, ideology, or both. Viewers construct ideological argumentation based upon the filmic data presented in the text. Throughout this process, spectators follow stylistic cues, which help these spectators to shape hypotheses appropriate for interpretation of the particular storyline. And each specific technique chosen—for example, an editing decision to connote transition, that uses a fade-in or fade-out as opposed to a dissolve—could affect how spectators cognitively process the stylistic prompts as well as possibly color those cognitions with ethical implications; the way film style is rendered provides additional relevancies about the rhetorical situation, and in the above option, of selecting either a fade-in/fade-out or a dissolve, the former device does not have so strong a narrative link as does the dissolve (Monaco 191). Fades tend to halt action temporarily, whereas dissolves are more continuous and fluid; they also are more likely to be selected for symbolic purposes.

Branigan describes this interpretive process as a means by which spectators assimilate the signals from style to produce a "plot," which ultimately leads to a story (i.e., an interpretation); he writes:

> when this stylistic account of narrative is itself viewed as an Aristotelian narrative, with a beginning in phenomenal form, a middle in plot, and an end in story, one may glimpse the true importance of "plot" as that "middle term" which separates style from story—preserving the integrity of each— while explaining the transformation of first into last. (120)

Bordwell, citing Noel Burch's *Theory of Film Practice,* states that technical parameters function as vitally as narrative ones for film form, and he argues further that the decoupage of film is an important process of dialectical structures that become as organized as narrative structures through a process of permutation (278–79). Such dialectics (or permutations) of film style can house any political meaning within them, so that paradigmatic choices become crucial in determining the filmmaker's argument.

An understanding of constructivist theory (a theory of psychological activity) can elucidate ways audiences might be guided to arrive at similar meanings that carry ideological or ethical import. In order for spectators to interpret in any way, they must be active, determined participants who draw conclusions about inferences based mainly upon inductive examination of data provided in the film and whose goal should be to construct meaning. The spectator, by definition, would be any person who has the abilities to assemble meanings from cues in the filmic text and who responds to the interanimation of chosen protocols of the filmmaker. Using not only stylistic markers but also borrowing from their own expectations and goals, spectators create, test, modify, reject inductive inferences, which can be held all at once or in succession, about spatial, temporal, or causal experiences made independently of screen time, since spectators' cognition is not limited to any particular moment (Branigan 37–38). Bordwell comments, in an argument reminiscent of Branigan's, that the plot—which he calls the "syuzhet" or the story's events or state of affairs and the style of cinematic devices—cues spectators to construct a fabula or story. A filmmaker can further construct a syuzhet so that certain fabula, resulting from understanding cues, framing and testing hypotheses, applying schemata (ways of knowing), will be inferred by spectators; fabula cannot be arbitrary, notes Bordwell (31–37, 49), because they have been generated from a revisionist process of constant scrutiny of the narrative and engagement with it. According to this argument, filmmakers, once again, have ultimate control of spectators' interpretations, albeit some interpretations may be parallel as opposed to identical and may also vary by the degrees to which spectators can generate politicized meanings. While constructing a story or meaning, spectators apply narrative schemata that help them to interrogate a text and decide whether to accept or to reject a given hypothesis. These schemata, which can be culturally biased, range from prototype schemata (identifiable persons, actions, locales, et cetera), template schemata (the canonical story), and procedural schemata (appropriate motivations and relations of causality/time/space), and they help the spectator construct meaning, along with the other two dynamic psychological processes: spectators' perceptual capabilities—involving physiological/ocular activities—and spectators' prior knowledge and experiences (Bordwell 49). Some shortcomings of the aforementioned system about schemata are that they do not necessarily address spectators' emotional responses (as noted earlier, spectators' emotional responses may be unpredictable), and they fail to account for effects of point-of-view manipulation upon viewers (Branigan 16). If schemata are lacking in these ways, might not a theory of film style as *ethos* help to buttress the notion of articulating ethical messages hidden within a text as well as of gauging possible effects upon spectators' states of mind?

By piecing together such cognitive data, essentially what viewers do is re-create their version of the filmmaker's terministic screen. As spectators gather all of this information, they assign value according to probabilities—the more probable or typical elements will be regarded as least significant and less apt to be recalled, and the more improbable or less typical elements will have the most significance assigned (Bordwell 35). Spectators, as Bordwell suggests, chunk films into structurally significant episodes while deriving pleasure from the reduction of probable hypotheses that are made (46). Thus, the entire process of interpreting narrative cinema involves the negotiating of stylistic devices, of physiological ones, of schematal ones, and of the circumstances of reception, all with respect to epistemological constraint; that is, these factors screen out certain interpretations as they direct spectator acceptance of a limited range of responses.

This constructivist theory may be observed in the ways in which Schumacher predisposes spectators to align themselves politically and empathetically with Carl Lee in the climactic sequence of jury selection that erupts into a racial riot in *A Time to Kill.* Spectators perceive prototype, template, and procedural schemata in this sequence as well as in the preceding scenes, one, at the mansion home of Judge Noose and, the other, at the black diner, Claude's. These schemata encourage the acceptance of hypotheses that exonerate Carl Lee and that expose Southern institutionalized racism and bigotry. Prototype schemata in these scenes and the editing sequence guide spectator reactions and sympathies toward the characters because viewers are repulsed by the rabid Klansmen, sympathetic with the so-called angry teen, (a black youth), who, on account of his moral outrage, takes the law into his own hands (like Carl Lee), supportive of the liberal lawyers who defend the underdog, resentful of Southern gentlemen like Judge Noose who benefit from institutionalized racism, and appreciative of persons (like Lucien Wilbanks) who regard blacks as equals and who have supported their cause in the past. Other prototype schemata—such as the locale of the Southern courthouse, which has historically been emblematized as a seat of injustice towards blacks, and the action of the civil-rights riot, which viewers have been conditioned by the media to regard as a righteous crusade—further signal spectators to desire the subversion of justice in the traditional courts and to support the cries of "Free Carl Lee!" that resound throughout the sequence. With regard to template schemata, *A Time to Kill* is a civil-rights drama and a courtroom drama and is typical of 1996 template films portraying fathers as heroic rescuers (such as *Fargo* and *Ransom*); all three of these examples shape spectator expectations that Carl Lee, as an abused black man and father, will probably be released, and the politics of these schemata suggest to viewers that he should indeed be released, due to the fact that he has experienced a lifetime of injustice. The procedural schemata—which may involve motivations, causality, time, and space—will be identified in the upcoming discussion of the riot sequence, but they too instruct the audience to screen in on inferences that support Carl Lee and that expose the white supremacists and racists as monsters.

At the mansion of Judge Noose, spectators are immediately cued to the fact that here is the home of a so-called Southern gentleman who is the heir of males who profited from the labor of blacks; he employs a maid and manservant, fittingly attired in gray, black, and white, emblematic of racial ambivalence and indifference on the part of Noose and people like him. The servants appear to be in a time warp of perpetual servitude, indicative of the inability of Noose to see blacks as anything but inferiors. Here, his name not only conveys his motivation to want to hang people but also his motivation to maintain a social and an economic stranglehold upon these people. The Judge's dimly lit house, evocative of the dimness of his wit, contains a grandiose spiral staircase, Persian rug, chandelier, iron railings, shutters, and a widow's walk; this mansion codes viewers to see the feudal Southern lifestyle as benefits derived from the suffering of others. These aspects of mise-en-scène guide spectators to disengage from the judge and from his values. The judge's words during this scene alienate him all the more from viewers, as he exposes his lack of impartiality and his cavalier attitude toward the suffering of others when he remarks to Jake, "You sure you want to be known as the man who defended that murderer? Could be very unpopular." When Jake, in support of Carl Lee's family, says, "How is his wife supposed to raise his family alone?" the judge replies, "Better than being a widow. Think about it—why toss away a promising career, hmmm?" Such a comment reinforces all the cues about the judge as a racist and as a supporter of his own kind.

Viewers are cued to support Jake's idea of vigilantism, his skewed sense of justice, in the luncheon scene at Claude's where Jake and Ellen Roark (Sandra Bullock) discuss capital punishment. In defense of his vision of justice, Jake argues, "Carl Lee Hailey does not deserve the death penalty; now the two men who raped his daughter did," thereby justifying Carl Lee's striking back as a father and as a black man. He adds, "I do not believe in forgiveness nor in rehabilitation. I believe in safety; I believe in justice." Some viewers may totally denounce capital punishment, yet the procedural schemata here motivate spectators to align themselves politically with the handsome and charismatic Jake by creating a partisan position that favors the brave father Carl Lee and condemns the cowardly rapists who attack a child walking home alone.

The sequence of the jury selection/race riot begins after the luncheon and is rife with motivational procedural schemata. Jake tells his colleagues that they must select jurors who are young, because young people are less bigoted, Jake surmises, and who are fathers, because they will share Carl Lee's motivation toward revenge. Schumacher hopes that viewers, like Jake, will believe in Carl Lee's innocence and that they will reject the arguments of the cheating, lying, and smug Buckley, who has rigged the jury selection in his favor. Scenes inside of the courthouse, where jury selection is being conducted, are intercut with scenes of the tense crowds gathering outside of the courthouse; these crowds are revealed in high-angle aerial shots that confine and restrict the movement of the crowds within the frames, connoting pressure and volatility to viewers. Spectators are framing hypotheses about a potentially explosive situation about to erupt. Schumacher cuts back to the courtroom, where all potentially sympathetic jurors (and black jurors) are eliminated from the jury pool, provoking Carl Lee's sarcastic comment "That's a jury of my peers," followed by a comment from Jake's friend, Harry Rex Vonner (Oliver Platt), "God bless America," building upon the sense of racial injustice that Schumacher develops in the spectators.

The riot scene, shot in rapid cutting, opens with a shot of a store window with the sign "Going Out of Business" posted upon it; Klansmen march past this sign, their reflections serving as a visual trope of their former "glory" as the "Invisible Empire." The Klansmen are subsequently equated with the words on the sign: their images in the glass window conveying their brittleness and antiquated ideology, and the sign conveying that their lifestyle is likewise "Out of Business." Stump Sisson, the Klan leader, shouts incoherent diatribes about law-abiding white Mississippians' victimizations by blacks, prompting the rage of the black supporters of Carl Lee in the crowd and, Schumacher hopes, the disgust of the spectators. Crosscuttings to the Klansmen are always cuts to the left, indicating leftist extremism, while shots of the black supporters are always cuts to the right, visually, literally, and figuratively in an ideological sense.

When Stump and his men approach the black supporters, he exclaims, "[M]ay that nigger be convicted and his black ass sent to the gas chamber," a comment that incites a black woman in the crowd to respond, "Who you callin' a nigger, you pointy-headed, white-faced, no good, wife beatin' son of a whore?" Stump rejoins by calling her a "wild animal." In her wrath, an anger of which Schumacher approves and which he justifies, she punches Stump in the face, providing the spark that ignites the riot, satisfying spectators' expectation that an explosive situation would occur and heightening their emotions. One viewer of the film, an African American native of Canton, Mississippi, where the film takes place, admitted that the film allowed her to vent repressed anger at the Ku Klux Klan, who had abused her father during nonviolent civil-rights protesting; Schumacher is pleased that his film allows the audience to release its fury against racism, especially in light of the O. J. Simpson acquittal (Malkin 35). This fury is paralleled in the actions of the characters, such as those on the bus labeled "Southern Christian Youth Conference," who do not act very Christian as they pump their fists and also yell out incoherent diatribes of hate towards the Klansmen, a hate that spectators have been cued by the film style and the narrative schemata to share. The use of the buses in the frames recalls the birth of the civil-rights movement aboard buses, and the fact that Stump is burned to death in front of a bus by an angry black teen not only signifies the spurious righteousness of the teen's actions but also signifies the purging of the white supremacist movement. This same teen is later observed at the final scene, the picnic; he has neither been accused nor convicted in the death of Stump Sisson, nor does it seem likely that he will be. Again, Schumacher invites spectators to excuse all racially retaliatory crimes of blacks against oppressors. In these shots and sequences, spectators acquire knowledge useful for the interpretation of the narrative based upon judgments made about time, space, and causality and determined by the techniques of film style, since these techniques aid in the way schemata are applied and hypotheses tested (Bordwell 33). Schumacher can sell his political views about racial revenge because spectators perceive the camera's reality as truth and therefore are less apt to question it (Branigan 74). Spectators witness and become inured to so many unpunished crimes in the name of eye-for-an-eye justice in *A Time to Kill* that they begin to reject hypotheses that would suggest meting out punishment for racial crimes and to accept hypotheses that favor vigilantism and justifiable violence when it comes to unrelenting racism.

The dialectics of film style that generate inductive inferences and that lead to ways of knowing about a film convey the *ethos* or the political agenda of a film-maker in the service of fostering consensus amongst the viewing audience. In the case of *A Time to Kill,* the interanimation of film style and film language presents the *ethos* of Schumacher, who wants spectators to accept a provisional justice system, one that should be color-blind and, when justified, retaliatory. He would then have the audience punish institutionalized acts of racism but pardon racially-motivated vigilantism. Because of the dialectics of film style and film language, viewers can arrive at essentially the same interpretations; *A Time to Kill* as such is a perlocutionary act that convinces spectators to vindicate Carl Lee. Politicized films like this one treat the plot as both narrative and as argument. The suasive nature of film can thus serve as a lure to spectators to the acceptance of the filmmaker's agenda through an artistic interplay of visual, aural, and psychological exigencies.

Works Cited

Aristotle. *The Rhetoric and Poetics.* Trans. W. Rhys Roberts. New York: Random House, 1984.

Austin, J. L. *How to do Things with Words.* Cambridge: Harvard UP, 1962.

Booth, Wayne. "Are Narrative Choices Subject to Ethical Criticism?" *Reading Narrative: Form, Ethics, Ideology.* Ed. James Phelan. Columbus: Ohio State UP, 1989. 57–78.

Bordwell, David. *Narration in the Fiction Film.* Madison: U of Wisconsin P, 1985.

Branigan, Edward. *Narrative Comprehension and Film.* New York: Routledge, 1992.

Burke, Kenneth. "Terministic Screens." *Language as Symbolic Action: Essays on Life, Literature, and Method.* Berkeley: U of California P, 1966. 44–62.

Chatman, Seymour. "The 'Rhetoric' of 'Fiction.'" *Reading Narrative: Form, Ethics, Ideology.* Ed. James Phelan. Columbus: Ohio State UP, 1989. 40–56.

Corbett, Edward P. J. *Classical Rhetoric for the Modern Student.* 2d ed. New York: Oxford UP, 1971.

Johnson, Brian D. "The Tale of a Mississippi Race War is Just Klu Klux Klumsy." *Macleans* 5 (Aug. 1996): 50.

Malkin, Marc S. "A Time to Kill." *Premiere* (Mar. 1996): 35.

Monaco, James. *How to Read a Film.* 2d ed. New York: Oxford UP, 1981.

Schumacher, Joel, dir. *A Time to Kill.* Perf. Samuel L. Jackson, Matthew McConaughey, and Sandra Bullock. Warner Bros., 1996.

Searle, John R. *Speech Acts: An Essay in the Philosophy of Language.* Cambridge: Cambridge UP, 1970.

15

Postmodern Dialogics in *Pulp Fiction:* Jules, Ezekiel, and Double-Voiced Discourse

Kelly Ritter

Filmmaking is invariably a rhetorical act. This is evident both in the way a film fosters momentary community in its relationship to the theater audience as a collective as well as in the way it fosters a partnership with the individual viewer via his or her own levels of internally persuasive discourse. In film studies, certain genres in particular are frequently theorized in terms of their persuasive elements. For example, *documentary footage,* once stylized and edited, is regarded as shifting from a record of the real to the phenomenon of *documentary cinema* (Rabinowitz 120). For decades, we have characterized nonfiction film as rhetorical. Because the scope of documentary traditionally functions via its impulse to educate and inform, to "record and interpret the actuality in front of the camera" (Ellis 2), we are quick to see this genre as one that operates with significant rhetorical agency. For example, in early U.S. government WPA projects such as Pare Lorentz's *The River,* a booming, eloquent voice-over serves to "educate" us about the possibilities of harnessing nature for, among other things, hydroelectric power. The hierarchical nature of this film's narrative, which is complemented by its overall educational subject matter and structure (because we are transfixed by the narrator's voice, we allow ourselves to be concurrently consumed by his poetic, repetitive rhetoric about "mules and mud"), seems perfectly in place in such an instructional film about an "actuality" in our collective histories. This power to create art and change points of view through a reorganization, or stylization, of true events has led theorists to recognize nonfiction cinema's rhetorical function, embodied either physically (as an aural presence) in the form of narrator or ideologically (in the mise-en-scène, outside character or narrator bodies).

But what of fictional film, especially popular Hollywood films that gain commercial success via financially proven means, such as stylized violence and high-profile stars? In these films, which succeed not necessarily because of overt political or social agendas but more likely because of profitable casting and an emphasis on recent cultural iconography, can there be a persuasive presence that seeks to elucidate a larger, more complex message than "you shall be entertained"? If we consider the historical given that rhetoric is present in all things and in all actions, we can see any film that is representative of any film genre as potential rhetorical space. Even within the Hollywood blockbuster there is room for the presence of a rhetorician, either within a specific character or a theme/motif woven through the film's larger narrative structure, such as the film noir genre and its obvious link to the rhetorical documentary. Often this rhetorical voice (or voices) is working at more than one linguistic level, however, and outside the overt conventions of voice-over. Thus, we may argue that rhetorical agency, while frequently grounded in just one character, may resonate throughout the larger space of the Hollywood film.

In Quentin Tarantino's 1994 film *Pulp Fiction,* a work popularly and critically acclaimed and almost immediately given the hyperpopular status of "cult" film, several manifestations of the persuasive are in place. *Pulp Fiction* deliberately and powerfully breaks with conventional Hollywood narrative style—one that serves linear, singular ends, guided by a singular narrative voice (either present or implied)—by designing a circular narrative around the rehearsed speech of one of its main characters, the hit man Jules (Samuel L. Jackson) and the consequences of this speech. By focusing on Jules as rhetorician in *Pulp Fiction,* we can see how this popular film not only makes room for rhetorical methodologies but also stops to analyze the place of rhetoric and language in its specific vision of today's postmodern world and the speakers within that world.

Recent criticism of *Pulp Fiction* typically has focused on the ultraviolent aspects of the film, and whether this attention to violence as a lifestyle (e.g., main characters who are in some ways perfectly "human" but are also by profession drug dealers, hit men, and gang or mob overlords) drives the film's box office and broad fan appeal. Reviews tend to focus on what the violence is *doing* in the film, taking as a given that this is its primary purpose; in other words, the message of the film that resonates for many critics is that this "cool" world that Tarantino creates is lawless, disdainful of laws, and acting out its postmodern sensibilities with great intertextual irreverence that thrives on the shocking, for the simple reason that we are no longer capable of *being* shocked.

There is another thread of criticism, however, that focuses not so much on the violence or self-referential and intertextual nature of the film, but instead on the characters' values and redemptive qualities. Indeed, this line of criticism is at odds with the mainstream reviews, in that it more thoroughly humanizes the main characters, Vincent and Jules, and thereby undercuts notions of widespread postmodern inhumanity that, for some, the film promotes. Todd Davis and Kenneth Womack's article "Shepherding the Weak: The Ethics of Redemption in Quentin Tarantino's *Pulp Fiction*" is representative of this school of thought. Davis and Womack assert that *Pulp Fiction,* particularly as reflected in Jules, employs its characters in the service of "exploring ethical and philosophical questions regarding faith, morality, commitment, and the human community" (60). They argue that Tarantino's choice to make Jules undergo a "metamorphosis" (60) at the end of the film shows that the values at work in *Pulp Fiction* resonate with notions of ethical criticism first put forth by Wayne Booth, Martha Nussbaum, and others. For Davis and Womack, Jules's recitation of Ezekiel 25:17, and his subsequent "conversion" after analyzing the passage, is key to understanding the redemptive powers at work in the film. This notion of redemption touches upon previous scholarship, such as that of Thomas Leitch, who argues that perhaps *Pulp Fiction*'s overall subject is "the possibility of self-discovery through moral conversion" (8), as evidenced in the three actions and their culminating transformations: Butch saving Marsellus, Vincent saving Mia (and Mia allowing herself to be saved), and Jules saving himself.

While these theories open the door to more textual, philosophical readings of *Pulp Fiction* than have previously been done—clearly advancing the potential purposes of the film far ahead of the violence-as-lifestyle critical reviews—there is perhaps more to these notions of the redemptive, which are directly tied to theories of language and rhetoric, specifically those that examine agency and discourse. Neither Davis and Womack nor Leitch tackle the actual *speech* that Jules recites, or its obvious errors in interpretation. While these critics, particularly Davis and Womack, do emphasize the reality of the dialogue (in its often mundane subject matter, which further humanizes the cartoonlike character types), little attention is paid to what Jules, clearly the spotlighted, transformative agent in the film, actually *says* and how this misinterpreted and wildly appropriated passage gives him an identity that ultimately rings quite false to the viewer, if not to Jules and his hit man and victim counterparts. This point of dissonance—between Jules's perceptions of his own rhetorical agency and his actual postmodern identity, which lacks agency, since Jules recites Ezekiel incorrectly and outside its original biblical context—is the true point of departure in the study of this film. Jules's dialogue not only with Ezekiel's words but also with himself exemplifies the role language has in an age that no longer has a concept of the "original" in any word, orator, or act. *Pulp Fiction* thus challenges us to see the seams between Jules's own speech and that which Jules appropriates for his own ends as cinematic agent, so that we may question in what ways language may actually fail rather than save us, due to rhetoric's limited ability to truly transform identity in a postmodern, heavily appropriated, linguistic universe.

Jules serves as a model for the way individuals may attempt, but fail, to manipulate speech in the service of particular ends. His Ezekiel speech, upon which his entire self-identity as a hit man is based, is voiced in two different versions spanning three key scenes in the film: the scene in the college boys' apartment near the start of the film; this replayed scene in the apartment, later in the film; and the diner scene at the close of the film. The various moments of delivery for this speech, as well as the accompanying commentary on the speech and its alterations, by Jules, makes the character of Jules stand out as the film's principal orator. As Dana Polan points out in his recent monograph on the film, the character of Vincent, in contrast with Jules, is often reticent to speak, particularly in order to threaten or intimidate others. Vincent is literally behind time, in that his words and actions are out of temporal sequence (30), most notably in his "reappearance" in the diner at the close of the film, which cycles viewers back to the beginning of the narrative, bringing us back to the time when Vincent was still alive. Thus Jules is one of the few characters who seems to control space and time vis-à-vis his speech and whom we follow throughout the atemporal arrangement of the film. However, his apparent ability to change through oration is the film's true red herring; Jules believes his changing of the Ezekiel speech allows him to walk away from the "life," but in reality, his changes result in nothing more than empty questions for which his linguistic postmodern universe has no answers. He does not spare his final victim-to-be because he is a changed man; he instead spares him because he has lost control of his own rhetoric and its delivery.

We may utilize three critical approaches to guide us through the dilemma Jules faces as a postmodern orator. Each of these addresses in some way the multiple relationships between orator and speech, and between individual and community discourse. First, Mikhail Bakhtin's notion of double-voiced discourse figures heavily in Jules's character. Jules believes the Ezekiel speech to be true and accurate, but in fact, the speech is a pastiche of biblical phrases and biblical-*like* phrases that Jules has melded together. The passage itself serves as an instance of double-voiced discourse, which, according to Bakhtin's definition,

> serves two speakers at the same time and expresses simultaneously two different intentions: the direct intention of the character who is speaking, and the refracted intention of the author. In such discourse, there are two voices, two meanings and two expressions [. . .] it is as if they actually hold a conversation with each other. (*The Dialogic Imagination* 324)

The Ezekiel passage also serves as an agent of change (or perceived change) for Jules; at the end of the film, Jules stops to consider what the words *mean*, and whether or not they are true. By seeing Jules as an agent of this type of discourse, we can see how he illustrates the postmodern speaker who knows no origins, who is motivated only by a recitation of words that connote power and authority in situations of need.

Jules perceives himself as authoritative agent because, according to Jean Baudrillard's concept of simulation and simulacra, postmodern (American) culture knows no original, for it is simply a culture of "copies" and re-creations of the real. According to Baudrillard, simulation is "the generation by models of a real without origin or reality: a hyperreal. The territory no longer precedes the map, nor does it survive it" (1), so we are doomed to live in a universe where things are "doubled by their own scenario" (11). This theory is crucial in an analysis of

Jules's character, as the majority of his rhetorical power comes from his "copied" speech, from his simulation, in which he feigns power he does not legitimately have (3) and relies on the "implosion of meaning" (80) that comes from hybrid, postmodern discourse. Jules operates as the "descriptive machine" (2) of simulation, which fuels the simulacra.

> It is no longer a question of imitation, nor duplication, nor even parody. It is a question of substituting the signs of the real for the real; that is to say of an operation of deterring every process via its operational double, a programmatic, metastable, perfectly descriptive machine that offers all signs of the real and short-circuits all its vicissitudes. Never again will the real have a chance to produce itself. (2)

Linked to Baudrillard's simulacra is Jean Lyotard's assertion that postmodern society has no need to remember its past and therefore presents itself as a pastiche of all that has come before, minus the social order (22). This vision of postmodern American society as arena of doomed re-creation is exemplified in Jules and his methodologies of double-voicing.

To tie these cultural theorists together, we can look to the rhetorician Kenneth Burke and his variations on the concepts of power and agency. Burke's idea of the Edenic paradigm, which provides for a "mutual conformity" that calls for a transformation of scene and agent via act (*A Grammar of Motives* 19), explains our analysis of the primary motivating factor for Jules at the end of the film, when he analyzes Ezekiel's words and plans to leave his life of crime. Applying Burke's theory within the larger notion of the pentad's power relations, we can see that while Jules believes if he speaks differently he will be changed, we realize as viewers that this is a false hope brought about by desperate circumstances. But Jules still believes in his own agency, since the passage, in his mind, holds the rhetorical power. The film's close, in which Vincent (John Travolta), Jules's hit-man partner, is still alive, reinforces this false hope, for we know that nothing Jules has said *will* change the damage he has done. Given the power via the film's nonlinear construction to see into the "future" (which now is seen as futile past), we realize Jules's attempt to enact the Edenic paradigm. He has transformed his rhetoric but cannot transform himself as a man. As a result, Jules symbolizes the postmodern victim of language *Pulp Fiction* says we will each become.

To clearly foreground ways that Bakhtin, Baudrillard, and Burke help us understand Jules's speech and actions, however, we must first turn to a further exploration of Ezekiel as character and mythical figure in Biblical studies and then the role of the postmodern in the attempted reification of Jules's language and character. Ellen F. Davis, in her study *Swallowing the Scroll: Textuality and the Dynamics of Discourse in Ezekiel's Prophecy*, comments on the style of the Biblical Ezekiel's words when she says that "Ezekiel's mind was saturated with the ideas and languages of the writers who preceded him, and when he wrote he reproduced thoughts and expressions as they came to him [. . .] he did not look up his quotations or verify his references" (45). She goes on to say that Ezekiel's genius can be measured by the fact that he "accommodate[d] his language to a changed discourse situation while producing a form of speech which [could] be recognized and assimilated by his audience" (147).

These very same descriptions of Ezekiel the Prophet could be used to describe Jules the hit man. Jules, like Ezekiel, relies on the words of others to create his speeches, without "verifying" his references. As can be evidenced from the way in which Jules modifies the Ezekiel 25:17 passage, it is clear that he similarly does not check his references. In fact, the true referent itself is unclear; viewers simply know that Jules has heard, or read, or been made to learn Ezekiel 25:17 at some point in his life and has internalized it and made it his own. As Jules himself says before each recitation of the passage in the film, "There's a passage I got memorized, seems appropriate for this occasion." Jules knows the validity of memorized words, the power of repetition and "reproduced thoughts." Further, he believes that the simple repetition of words bestows upon him a more powerful (here, violent) presence and a more secure rhetorical agency.

In fact, Ellen F. Davis's study of Ezekiel may further link Jules's power as postmodern orator and Ezekiel's oratory power as prophet as she states that oral prophecy relied on "repetitions [which in some cases were] 'reifications' of images taken from earlier prophecy" (45). This ties directly into Baudrillard's notion of simulation, which "threatens the difference between the 'true' and the 'false,' the 'real' and the 'imaginary'" (3). Jules reworks and revises Ezekiel's words in such a way as to leave their original *power* intact while erasing their original context and "true" meaning in Biblical prophecy. Perverting Augustine's notion that it is better to read a single verse *spiritually* than the whole psalter *literally* (Carruthers), as well as Augustine's emphasis on invention as an activity of memory (Augustine xiii), Jules takes liberties with Ezekiel's original brief passage to elevate his status as orator. He relies upon the tools of rhetoric more than the words of Ezekiel and in doing so further troubles the boundaries between his identity and the language that he uses to create identity in his oration.

The second important connection between Jules and Ezekiel is the idea of recognition by and assimilation for an audience. Even though at times Jules seems to be speaking to himself (as the final scene in the diner illustrates, as Jules is in a trancelike state, he contemplates the meaning of the passage for the first time while Pumpkin merely watches him speak), he certainly designs his words for his audience. He means for the passage to frighten, intimidate, and demean his victims before they are killed. Because Ezekiel was a man of God, not a killer-for-hire, this idea of empowering the speaker via recognizable rhetorical tools becomes clearly ironic: Jules uses his audience's familiarity with God and the Bible to elevate himself, with both Jules and his audience employing the canon of memory in making meaning from the message, whereas Ezekiel used audience familiarity in his prophetic speech to persuade them to trust and respect him as God's messenger.

We can look to Baudrillard for the significance of this methodology for the postmodern speaker, as he asserts that "the circularization of power, of knowledge, of discourse, puts an end to any localization of instances and poles [. . .] the 'power' of the interpreter does not come from any outside instance but from the interpreted himself" (41). In other words, if Jules has gained any power from his speech, it is the original power of God's words and Ezekiel's role as prophet. He deliberately uses this passage instead of a colloquial, non-Biblical passage or speech because he seeks to capitalize on the original power of the Bible in his community of victims. He is simply a receiver of past messages, now taken and appropriated for vastly different ends. Jules is counting on the notion that in God's absence (which is one of the givens in a postmodern universe), *he* will serve as the ultimate messenger, a symbol of God's words. This stems from rhetorical principles such as those of Augustine, who recognizes that in spiritualized discourse, God himself is ineffable (11). Postmodern culture, which relies on representations of the original gesture or thought that erase the idea of the original, allows for Jules to step in here, as the conductor of the question that behind all religious ritual always lingers, what if "God himself can be simulated [. . .] reduced to the signs that constitute faith" (Baudrillard 5)?

As simulator, Jules introduces the notion of double-voiced discourse into the larger narrative structure of the film. This introduction is seamless, since, in *Pulp Fiction,* the world is a series of copies. The copy motif is evident early in the film, when Vincent and Mia visit Jack Rabbit Slim's and Vincent notices the Marilyn Monroe, Mamie Van Doren, and Buddy Holly figures, among others. This sort of themed restaurant, which likely purports to be a "nostalgic" experience for its patrons, is a world built upon copies, but more importantly, *simulacra;* the waiters and performers are not seen by Vincent as actors playing roles, but as the actual historical figures themselves, and thereby substitutes for the original(s). Vincent and Mia ignore the oddities around them and instead engage in a detailed discussion of how the telling of narratives may change from person to person (e.g., how and why Marsellus threw Antoine out a twelfth-floor window) and how these linguistic variances affect the construction of self (Is Marsellus justified in his actions? Is Mia an adulterer?). This discussion foreshadows, in many ways, Jules's struggle with the construction of his own identity, which is based on a misquotation or altered translation of the words (and by extension, the story) of Ezekiel. Vincent and Mia seem to move effortlessly through the world of Jack Rabbit Slim's, ignoring the crucial difference between appropriation (as in the "Amos and Andy" shake that Mia orders) and larger simulation (the waiters and performers) as postmodern citizens generally do. This erasure of the boundaries between present and past sets up the overall trajectory of the film, which disrespects filmic laws of space and time in order to allow for language and rhetoric to take center stage.

The crucial diner/robbery scene, which frames the film, provides Tarantino with a central opportunity to lean on the past in order to reconstruct the present, which becomes emblematic of Jules and his struggle to overcome his past actions by revising his present discourse. By stopping and starting time, Tarantino here duplicates the diner scene with two very different rhetorical effects. When viewers see the first "version" of the scene in the beginning of the film, it is simply a brief look into the lives of two petty thieves. However, when viewers see the second "version" of the scene at the *end* of the film, it becomes a story within the larger story, a final episode outlining Jules's analysis of the Ezekiel passage and a look at the "future" (Jules plans to leave his life of crime and gestures toward this by walking out of the diner at the close of the film) within what *must be* the past (Vincent is alive in this scene; previously, viewers have seen Vincent die at Butch's house). By manipulating scene and time in this way, giving us a slice of the past, but then heralding this past as the promise for Jules's future, Tarantino designs the film to be a world built on simulation, a space in which the past is re-enacted in such a way that, according to Baudrillard, "the real is no longer what it was, [and] nostalgia assumes its full meaning" (6). In Lyotard's terms, *Pulp Fiction* attempts to construct a new "presentation" of the collective unattainable— the past and its litany of mistakes (81).

Within this larger world of the simulacra, the "copy" that blurs the boundaries between past and present, between the real and the re-enacted and the linear and the circular narratives, Jules stands as the apparent leader, particularly since, unlike Vincent and Mia, he *recognizes* the oddity of simulated events that stand in for the real (such as the bullet holes in the college boys' apartment, which represent gunfire but are not the by-product of death or injury; this to Jules is a "miracle," while to Vincent it is "luck"). However, Jules, unlike Vincent, believes that *his* "copy" (the Ezekiel speech) is in fact *real;* thus his ability to change the speech alters not Ezekiel's past original but Jules's present creation. In this way, by bowing to a world of copies, even unwittingly, Jules is allowed to survive intact (alive, moving forward on his own, through time) by the film's end, whereas Vincent is explicitly destroyed (gunned down by Butch) and then "recreated" as his own simulacra (dead, as a result of *being moved* backward into time, "alive" but without agency) in the diner scene.

But at what cost is Jules allowed to survive? To examine Jules's actions and motivations in his recitations of the Ezekiel passage, it is crucial to understand, additionally, Jules as an agent of double-voiced discourse. He follows in the footsteps of the prophets as he engages in this type of discourse, as Davis points out the words of Ezekiel and other prophets "passed through the double filter of prophetic and divine speech" (86). This filter is an example of Bakhtin's theory of double-voiced speech. If we look at Ezekiel as prophet *and* agent, someone who cannot exactly mimic the word of God, for he and God use distinct languages, then the prophet alone, before he is quoted by Jules, is an agent of double-voiced discourse. As Ezekiel seeks to validate his own position through "new" language of his own (Davis 90), he serves as the perfect model for Jules, who takes similar liberties with his own discourse. If Ezekiel's text is a series of "voices within voices" (Davis 86), so too is Jules's text, as he seeks to appropriate Biblical prose for its cultural rhetorical power while modifying the original text to serve more contemporary, specifically violent, needs.

In Jules's version of Ezekiel 25:17, one can see the seams that quietly exist between the real and the simulacra, or the original speech and the double-voiced version of it. Jules fundamentally adds, rather than deletes or substitutes, within the passage, and so what results is a true hybrid construction, with Jules's biblical-sounding words effectively mimicking the style of scripture. In fact, while viewers who are familiar with the Bible may stop and think, "that doesn't *sound* right," it is only through the absurdity of the three recitations, and its final analysis by Jules, that we as viewers are signaled to the meaning-making being done by Jules. His changes make him a participant in Lyotard's "language games," the games that make up postmodern life. Jules illustrates the possibility for simulacra to exist *within* a speaker—this follows recent observations of simulacra that point to its manifestation in persons as separate *selves* (Murphy 14–16).

To explore how Jules changes Ezekiel 25:17 not only to gain rhetorical agency but also to gain a "new" self for his new life, one may compare two original 25:17 passages to Jules's version. According to *The Holy Bible Revised Standard Version,* Ezekiel 25:17 states, "I will execute great vengeance upon them with wrathful chastisements. Then they will know that I am the Lord, when I lay my vengeance upon them." In *The New English Bible,* the passage reads "I will take fearful vengeance upon them and punish them in my fury. When I take my vengeance, they shall know that I am the Lord." Both versions utilize "vengeance," whether it be "executed" or "take(n)," and both versions assert that the speaker somehow communicates the power of the Lord by stating "I am the Lord." The forceful nature of the passage imparts certainty, directness, and power; there is no mistaking the intentions of the speaker. It is a wrathful passage, one which seems to allow no space for mercy or forgiveness. In principle, it fits nicely with Jules's frame of mind before killing his victims, in that it communicates a sealed fate for those recipients of his address.

However, notice how Jules's version of Ezekiel 25:17 differs from that of either version of the Bible. Again, Jules makes no mention of any changes made to the passage when he recites it; it is "memorized" and by virtue of this, we as viewers are made to believe it is *true.* Jules's version, which he recites for the first time right before killing Brad at the apartment (where he and Vincent have gone to retrieve the mysterious briefcase), is as follows:

> The path of the righteous man is beset on all sides by the inequities of the selfish and the tyranny of evil men. Blessed is he who, in the name of charity and good will, shepherds the weak through the valley of darkness. For he is truly his brother's keeper and the finder of lost children. And I will strike down upon thee with great vengeance and furious anger those who attempt to poison and destroy my brothers. And you will know that I am the Lord when I lay my vengeance upon you.

Some important changes have been made here. The message of Ezekiel remains in spirit—at least the second half of it—in "And you will know that I am the Lord when I lay my vengeance upon you." However, before Jules says this, he adds a multitude of biblical-like words and phrases that sound very plausible, in that their tenor rings true to biblical discourse, but do not appear in the original passage. The additions significantly change Jules's role in the speech, as he becomes, through his imitation of Ezekiel, both a "shepherd" and a "finder of lost children." Why does he make these changes?

To investigate this question, it helps to raise another key question that comes to mind after viewing the film. Does Jules *know* that he is misquoting? Or, alternatively, does he believe in what he says? The fact that Jules claims to have memorized the passage and the fact that he "doesn't know what [it] means" later in the film, in the final diner scene, point toward the notion that Jules *believes* in the message he communicates and in the truth of his words. The implication is that Jules either has heard this message "passed down" through cultural recitations, within his own discourse communities (African Americans, religious orators, criminals, one of these or a combination of all three, like Jules himself), and that, however modified, it now exists as his own truth. If this is true, the additions are not intentional, but a collage of biblical phrases he has heard, learned, and fused together to create this passage. As in larger postmodern culture, Jules has no need to "remember the [passage's] past" in his act of recitation (Lyotard 22).

Indeed, biblical discourse is one of the fundamental discourse communities that shapes Jules as a speaker. At the very least, Jules realizes the implicit conventions in religious oratory; the same constraints that privilege and empower the institution of the church also limit the way in which that institution's messages are voiced (Lyotard 17). The irony in Jules's character is that even though he knows the tone and sentiment of God's words, he is unable to be a *true* speaker for God, because he has lost the original intent of the passage.

However, as a kind of "master code" for Jules, Ezekiel's words, originally filtered from God to Ezekiel, and now situated in Jules, constitute Bakhtin's secondary notion of internally persuasive discourse. Whether or not Jules realizes how *much* the passage is inaccurate is another question entirely; by constructing this passage for himself to say to his victims, by verbalizing the sentiments in the passage in order to represent himself as dual, as a killer-savior, Jules undertakes a dialogic action and creates internally persuasive discourse. Jules's choice to fuse his own identity with that of a religious orator is significant here, as it represents a fusion with the *image* of an actual speaking person via ethical discourse. As Bakhtin emphasizes, this type of fusion allows the orator to "creatively styliz[e] and experimen[t]" (347) with the discourse in order to cast the original speech in a new light. Because Jules is the speaker who holds the power (the gun) and because his power is fused with God's power (biblical rhetoric), the message of the fused passage therefore connotes double strength, physical and spiritual.

By the end of the film, Jules has recited the Ezekiel passage three times. What is key about these three recitations is that the speech changes slightly; in the first two recitations, Jules says "and you will know my name is the Lord." In the final recitation, Jules says "And you will know that *I am* the Lord," which signals an important change in self-definition for Jules as orator. He has now come closer to the original passage as stated in both of the biblical versions previously discussed—which do equate Ezekiel linguistically with God—and this additional found power makes Jules's rhetoric even more seemingly self-transformative. But Jules is not satisfied with simply changing the words of his speech, with this slight modification in language that continues his amendment of the original Ezekiel passage. Not only is Jules now amending his *amended* version of Ezekiel 25:17, at the end of the film, but now he wants to know what it all *means.* He thus launches into a monologue, which is actually a dialogue with his two selves—the hit man and the (pseudo-) religious orator—in the tradition of double-voicing:

> I been sayin' that shit for years . . . I never really questioned what it meant. Now I'm thinkin', it could mean you're the evil man. And I'm the righteous man. And Mr. .45 here, he's the shepherd protecting my righteous ass in the valley of darkness. Or it could be you're the righteous man and I'm the shepherd, and it's the world that's evil and selfish. I'd like that. But that ain't the truth. The truth is you're the weak. And I'm the tyranny of evil men. But I'm tryin'. I'm tryin' real hard to be the shepherd.

The significant qualities that pervade this speech are indecisiveness and instability. Jules is unsure of the meaning of his own words, as well as who is who, who is good and who is bad, who is saved and who is damned. Jules's three versions of the scenario are strikingly different: If Jules is righteous, and Pumpkin, the petty thief, is evil, then the gun (violence) becomes a justification for Jules. If Pumpkin is righteous, and Jules is the shepherd, then the gun disappears as agent, and it is the world that has made the two men the way they are, both men are blameless. Finally, though, Pumpkin is "the weak" and Jules is "the tyranny of evil men," but Jules is "tryin' real hard" to be the shepherd. This changes the scheme of all actions before this, because if Jules is evil but capable of redemption vis-à-vis rhetoric, then there is no justification in continuing violence, and Jules must walk away—he must try harder—and so he decides to give up his life of crime.

However, the fact that Jules questions his words at all is the most fascinating element in the scene. Up to this point, Jules has been the focal point, the spokesman for the postmodern pastiche that comprises the narrative, which relies heavily on the notion of intertextuality. As widely noted among most critics of the film, Tarantino's multiple references to popular culture (the soundtrack, populated with songs from previous decades) and to popular genres in film and fiction (the pulp novel, whose definition is outlined on-screen in the pre-credit sequence, as well as the *film noir*) and use of well-known cultural icons (most notably John Travolta) not only symbolize a tangible nostalgia for the original but also serve to solidify the film's role within the world of copies, repetition, and simulation that constitute postmodern society. But when Jules questions his own double-voicing, his own simulation, and the notion that he himself, by extension, is then only *simulacra,* the narrative takes a turn toward questioning Jules's rhetorical strategies and Jules's role as orator.

Jules uses discourse as an element of change; he "talks through" who and what he will become, who he has decided to be, who he is. Pumpkin, the petty thief, has no say; he is one in a series of unfortunate listeners. Jules's power as hit man is as much in his words, his rhetoric, as in his capability for brute force. Each listener falls victim, therefore, not only to his gun but to his false rhetorical agency. But Pumpkin, in this final scene, is *not* a victim; Jules lets him go. This gesture, combined with the interpretation of his words, allows Jules to perceive that he has reified his agency; his empty words, to employ Burke, have been shown to have an "emotional connective for him [. . .] best observable when words refer to no specific thing, such as 'liberty, fraternity, equality'—the good of society" (*Counter-Statement* 159). Even though what Jules has said, and analyzed, makes little sense to viewers of the film, and his victims within the film, it makes an *emotional* sense to him and changes who he thinks he is.

This sense of closure is key to one's interpretation of the final diner scene in the film, as Jules's analysis of the passage is twofold: it unites on- and off-screen witnesses to Jules's language by verifying that Jules is powerless to his own rhetoric, thus solidifying Jules's rhetorically-constructed community, while simultaneously convincing Jules that he alone holds power *over* this same language. The subject matter of his speech, like all subject matter for Burke, is "categorically charged, in that each word relies for its meaning upon a social context, and thus possesses values independently of the work in which it appears [. . .] it is a matter of degree" (*Counter-Statement* 164). Jules creates meaning for the passage and then creates new meanings for himself; each of these situations produces a new "charge" for him and new personal definitions. In terms of double-voiced discourse, an inherently open construction in its capability for new persuasive occasions in speech, Jules experiences the possibility of "translating [his] own intentions" by fusing language, saying "I am me" *and* "I am other"—the creation of two simultaneous selves from which he can choose (Bakhtin 315).

But, unfortunately, Jules can never truly choose who he is via language, nor can he experience complete change in himself through his rhetoric. While Baudrillard serves to foreground the presence of simulation in all cultural utterances, and Bakhtin serves to extrapolate the lengths of that simulation in double-voiced discourse—the ultimate simulated utterance—Burke's theory of the Edenic paradigm helps us understand Jules's attempt to remake himself and explains the closure that some viewers feel upon witnessing Jules's attempt to transform his identity and his life. According to Burke, even though "[an individual's] acts can make him or remake him in accordance with their nature; they would be his product and/or he would be theirs" (*Grammar* 16), complete change via rhetorical acts is impossible. Thus, the transformation we see—and Jules believes he completes—is only a partial one.

As Burke states, "In reality, we are capable of but partial acts, acts that but partially represent us and that produce but partial transformations" (*Grammar* 19). Burke conceives of this impossibility as an "unending moment" of idyllic conformation between agent and scene, between agent and act. His Edenic paradigm is the straw man Tarantino sets up in Jules's words and actions, which is then designed to be knocked down by viewers who recognize the linguistic and social impossibilities of Jules's transformation from hit man to true preacher, the visual and spiritual core of his agency. Jules embodies in his analysis of Ezekiel's words the preparation for an act, a movement toward a symbolic act (Burke, *Grammar* 20), but is not able to follow through past his own preparation to change his life. He is full of emptiness, as his primary mission in life is to kill or be killed. Jules represents annihilation and erasure—an inescapable position for postmodern men who cannot create anything new, who can only recycle and rearrange the past, as represented in other Hollywood films that illustrate postmodernity and that also conflate violence and everyday human existence.[1] Jules believes, therefore, that if he is able to *withdraw* his threats always—if always he is able to "be the shepherd"—that his past life will cease to exist, as his victims ceased to exist in his work as hit man. This attempt to escape his true self is part of Jules's desire for what Burke labels the Edenic paradigm.

Jules also attempts to literally "deflect attention from scene matters" by "deriving [his] attitude from not the traits of [himself as] agent, but from the nature of the situation" (Burke, *Grammar* 17). In other words, Jules sees himself as a situational speaker, much as Ezekiel and other prophets were situational speakers in times of moral and spiritual crisis. But unlike Ezekiel, whose place in rhetoric was fixed by God's messages to him, and whose position was designed to change *others* through rhetoric, Jules uses his role as double-voicing agent to incite self-change by challenging his words to have varied meanings in varied contexts, whatever "fits the situation." He temporizes and recruits momentary allies—the petty thief, the diner customers—in his mission to change. It is doubtful, to cite Burke's notion of time-essence ambiguity, that these same persons would back his position "in the absolute" (*Grammar* 440).

The absurdity of Jules's situational motivation is reinforced within the space of the film's narrative by the simulated structure the plot employs, as mentioned earlier. By *first* showing Vincent's death, *then* showing him "alive" in the final scene, we as viewers can surmise that Jules is ignorant of the forces at work around his life and that he is equally ignorant of the position he occupies in keeping Vincent alive. Jules professes to suddenly be able to interpret his Ezekiel passage, thereby positioning himself as a man of knowledge, but he is unable to "know" many of the film's forthcoming events. By placing Jules's self-realization at the end of the film, but *not* at the end of the narrative's trajectory in "real" time and space, Tarantino acknowledges the futility of Jules's words and actions and thus ends the film with Jules in a position of ignorance, as a vessel of regurgitation. Jules is therefore symbolic of the postmodern man who is only a shadow of his original model.

As dialectic concerns a *specific* other (Burke *Grammar* 33), all three critical approaches here, which in some shape or form employ a dialectical framework as point of fact, can be seen as a means of situating Jules against that which represents the ordinary, the traditional, or the Hollywood linear. By creating a main character who exemplifies the complexities of the postmodern identity, Tarantino's *Pulp Fiction* has set forth its own dialogue between rhetoric and contemporary filmmaking. By utilizing a speaker such as Jules to guide its unconventional use of time and narrative to its equally unconventional *lack* of closure, *Pulp Fiction* represents a series of ultimate rhetorical questions: Is any speech true? Do words alone have the power to change? Is language itself a cycle of futility? By allowing Jules to fuse multiple discourses and then disallowing him the power over this hybrid of discourses, the film makes one clear assertion: what we call "voice" has already been spoken, and that "voice" will quickly reformulate again and disappear.

Note

1. See the films *Repo Man* and *Blade Runner* for examples of postmodern protagonists who are defined in terms of their mission to fight the alien "other" for survival.

Works Cited

Augustine. *On Christian Doctrine.* Trans. D. W. Robertson Jr. Upper Saddle River, NJ: Prentice-Hall, 1958.

Bakhtin, Mikhail. "Discourse in the Novel." *The Dialogic Imagination.* Ed. Michael Holquist. Trans. Caryl Emerson and Michael Holquist. Austin: U of Texas P, 1981.

Baudrillard, Jean. *Simulacra and Simulation.* Trans. Sheila Faria Glaser. Ann Arbor: U of Michigan P, 1994.

Burke, Kenneth. *Counter-Statement.* 1931. Berkeley: U of California P, 1968.

———. *A Grammar of Motives.* 1945. Berkeley: U of California P, 1969.

Carruthers, Mary. "From *The Book of Memory.*" *Rhetoric: Concepts, Definitions, Boundaries.* Ed. William A. Covino and David Jolliffe. Boston: Allyn and Bacon, 1995. 199–212.

Davis, Ellen F. *Swallowing the Scroll: Textuality and the Dynamics of Discourse in Ezekiel's Prophecy.* Bible and Literature Ser. 21. Worchester, UK: Almond, 1989.

Davis, Todd F., and Kenneth Womack. "Shepherding the Weak: The Ethics of Redemption in Quentin Tarantino's *Pulp Fiction.*" *Literature/Film Quarterly* 26.1 (1998): 60–67.

Ellis, Jack C. *The Documentary Idea: A Critical History of English-Language Documentary Film and Video.* Englewood Cliffs, NJ: Prentice-Hall, 1989.

Leitch, Thomas M. "Know-Nothing Entertainment: What to Say to Your Friends on the Right, And Why It Won't Do Any Good." *Literature/Film Quarterly* 25.1 (1997): 7–18.

Lyotard, Jean. *The Postmodern Condition: A Report on Knowledge.* Trans. Geoff Bennington and Brian Massumi. Theory and History of Literature 10. Minneapolis: U of Minnesota P, 1991.

Murphy, Cullen. "The Real Thing." *The Atlantic Monthly* 280.2 (Aug. 1997): 14–16.

Polan, Dana. *Pulp Fiction.* BFI Modern Classics Ser. London: British Film Institute, 2000.

Rabinowitz, Paula. "Wreckage Upon Wreckage: History, Documentary and the Ruins of Memory." *History Today* 32 (Fall 1993): 120.

Tarantino, Quentin, dir. *Pulp Fiction.* Perf. Samuel L. Jackson, Uma Thurman, John Travolta, and Bruce Willis. Miramax, 1994.

Contributors
Index

Contributors

Thomas W. Benson is the Edwin Erle Sparks Professor of Rhetoric at Pennsylvania State University. He is the coauthor/coeditor of *Reality Fictions: The Films of Frederick Wiseman* and *Documentary Dilemmas: Frederick Wiseman's Titicut Follies.* He is the author/editor of *American Rhetoric: Context and Criticism; Rhetorical Dimensions in Media; Landmark Essays on Rhetorical Criticism;* and *Rhetoric and Political Culture in Nineteenth-Century America.*

David Blakesley is an associate professor of English and director of professional writing at Purdue University. He is the author of *The Elements of Dramatism;* the editor of Rhetorical Philosophy and Theory, a Southern Illinois University Press series; the coeditor of *The Writing Instructor;* and the founder and moderator of the Kenneth Burke Discussion List (KB) and the Virtual Burkean Parlor. His articles on film have appeared in *Enculturation* and *Encyclopedia of Novels into Film.*

Ann Chisholm is an assistant professor of communication studies at California State University, Northridge, where she teaches rhetoric, media studies, and gender studies. Currently, she is conducting research pertaining to body doubling in the U.S. film industry. Her work in that area has appeared in *Camera Obscura* and in the *Aura Film Studies Journal.* She also is writing a book about U.S. women's gymnastics.

Ekaterina V. Haskins is an assistant professor of communication at Boston College. She has authored articles on rhetorical history and theory that have appeared in *Quarterly Journal of Speech* and *Rhetoric Society Quarterly.*

Byron Hawk is an assistant professor of English at George Mason University. He is the author of articles on rhetoric, film, and media/digital culture in journals such as *Post Script, Technical Communication Quarterly, Pre/Text: Electra-(Lite),* and *Kairos.* He is also the cofounder and editor of the online journal *Enculturation.*

Davis W. Houck is an assistant professor of communication at Florida State University. He is the author of *FDR and Fear Itself* and *Rhetoric as Currency: Hoover, Roosevelt, and the Great Depression* and the coauthor of *A Shining City on a Hill: Ronald Reagan's Economic Rhetoric, 1951–1989.* He has published articles in *Advances in the History of Rhetoric* and *Rhetoric and Public Affairs.*

Bruce Krajewski is a professor and department chair of the literature and philosophy department at Georgia Southern University. He is the author of *Traveling with Hermes: Hermeneutics and Rhetoric,* editor of *Gadamer's Repercussions: Philosophical Hermeneutics Reconsidered,* and coeditor of *Gadamer on Celan.*

Harriet Malinowitz is an associate professor of English at Long Island University, Brooklyn. She is the author of *Textual Orientations: Lesbian and Gay Students and the Making of Discourse Communities.* Her essays and reviews have appeared in numerous periodicals and anthologies, including *College English; Journal of Advanced Composition; Pre/Text; Rhetoric: Concepts, Definitions, Boundaries; Composition Studies in the 21st Century: Rereading the Past, Rewriting the Future; The Women's Review of Books; NWSA Journal; Frontiers; Conditions; The Right to Literacy; Feminism and Composition Studies; Sissies and Tomboys: Gender Nonconformity and Homosexuality;* and *The New Lesbian Studies.*

Martin J. Medhurst is a professor of speech communication and coordinator of the Program in Presidential Rhetoric at Texas A & M University. His areas of research include Cold War rhetoric, presidential discourse, the language of civil religion, and media criticism. His articles on film have appeared in *The Quarterly Journal of Speech, Communication Monographs, Critical Studies in Mass Communication,* and *Southern Communication Journal.*

Alan Nadel is a professor of language, literature, and communication at Rensselaer Polytechnic Institute. He is the author of *Containment Culture: American Narrative, Postmodernism, and the Atomic Age; Invisible Criticism: Ralph Ellison and the American Canon;* and *Flatlining on the Field of Dreams: Cultural Narratives in the Films of President Reagan's America* and the editor of *May All Your Fences Have Gates: Essays on the Drama of August Wilson.*

Caroline J. S. Picart is an assistant professor of English and courtesy assistant professor of law at Florida State University. She is the author of *Resentment and the "Feminine" in Nietzsche's Politico-Aesthetics; Thomas Mann and Friedrich Nietzsche: Eroticism, Death, Music, and Laughter; The Cinematic Rebirths of Frankenstein: Universal, Hammer, and Beyond; A Frankenstein Film Sourcebook;* and *Remaking the Frankenstein Myth on Film: From Abbott and Costello Meet Frankenstein to Alien Resurrection.* Her articles have appeared in the *Journal of Aesthetics and Art Criticism, Critical Studies in Media Communication,* and *Qualitative Inquiry.*

Granetta L. Richardson is a lecturer in American literature and the academic program coordinator for the film studies program at the University of North Carolina at Wilmington. She served on the editorial team for the 3d edition of Bernard F. Dick's *Anatomy of Film,* and she has written numerous articles about the rhetorical, cultural, and ideological aspects of film.

Kelly Ritter is an assistant professor of English at Southern Connecticut State University. Her articles, poetry, and reviews have appeared in *The Journal of Popular Film and Television, College English, M/MLA, Notre Dame Review,* and *CutBank.*

James Roberts teaches international film at Georgia State University. He has authored articles on film in *Enculturation* and the *Journal of Popular Film and Television*. He was also the guest editor of *Enculturation*'s special issue on film.

Philip L. Simpson is an associate professor and department chair of communications, humanities, and foreign languages at the Palm Bay campus of Brevard Community College in Florida. He is the author of *Psycho Paths: Tracking the Serial Killer Through Contemporary American Film and Fiction.*

Friedemann Weidauer is an associate professor of German at the University of Connecticut. He is the author of *Widerstand und Konformismus: Positionen des Subjekts im Faschismus bei Andersch, Kluge, Enzensberger, und Peter Weiss* and the coeditor of *Fringe Voices—An Anthology of Minority Writing in the Federal Republic of Germany.* His articles have appeared in journals such as *Seminar: A Journal of Germanic Studies* and *Modern Language Studies.*

Index